ISBN 978-1-332-31197-2
PIBN 10312513

1 MONTH OF
FREE
READING

at

www.ForgottenBooks.com

By purchasing this book you are eligible for one month membership to ForgottenBooks.com, giving you unlimited access to our entire collection of over 700,000 titles via our web site and mobile apps.

To claim your free month visit:

www.forgottenbooks.com/free312513

English
Français
Deutsche
Italiano
Español
Português

www.forgottenbooks.com

Mythology Photography **Fiction**
Fishing Christianity **Art** Cooking
Essays Buddhism Freemasonry
Medicine **Biology** Music **Ancient**
Egypt Evolution Carpentry Physics
Dance Geology **Mathematics** Fitness
Shakespeare **Folklore** Yoga Marketing
Confidence Immortality Biographies
Poetry **Psychology** Witchcraft
Electronics Chemistry History **Law**
Accounting **Philosophy** Anthropology
Alchemy Drama Quantum Mechanics
Atheism Sexual Health **Ancient History**
Entrepreneurship Languages Sport
Paleontology Needlework Islam
Metaphysics Investment Archaeology
Parenting Statistics Criminology
Motivational

TAMMANY'S TREASON

IMPEACHMENT OF

GOVERNOR WILLIAM SULZER

he complete story written from behind the scenes, showing
how Tammany plays the game, how men are bought
sold and delivered

By

JAY W. FORREST and JAMES MALCOLM

Foreword by
CHESTER C. PLATT
Private Secretary to Governor William Sulzer

Illustrations by
W. K. STARRETT

THE FORT ORANGE PRESS
ALBANY, N. Y.

"Out of the night that shelters me
   Black as a pit, from pole to pole,
I thank whatever Gods there be
   For my unconquerable soul.

In the fell clutch of circumstance
   I have not winced or cried aloud;
Beneath the bludgeonings of chance
   My head is bloody, but not bowed.

However straight may be the gate,
   How charged with punishment the scroll,
I am the master of my fate,
   I am the captain of my soul."

HENLEY, who was denied the Laureateship because
he was not Orthodox; in defiant scorn flung out these
lines which tell so much to those who can comprehend.

CONTENTS

CHAPTER I   PAGE
WILLIAM SULZER'S ENTRANCE INTO PUBLIC LIFE................... 19

CHAPTER II
GOVERNOR DIX'S TAMMANY ADMINISTRATION...................... 23

CHAPTER III
MARTIN H. GLYNN'S AMBITION TO BE GOVERNOR................. 27

CHAPTER IV
DEMOCRATIC STATE CONVENTION AT SYRACUSE, OCTOBER, 1912...... 32

CHAPTER V
SULZER'S CAMPAIGN FOR GOVERNOR AND HIS ELECTION............. 37

CHAPTER VI
MURPHY OFFERS TO PAY SULZER'S DEBTS....................... 41

CHAPTER VII
SULZER TRIED TO BE AT PEACE WITH MURPHY................... 46

CHAPTER VIII
GLYNN PREDICTS IN FEBRUARY HE WILL BE GOVERNOR............ 51

CHAPTER IX
SULZER'S SECRET MEETINGS WITH MURPHY...................... 57

CHAPTER X
SULZER'S LAST MEETING WITH THE BOSS....................... 67

CHAPTER XI
IMPEACHMENT COURT AT DELMONICO'S.......................... 74

CHAPTER XII
" WE'RE GOING TO GET THAT FELLOW."—MCCABE................ 81

CHAPTER XIII
EUGENE D. WOOD'S LETTER TELLS OF DELMONICO CONFERENCES... 86

x CONTENTS

CHAPTER XIV
MURPHY SENDS MESSENGERS TO THREATEN SULZER..............

CHAPTER XV
NORMAN E. MACK ACCEPTS AND THEN DECLINES PLACE ON SULZER
PRIMARY COMMITTEE..

CHAPTER XVI
THE FRAWLEY COMMITTEE AND ITS WORK.......................

CHAPTER XVII
CHARGES OF GRAFT MADE AGAINST JUSTICE DANIEL F. COHALAN..

CHAPTER XVIII
FRAWLEY COMMITTEE DELVES INTO SULZER'S CAMPAIGN ACCOUNTS.

CHAPTER XIX
GOVERNOR SULZER'S LAST SPEECH IN THE EXECUTIVE CHAMBER....

CHAPTER XX
MURPHY'S ASSEMBLY ORDERED TO IMPEACH THE GOVERNOR........

CHAPTER XXI
"GOVERNMENT BY INVESTIGATION SHOULD NOW CEASE."—GLYNN..

CHAPTER XXII
THE HIGH COURT OF IMPEACHMENT CONVENES...................

CHAPTER XXIII
ASSEMBLY DENOUNCED FOR USURPATION.........................

CHAPTER XXIV
SULZER CHAFES UNDER BAN OF SILENCE.......................

CHAPTER XXV
SUMMING UP AND REMOVAL...................................

CHAPTER XXVI
SULZER SAYS HIS REMOVAL WAS A POLITICAL LYNCHING...........

CHAPTER XXVII
DEPOSED GOVERNOR GREETED AS A HERO.......................

CHAPTER XXVIII
SULZER NOMINATED AND ELECTED TO ASSEMBLY..................

CONCLUSION
PAGE

THE PEOPLE DEMAND SOCIAL JUSTICE, ECONOMIC FREEDOM AND
POLITICAL LIBERTY...................................... 202

APPENDIX

ARGUMENT OF HON. HARVEY D. HINMAN OF COUNSEL FOR GOVERNOR
SULZER... 209
ARGUMENT OF HON. LOUIS MARSHALL OF COUNSEL FOR GOVERNOR
SULZER... 212
ARGUMENT OF HON. ALTON B. PARKER, CHIEF COUNSEL FOR IM-
PEACHMENT MANAGERS....................................... 219
ARGUMENT OF HON. D- CADY HERRICK, CHIEF COUNSEL FOR GOV-
ERNOR SULZER... 225
ARGUMENT OF HON. EDGAR T. BRACKETT, COUNSEL FOR IMPEACH-
MENT MANAGERS.. 240
CHIEF JUDGE EDGAR M. CULLEN IN EXPLAINING VOTE............. 253
BIOGRAPHY OF GOVERNOR WILLIAM SULZER...................... 259
HENNESSY'S REPORT IN RELATION TO CAPITOL CONTRACTS......... 279
HENNESSY'S REPORT ON HIGHWAY GRAFT........................ 295
BLAKE'S REPORT ON PRISONS................................. 303
LIST OF MEN AT DIRECT PRIMARY CONFERENCES................. 319
HOW THE LEGISLATURE VOTED ON THE PRIMARY BILL............. 327
SULZER'S SPEECH AT BUFFALO, MAY 19, 1913.................. 339
FORREST'S SPEECH AT SCHENECTADY, MAY 21, 1913............. 346
SULZER'S SPEECH AT ROCHESTER, JUNE 11, 1913............... 353
SULZER'S MESSAGE TO LEGISLATURE—EXTRAORDINARY SESSION..... 360
FULL CREW BILL—THE MAN ABOVE THE DOLLAR.................. 374
SULZER'S LAST MESSAGE TO THE LEGISLATURE PREVIOUS TO IMPEACH-
MENT.. 377
ARTICLES OF IMPEACHMENT AGAINST GOVERNOR WILLIAM SULZER... 383
INDICTMENT OF THE ROCKLAND COUNTY GRAND JURY ON THE HIGHWAY
FRAUDS.. 393
ROOSEVELT'S LETTER TO GOVERNOR SULZER..................... 396
EDITORIALS BY LEADING PAPERS OF THE COUNTRY..... ....397, 416
TICONDEROGA MASS MEETING DENOUNCING TAMMANY'S TREASON... 417
LETTERS RECEIVED BY GOVERNOR SULZER FOLLOWING HIS IMPEACH-
MENT BY THE ASSEMBLY................................421, 446
CONTRIBUTIONS TO THE ALBANY KNICKERBOCKER PRESS FUND...... 447
ALBANY MASS MEETING AGAINST TAMMANY'S TREASON............. 448

ILLUSTRATIONS

PAGE

William Sulzer..*Frontispiece*

Facsimile letter of Governor William Sulzer........................ 15

Facsimile letter of Martin H. Glynn to Jay W. Forrest...............30–31

"If he does not do these things I will be governor of the state"........ 53

"I will disgrace and destroy you"................................. 69

Governor Sulzer and Lieutenant-Governor Glynn................... 73

"We are going to get that fellow before we are through with him"..... 79

"At Delmonico's—Murphy, Glynn, McCabe, McCall, McCooey and Wagner"... 87

Facsimile letter of Eugene D. Wood...........................90–92–93

Matthew T. Horgan and William H. Fitzpatrick.................... 105

Isodor Kressel, William T. Jerome and Judge Cohalan.............. 111

"Al Smith getting orders from Delmonico's"...................... 127

Aaron J. Levy's sunrise speech.................................. 139

Lawyers for Impeachment Managers............................. 151

Senators Wagner and Frawley.................................. 155

Lieutenant-Governor Martin H. Glynn and Frank Tierney........... 165

Aaron J. Levy... 169

Patrick Edgar McCabe... 179

The capitol and the executive chamber.......................... 205

Hon. Harvey D. Hinman....................................... 209

Hon. Louis Marshall... 212

Hon. Alton B. Parker.. 219

Hon. D. Cady Herrick... 225

Hon. Edgar T. Brackett.. 240

Jay W. Forrest.. 347

CARTOONS REPRODUCED

	PAGE
"The Constitutional Governor"	18
"The New Arson Trust"	65
"The Gang—'Lynch Her' "	94
"A Man, the State, the Mob and the Beast"	97
"What Are You Going To Do About It? "	100
"And He Used Campaign Funds To Gamble in Wall Street, and"	117
"His Master's Voice"	123
"Breaking the Penal Law"	133
"Impeaching Sulzer"	134
"How Murphy Impeached Sulzer"	137
"Impeaching Sulzer"	145
"The Governor and the Pretender"	147
"The Court of Impeachment"	159
"Doomed₁ "	191
"The Deluge"	193
"Fear Hath Torment"	199
"The Great S(t)eal of the Empire State"	208
"Ring-a-round-the-rosy"	261
"The Climbers"	280
"It Is To Laugh"	294
"Darby and Jonah₁ "	304
"The State Government"	318
"He's Good Enough For Me"	326
"King Cannot"	338
"Bill Sikes Murphy—'Don't I Own Yer? ' "	413

October 21, 1913

Jay W. Forrest, Esq.,
    Albany, N. Y.

My dear Mr. Forrest:

        Information has just come to me that
you are preparing for publication the history of my Removal
from Office by an arrogant and relentless Boss because I
refused to do his bidding.

        You are peculiarly qualified to do this
work, and I know you will do it in such a way as to present
the facts and the whole case to the people. No one is more
anxious than I am to have this done so that the people of the
Country shall understand the real reasons for my impeachment
as the Governor of the State.   You know my trial was a
political lynching.

        I sincerely hope your book will be published
at an early date, and I feel confident it will have a large
distribution and a wide circulation.

        The story of Bossism run mad will be as in-
teresting as it will be instructive to the believers in honest
government from one end of the land to the other.

                    With best wishes, believe me,
                            Very sincerely your friend,

GOVERNOR SULZER: "I have lost my office, but I have kept my self-respect. I would rather lose the governorship than lose my soul and no governor can serve God and Mammon, the people and the boss, the visible and invisible government. Had I but served the boss with half the zeal I did the state, William Sulzer would not have been impeached."

JUDGE EDGAR M. CULLEN, presiding judge of the high court of impeachment: "Never before the present case has it been attempted to impeach a public officer for acts committed when he was not an officer of the state. No suggestion to that effect can be found in any opinion of courts of impeachment in the arguments of counsel on such trials, or in the text writers. In several cases where it has been sought to remove the officers for such acts for judicial proceedings, the right has been expressly denied."

JOHN A. HENNESSY, special investigator for Governor Sulzer: "No one better than I knows that had the governor agreed not to execute his oath of office he would be today unchallenged in his place as executive, no matter what other bitterness might be displayed against his independence of boss control. 'It is his life, not ours,' was the way one Murphy leader put it to a group of newspaper men."

FORMER JUDGE D-CADY HERRICK, chief counsel for Governor Sulzer: "If there is a determination to convict this man here, do it without any violation of the law. It is related that one of the judges of the old Court of Appeals not one of the present court said that 'when me and Judge So-and-so make up our minds to beat a man, we can always find a way to do it.'"

INTRODUCTION

In the impeachment and removal of Governor William Sulzer the arrogance of corrupt bossism in New York state reached its zenith in boldness and brutality. Up to that time political bosses had controlled party organizations; they had commanded legislatures and administrative officers of the state government; they had nominated, for a consideration, justices of the supreme court, but it remained for Charles F. Murphy, the reigning boss of his period,, to impeach and remove a governor only because the governor refused to do the bidding of the boss.

In that respect and for many other reasons the removal of Governor Sulzer is without a parallel in the history of impeachments or since civilized government began.

It is one of the crises in human affairs, an event of epochal importance in the evolution of popular government. Only the perspective, which time and vision create, can reveal its tremendous significance.

The purpose of this book is to bring clearly to the attention of the reader the vital happenings, preceding and immediately following the impeachment. One of its objects is to make plain to the ordinary citizen the underground or hidden causes that make such events possible in a country where the people are supposed to be sovereign.

Governor Sulzer was nominated in a convention controlled by the boss, who in less than ten months from the date of his inauguration brought about his removal.

Whatever may have been the governor's shortcomings before he was installed as chief executive there was no evidence adduced to prove that he was faithless to his trust after he became governor.

On the contrary, it is doubtful whether any executive of New York state ever accomplished so much of permanent good to the public as did William Sulzer by his courageous and unswerving assault upon bossism during the seven and a half months he was permitted to exercise the functions of the office.

History will record that he was the powerful instrument

9

during that brief and interrupted term to strike the fatal blow
to a political oligarchy and to inaugurate a new era of freedom
in the state government.

The following pages narrate accurately and dispassionately
the big and controlling events surrounding the tragedy of the
impeachment. Much of the story here related has never
before been told.

It lays bare the connection between bossism and invisible
government. It supplies the facts to prove that the boss
could not persist and so long defy public sentiment, if indeed
he were not the agent and the servant of greedy special interests which in their political activities always are invisible.

Governor Sulzer immediately was the victim of a corrupt
boss, but primarily he was the victim of those sinister forces
which stealthily and powerfully operate through the bosses.

His fate was designed by his assailants to be a warning
forever to governors who dared to harbor any notions of independence.

All signs indicate that his refusal to obey the command of
those who set themselves up as his masters marked the beginning of the end of irresponsible government in New York
state.

FOREWORD

BY CHESTER C. PLATT, SECRETARY TO GOVERNOR WILLIAM SULZER

The impeachment of William Sulzer as governor of New York state marks an epoch in the history of the commonwealth. Corrupt political bossism had shown amazing power in many ways, in many states, but never in such a startling manner as in the removal from office of a duly elected governor of the greatest state in the Union. Mr. Sulzer was elected by a plurality of over 200,000, the largest ever given to a gubernatorial candidate. His administration had won popular approval, and when the impeachment resolution was passed in the assembly, Governor Sulzer was stronger with the rank and file of the voters of the state than he was on election day.

In the fall of 1912, when the defeat of the democratic party seemed impending owing to the high character, the broad democratic instincts, and the wide-spread popularity of Oscar S. Straus, the leaders of the democratic party turned to William Sulzer who had won such notable victories in the Tenth Congressional District in New York city and nominated him for governor. He not only saved the party from defeat, but led it to a triumphant victory, and Woodrow Wilson for President, carried the state by a majority almost as large as that given to Mr. Sulzer.

And then what startling events followed! No sooner was William Sulzer made governor than it at once appeared that he meant what he had said in his campaign speeches, when he declared that if elected governor he would be THE governor, that he never had had a boss and never would have one. Not such a startling utterance to come from a candidate for public office; but it was surprising to many who did not thoroughly know the man; that the implied promise in this utterance was faithfully carried out by Mr. Sulzer. And it was carried out, although to do so Mr. Sulzer often calmly sat and looked political death in the face, and although carrying out the promise brought attacks from Charles F. Murphy, the state boss, calculated to ruin Mr. Sulzer's reputation and to drive him in disgrace from public life.

Yet none of these things moved him, nor tempted him to depart from his steadfast purpose, to be the people's, and not the bosses' governor.

He was determined to administer the duties of his high office, to promote all the reforms so much needed to remedy the corrupt political conditions of the times—reforms in line with those for which he had been struggling during eighteen years of faithful service to the people in the halls of congress—reforms calculated to make easier the hard and cruel conditions surrounding the life of the wage-earners of our great city—reforms calculated to curb the power of arrogant, avaricious wealth, of wealth gained by grinding the faces of the poor, of wealth gained through evasions of law, of wealth gained through the insidious passage of laws granting special privileges to the few, at the cost of the many—of reforms calculated to abolish political, economic and social injustice, to give uplift and succor to the friendless poor, to give to the world workers a fair share of the wealth they produce, that the homes of the honest toilers of our land may be the homes of happiness and plenty, and not homes of poverty and squalor.

" To make a happy fireside clime for weans and wife
" That's the true pathos and sublime of human life."

How often had these immortal words of Burns been quoted by William Sulzer in his pleas for social justice, for conditions of employment uplifting and not degrading, for wages enabling the toiler to give to his loved ones some of the comforts as well as the bare necessities of existence; for remuneration that may place some adornments in the homes of the wage-workers; that may place some good books and magazines by the fireside; that may give him some hours of leisure to enjoy the pleasures of home, or to go to theatre, lecture or concert, and that may also give him that which is dearer to the human heart than all else, the opportunity to give his children a better education, a better training and a better start in life than he had himself, in the years gone by.

Mr. Sulzer's career in congress has demonstrated the truth of this characterization. He was the author of measures to grant liberal pensions to the old soldiers; to increase the pay of letter-carriers; to curb trusts and monopolies; to place government close to the people through the direct election of United States senators; to reduce tariff taxes; to provide an income tax; to establish postal savings banks and the parcel post and to establish a department of labor, with a secretary having a seat in the cabinet. He showed himself the friend of the poor and oppressed of all nations by his resolutions of sympathy for the Cuban patriots, for the oppressed Jews in Russia, for the abrogation of the Russian treaty and for the recognition of the Chinese republic.

Therefore, when Mr. Sulzer went to Albany and became governor none of those who knew him best were surprised that a battle against corrupt bossism was begun. It was this battle, coupled with his determination to secure the enactment of measures that would give the people of the state an opportunity to nominate all state officers that aroused the vindictive hatred of all the bosses of the state.

Muttered warnings of hostility were heard when the governor refused military pageantry at the inauguration ceremonies.

The threat direct came in Murphy's message, " Gaffney or war"—a message meaning that a state highway commissioner was to be appointed who would be indulgent to such men as Bart Dunn, the Tammany Hall member of the state committee, and William H. Whyard, the democratic boss of Rockland county, who were both indicted for highway frauds.

There were warnings which preceded the threat direct when the governor removed Hoefer for frauds in the state architect's department, and Superintendent Scott for corruption in the Prison department, and thus took the first step which resulted in twelve indictments in connection with Great Meadow Prison and five indictments in connection with the management of Sing Sing Prison.

There were more warnings when the governor removed C. Gordon Reel of the highway department, and just in the nick of time to prevent the letting of a big bunch of bonanza highway contracts open war began soon after the governor placed John N. Carlisle at the head of the reorganized highway department.

It grew more vindictive when the governor refused to turn the public service commission over to the railroads by appointing George M. Palmer chairman of the commission. To remove the governor from office was fully determined upon when he appointed a practical railroad man and a union wage worker as a member of the Public Service Commission, and signed the Full Crew bill.

William Sulzer was governor of New York State for only nine months, but they were months big with accomplishments. During the three quarters of a year that he occupied the governor's chair, in pursuance of the advice and counsel of the best authorities in the field of sanitary science, the governor secured the passage of a bill reorganizing the public health department and increasing its efficiency to a degree that promises to check preventable diseases, prolong human life and greatly increase the general health of the people.

The governor secured the passage of a bill reorganizing the labor department, which John Mitchell and James Lynch declare will make that department the most efficient and helpful to wage earners of any labor department of any state in the Union.

The governor started a movement to reform prison management, to reform our banking laws, and our laws relating to taxation. It is needless to say that none of these things won any approval from Charles F. Murphy nor his manikins of the court of impeachment. They should have been particularly interested in the movement to make our prisons more decent, but they were not; they were concentrating all their endeavors to prevent grand jury investigations, from Lake Erie to Long Island—investigations which promised to greatly augment the overcrowded condition of the prisons of the state.

The governor was not seriously charged with any wrong doing in office, except in trying to secure the passage of a bill to destroy boss rule.

It was not claimed at the time of the impeachment that corruption existed then in any department of the state, except the department of public works, and it was known that evidence for a grand jury investigation of this department had then been obtained, by a commissioner appointed by the governor for this purpose, and that except for the starting of the impeachment proceedings, the removal of Duncan W. Peck, the head of the department, would have been made.

It was not claimed that directly or indirectly the governor had connived at corruption or wrong doing in any department or office of the state. It was not charged that any campaign contribution made to the governor, which he omitted to report, wrongly influenced him in the slightest degree in any official acts.

On the contrary it was his integrity, his incorruptibility and his refusal to turn the state over to public grafters, coupled with his efforts to send the grafters to prison, that led to the impeachment proceedings. He sacrificed himself and his official career in an endeavor to save the state from civic pollution.

He was convicted by an unfair court. A large proportion of the members of that court, although in form selected by the people, yet, in reality, they were placed where they were by the appointment of the governor's arch enemies, Charles F. Murphy, William H. Fitzpatrick and William Barnes.

In violation of the common law, and of common sense, even the governor's vindictive accusers, who had declared him guilty before the trial began, were allowed to sit as his judges, and to join in the issuance of a verdict which they determined should be rendered before a word of testimony had been taken. With these men admitted as duly accredited members of the court, ready at every executive session to attack the governor, what a travesty it was for the presiding judge to warn members of the court, after the testimony had all been taken, that they should not discuss the case with any outside their own numbers.

No wonder that even that conservative newspaper, the " Boston Transcript," declared that " not since the days of King John has there been a greater travesty of justice than was presented by the composition of the New York court of impeachment." The governor was in fact deprived of the right which is accorded the meanest criminal in a jury trial—the right to an unprejudiced court. Prejudice, vindictiveness and political hatred were all deeply rooted in the composition of the court of impeachment, which, according to all established standards of justice, should have been impartial.

With regard to questionable evidence, unfavorable to the governor, the court adopted the convenient theory, most

agreeable to the governor's enemies, that the evidence should
be received, and go on record, but the validity of it was not to
be determined until the close of the trial.   The principle of
this ruling, however, was not followed with respect to proffered
testimony in the governor's favor, which would have been given
by John A. Hennessy, Samuel A. Beardsley, John N. Carlisle, and others.

The prosecution was permitted to roam at will, and go on
all sorts of fishing expeditions, but the governor's lawyers
were promptly checked, when they sought to introduce testimony contradicting this questionable testimony.

To impeach an official for offenses committed before he as-
sumes the duty of the office, was in violation of all law and
precedent.   Furthermore, the court was without proper
jurisdiction to try the governor, on the impeachment resolutions passed at an extraordinary session of the legislature.
The constitution plainly says:

"At extraordinary sessions, no subject shall be acted upon,
except such as the governor may recommend for consideration."

The attorneys for the prosecution were unable to explain
away the plain meaning of these words to the average citizen
of the state.

During his short career as governor, Mr. Sulzer made a
peculiarly effectual appeal to the moral and religious sentiment
of the state.   After the verdict of the impeachment court,
every mail brought testimonials of confidence and esteem
from ministers, teachers and others, who were devoting their
lives to political, social and moral reforms.

The country weeklies, generally, throughout the state,
defended the governor in their editorial columns.   He also
received the support of such independent and fair-minded
daily newspapers as the Albany Knickerbocker Press, the
Albany Argus, the Troy Standard Press, the Troy Observer,
the Rochester Herald, the Rochester Union & Advertiser, the
Buffalo Courier, the Buffalo Inquirer, the Buffalo News, the
Elmira Gazette, the New York Evening Mail, the New York
Globe, and nearly all the progressive daily papers in the state.

Why the governor's case looked so differently to the editors
of the New York Times, Sun, World, and other metropolitan
dailies, I will not undertake to explain, except to say, that the

moral and intellectual standard of such editors as Albert Shaw of the Review of Reviews, Lyman Abbott and Theodore Roosevelt, of the Outlook, Henry W. Stoddard and James Creelman, of the Evening Mail, will compare favorably with those of the editors of the daily newspapers of New York city, that began to turn against the governor, about the time that he signed the full crew bill.

I have outlined the causes which led to Governor Sulzer's expulsion from office, by what will be known to future historians, not as it was called at the time "the high court of Impeachment," but as "Murphy's high court of infamy."

Soon after the close of the trial, in a notable speech delivered at the Broadway Theatre on Sunday morning, October 26th, Governor Sulzer uttered these impressive words:

"The judgment of that court will not stand the test of time. The future historian will do me justice. There is a higher court than Murphy's—the court of public opinion. I have appealed from Murphy's court of political passion to the calmer judgment of posterity, and the sober reflection of public opinion."

A few days after this, Mr. Sulzer was elected a member of assembly, from the sixth assembly district of New York city, a district forming part of the tenth congressional district which he represented for many years at the national capital. He was elected by a majority of almost two to one over his nearest competitor, in a campaign unparalleled in the history of New York city. At every meeting at which he spoke he was given a great ovation. No halls in the district could hold one tenth of the people who turned out to do him honor. The streets were choked with people for blocks in the neighborhood of the meeting places. Before and after each meeting, Mr. Sulzer from his automobile addressed thousands of cheering men and women.

The campaign was a striking demonstration of the fact that his old friends and supporters on the East side considered his impeachment a badge of honor. His election was a vindication. The verdict of the people reversed the verdict of Murphy's court, and William Sulzer will take a place in history as one of the most faithful, fearless and courageous of America's public servants.

HE CONSTITUTIONAL GOVERNOR

From the Albany Knickerbocker Press.

CHAPTER I

WILLIAM SULZER'S ENTRANCE INTO PUBLIC LIFE

John Riley was the Democratic boss in the old Tenth Congressional District of New York State in the early nineties. He was a political lord of the manor, so to speak. The population which occupied the territory along a portion of the lower East Side of Manhattan Borough was almost entirely foreign and the people looked to Riley as their public protector and guide.

During the late summer of 1889 Riley was on the lookout for a candidate for the Assembly and sent for John Leary, who had just been admitted to the bar, and offered him the nomination. Mr. Leary declined the offer, saying that he had laid all his plans to devote ten years more to study and travel.

" But," said he to Riley, " there is my young friend, Sulzer, who has just been admitted to the bar and has a taste for public life. He would be a good man for you to nominate for the Assembly."

- Riley sent for Sulzer and the result of the conference was that he was nominated and elected from what was known as the Fourteenth District. In 1893 the young assemblyman was elected speaker.

There was always some friction between John Riley and Tammany although the local boss usually fell in line with the organization, but not until he had received the recognition to which he held he was entitled. Mr. Sulzer was afterwards nominated for congress by Riley. That was in the fall of 1894. When Mr. Riley died the leadership of the district fell largely on the shoulders of Congressman Sulzer. It was one of those districts where personal attention on the part of the leader was needed a l the year round. Campaign contributions were made and the money quickly disbursed to meet the needs of the local leaders. As was the custom in those days, no strict account was kept of these receipts and expenditures, the laxness being a part of a system, if it might be styled, which had grown up for many years.

William Sulzer, who in a few years had advanced from being a young and obscure lawyer to assemblyman, speaker of the assembly and then congressman, began to feel that he was called upon to be governor of the state. At the Democratic state convention in 1896, held in Buffalo, there was the first mention of his name for the office.

In 1898, however, he announced himself as a candidate. Richard Croker, then the Tammany chief, and all the politicians allied with him, openly referred to the Sulzer candidacy as a joke.

Augustus Van Wyck was nominated by Tammany and defeated by Theodore Roosevelt, who had just returned from the Spanish-American war as one of the heroes of the hour.

Every two years thereafter William Sulzer's name was prominently before the voters of the state as a candidate for the Democratic nomination for governor. On every occasion, in spite of the fact that he developed considerable upstate strength, he was rejected by Tammany.

Meanwhile Congressman Sulzer was steadily adding to a legislative record at Washington calculated to attract the attention of radicals and advanced thinkers all over the state. He was the first congressman from this state to introduce a resolution in congress in favor of amending the United States constitution to permit the voters of each state to elect United States senators. He was diligent in his efforts to promote labor legislation; to protect immigrants in this country and never hesitated to take an advanced stand on economic questions under public discussion. He announced himself for the referendum, for the short ballot and for kindred reforms calculated to give the voters more control over their public affairs.

At a time when such measures were hardly ever mentioned by public men their advocacy by Congressman Sulzer set him down as a "crank" by the "politically wise" but steadily gained him friends among progressives of all parties. From the Tammany viewpoint any public man, especially one elected from Tammany territory, who held opinions of that sort was either a fool or insincere.

Twice during his congressional career the Tammany organization tried to shelve Sulzer by defeating him for renomition, but he had so won the confidence of the voters of the district that he was elected in spite of the organization.

Every two years, beginning in 1898, Mr. Sulzer was on hand at the Democratic state convention to promote his candidacy for governor. Tammany leaders on all these occasions never failed to ridicule his ambition, although they professed to be constantly on the lookout for a candidate popular with upstate voters.

Mr. Sulzer and his friends suffered these repeated rebuffs from Tammany at state conventions with patience. They always predicted that his time would come; that public opinion would eventually force Tammany to nominate Sulzer because of his growing popularity among the voters who were not in the habit of taking an active part in organization affairs.

Owing to the anti-Republican feeling which set in early in 1909 and continuing in 1910, due largely to the clash between Governor Charles E. Hughes and the Old Guard members of the party over a direct primary law, it became apparent that the Democratic party could elect a governor and other state officers at the election of 1910. Not merely was there an open break between the conservative and progressive elements in the party but this feeling had been intensified by what was known as the Allds scandal.

Senator Jotham P. Allds, representing the thirty-seventh district, made up of the counties of Chenango, Madison and Otsego, and one of the party leaders in the senate, was accused by Senator Conger, one of his Republican colleagues, of having accepted bribes while a member of the senate. As the result of a trial by the senate Senator Allds was expelled.

The details developed at the trial contributed greatly to the unpopularity of the Republican state machine and increased the confidence of the Democratic leaders in their ability to win the state election.

Congressman Sulzer was more active as a candidate during the pre-convention period than he had ever been before. Democratic victory seemed to be assured and the congressman's supporters again pointed out that he was the one man to solidify upstate Democrats and attract independents while not driving away Tammany voters.

The principal candidates considered by the leaders were the

late Edward M. Shepard and John A. Dix, then chairman of
the Democratic state committee. Charles F. Murphy, as
Tammany boss, sat in his room daily at a Rochester hotel
during the convention in September of that year, pretending
to listen to suggestions from upstate Democrats.

It is recalled that Martin H. Glynn of Albany, who had
served two years as state comptroller during the first Hughes
administration—1907 and 1908—appeared for the first time at
this convention as a candidate for governor. He had headquarters at one of the hotels, and his promoters touted him
as the "independent, up-state candidate."

Murphy finally selected John A. Dix and the convention
went through the form of ratifying his choice. Sulzer's friends
were greatly disappointed at the outcome, as they had been
led to believe that their candidate would be nominated. Congressman Sulzer is said to have walked the streets of Rochester,
after Murphy had issued the Dix edict, accompanied by one
or two friends, contemplating whether he would continue to
maintain even the appearance of friendly relations with Tammany which had so often deceived and repudiated him.

CHAPTER II.

GOVERNOR DIX'S TAMMANY ADMINISTRATION

The administration of John A. Dix, democratic governor of
New York for the years 1911 and 1912, will be noteworthy in
history chiefly because of the avenues to graft and public
plunder which were opened to Tammany. In order to fully
appreciate the difficulties which beset the path of Governor
Sulzer it is necessary to know what was going on in the state
government while Mr. Dix was the nominal governor.

Personally an amiable and honest man, it seemed to be the
crowning misfortune of John A. Dix, while governor, that he
permitted his underlings to conduct the state's affairs upon
orders from Charles F. Murphy and for the benefit of the
Tammany organization.

When he was nominated at Rochester in 1910, Mr. Dix was
chairman of the democratic state committee, having succeeded
in that office William J. Conners, of Buffalo. At the time
Mr. Conners was deposed by Murphy, for betraying signs of
independence and a disposition to tell out of school Tammany
secrets of how nominations were bought and sold, Dix was a
member of the democratic state league, composed for the most
part of up-state democrats of anti-machine tendencies.

This membership in the league was presumed to insure Mr.
Dix against Tammany taint and as the head of the state organization was hailed by many simple-minded democrats, un-
schooled in Tammany wiles, as a coming state leader to wrest
the party organization from Tammany control—a dream
often indulged in by sincere democrats since the days of
Tilden, Cleveland and Hill.

But all who are versed in the political game know that
Murphy would never have selected Dix for state chairman
had he not been certain of the subserviency or pliability of
his man. That was why he was nominated at Rochester in
preference to Edward M. Shepard, James S. Havens and
other democrats of high character and intellectual independence.

The first shock experienced by progressive democrats, who
had hoped for the beginning of a new era for the party under

Governor Dix, was when he cringed to Murphy, while the deadlock was on in the legislature over the candidacy of William F. Sheehan for United States senator. Edward M. Shepard was the candidate of the progressives in his party, and it had been assumed that Mr. Dix was friendly to him and opposed to Sheehan, but the governor chose to give aid and comfort to the Sheehan candidacy. For this unexpected attitude, Governor Dix was condemned by his former upstate political associates and especially those in the democratic league.

But his support of the Tammany candidate for the United States senate proved to be merely a prelude to a consistent and complete Tammany policy in the executive chamber. Under the Dix administration, Charles F. Murphy was allowed to pick all the important appointees who not merely filled the big departments with loyal Tammany henchmen but instituted the system of graft discovered and exposed by Governor Sulzer's investigators.

It was under the Dix regime that William H. Fitzpatrick was installed and entrenched as the Murphy boss in Erie county, having been made by the Tammany chief the sole distributor in that county of state patronage.

It was while Governor Dix was in office that William H. Kelley in Onondaga county, Patrick E. McCabe in Albany county, Michael J. Walsh in Westchester county, and a score of lesser Tammany satraps were strengthened and their power extended over the democratic organization.

Never in the history of the state, not even in the heyday of William M. Tweed, did a corrupt Tammany system find it so easy to ramify all sections of New York state. At the conclusion of Governor Dix's term of two years and the beginning of Governor Sulzer's term, Charles F. Murphy had more subject provinces in the empire state than any boss who preceded him. More than that, he had more complete control of the state departments than any Tammany organization ever had.

Applicants for the smallest jobs in the exempt class had to go to Murphy for his approval or to the men who directly represented him before the heads of department would dare make the appointment. These methods put in force during the Dix administration were sought to be justified by Tammany men as necessary to " build up an organization.''

Long before he began his active campaign for the nomination for governor in 1912, Congressman Sulzer was well aware of the democratic dissatisfaction with Governor Dix. He knew that the reason for the growing unpopularity had, in a word, been the truculence of Dix to Boss Murphy, demonstrated in a series of sins of omission and commission on the part of the executive. By an investigation in about forty counties of the state, by a staff correspondent of the Albany Knickerbocker Press during the summer of 1912, it was shown that Governor Dix was opposed for renomination by the great majority of the party. The demand was for a governor who was his own master and would not take orders from a boss.

Governor Dix had been one of the ninety delegates to the democratic national convention at Baltimore in June and July to whom William J. Bryan had referred to in a speech at the convention as " Mr. Murphy's ninety wax figures." After the convention the governor, in an interview, condemned Mr. Bryan, saying that he should be put out of the democratic party.

Perhaps no single utterance during his public career did so much to bring about the political undoing of Mr. Dix as this reference to Bryan. It was commented upon extensively throughout the country and the New York state newspapers, both democratic and republican, made the most of it.

New York state had been humiliated at Baltimore by the antics of the ninety "wax figures" whom Mr. Murphy had used desperately to resist the nomination of Woodrow Wilson. Early in the convention and in the balloting it was made plain that Murphy, with his ninety delegates, bound and gagged by the unit rule, were operating with Roger Sullivan of Illinois, Thomas Taggart of Indiana, and similar state bosses to bring about the nomination of a presidential candidate satisfactory to the great financial interests.

It is conceded that Mr. Bryan's opportune and vigorous denunciation of the plot in a series of speeches carried by storm the convention against these marplots and resulted in the nomination of Wilson. The dramatic scene when, from the platform, he pointed to Thomas F. Ryan and August Belmont among the delegates, as schemers to sell the party into bondage to the financial interests will never be forgotten by those who witnessed it. It was the turning point in proceedings which had evidently been "framed up," to speak in the political vernacular, for the nomination of Champ Clark, Oscar W. Underwood or some other candidate preferred by the reactionary element in the convention.

Woodrow Wilson received the necessary two-thirds vote of the delegates before New York state cast a single vote for him. Charles F. Murphy opposed him to the last and only consented to the casting of the ninety votes for the winner when the motion was made to make the nomination unanimous.

Discredited in the eyes of the country and condemned by the democrats of the state, the "wax figures" returned to their homes. Then began the campaign for governor and the other state offices to be filled at the November election.

CHAPTER III

MARTIN H. GLYNN'S AMBITION TO BE GOVERNOR

Up until April, 1913, Martin H. Glynn of Albany had been regarded by up-state Democrats as a progressive in his political ideas and independent of Tammany. In his speeches and occasionally in his Albany newspaper he had given evidence of his sympathy with direct nominations and kindred reforms Mr. Glynn had served one term in congress without attracting pub'c attention, but during his te m as state comptroller, in 1907 and 1908, he manifested independence in some of the investigations he instituted into county affairs especially into the public records of Oneida county, which pleased the people generally.

About August 20, 1912, Mr. Glynn sent word to Jay W. Forrest of Albany that he would like to see him at the newspaper office of the former. Mr. Forrest had been promised by Glynn and Patrick E. McCabe the year previous, 1911, that he would be made the Democratic candidate for congress in the Albany-Troy district, and the interview sought by Mr. G ynn was ostensibly on that subject.

August 20 was within a few days of the date when designations for congress were to be made by political committees. In the course of the conversation, Glynn confided to his friend, Forrest:

" Jay, I think I will be nominated for governor this year. If I am not nominated for governor I can surely be nominated for lieutenant-governor. Would you advise me to take it? "

" Yes, I would advise you to accept the nomination for lieutenant-governor," Mr. Forrest replied. " There is always possibility of death and then you would be governor."

" Yes, or removal," instantly added Glynn.

That conversation took place between the two men when they were on very friendly terms and six weeks before the Democratic state convention was held at Syracuse. Mr. Forrest said that although he gave no thought to Mr. Glynn's prediction that he would be nominated for one office or the other at the time, his remark "or removal" took on a new and more serious significance when Charles F. Murphy's plot to impeach Governor Sulzer revealed itself.

Was the plot to impeach and remove Governor Sulzer being considered by Tammany leaders even in the summer of 1912?

Did they foresee two months before the convention that Sulzer, always active as a candidate, was the most available man in that year of independent upheaval in politics and that if Martin H. Glynn, their first choice, could not be nominated it might be wise to take a chance on Sulzer?

These and similar questions naturally force themselves on the mind in view of what has subsequently happened.

Mr. Glynn's conversations with Mr. Forrest all during this period as well as with other close friends showed that the Albany editor was in the confidence of Charles F. Murphy, Tammany boss; with Justice Daniel F. Cohalon and other "king-makers" in Tammany. They showed also that plans for the Syracuse convention and for events after the convention and even following the election of that year were all being laid out carefully by the Democratic bosses and that Mr. Glynn was being advised of all their political projects, if indeed he was not one of the chief planners.

Six weeks ahead of the convention, Glynn was sure that if he could not be nominated for governor he certainly would be named for lieutenant governor, and even then was considering the possibility of removal of the governor. That thought would hardly come to his mind had it not been discussed between himself and those who were pushing him to the front as a candidate. Taken in connection with other significant facts to be recited further on in this book, Mr. Glynn's contemplation of what might happen to the elected governor sheds a flood of light on the situation.

Jay W. Forrest, although promised the Democratic nomination for congress by both Glynn and Patrick E. McCabe the year before, was not designated by the Democratic committee which met late in August, 1912. Thereupon, Mr. Forrest became an independent candidate by petition and opened headquarters in Albany for the promotion of his campaign.

Immediately after the Democratic state convention in Syracuse, at which William Sulzer was nominated for governor and Martin H. Glynn for lieutenant-governor, Patrick E McCabe telephoned to Mr. Forrest that he would like to see him at his office (clerk of the senate) at the Capitol. When Mr. Forrest arrived at the office, Mr. McCabe asked him to go with him to the senate chamber where the following conversation, substantially, ensued:

"Now, Jay, you will have to stop being an independent candidate for congress and help us to win," began McCabe. "My advice to you is to go down to your headquarters on State street and take that sign off and shut the place up. You have no chance of being elected. I am going to be boss in this section. Do as I tell you and I will take care of you. We are going to carry this state. Murphy told me at Syracuse he would make me clerk of the senate again and that I would have absolute power to represent him at Albany. Come with me and I will take care of you. Pick out your job and I will see that you get it."

"That is putting it pretty strong," replied Mr. Forrest. "I don't see how I can shut up my headquarters. You must remember that I have friends who have backed me in this fight and that I have been put to big expense."

"That's nothing," interrupted McCabe. "Give me your bill and I will pay it if you shut up your headquarters and line up for the ticket."

Forrest promised to take the matter under consideration for a few days, reminding McCabe that he would have to confer with his friends before he could do anything to change his plans.

McCabe again urged him to withdraw, saying: "I will have Martin H. Glynn write you a letter asking you to retire and you can answer it announcing that you will withdraw for the good of the party. It ought to be done four or five days before the time has expired for the filing of petitions for independent nominations."

Mr. Forrest called a meeting of his political friends and informed them of the offer of McCabe. Not one of them advised him to accept the offer of the senate clerk. On the contrary, they were unanimous in the decision that the McCabe proposition should immediately be declined and the campaign for Forrest continued with vigor until election day.

To avoid attack from the McCabe organization on the Forrest petition it was resolved not to give Mr. McCabe a definite answer until the last day for filing objections to the petition. Meanwhile, Mr. Forrest received the following letter from Martin H. Glynn:

"Albany, N. Y., October 12, 1912.

" My dear Mr. Forrest:

I wish you would consider the advisability of withdrawing your name as a candidate for representative in congress in this campaign. In the opinion of many of your friends and admirers, your withdrawal, though undoubtedly distasteful to yourself, would be productive of good results for the national, state and local democratic tickets. If you can see your way clear to withdraw you will make a handsome contribution toward democratic success.

" Respectfully yours,

" Martin H. Glynn.

To Hon. J. W. Forrest,
89 Manning Boulevard, Albany."

When McCabe discovered that Forrest had not withdrawn as a candidate for congress he was furious. He demanded that Forrest write out his resignation as a member of the democratic county committee, which he refused to do. Subsequently, Forrest was expelled by the committee itself which was controlled by the Albany boss.

AFTER FIVE DAYS RETURN TO
THE TIMES-UNION
COR BEAVER AND GREEN STS.
ALBANY, N. Y.

$5,000 will be paid to any Charity in the United States if the net paid circulation of The Times-Union is not larger than the combined net paid circulation of the other Albany Dailies.

THE TIMES-UNION HAS AN AUDITED CIRCULATION GUARANTEED TO BE LARGER THAN THAT OF ALL THE OTHER DAILIES
IN ALBANY COMBINED

The Times-Union
Consolidated by JOHN H. FARRELL
(60th Year. Every Evening except Sunday)
Times-Union delivered at your door for
$3.00 a year
MARTIN H. GLYNN
EDITOR AND PUBLISHER

TIMES-UNION BUILDING
COR. BEAVER AND GREEN STREETS

Albany, N. Y. _____ Sept 12 191 2

My Dear Mr Forrest:— Will you now re-
consider the advisibility of withdrawing
your name as a candidate for Representative
in Congress in this campaign. In the
opinion of many of your friends, and
admirers your withdrawal, though undoubtedly
distasteful to yourself would be productive
of good results for the National, State and
local Democratic tickets. If you can
see your way clear to withdraw you
will make a handsome contribution
toward Democratic success.

Respectfully Yours
Martin H Glynn

Hon J. N. Forrest,
89 Manning Boulevard,
Albany

CHAPTER IV.

DEMOCRATIC STATE CONVENTION AT SYRACUSE, OCTOBER, 1912

Both republicans and progressives had held their state conventions and nominated candidates for state office prior to the assembling of the democratic state convention at Syracuse, October 1.   Unexpectedly, and as a result of a stampede of the delegates, the progressives named for governor Oscar S. Straus, eminent as a philanthropist and independent in politics, and for lieutenant-governor, Professor Frederick M. Davenport, of Clinton, a former state senator and supporter of former governor Charles E. Hughes.

The republicans named for governor, Job E. Hedges, and James W. Wadsworth, Jr., for lieutenant-governor.   It was conceded on all hands that the republican party, on account of the unpopularity of the administration of President William H. Taft, due to its reactionary record, was hopelessly divided in state and nation.   Political students at once perceived that the struggle for the governorship in New York state lay between Mr. Straus and whoever was to be the nominee of the democratic party.

The selection of Straus, a man of high character and ability as a statesman, thoroughly frightened Tammany leaders. Charles F. Murphy had evidently concluded before the holding of the progressive convention to nominate Martin H. Glynn for governor.   But the nomination of Straus caused the democratic boss to hesitate.   He was reminded that selection of Mr. Glynn, a Roman Catholic, against Straus, a Jew, would project into the campaign a religious issue full of peril to the democratic candidates.

The boss was also reminded that Straus would draw nearly all of the Jewish voters to his support unless a candidate were named by the democratic convention who could hold at least the party's usual share of that nationality on election day.   It was pointed out to him that Sulzer was the candidate who could do this because of his championship of the Jewish cause while a member of congress and his familiarity with the needs of that race.

" If you don't nominate Sulzer for governor this year when the democratic party is so much in need of the independent vote in the state, Sulzer is likely to come out for Straus," was one of the threats held over Murphy and his Tammany advisers at the beginning of the convention.

"And you must remember," the boss is reported to have replied, " Sulzer must always come back to our organization for a renomination to congress."

" But three-fourths of his constituents are Jews and they could send him to congress no matter what your organization could do to prevent it," was the rejoinder of the Sulzer men.

John Leary—the same John Leary who had been instrumental in starting Sulzer on his political career—was foremost among the Sulzer boosters at Syracuse. He went directly to the room of Charles F. Murphy at the Onondaga hotel and plainly told the boss why he thought Sulzer was the most available candidate and why he believed there was danger to the party's success with any other nominee for governor.

That up to a few hours before the convention assembled Martin H. Glynn and his friends were confident he would be nominated for governor was shown by more than one incident happening within the inner circle of Tammany politicians. Glynn was posing as the up-state independent, although all the time in close and confidential communication with Charles F. Murphy and other Tammany leaders. Until the holding of the convention there had been nothing that Mr. Glynn had done or said which would have identified him with Tammany. Indeed, he had been set down by the great mass of up-state voters, who thought of him at all, as a reformer and progressive democrat.

But in a literal as well as in a metaphorical sense, the stage of the Syracuse convention had all been prepared by Tammany for the nomination of Martin H. Glynn for governor. Rolled up at the rear of the stage was a huge banner bearing the picture of Glynn and the words: "WE CAN WIN WITH MARTIN H. GLYNN."

The banner was ready to be let down at the moment when the convention was supposed to be aflame with irresistible

enthusiasm for the " up-state candidate and independent."
But the string was never pulled.   Murphy reluctantly reached
the conclusion that Glynn could not be elected.

The day before nominations were to be made, Murphy and
Patrick E. McCabe, his Albany county representative and
political mentor of Glynn, took a long automobile ride in
Syracuse.   When they returned to the hotel the talk for Sulzer
grew stronger and from that time on the Tammany delegates
felt free to express a preference either for Sulzer or for any
other candidate not opposed by Tammany.   The result was
that Tammany delegates for a time expressed their individual
preference for the nomination

Meanwhile, however, the cause of Sulzer had made considerable progress among the up-state delegates.   This was due to
the industry of Edward E. Perkins of Poughkeepsie, chairman
of the Dutchess democratic county committee and state
committeeman from that district.   Mr. Perkins had also been
elected chairman of the association of democratic county
chairmen and he was in a position of advantage, as the delegates arrived, to reach them through these county chairmen
and sound them on their attitude toward Sulzer.

Gradually, after the boss graciously let it be known that his
delegates might act for themselves, the tide set in for Sulzer.
Sporadic attempts had been made to start a boom for Victor
H. Dowling, one of the Tammany justices of the supreme
court, for Herman A. Metz and for other out-and-out Tammany
men, but these efforts were all repelled by the delegates not
tied to Murphy.   Nearly all of the up-state men wanted Sulzer
because, while he came from a Tammany congressional district, his record at Washington had been such as to make it
clear that he was independent and seldom paid heed to orders
from the organization.

Although Martin H. Glynn had been the first choice of Murphy, he pretended to many of the up-state delegates who
called on him at his rooms that he still favored the renomination of Governor John A. Dix.   During the summer, however,
the close lieutenants of the boss concluded that Dix could not
be renominated and Murphy came to Syracuse with his mind
fully made up on that question.   To the democrats who called
on him to protest against renomination of Dix, a favorite reply

of the boss, when informed that Dix could not be re-elected because he had not been independent enough, was: "You've got to bring some other argument against Dix than the one that he has been a friend of the organization. I am not going to turn a man down because he has been my friend."

The preliminary ballots at the convention gave Governor Dix a "consolation" vote, all of the Tammany men making it appear that they wanted to " let him down easy." There was little or no talk in behalf of Glynn's candidacy for governor. Apparently his friends wanted his nomination to come as a surprise if it came at all.

Long before the convention met, Mr. Glynn had been selected for temporary chairman and Alton B. Parker, of counsel, a year later, in the impeachment proceedings against Sulzer, for permanent chairman. There had been a bitter fight over the election of Parker for temporary chairman of the national democratic convention at Baltimore three months previous, Parker being regarded by William J. Bryan and his progressive following as the representative of invisible government.

Selection by the boss of Parker for permanent chairman at Syracuse revived the struggle between the Tammany men and progressives, but not more than thirty-five votes in a total of 450 could be mustered against Parker. Many of the anti-Tammany men explained this by saying that they did not care to make an issue of what they regarded as a non-essential.

There was no opposition to the election of Martin H. Glynn as temporary chairman, so well had he and his friends been able to conceal his political views and his underground connection with Tammany. His speech was of the good-lord, good-devil type. John A. Dix and his administration were praised to the skies in spite of the fact that the temporary chairman had predicted and at that moment knew that the convention was to deny him renomination.

There were several dramatic incidents during the preliminary sessions of the convention. One came in the election of Alton B. Parker as permanent chairman when John K. Sague, former mayor of Poughkeepsie, Frank H. Mott of Jamestown and other anti-Tammany delegates opposed Parker's election because they held it would mean notice to the state that

Charles F. Murphy controlled the convention. Judge Parker was held up as a reactionary and the bitter fight waged against his election as temporary chairman of the democratic national convention at Baltimore, only three months before, by William J. Bryan and other progressive democrats, was recalled again and again by the anti-Tammany men at Syracuse. The persistent exaltation of Parker by Tammany, it was pointed out, was an affront to the progressive members of the party.

Another sensational episode came while the convention had before it the majority and minority reports of the committee on resolutions. Thomas M. Osborne, spokesman for the minority, pleaded in vain for a more explicit declaration for direct primaries and for other reforms. At one point in his speech from the platform he pointed his finger at Charles F. Murphy, seated at the head of the Tammany delegation, and exclaimed: " There sits Charles F. Murphy; look at him well. It is the last time he will ever control a democratic state convention."

Murphy sat motionless and apparently undisturbed throughout the excoriation of bosses and bossism by Osborne, who was interrupted by applause and hisses. Among the interruptors was Patrick E. McCabe of Albany, who taunted Osborne for having accepted an appointment on the public service commission during the administration of Governor Charles E. Hughes.

CHAPTER V.

Returning Tammany leaders and delegates from the Syracuse convention were heard to ridicule Sulzer and otherwise express contempt for the man they had just nominated for governor. They spoke of him as a " joke," and freely predicted that he would never be able to get along with the organization. They made it plain that Sulzer had been forced on them by political events and that they thoroughly distrusted him.

The campaign was without important incident. Sulzer and Glynn toured the state in a special car, accompanied by political friends and newspaper correspondents. Their speeches were óf the usual pre-election character, platitudinous and non-specific. Confident of election, owing to the republican schism, the democratic candidates felt that they did not have to be either emphatic or definite in their pledges. They did refer occasionally to the need of carrying out the pledges of the party for direct primaries, but as to just what those pledges meant the candidates did not attempt to particularize.

Even at that time the feeling between the Sulzer and the Glynn followers cropped out. Glynn's friends at various times during the state journeyings referred to Sulzer as a joke— a favorite word in their allusions to the candidate for governor —and frequently remarked that Glynn should have been at the head of the ticket. Mr. Sulzer afterwards discovered that some of the men in his confidence during that tour were Tammany spies.

The vote for the candidates for governor at the election in November, 1912, was as follows:

William Sulzer, democrat..................649,559
Job E. Hedges, republican.................444,105
Oscar S. Straus, progressive..............393,183
Charles E. Russell, socialist............. 56,917
T. A. MacNicholl, prohibitionist.......... 18,990
John Hall, socialist labor................ 4,461

No sooner had the result of the election been announced than the governor-elect began to hear from Charles F. Murphy and other Tammany men about appointments. They made it manifest that they intended to take charge of his administration; to lay down the law as to whom in the various counties he was to recognize in the distribution of patronage and even went so far as to pick out beforehand the men who were to surround him in a confidential capacity in the executive chamber.

Charles F. Murphy wanted John A. Mason, who had been secretary to Governor Dix, continued in the same position under the new governor. Mr. Mason, who had been secretary of the democratic state committee, was an intimate of the Tammany chief and had proved himself invaluable to Murphy during the Dix administration.

Governor-elect Sulzer objected to this arrangement and asked Murphy whether George W. Blake, a political writer on one of the New York newspapers, would not do for the place. Murphy replied that almost anybody but Blake would be satisfactory to him. He explained Blake had always fought him and his appointment as private secretary to the governor would be considered an insult to the organization.

The governor-elect also wanted E. Boardman Scovell, a Buffalo and Niagara county lawyer, as his legal adviser, but this likewise was vetoed by the boss. At this time Mr. Sulzer wanted to keep the peace between himself and the Tammany organization, and, in large measure, acquiesced in the demands of Murphy, hoping all the while that he would be able to obtain more from the Tammany legislature than if he antagonized it from the outset.

The first appointments of the governor-elect were Chester C. Platt, of the " Batavia Times," for secretary, and Valentine Taylor, of the attorney-general's office, for legal adviser. Mr. Platt was well known for many years as one of Mr. Sulzer's indefatigable supporters for the nomination for governor. He had also proved himself a sincere progressive in politics and economic beliefs. His selection was hailed throughout the state by the anti-Tammany democrats and political reformers of all schools as the first omen of a desire by the new governor to be truly independent of Tammany.

Of Mr. Taylor less was known by the public. He was formerly a New York city man, having received his first appointment from Senator Robert F. Wagner, the Tammany leader in the senate, as a clerk of a committee. Subsequently he was appointed a deputy attorney-general, which position he held when selected by Mr. Sulzer as his legal adviser. Although Mr. Taylor was undoubtedly unobjectionable to the Tammany leaders there is no evidence that he was disloyal to Governor Sulzer.

Governor-elect Sulzer spent considerable of his time after election at Washington winding up his affairs there. During that time he was besieged by office-seekers and politicians desiring appointments for their friends. Some democrats declared that he made promises of places which he afterwards was forced to rescind on account of a conference with Tammany leaders in New York city two or three weeks before he went to Albany.

At that conference, Charles F. Murphy, Senator Robert F. Wagner, Norman E. Mack, William H. Fitzpatrick and the governor-elect were among those present. Mr. Sulzer was not then in a fighting mood, fearing to have a break with the boss so early in his administration.

He readily acquiesced in the wishes of those present.

" Of course you understand, governor, that Mr. Fitzpatrick is to distribute all the patronage for Erie county," was the way one of the commands was conveyed to the new governor. Sulzer agreed to recognize Fitzpatrick. There was some fear then that he might permit William J. Conners, former state chairman, to have some of the patronage. Conners for several years had been bitterly opposing both Murphy and Fitzpatrick but had supported Sulzer during the campaign, hence the fear that he might get some of the places away from the Tammany lieutenant in Buffalo.

Care was also taken to point out to the governor-elect who were the accredited Murphy agents in other counties. These included William H. Kelley in Onondaga; Patrick E. McCabe in Albany; and Michael J. Walsh in Westchester.

At that conference, governor-elect Sulzer ventured to suggest that the up-state democrats of the independent kind, like Carlisle, Osborne and Sague, ought to be recognized, even if it were only in a small way for the sake of party harmony. But his suggestion was frowned upon and he did not press it. The policy of the Tammany men was to allow no quarter to the enemies of the organization and they impressed upon the mind of the governor-elect that he would have to unite with them in the war of extermination.

CHAPTER VI.

Murphy Offers to Pay Sulzer's Debts

After Sulzer had been elected governor and before he was inaugurated the governor-elect had a memorable conference with Charles F. Murphy in Delmonico's. He spent the afternoon with the boss in his private rooms and Mr. Murphy on that occasion grew very confidential. It was just prior to the time when Mr. Sulzer was to go to Albany to assume his duties as governor.

There was a friendly talk concerning the result of the election and plans for the session of the legislature. Suddenly Mr. Murphy referred to the financial difficulties of the governor-elect and in a friendly way expressed his desire to assist him. Mr. Sulzer afterwards admitted that he was amazed at the knowledge which Murphy had gained of the details of his money troubles.

" I am willing to put up $100,000 to pay off your debts and start you right as governor of the state," Murphy is declared to have said. When he saw that Sulzer was inclined to demur to acceptance of the offer, the boss instantly added: "You know this really is a party matter. The organization should do that much to set you on your feet. You have been elected at less expense to the organization than any candidate for governor within my recollection."

Sulzer continued to indicate his objection to the proposition, knowing well what it meant; that if he in any degree accepted it that moment would he cease to be a free agent at Albany.

Mr. Murphy continued to argue that there was nothing wrong in the governor receiving the benefit of the money contributed to the organization. " Nobody need know anything about it," Murphy pointed out to Sulzer. " The organization is glad to help its friends when they need it." The boss showed he was familiar with Sulzer's financial troubles, a fact which all the more aroused the latter's suspicion as to the motive for making the offer. The governor-

elect remarked that while he was deeply in debt he was paying
it off gradually.

Murphy repeated the offer, asking Sulzer to remember it
was for the good of the democratic party.

"The organization," said Mr. Murphy, "doesn't want you
to be hampered by these debts when you go to Albany. We
would be willing to allow you $1,000 a month for living ex-
penses at the executive mansion. The organization wants
you to live as you ought to live while you are governor of the
state.

"We cleaned up a lot of money out of your campaign. I
could afford to let you have what you want and never miss it."

During a large part of the afternoon the boss urged upon
the governor-elect the advisability of accepting money enough
to pay his debts and to pay his living expenses at the mansion.
Governor Sulzer made it plain that he did not want to accept
the aid of Mr. Murphy or the organization to get him out of
financial difficulties.

This conference between the two men took place either
just before Christmas of 1912 or between Christmas and
New Year.

Mr. Murphy's bold attempt to place the elected governor
of the state under financial obligations to himself left a lasting
impression on Mr. Sulzer's mind. Even then he foresaw
trouble with the boss and wondered how he was going to
maintain peace and be his own master.

For his inauguration ceremonies, Governor Sulzer established
several precedents. He dispensed with the military parade,
which had been a spectacular event in the inauguration of
governors from the beginning of the state government. Accompanied merely by the immediate members of his military
staff, he walked from the executive mansion to the Capitol,
where he was inaugurated in the assembly chamber. Never
before, within the memory of the oldest inhabitant of Albany,
had a governor been so democratic as to walk to the Capitol
for his inauguration. Charles F. Murphy did not attend the
inauguration.

After the ceremonies in the assembly chamber, the governor
established another precedent by appearing at the top of the
great staircase at the front of the Capitol, and delivering an

address to the waiting multitude which extended far out into the park and beyond the range of his voice.

The new governor's inauguration speech was brief, and is now interesting in the light of subsequent events. Between the lines one may read that the governor feared that his path was not to be a rosy one, and that he was on his guard for attacks from within as well as without his party.

His inauguration address was as follows:

FELLOW CITIZENS:—I realize to the fullest extent the solemnity of the obligation I have just taken as the governor of New York. Conscious of my own limitations I keenly appreciate the responsibilities it entails.

Grateful to the people who have honored me with their suffrages, I enter upon the performance of the duties of the office without a promise, except my pledge to all the people to serve them faithfully and honestly and to the best of my ability. I am free, without entanglements, and shall remain free. No influence controls me but the dictates of my conscience and my determination to do my duty, day in and day out, as I see the right, regardless of consequences. In the future, as in the past, I will walk the street called straight, and without fear and without favor I shall execute the laws justly and impartially—with malice toward none.

Those who know me best know that I stand firmly for certain fundamental principles—for freedom of speech; for the right of lawful assembly; for the freedom of the press; for liberty under law; for civil and religious freedom; for constitutional government; for equality and justice to all; for home rule, and the reserved rights of the state; for equal rights to every one, and special privileges to no one; and for unshackled opportunity as the beacon light of individual hope and the best guarantee for the perpetuity of our free institutions.

New York is the greatest state in the Union. It should always stand as an exemplar of economical and efficient and progressive administration. As its governor I shall, in so far as I can, give the people of the state an honest, an efficient, an economical and a business-like administration of public affairs. I say business-like advisedly, because I assure the business men in every part of our state that they can rely on me at all times to do my utmost to promote the commercial interests of our commonwealth. I realize how important they are, and shall always be exceedingly careful to take no step that will jeopardize the financial and the commercial supremacy of the first state in the republic.

Suffice it to say that I am a friend of every business, whether big or little, so long as it is legitimate, and will always have its welfare in view in the administration of state affairs. To this end I shall work unceasingly for quicker and better transportation agencies, and for improved and larger terminal facilities, in order that New York shall continue to receive her just share of the trade and the commerce of the country.

It is my purpose to be the governor of all the people, and, in so far as possible, to follow in the footsteps of Silas Wright in the honesty and the simplicity of my administration; and to the best of my ability try to emulate the example of Samuel J. Tilden in my efforts for progressive reforms along constructive and constitutional lines.

Let me ask all to be patient and charitable. To avoid mistakes I must go slow. It is better to be slow than to be sorry.

I know that I am human, and that I shall make mistakes in human ways. Being human I believe in the welfare of my fellow man, and whatever concerns the good of humanity appeals to me, and will ever have my constant care and earnest consideration.

Whatever I do as governor will always be open to all and above board. I shall confide in the people, and I indu'ge the hope that when my official term, this day begun, comes to an end, that I shall have accomplished something to merit their approval, and to justify the confidence they have reposed in my intentions. Hence I shall promise little, but work unceasingly to secure the things now demanded by the people. They know an ounce of performance is worth a ton of promise, and they will judge my administration not by what I say now but what I do hereafter.

The hour has struck, and the task of administrative reform is mine. The cause is the cause of the state, and is worthy of the zealous efforts of any man. I grasp the opportunity the people now give me, and am resolved to shirk no responsibility; to work for the welfare of the people; to correct every existing abuse; to abolish useless offices, and wherever possible consolidate bureaus and commissions to secure greater economy and more efficiency; to uproot official corruption and to raise higher the standard of official integrity; to simplify the methods of orderly administration; to advance the prosperity of all the people; to be ever dissatisfied with conditions that can be improved; to promote the common weal; to guard the honor, and protect the rights of the Empire state; and last but not least to reduce governmental expenditures to the minimum, and thus lessen as much as possible the heavy burdens of taxation.

CHAPTER VII

SULZER TRIED TO BE AT PEACE WITH MURPHY

From the beginning of the Sulzer administration the foes of Tammany confidently predicted that the governor would be a typical organization executive and that his policy would differ little from that of Governor Dix. Sulzer's appointments made during the first two months confirmed these predictions. All the principal appointees bore the Tammany tag, whether they were from New York city or upstate districts, and the organization leaders were delighted.

Those intimate friends of the governor who claimed to know that he was not a Tammany man; that he would sooner or later assert his independence of Charles F. Murphy, and be the real governor of the state, admitted their disappointment at the manner in which Governor Sulzer had begun his term of office in Albany. Still, they counseled patience, pointing out that Dix had permitted Tammany to be so entrenched in the state government, that the new executive had to proceed cautiously to undo what his predecessor had done.

Many of Mr. Sulzer's progressive friends, during this period complained to him of his apparent friendliness to Murphy and the under-bosses, and the governor's usual reply was he was trying to keep peace with the boss and at the same time carry through the legislature a program of reform. To one progressive democrat, long known throughout the state, as an unrelenting opponent of Tammany, Governor Sulzer said:

" Charles F. Murphy will soon discover, if he doesn't know it now, that I intend to be the democratic leader and the real governor in this state."

To another democratic chairman of a county committee, Governor Sulzer, early in the year, declared:

" I agree with Thomas M. Osborne that Charles F. Murphy will never control another state convention. A real direct primary law will prevent that."

These remarks, made occasionally to his visitors, were an index of Mr. Sulzer's real attitude toward the boss, even when he was trying to live in harmony with him. But he was careful not to indicate this feeling publicly, and to all direct questions put to him by newspaper men, calculated to test his relations with Murphy, his customary reply, in substance, was: " I am not seeking a quarrel with any representative of the organization; I am a man of peace."

Meanwhile, Lieutenant Governor Martin H. Glynn was a frequent visitor to the executive mansion which Governor Sulzer had renamed the " People's House." At these conferences between the governor and the lieutenant governor various affairs of state were discussed. At nearly all of them Mr. Glynn urgently pressed upon the governor the importance of using his influence to obtain from the legislature a genuine primary law. He reminded Mr. Sulzer that the democratic platforms in 1910 and 1912 had promised the people of the state that such a law would be passed, and that the Dix administration had been greatly criticised because it failed to fulfill the promise.

At these conferences the lieutenant governor professed to be zealously for such a law, and made it plain that his sympathies were with the upstate fight upon Tammany bossism. The governor was then busying himself in getting other legislation through which he deemed vital to the state, included among which were the stock exchange bills, measures to reorganize the labor and health departments, and providing for workingmen's compensation.

In his consultations with Tammany leaders in the legislature about this time, Governor Sulzer advised a policy of harmony, saying that while he was willing to give Tammany the larger share of appointments, some should go to the leaders known to be opposed to Tammany dictation upstate. He contended that such men as John N. Carlisle, Thomas M. Osborne and John K. Sague should be made to feel that they were a part of the organization.

From the average Tammany man the names of these men invariably brought angry comment. The governor was informed that any recognition of these enemies of the organization would be very objectionable to Mr. Murphy. Mr. Carlisle, however, was appointed by the governor chairman of a committee of inquiry to investigate state departments for the purpose of improving administrative methods. The other two members of the committee, John H. Delaney and H. Gordon Lynn, were Tammany men.

February 2, after having been a month in office, Governor Sulzer in an interview with a reporter for " The Knickerbocker Press" expressed his confidence in being able to carry through, the nine big pledges made in the democratic platform and in his speeches before election.

At that time he was in a dickering frame of mind in his attitude toward Tammany, for he said:

" Some of the newspapers seem to be growing impatient over what they consider delay in my getting into a fight with somebody right away, but it isn't my place to seek a quarrel. I am endeavoring to co-operate with all who want to accomplish what we promised to do. Depend upon it, I shall not back away from a position, once I make up my mind that I am right."

Among the pledges which the governor then admitted he considered vital was the one on direct primaries, but he declined to discuss the details of the measure. He was more willing to talk of the work being done by his committee of inquiry appointed to examine the state departments for the purpose of bringing about efficiency and economy.

It is conceded now that the first bitter hostility on the part of the Tammany leaders toward Governor Sulzer came when John A. Hennessy, appointed executive auditor, testified before the committee of inquiry concerning the graft he had discovered in contracts for restoration of burned portions of the state Capitol. The revelations resulted in the resignation of Herman W. Hoefer, the state architect, and a thorough reorganization of that department.

*NOTE—For Hennessy's report on Capitol graft see index.

FIRST PROOF OF COURAGE

Here was the first proof that Governor Sulzer dared to investigate a department over which a Tammany man presided, and to direct his investigator to make the facts public. This, indeed, was political " treason," as incomprehensible as it was unpardonable to the normal Tammany mind.

But the governor continued to show evidences of his desire to award Tammany a share of the offices, with the expectation

that he would be able to get through the legislature his fundamental reforms.

"My administration," he said in February, "will not be
remembered so much by the appointments I make to office as
the fundamental laws I am able to get, of lasting benefit to
the people. What I say for publication from day to day will
not be considered of much consequence unless it is followed by
the doing of the things desired done."

Governor Sulzer, it will be observed, was willing to give
Tammany offices if, in return, he could get the legislative
reforms he had set his heart on.

In the meantime he was being condemned by his reform and
progressive friends for handing over the spoils of office to his
enemies. They predicted that he would soon find himself in
the same predicament into which Governor Dix had been
forced—entrenchment of Tammany behind powerful offices,
with no substantial legislation to benefit the people in return.

When he named Edward E. McCall, a Tammany justice of
the supreme court, to succeed William R. Willcox as chairman
of the public service commission of the first district, there was
a howl of dissent from the anti-Tammany democrats and
especially from New Yorkers, who were fighting against the
pending contract between the city and the Interborough
company. Appointment of McCall is said to have severed a
long political and personal friendship between the governor
and William R. Hearst.

At this time it was assumed that John N. Carlisle, of Watertown, whom the governor had made chairman of his committee of inquiry, was to be appointed chairman of the upstate
public service commission to succeed Frank W. Stevens.
Carlisle was offensive to Charles F. Murphy because of his
independence. Governor Sulzer was informed by Murphy
that Tammany's choice for the chairmanship was George M.
Palmer, chairman of the democratic state committee. The
governor, still in a mood to compromise, is said to have offered
Palmer a place on the commission to succeed Curtis N. Douglas,
brother-in-law of Governor Dix, who had been appointed by
Mr. Dix during the closing days of his administration. Palmer
refused the appointment, still confident that he could get the
chairmanship.

Lieutenant Governor Martin H. Glynn, according to the governor, appealed to him to appoint Patrick E. McCabe to succeed Mr. Douglas as public service commissioner. McCabe, as was well known, was the factotum of Charles F. Murphy in Albany county, and the one man, more than any other, responsible for the political advancement of Mr. Glynn.

Governor Sulzer declared afterwards that he was astounded at the proposition of the lieutenant governor that Mr. McCabe should be appointed to a position so important, for, outside of his utter lack of experience and training for the place, it was pointed out that the people would never tolerate the appointment of political bosses on a commission dealing directly with public service corporations.

CHAPTER VIII

Although there was already evidence of friction between the governor and Charles F. Murphy early in February, Mr. Sulzer and Mr. Glynn, so far as outward appearances could be judged, were still on friendly terms. Governor Sulzer trusted his associate implicitly, and, during their conferences from day to day, confided to the lieutenant governor all his legislative plans, the latter continuing to urge on the governor the question of direct primaries as the pressing and popular pledge of the democratic platform to carry out.

But while Mr. Glynn appeared to Governor Sulzer as being in sympathy with his program, and indicated a desire to assist him in giving it effect, the lieutenant governor, according to other witnesses, was all the while on the most confidential relations with the governor's political enemies. Toward the latter part of February, Mr. Glynn sent for Jay W. Forrest, of Albany, to come and see him in his office at the Capitol. Mr. Forrest had been applying to the courts for a writ of mandamus to reinstate him as a member of the Albany county democratic general committee from which he had been removed by Patrick E. McCabe. The proceedings evidently were annoying to the McCabe organization, as the leaders were anxious to stop them.

The lieutenant governor gave Forrest the usual lecture about the futility of being an independent in politics, advised him to stop his court proceedings and come into the organization.

"I have talked this thing over with Sulzer," he said to Mr. Forrest, "and he says he is going to take care of you. There will be a good appointment for you."

Mr. Forrest says that the place referred to was that of state sealer of weights and measures, but that Governor Sulzer afterwards told him he wanted to give him something better. The lieutenant governor was very anxious on this occasion to persuade Mr. Forrest to come into the McCabe

organization and "be good." Mr. Forrest quotes Mr. Glynn
as follows:

"Jay, you are making a great mistake in fighting the organization. Those fellows in New York city are the ones you have
got to be with, if you ever expect to amount to anything in
politics. McCabe is their representative and you have to be
with him if you expect to get any office or favor of any kind.
What is the use, Jay, of running your head up against a stone
wall.

"*You know I once had an idea that I could get somewhere by
being independent, but I gave that up long ago. Why don't you
come in and be with the organization? If you do, even now, you
will be well taken care of.*"

Forrest, it will be remembered, after having been promised
the democratic nomination for congress by the McCabe
organization, was refused it at the last minute, and had become
an independent candidate. In February he was preparing to
make further trouble for the McCabe organization in the
courts which led to the fervent plea of the lieutenant governor.

"We got talking about Governor Sulzer," said Mr. Forrest,
"after Mr. Glynn delivered that lecture to me about the
foolishness of being independent in politics. At the beginning
of the governor's term, I, with many other democrats, was
disappointed at the way he was giving pretty nearly everything
to Murphy. The lieutenant governor, I recall very distinctly,
said:

"'I have tried to get that fellow downstairs (the governor)
to do certain things and if he does not do these things I will be
governor of the state.'"

"That happened toward the last of February and it was not
known just how Governor Sulzer was going to act. As I say,
I was against him then. He hadn't been living up to what I
considered the promises of the platform, and it looked as if
Sulzer was going to be another Dix. For that reason I attached
no particular significance to the words of Mr. Glynn. But
what he said before election about the possibility of the governor's removal and what he said at that meeting in his office in
the Capitol in February, come home to me with re-inforced
meaning, in the light of the events of the last few months.

"I am stating the facts in as nearly the language as I can

"If he does not do these things I will be governor of the state."

now put them and I leave the people to draw their own inference. For some years past, Mr. Glynn often undertook to tell me what a fool I was not to get inside the organization, and I could have pretty near anything I wanted. At all of these conversations he set himself down as being in harmony with Tammany, with Murphy and McCabe, and told me again and again that my only salvation was to get into the Tammany band wagon. He particularly wanted to impress on me that McCabe was the whole thing in Albany county, and that McCabe was the authorized agent of Charles F. Murphy.

"In the summer of 1912, weeks before the democratic state convention at Syracuse, I met Mr. Glynn and he said to me:

"'I have a good chance to be nominated for governor. Murphy is the whole thing in this state, and if you want anything you have got to be with him. Dix can't be renominated because he can't be re-elected. If you want anything you have to be with McCabe in Albany county.'"

DINGED IN EARS ALL SUMMER

"That kind of talk was dinged into my ears all that summer. Mr. Glynn seemed to know the inside of the Murphy game, and he was giving it to me to persuade me to come out in the open for the organization.

On the 31st of October, 1910, Martin H. Glynn wrote the following and printed it in his paper, the "Albany Times-Union."

"Mr. Forrest is a powerful speaker and has a blistering way of saying things. When so minded he makes language sizzle and facts cut like a rapier."

In August, 1911, Martin H. Glynn requested Mr. Forrest, as a personal favor, to become a member of the democratic general committee of Albany county. And on August 26th, 1911, Mr. Glynn printed Mr. Forrest's picture in his paper, with the following underneath:

"With Jay W. Forrest as a member of the democratic general committee, the democrats will have the distinction of being represented by one of the foremost thinkers of the day along the line of economic thought. As an orator he is the equal of any man on the public platform. He has a repu-

CHAPTER IX

SULZER'S SECRET MEETINGS WITH MURPHY

Governor Sulzer afterwards outlined more in detail his secret meetings with Charles F. Murphy and their conversation on those occasions. He was being condemned by both Tammany and anti-Tammany men for his policy at the outset and it was evident that he would soon have to announce himself on one side or the other. The public would demand to know whether he was with the democratic state organization or whether he was to make an effort to emulate the example set by President Woodrow Wilson in his war upon bossism in politics.

As he tells the story himself, Governor Sulzer's conversations with Mr. Murphy during the early months of his administration were stormy and prolonged.

"Mr. Murphy did not attend my inauguration," declared Mr. Sulzer, "I first saw him after I was governor when he came to Albany to attend the presidential electors' meeting January 13. We had a brief conversation at the executive chamber and at the executive mansion. He telephoned from the Ten Eyck hotel that he did not think it advisable to meet me at the mansion and asked me to come to the hotel that night. I told him it would be impossible for me to do that.

"The next time I met him was at Judge McCall's house in New York City about the beginning of February. Judge McCall met me at the 125th street station with an automobile to take me to his house. On the way over I remember that the judge advised me to be firm with Murphy. I had come to see Judge McCall about appointing him public service commissioner and the judge confided to me that he would accept if I insisted upon it, but he wanted Murphy's consent so that there would be no trouble about confirmation by the senate.

"When we reached Judge McCall's house we went upstairs and I met Mr. Murphy in the front room. We talked over several matters. Judge McCall was present part of the time. Then we had dinner.

"After dinner Mr. Murphy and I discussed matters at considerable length regarding appointments. Mr. Murphy urged me to .appoint his friend, John Galvin, public service commissioner, in place of Mr. Willcox, whose term had expired.

\\" The subway question was very acute in New York and great pressure had been brought to bear on me by prominent citizens to reappoint Mr. Willcox, or to let him remain in office until the subway contracts were disposed of.]

" I urged the appointment of Henry Morgenthau or George Foster Peabody or Colonel John Temple Graves. Mr. Murphy would not hear of these men. !He talked long and earnestly in behalf of Mr. Galvin.

" Finally I suggested as a compromise Judge McCall. McCall himself said that he would accept, provided it was agreeable to Mr. Murphy. √ √

"We discussed the subway question, the proposed contracts and various other matters. The hour was getting late and I finally said that unless Judge McCall was agreeable to Mr. Murphy I would send in the name of Henry Morgenthau to the senate the following Monday night. and if he was not confirmed, of course Mr. Willcox would not hold over, and that that would be agreeable to a great many prominent citizens in the city.

" Mr. Murphy was agreeable to the appointment of Judge McCall, and it was understood that the judge should send me his resignation by messenger Monday afternoon.

" It was near midnight when I left the McCall house in an automobile, both Murphy and McCall accompanying me to the grand central depot, where I took the midnight train for Albany.

"At this meeting and subsequently, Mr. Murphy demanded from me pledges regarding legislation, and especially concerning appointments to the public service commissions, the health department, the labor department, the state hospital commission, the department of state prisons, and the department of highways. He insisted that George M. Palmer should be appointed chairman and Patrick E. McCabe a member of the public service commission of the second district. This is the 'Packy' McCabe who is Murphy's political lieutenant in Albany.

" Mr. Murphy further insisted upon having ' The ' McManus

for labor commissioner, a man named Meyers for state architect, a man from Brooklyn whose name I forget for state
hospital commissioner, and James E. Gaffney for highway
commissioner, in case I wished to supplant Mr. Reel. Mr.
Murphy said that Reel ought to be kept, as he was a good man.
This is the same Reel whom I subsequently removed.

"Mr. Murphy added that if I wished a new commissioner
of highways 'Jim' Gaffney was the best all-around man for
the job. Subsequently he demanded the appointment of
Gaffney, and still later a prominent New Yorker came to me
in the executive mansion bringing the message from Mr. Murphy that it was 'Gaffney or war.' I declined to appoint
Gaffney.

"This is the Gaffney who, only a few months afterwards, on
September 4, 1913, in undisputed testimony before the Supreme
Court at Nyack, was shown to have demanded and received
$30,000 in money (refusing to take a check), from one of the
aqueduct contractors, nominally for "advice." This is the
man who Mr. Murphy demanded should be put in a position
where he would superintend and control the spending of
sixty-six millions of the money of the state in road contracts."

"When I removed Reel from the office of commissioner of
highways I began to hear pretty vigorously from Mr. Murphy,
who was more determined than ever to secure the place for
'Jim' Gaffney.

"About the fifth of March, just after President Wilson's
inauguration, I visited the President in the White House.
When I came out I met Thomas F. Smith, secretary of Tammany Hall, in front of the White House. He wanted to know
what I had said to the President and what the President had
said to me. I told him I made it a rule never to discuss conversations that I had with the President.

"Mr. Smith said Mr. Murphy wanted me to meet him and
some of the democratic state leaders at Senator O'Gorman's
rooms in the Shoreham hotel at 8 o'clock that night. He
asked me if I would be there and I said 'Yes.'

"I went to the Shoreham that night. There were present
Senator O'Gorman, Mr. Murphy, Norman E. Mack, the Murphy leader in Buffalo; Mr. McCoohey, the Murphy leader of

Brooklyn; Thomas F. Smith and myself. State affairs were discussed in a general way. I took very little part in the talk.

" I had made arrangements to leave for New York with my staff and Mrs. Sulzer and about 11 o'clock I shook hands with all and bade them good night.

"As I went out Mr. Murphy followed me into the hall. He told me he was very anxious to get away to Hot Springs but didn't want to go until Albany matters were straightened out.

" He asked me if I would give him assurance that I would appoint his friend ' Jim ' Gaffney, commissioner of highways. That place, you will remember, controlled the immediate spending of $66,000,000 for good roads, the very same work in which Mr. Hennessy's investigations have recently uncovered frauds amounting to millions of dollars in twenty-two counties under the Reel administration.

" Mr. Murphy seemed very much aroused. He said he would like to have the matter settled before he went away; that if I would appoint Mr. Gaffney I could have my own way regarding other matters.

" Mr. Murphy assured me that he was more interested in Gaffney's appointment than in anything else in the state; that Gaffney was a good all 'round man for the job, knew what to do and could get results!

" I told him that in my opinion it would be a mistake to appoint Mr. Gaffney. I repeated to him practically what I had said at Judge McCall's house and also at his own house a few days before.

" Mr. Murphy said to me, ' I want you to appoint Gaffney. It is an organization matter. I will appreciate it.'

" I said, ' I will consider all you say about the matter. I want to go slow and get the very best man I can find for that position. I would rather be slow about the appointment than be sorry.'

And he answered: ' If you don't appoint Gaffney you will be sorry.'

" I told him that I thought the appointment for highway commissioner should be to an upstate man, that the people up the state expected the governor to appoint an upstate man; that there was a prevailing sentiment to that effect.

"He replied that there was nothing in that; that New

York city paid most of the money and was just as much entitled
to the place as the upstate people.

"Again, Mr. Murphy said that Gaffney, in his opinion, was
the best man for the place; that he would see to it that Gaffney
was promptly confirmed; that Gaffney would make good, and
that I would never have cause to regret it.   He asked me again
to give him a promise to appoint Gaffney.   I told him I would
not make a promise about it; that I would consider all he said,
but that in my opinion Mr. Gaffney would not do; that it
would be a mistake to appoint him; that the people would not
stand for it; that Mr. Gaffney was too close to him.

"Mr. Murphy finally said, 'I am for Gaffney.   The organization demands his appointment and I want you to do it.'

"I replied: 'I will make no promise about it.'

He said: 'It will be Gaffney or war.'

"He laughed at me and rebuked me for asserting my independence and said that I might be the governor but that he
controlled the legislature; that unless I did what he wanted
me to do regarding legislation and appointments I could not
get my nominations confirmed and that he would block everything.

"I listened to those boasts and threats from Mr. Murphy,
not once but frequently.   It was all disheartening and dis-
couraging, but I tried to be patient, to get along with him, and
do my best.

"While I was governor, Mr. Murphy communicated with me
frequently, and always along these lines.   From the beginning
of January to April 13, there was hardly a day that he did not
send some one to see me with peremptory demands to do this
or that.   Some requests were reasonable and I granted them;
some were so unreasonable and so much against the people's
interest that I refused to consent.

"Prior to April 13 our relations politically were badly
strained.   I could not comply with his demands.   I realized
that we had come to a parting of the ways.   I was determined
to be governor, to make a good record, to do my duty according
to what I believed to be right and to carry out, as far as possible,
the platform upon which I was elected.   I also wanted to
treat all the upstate democratic county organizations squarely,

whether these county organizations were friendly to Mr. Murphy or otherwise. That was not his plan.

"One talk with Mr. Murphy, which I remember very distinctly, was at his house in New York on March 18.

"He expressed great indignation because I had removed Colonel Scott, the superintendent of prisons. I told him the reasons. He pooh-poohed them, and said Scott was a friend of his.

"That was the occasion when Mr. Murphy objected to John Mitchell for commissioner of labor.

"I talked to Mr. Murphy about a new commissioner of labor and said we ought to appoint the very best man in the state. I spoke to him about John Mitchell. He wanted to know. what was the matter with 'The' McManus for labor commissioner.

"I replied that, in my judgment, that it would never do to appoint McManus. He told me that he thought McManus was the best man for the place, and his appointment would be satisfactory to the labor organizations as well as to the 'organization,' meaning, of course, himself.

"I told him under no circumstances would I agree to appoint McManus, that McManus had been to see me several times about it and had told me that he had come direct from Mr. Murphy and that Mr. Murphy wanted me to appoint him.

"I urged the peculiar qualifications of Mitchell, and he said Mitchell was not a democrat, and that he was a Roosevelt man, adding: 'He is a progressive and you are heading the same way.'

"I replied that Mitchell was a good enough democrat to get every democratic vote in the legislature of Illinois for United States senator, and to be offered the democratic nomination for vice president at the Denver convention. 'However,' I said, 'it is immaterial to me whether he is a democrat or not. He is the most experienced and competent man in the state in my opinion for the place.'

"We talked over the appointments to vacancies on the supreme court bench for the first department. Mr. Murphy was very anxious that I should appoint Michael J. Mulqueen and Mr. Gillespie to two of these vacancies, and urged the matter on me very strongly. In talking about these appointments to the supreme court bench I told him under no circumstances would I appoint any lawyer to the supreme court unless it met with the approval of the bar association.

"As a matter of fact I refused to name Mr. Murphy's candidates for the supreme court vacancies, but appointed Bartow S. Weeks and Eugene S. Philbin.

" It was in this very conversation that Mr. Murphy said to me: ' Unless you do what I want you to do I will wreck your administration as governor, block all your legislation, and defeat all of your appointments.'

" He said, ' Remember, I control the legislature, and the legislature can control the governor.'

" He also threatened me with public disgrace unless I agreed to his program on legislative matters and appointments.

" It was at this conference, too, that he talked about the things he ' had on me,' and said that I had better listen to him and not to enemies up the state; that if I did what he told me to I would have things easy, and no trouble, and that if I didn't do what he wanted me to I would have all the trouble I wanted.

I told him that I was the governor and that if he would let me alone I could succeed, but that I could not succeed if I was to be a catspaw for him. I told him that I wanted to give the state an honest and efficient administration; that in my opinion that would do more to help the party than anything else.

" He was very insulting. Then I asked him what he could do to destroy me. And he said: ' Never mind, you will find out in good time. Stand by the organization and you will be all right. If you go against the organization I will make your administration the laughing stock of the state.'

" I told him that all I wanted was to do right, be honest, and carry out my oath of office. He laughed at this, and said that some of the men I had around me would run away from me just as soon as trouble began.

" It was at this time that he asked me to call off George W. Blake, the commissioner who was investigating the prisons. He said that Blake must be called off and that he didn't want the prisons investigated unless we could agree upon some man to do it. I told him that Blake was an efficient man and that I was going to let him go on with his work, and he said: ' If you do you will be sorry for it. Mark what I am telling you now!'*

"I told him what I had heard about the vileness of things in the Sing Sing and Auburn prisons. I said: 'We certainly ought not to stand for them. I want to get at the facts and if there is anything wrong, stop it; if there is any graft, eliminate it.'

"Mr. Murphy told me that he didn't want anything done in connection with Sing Sing prison by Blake or any other man; that the warden there, Mr. Kennedy, was a friend of his and a good man and he wanted him left alone. This, remember, was the warden whom I afterward removed from his place on charges and who was since indicted by the Westchester grand jury.

"When Mr. Murphy found that he could not use me and control me he sent emissaries to see me frequently to demand that I do certain things, and to threaten me if I refused. These threats began in a small way in February and continued with greater vehemence up to the very night the assembly passed the resolution of impeachment in obedience to Mr. Murphy's orders.

"One of the agents through whom Mr. Murphy most frequently communicated with me was Judge McCall. Judge McCall usually spoke of Mr. Murphy as 'the chief,' and would say to me that 'the chief' wished such and such a thing done or demanded that I follow such and such a course of action.

"Every Tammany member of the legislature of either house who approached me from day to day used the same language, saying that 'the chief' demanded this or demanded that, or that 'the chief' had telephoned to put through such a piece of legislation, or kill some other piece of legislation.

Governor Sulzer said he knew what Mr. Murphy and his agents in the legislature were trying to do long before open hostilities began, and that he was in for a long, hard fight. He declared, however, he had resolved to go through with it and rely on public opinion to back him up in his battle for such reforms as a real primary law and especially his work in uncovering graft in the state departments.

It was recalled that Patrick E. McCabe was the first of the

* Note—For Blake's report on prison see index.

THE NEW ARSON TRUST

Tammany men to accuse the governor of the Vermont perjury
affair. Later developments indicated that he had been selected
at the Delmonico conference held a short time prior to that
accusation, to take the first opportunity to embarrass Sulzer.

That was followed quickly by the Philadelphia breach of
promise suit, the inspiration for which was later traced to a
political agent of Charles F. Murphy. These two accusa-
tions served, as was intended, to distract public attention in a
measure from the campaign then going on throughout the
state for the governor's primary bill. Notwithstanding the
prompt replies of Mr. Sulzer to both charges, public discussion
of the details did not cases.

Referring to these two attacks afterwards, the governor said
he had reason to believe that Mr. Murphy hoped they would
be sufficient to compel his surrender to the boss; that he would
be willing to tell Judge McCall—still on friendly terms with the
governor—that he would stop the investigators and agree to
some compromise on a direct primary law if no more charges
were made against him.

When he declined to heed these threats, the Frawley committee was directed by Murphy to go deeper into the Sulzer
record. Matthew T. Horgan, deputy efficiency and economy
commissioner, who had been intimate with Sulzer during his
campaign for governor, was appointed secretary to the Frawley
committee and the work of uncovering the campaign receipts
and expenditures of Mr. Sulzer was begun.

CHAPTER X

SULZER'S LAST MEETING WITH THE BOSS

Even after he had been insulted and threatened with destruction by Murphy during his interviews with the boss in January, February and March, Governor Sulzer and the mutual friends of the two men still indulged the hope that harmony might be restored. It was known among the democratic leaders at Albany that there was serious friction between the governor and Murphy. C. Gordon Reel, superintendent of highways, had been removed by the governor March 7th. Col. Joseph F. Scott, superintendent of prisons, had also been forced out and the air was full of rumors that wholesale removals of Tammany men at the head of other departments were to be made. These disquieting reports disturbed the democratic leaders all over the state, especially those responsible for office-holders as well as those through whom important contracts were awarded to friends.

Governor Sulzer attended the Jefferson banquet at the Hotel Waldorf, New York city, April 13th, given by the National Democratic Club. Charles F. Murphy was present and Governor Sulzer was one of the speakers. It was observed that the two men did not recognize each other.

After the governor had spoken, Norman E. Mack, of Buffalo, came to the governor's table to greet him and said he was very sorry to know that there was a difference between him and Mr. Murphy.

" I should think," suggested Mr. Mack, " that this trouble could be fixed up before it became public and a working agreement made between you for the good of the party. Will you meet Mr. Murphy after the dinner? " the Buffalo man inquired of the governor.

Governor Sulzer replied he was willing and suggested that they meet in the cafe downstairs. Mr. Mack carried the message to Murphy, who sent back word that it was too public a place and wanted to meet the governor at his own rooms at Delmonico's. Governor Sulzer refused to do this

and proposed to Mr. Mack that Mr. Murphy come to his room at the Waldorf after the banquet was over.

When the governor left the dining room and was on his way upstairs he met Judge Edward E. McCall and former Governor Spriggs, and invited them to his room. While the three men were talking, Mr. Mack arrived and announced that Mr. Murphy was in the cafe but did not want to come to the governor's room as newspaper men were there and they would be likely to find out where he went if he went upstairs. Mr. Murphy again asked through Mack why the governor could not meet him at Delmonico's.

Governor Sulzer once more declined to go there and asked Mr. Mack to try again to bring Mr. Murphy up to the room in the hotel. Mr. Mack went away and returned soon to say that Mr. Murphy had left the cafe.

Judge McCall called Mr. Murphy up at his home on the telephone and the latter suggested that he and the governor meet him there.

It was the last time the governor and Mr. Murphy met. Governor Sulzer described the conference and recalled what was said as follows:

" Judge McCall and I got into a taxicab and went to Mr. Murphy's residence. It was after midnight and Mr. Murphy let us in at the door. We sat in the front parlor and talked over the situation at Albany—appointments, legislation and so on. Mr. Murphy would agree to nothing I wanted, and I didn't agree to anything he wanted.

" I asked him not to interfere with the trial of Stilwell in the senate. I said:

" 'What are you going to do about him? '

" ' Stand by him, of course,' replied Mr. Murphy. ' Stilwell will be acquitted. It will only be a three-day wonder. How do you expect a senator to live on $1,500 a year? That is only chicken feed.'

"At this conference," said Mr. Sulzer, " I urged Mr. Murphy to let me carry out in good faith the platform pledges of the democratic party for direct nominations. We talked over the bill. I told him there was a strong sentiment throughout the state in favor of this legislation. He said I was mistaken, that

"I will disgrace and destroy you."

THE NEW YOR

there was no sentiment for direct primaries except from a few cranks.

"I called his attention to the pledge in the platform. He said he was opposed to any bill that abolished the state convention, and eliminated the party emblem.

"I said that there could be no honest direct primary law unless that were done. He answered that the organization would never agree to any bill that did it, and that such a bill would be overwhelmingly defeated in the legislature. I said to him that unless we made good on direct primaries we would lose the State. He replied that I did not know what I was talking about.

"We again talked over appointments to vacancies on the supreme court bench, and I said that I was being criticised by the judges and others for not filling the vacancies. He talked over several names that would be agreeable to him, Mulqueen, Gillespie and others. I told him that I thought I ought to select the very best lawyers I could get, and said again that I would make no appointments unless the names were approved by the Bar Association. That was the last time I saw Mr. Murphy, and I returned to the hotel very much disheartened.

"Before we parted that night I warned Mr. Murphy that he would wreck the party and accomplish his own destruction if he persisted in shielding grafters and violating platform pledges. His angry retort was that I was an ingrate, and that he would disgrace and destroy me.

"Every man who has borne the weight of a great office like that of the governor of New York will appreciate my position. I wished to keep in with the organization; I was anxious to avoid a break with it. I knew only too well the legislature would obey Mr. Murphy's every order, whether given over the telephone or in person. I knew the terrible odds against me in the fight which I courted when I declined to submit to Mr. Murphy's dictation; when I declined to turn my office into an instrument for the corruption of government and the debauching of the state. I was reluctant to break with Mr. Murphy. I did it only because it became impossible to do otherwise, and not betray my oath of office and forfeit every shred of self-respect.

...to Illinois after my last interview with ...ako considered my object and the whole ...our only at that time, nor since, that any ...any office was in my mind.

...proper for me to bow?: to surrender to ...mindful to everything except his orders; ...believed was right, regardless of Murphy, ...to tell them the people my reasons.

...the way to determine not to surrender. I ...not maintain my self-respect.

...it over. It did not seem possible. I knew ...old the liars when he said he could and would ...legislature. I knew also that every state ...nder his control, were the law I managed to

...More than all, I knew from many years' ...my methods, that when desperate, he would ...thwart me, even to the extent he has done,

...ing and seriously about it all. My impulse ...knowledge of Murphy's control of everything, ...which he was held by every legislator and ...e fight seem hopeless.

...d be the victim in the end. I was deeply in ...hy knew it. I was without power over the ...Murphy knew it. Even friends of good govern- ...cynical, offering much criticism but little real

...me out and signed my resignation as governor. ...thought it all over finally it looked cowardly. ...resignation. The old determination to fight ...d I made up my mind that no matter what the ...wardly I would fight and fight hard. ...fought hard from that moment to the present

GOVERNOR SULZER AND LIEUTENANT-GOVERNOR GLYNN

Taken January 1st, 1913, on the north porch of the "People's House." Governor Sulzer had just arrived from New York City and Mr. Glynn had called to greet him.

"When I returned to Albany after my last interview with Mr. Murphy I carefully considered my plight and the whole state situation. It was only at that time, not since, that any thought of resigning my office was in my mind.

" There were three paths for me to travel; to surrender to Murphy and be unmindful to everything except his orders; to fight for what I believed was right, regardless of Murphy, or to resign my office and give the people my reasons.

" It did not take me long to determine not to surrender.   I could not do that and maintain my self-respect.

" Could I fight and win?   It did not seem possible.   I knew that Mr. Murphy told the fact when he said he could and would block me in the legislature.   I knew also that every state department was under his control, save the few I managed to hold against him.   More than all, I knew from many years' knowledge of Murphy methods, that, when desperate, he would stop at nothing to thwart me, even to the extent he has done, which is not his limit.

" I thought long and seriously about it all.   My impulse was to fight; my knowledge of Murphy's control of everything, and the fear in which he was held by every legislator and officeholder, made fight seem hopeless.

" I alone would be the victim in the end.   I was deeply in debt and Murphy knew it.   I was without power over the legislature and Murphy knew it.   Even friends of good government stood by, cynical, offering much criticism but little real help.

" Then I wrote out and signed my resignation as governor.

" But as I thought it all over finally it looked cowardly. I tore up my resignation.   The old determination to fight came to me and I made up my mind that no matter what the cost to me personally I would fight and fight hard.

"And I have fought hard from that moment to the present day of my unjust condemnation—how hard is proven by the enemies I have made and the conspiracy they have worked out against me.   Every agency these enemies could use to destroy me has been used.   It is a long, pitiable story, miserably contemptible in its meanness and pettiness."

GOVERNOR SULZER AND LIEUTENANT-GOVERNOR GLYNN

Taken January 1st, 1913, on the north porch of the "People's House." Governor Sulzer had just arrived from New York City and Mr. Glynn had called to greet him.

CHAPTER XI

IMPEACHMENT COURT AT DELMONICO'S

After his break with Charles F. Murphy, Governor Sulzer took every opportunity to prove to the people of the state that he was no longer consulting the wishes of the boss. He had already sent to the legislature, three days before the last meeting with Mr. Murphy, the vigorous message disapproving the Blauvelt primary bill. When he finally resolved to burn all his bridges and to resist Murphy at every point he concluded to make the fight for a genuine primary law the main issue between him and his enemies in the democratic party.

He called into conference all the democratic county chairmen, all the members of the democratic state committee and representatives of all political parties and organizations in favor of a state-wide primary law. These meetings, held in the executive chamber and addressed by Governor Sulzer, stirred the state from end to end. Committees were appointed to prepare a primary bill and to promote its enactment by the legislature.

Lieutenant-Governor Glynn was offered the chairmanship of the publicity committee. As he had always loudly proclaimed his belief in direct primaries and had urged Governor Charles E. Hughes to use the axe on the bosses to hasten the realization of the reform it was assumed that he would be found working side by side with the governor for the Sulzer bill.

Greatly to the surprise of direct primary advocates all over the state the lieutenant-governor paid no attention to the invitation to become chairman of the publicity committee. His silence was all the more astonishing from the fact that since the beginning of the year he had constantly urged upon Governor Sulzer the desirability of sending a strong message to the legislature for a state-wide direct primary law.

It soon dawned on the minds of the people that Mr. Glynn had gone completely over to the side of Charles F. Murphy

NOTE—For complete list of all those in attendance see index.

and that he would be found with the boss against whatever
the governor attempted to persuade the legislature to do.
Beginning of the direct primary campaign, in large measure,
lined up the sheep and the goats, so to speak, and the lieutenant-governor for the first time during his public career
openly chose the side of the Tammany boss.

Every time Governor Sulzer spoke for direct primaries he
spoke with a feeling and earnestness that impressed those who
listened to him with the idea that he had recently undergone
a radical change in his opinions. He no longer veiled these
opinions with equivocal language, but made plain in lucid and
forceful English that he was for an honest, thoroughgoing
direct primary law, because it was the only instrument by which
the people could drive the bosses from power and restore
popular government at Albany.

Those who listened to his fervent plea for a direct primary
law and denunciations of bosses were not aware at the time of
his secret conferences with Charles F. Murphy and his many
tribulations resulting from the arrogance of the boss. The
public began to sit up and take notice of the fact that a real
war had at last broken out between the two men, but it was
ignorant of the events since the beginning of the year, which
gradually led up to and provoked the opening of hostilities.

It subsequently developed that it was the governor's determination to carry the direct primary war into the Africa of
Tammany and especially his refusal to call off his special investigator, John A. Hennessy, from the pursuit of grafters
that was the direct cause of the notorious Delmonico conference
held May 20th. By a man who claims to have obtained all
the names of those present from one of the conferees, those
who attended were: Charles F. Murphy, Norman E. Mack,
Edward E. McCall, William H. Fitzpatrick, Patrick E. Mc-
Cabe, Martin H. Glynn, John H. McCooey, Thomas Foley,
Robert F. Wagner, James J. Frawley, Senator James A. Foley,
Alfred E. Smith and Aaron J. Levy.

Mr. Glynn afterwards vehemently denied that he was present
at any conference in Delmonico's. Certain it is that such a
conference was held and that it took the first steps toward
procuring impeachment of Governor Sulzer, who at that time
was out on his first tour of the state in behalf of the direct

primary bill which had been defeated at the regular session of the legislature. The legislature adjourned May 3rd and within a few days thereafter the governor issued a call for an extraordinary session to meet June 16th, its principal purpose being to consider the direct primary bill.

Governor Sulzer addressed the first public meetings in Buffalo, May 19th. At these gatherings, all of them being large and enthusiastic, he vigorously attacked the bosses, mentioning by name Charles F. Murphy, William H. Fitzpatrick and William Barnes. He also set forth the main features of the direct primary bill and called upon the people of Erie county to demand of William H. Fitzpatrick, the local Tammany boss, that he permit his seven assemblymen to vote as their constituents wanted them to vote on the primary bill.

"When the bosses permitted my nomination,' he said, " I suppose it was their idea that they could control me and I sometimes think if I were not so foxy they would control me. When they found out they could not control me they were the maddest men on earth. They said they were going to destroy me, but I say to you the only man who can do that is myself.

" The power to nominate is the power to control. The bosses want to control the governor and other state officers. That is why they insist upon retaining the state convention.

" Here and there a man slips into office who cannot be controlled. It took the bosses a long time to pick me. Now they are sorry they did it.

" I told the gentleman (Murphy) in New York in a speech that the best place for him was his own bailiwick. I know the tiger and best place for him is a cage.

" Some of the politicians are doing the cuttle fish act. They are muddying the water not to get away but to get something that doesn't belong to them."

This plain talk infuriated the Tammany men. No governor had ever dared to go before the people and hold the bosses up to contempt in that fashion.

The next day, May 20th, Charles F. Murphy and his aides held a council of war at Delmonico's, the private political headquarters of the boss. It was then and there resolved to " get something" on Sulzer and endeavor to have him impeached

NOTE—For Sulzer's speech in full at Buffalo see index.

and removed from office, if in the meantime he did not cease his attacks on the organization and stop his investigations into the highway, prisons and other state departments. As Senator Frawley is quoted as having remarked a few weeks later to former fire chief Croker: "Yes, we are going through with this impeachment because it is either Sulzer's life or ours."

It was determined at the conference of Tammany leaders first to threaten the governor with exposure of petty offenses and if he did not then take warning, to continue the attacks and remove him from office, if necessary. The Frawley committee, made up of senators and assemblymen, had been appointed before the legislature adjourned to pry into various matters. This committee, it was decided at the Delmonico conference, was to attempt to counteract the Hennessy and Blake investigations into the highways and prisons by holding hearings and assailing the data collected by the investigators. There was no intimation at the time that the governor's campaign expenses were to be made the subject of inquiry.

Soon after his return from the speaking tour for the direct primary bill, Governor Sulzer began to hear from the emissaries of Charles F. Murphy. At first the men who called on him pretended to be his friends more than they were friends of Murphy. They pleaded with him, " for the sake of the party," to cease his attacks on Murphy and the Tammany organization and especially not to "imperil democratic success" by investigations and making trouble over a direct primary law.

But the governor convinced all of these messengers that he had resolutely set his face toward the goal of an honest primary law and that he would not let up his efforts to uncover graft.

Then followed another train of Tammany agents who were more blunt in their threats. They repeated what Murphy had told him in private in April; that the boss "had something on him," and that it was the height of folly for even a governor to continue fighting the organization if he did not want to be destroyed. Speaking of his experience at this time, Governor Sulzer said:

" Every agency known to these political conspirators was set in motion. My life was raked from the time I was born down to the present day by detectives, investigators and various sleuths, with a view of finding out something that would

injure me. Criminals and perjurers were utilized to defame
me. I was hampered and obstructed in my official duties and
privately hounded, denounced and threatened.

"The first thing the conspirators did in the plot to poison
the public mind against me was to put out that Vermont
business. I promptly told the truth about the matter and it
fell flat. It was a forgery and I have sworn proofs to that
effect. Then came the Philadelphia breach of promise frame-
up. That also fell flat when I told the truth about it."

"We are going to get that fellow before we are through with him."

THE

CHAPTER XII

"WE'RE GOING TO GET THAT FELLOW"—McCABE

After Governor Sulzer had addressed direct primary meetings at Buffalo, Hornell, Corning and Elmira, he returned to Albany for a day before addressing two meetings in Schenectady. Among the speakers who accompanied the governor to Schenectady were John Mitchell, whom he had appointed commissioner of labor, and Jay W. Forrest of Albany. The newspapers for several days had contained notices of the meetings, giving the names of the speakers.

Patrick E. McCabe met Mr. Forrest a few days before the meeting in the Capitol and asked him whether it was true that he was going to address a Sulzer direct primary meeting at Schenectady.

"Yes, I am going to speak at that meeting," replied Mr. Forrest. "I have always been for direct primaries."

"I thought we had all that foolishness stopped," was McCabe's comment.

"You are mistaken; there is nothing foolish about direct primaries and you people will soon find it out," retorted Forrest.

"Well, Jay, if you are for direct primaries you can't expect any favors from Murphy or the organization. You have either to be for us or against us. This is a fight to the finish and we are going to get that fellow before we are through with him."

Mr. Forrest said that Mr. McCabe was excited. At that time there had been no public talk about impeachment but McCabe's parting prediction has since become significant of what was then going on in the inner Tammany circles.

McCabe's outbreak recalled to Forrest's mind that during Governor Charles E. Hughes' administration Martin H. Glynn, the senate clerk's friend, had been very much for direct primaries. He immediately began to look for an editorial published in Mr. Glynn's Albany newspaper, the " Times Union," April 9, 1909.

NOTE—For Forrest's speech in full see index.

Failing to find the files of the paper in the local libraries, he visited the " Times Union" office and asked for the file of that year. He had copied three or four lines of the editorial when he heard a voice behind him, asking: "Jay, what are you doing? "

Lieutenant Governor Glynn stood in the doorway, asking the question. " I am copying this editorial," Forrest replied, " that you wrote on direct primaries in 1909."

"What are you going to do with it," demanded the lieutenant governor.

" I am going to use it in the interest of direct primaries," replied Forrest.

Mr. Glynn.—" How do you know I wrote the editorial ? "

Mr. Forrest.—" Surely you are not going to deny your own child."

The lieutenant governor declared that he was not responsible for everything that appeared in the " Times Union," and ordered Forrest not to copy any more of the editorial. He then asked him into his private office.

" Now, Jay," began the lieutenant governor in his most confidential tone, " I have always been your friend and I don't see why you should want to get me mixed up in this direct primary fight. I don't want to be in this trouble between Sulzer and the people in New York city. If I get into it at all it will ruin my political future."

"Your future is gone now after you took part in that conference last week in Delmonico's," interrupted Forrest.

Mr. Forrest said that the lieutenant governor jumped from his chair in excitement at the mention of the Delmonico conference and denounced any statement to that effect as a lie. He demanded to know Forrest's authority for the report that he had been at any such conference.

Forrest refused to give it, but insisted that it was reliable authority. "And the same authority tells me," added Mr. Forrest, " that with you at that conference were Charles F. Murphy, Edward E. McCall, Robert F. Wagner, Patrick E. McCabe, and John H. McCooey. Martin, I know what I am talking about when I say you were there."

"And I say as positively that you don't know what you are

talking about when you say I was there," shouted the lieutenant governor.

Mr. Forrest returned to the subject of the editorial and wanted to know why he couldn't be permitted to copy it. " Remember," he warned Mr. Glynn, " that if I don't get it here I can hunt up another copy of the paper."

" Let me look at that editorial again," said Glynn, walking out to the file of the paper. After reading it over he turned to Forrest and said: " No, Jay, you can't copy that editorial now. And I want to ask you not to do anything about it until Monday night, when I will call you up and let you know my decision."

Mr. Forrest never heard from the lieutenant governor one way or the other on the subject. He thereupon advertised in the three Albany newspapers, the Knickerbocker Press, the Argus, and Evening Journal, for a copy of the Times Union of April 9, 1909, offering a reward of $5 for it. The following day a copy was brought to his home.

Governor Charles E. Hughes, who was then beginning his second term of two years, had been obstructed at every step by a combination of republican and democratic bosses in his efforts to get a direct primary bill enacted into law. Mr. Glynn then professed to be zealously for such a law. Here is the editorial which he had in his newspaper at the time and refused to allow Mr. Forrest to copy four years later:

MARTIN H. GLYNN IN 1909

Editorial Printed in his Newspaper the Albany Times-Union, April 9th, 1909.

" THE AXE, GOVERNOR, THE AXE."

" The political power and prestige of the governor of this state is second only to that of the President of the United States.

So potent is the authority of the governor—in the hands of one who knows how to use it, and who will use it like a man and not like an angel—that no machine politician can successfully oppose a governor's measures, particularly when such measures are framed in the interest of the whole people.

The test vote yesterday of 112 to 28 against Governor Hughes on his direct primary bill should be proof conclusive that the governor must change his methods before he can possibly pass any of the measures for which he has become personally responsible.

Yesterday's defeat was too emphatic to leave any excuse for an extra session of the legislature. To call an extra session under such circumstances would almost be an abuse of executive power.

Yesterday's vote was not a defeat. It was the most humiliating rout—horse, foot and dragoons—which has been administered to any governor of this state in thirty years.

It should convince Mr. Hughes that he can't tickle the bosses and fight them at one and the same time. MOST OF THE BOSSES ARE VAMPIRES—THEY KILL YOU IF YOU DON'T KILL THEM. ALL OF THEM ARE SHYLOCKS, ALWAYS DEMANDING THEIR POUND OF FLESH, BUT EVER FEARING TO SHED A DROP OF BLOOD— PARTICULARLY THEIR OWN.

If Governor Hughes thinks he can fight the bosses by giving them all the political pap in sight for three hundred and sixty-four days in the year and then wrestling them one day on scholastic questions he is sadly mistaken. This game of political warfare is not conducted on the lines of a college professorship. It is, as in all other kinds of warfare, the God of victory is with the heaviest artillery, and the General in a battle who refuses to fire his heaviest guns for fear of fracturing some rule of etiquette or of besmoking some lofty principle of conduct has no business to enter a battle himself or to lead his friends up against the lines of the enemy.

This political fight for good laws is not a game of parlor battledore and shuttlecock with all the social amenities. It is stand up, knock down and drag out fight, and you must do the other fellow before he does you. It may be all right in the religious life to turn the left cheek when your enemy smites you on the right. But in politics this course butters no parsnips and wins no victories. And it is high time for Governor Hughes to write this fact down in his diary.

Yesterday's defeat has injured the cause of direct primaries and made STRONGER THE RULE OF THE MACHINE IN THIS STATE.

THE PEOPLE ELECTED MR. HUGHES GOVERNOR, AND PLACED IN HIS HANDS ALL THE POWER WHICH THE LAW GIVES HIM TO WORK FOR THEIR INTERESTS. AND THIS POWER SHOULD BE USED TO WEAKEN THE ENEMIES AND STRENGTHEN THE FRIENDS OF MOVEMENTS FOR THE PUBLIC GOOD. What else can it mean? And isn't it nonsense to indulge in mental philosophical distinctions that prevent a common sense course looking to results for the public welfare?

Some of Governor Hughes' overzealous friends maintain that every time he is beaten by the machine he is stronger with the people. This is nonsense, and, if it were true, such warfare with such a purpose would be contemptible. We don't believe Governor Hughes fights with any such motive. But defeat never strengthened any leader or any cause, and Mr. Hughes and his issues are no shining exception to this rule.

GOVERNOR HUGHES HAS CONVINCED THE PEOPLE, BUT HE HAS FAILED TO CONVINCE THE POLITICIANS.

There is only one way to convince the politicians, and that is the way of the axe.

THE AXE, GOVERNOR, THE AXE."

CHAPTER XIII

EUGENE D. WOOD'S LETTER TELLS OF DELMONICO CONFERENCES

Eugene D. Wood, familiarly known in Albany as " Gene Wood," was a lobbyist at the Capitol for many years at a time when that calling was recognized as more legitimate than in these later years. In the early days when the New York Central railroad owned the legislatures, the genial Wood was the distributor of passes and of other favors. Mr. Wood probably knows more about the Black Horse Cavalry, in-famous in New York state's legislative annals, than any member thereof.

Mr. Wood had large interests in the Albany and Troy gas companies and was intimately connected with the late Anthony N. Brady, gas and electric light magnate, in both business and politics.

Soon after the legislature of 1913 assembled, what is known as the Capitol district hydro-electric bill was introduced in both the senate and assembly by Senator John F. Murtaugh of Elmira and Assemblyman J. Lewis Patrie of Greene county. Briefly described, the measure was intended to authorize the state conservation commission to utilize the water power at two barge canal dams, at Vischer Ferry and Crescent, near Albany and Troy, for the production of electric power to be sold to Capitol district municipalities at cost. The plan was to be modeled on the hydro-electric plan in operation for five or six years in the province of Ontario, Canada, where cheap power was insured to consumers.

A similar bill had been introduced in the legislature of 1912 by Senator Howard R. Bayne of Richmond county and had stirred up intense opposition from the electric power interests not only in New York state but from electric power companies throughout the east.

When the measure was re-introduced in 1913, the power interests were well organized to oppose it. Eugene Wood, not merely on account of his personal interest in the Albany and Troy companies, but because of his business relations with

"At Delmonico's—Murphy, Glynn, McCabe, McCall, McCooey and Wagner."

Mr. Brady and other prominent financial men, fought the bill in a political way from the outset. Like the trained lobbyist that he was, he went directly to the seat of power, Charles F. Murphy, and asked that the hydro-electric power bill be killed. Murphy and Patrick E. McCabe, clerk of the senate and Murphy's agent in Albany county, both promised to see that the bill never passed the senate.

All of this was unknown to the advocates of the plan in the cities of the Capitol district, who held meetings, appointed committees and conducted a systematic campaign in its behalf.

Suddenly there came a change in the attitude of the Tammany leaders in the legislature and, despite the promise of Murphy and McCabe to Wood, the hydro-electric bill was allowed to go through both houses. Brady and Wood were furious at this breach of faith on the part of Murphy. With Samuel A. Beardsley of Utica, legal and political representative of Brady, they execrated—all under cover of course—Murphy and his gang at Albany for this " double cross," and vowed vengeance.

Meanwhile, Governor Sulzer had in various ways endorsed the hydro-electric bill so far as an executive, with propriety, could endorse a measure before it came to him. He said he was in favor of the principle of the bill and vigorously denied rumors that he had made up his mind to veto it.

But as the day of a public hearing on the measure before the governor approached, these rumors of a veto multiplied and were more persistent. Unable to impress the governor with the usual arguments employed by private corporations against state competition the electric trust shrewdly appealed to Governor Sulzer from the political angle. They knew he was already in the thick of a fight with Murphy over direct primaries and one of them wrote in substance:

" *I have no use for the governor's direct primary ideas but we are willing to do what we can at this time to assist him in destroying Murphy. Murphy, McCabe and Glynn are interested in this hydro-electric bill and that is why it passed the legislature. Murphy and McCabe promised faithfully that it would never pass the senate and now we are out to fight them.*"

Lieutenant Governor Glynn, from the beginning of the year, was in the forefront of the battle for the hydro-electric bill. When Governor Sulzer saw this and that the lieutenant governor did not want to help him in his fight for a primary law his suspicions were aroused and daily confirmed in his mind by the stories brought to him by Beardsley and others interested in the veto of the hydro-electric bill.

A letter from Eugene D. Wood at this time throws some light, not merely on the manner in which Governor Sulzer was bombarded, but on the anxiety of Wood and his friends to keep the governor posted on the Delmonico conferences. It is as follows:

Envelope of letter written by Eugene D. Wood, and mailed from New York city Sunday evening, May 18th, 1913, at 10:30 P. M.

"Sunday Eve.

"EUGENE D. WOOD"

"My Dear John:—

I hope the governor is to veto Murtaugh's hydro-electric bill. It is surely to his political benefit and advantage to do so. They had a meeting last Wednesday eve. at Delmonico's regarding that bill and the primary bill. Glynn and McCabe were present. So was McCall, McCoohey, Wagner and Murphy.   It hits many of his enemies by veto—and makes many friends and no enemies by doing so.   I wish you would make it strong with the governor how important it is to him.   Of course, I am thinking of how it hurts me.   Let me hear if you think I can do anything that will help him to veto the bill. He can for sure make many friends and get much help by vetoing it, and gain nothing the other way, but help his enemies and give them a club for future use.   With best wishes I remain,

" Yours Sincerely,

" Eugene D. Wood "

Sunday Eve

My Dear John— I hope the
Governor is to Veto Murtaughs
Hydro Electric Bill— It is
surely to his political bene-
-fit and advantage to do so.
They had a meeting last
Wednesday Eve at Delmonicos
regarding that Bill and the
Primary Bill. Glynn and
McCabe were present. So was
McCall. McCooey, Wagner
and Murphy. It hits many
of his enemies by Veto—
And makes many friends
and no Enemies by doing
so— with your majority
of strong with the

EUGENE D. WOOD

Governor how important it is to him. Of course, I am thinking of how it hurts me = Let me hear if you think I can do anything that might help him to Veto the Bill. He can, for sure, make many friends and get much help by Vetoing it, and gain nothing by approving it. But help his enemies and give them a club for future use. With best wishes I remain Yours Sincerely,

Eugene D. Wood.

THE GANG—"LYNCH HER!"

From the Albany Knickerbocker Press.

CHAPTER XIV

MURPHY SENDS MESSENGERS TO THREATEN SULZER

For at least two months before the seventy-nine assemblymen in the gray dawn of August 13th passed the articles of impeachment, Governor Sulzer had received messages from Charles F. Murphy, all bearing an open or covert threat of what would happen to him if he did not change his course at Albany. The governor frequently confided to his friends that the boss was preparing to destroy him politically, but that he had resolved to keep right on with his campaign for a real primary law and with the investigations.

His addresses before the direct primary campaign committee in June a few days before the convening of the extraordinary session all had the ring of a man heavy of heart but resolute in spirit.

Spies were put on the trail of John A. Hennessy and George W. Blake, who were conducting the investigations so much feared by Murphy.   Every step of Hennessy was dogged by one or more sleuths and his movements reported to the boss or his agents. Members of Mr. Hennessy's family were watched by spies all with the idea of getting information which could be used against the investigator and his work rendered futile.

All kinds of men, willing to be messengers for the boss, were sent to the governor.   By some of the more suave he was told that all this investigating business would wreck the democratic organization in the state; that it would surely react on the governor himself without accomplishing very much.   He was told that Hennessy was a bitter enemy of Tammany and was not the right kind of man to collect evidence of that sort anyhow.

Governor Sulzer also received indirect threats.   Men pretending to be mutual friends of himself and Murphy begged the governor to let up in his campaign for direct primary legislation and especially not to pursue his highway and other probes until he took time to consider what might be brought down on his head in consequence of that policy.

In most of his speeches in May and June on direct primaries the governor referred to these threats without going very much into their character. He afterwards said that he knew what was coming because the nature of the attacks had been specified in some of the threatening letters received at the executive chamber and by Tammany men sent to tell him.

Newspapers in the bipartisan alliance, belittled the big meetings addressed by Governor Sulzer in May and June. The impression sought to be given was that few attended the meetings and that many were progressives, hence there was no indication, according to these press reports, that either democrats or republicans were taking any interest in state-wide direct primaries.

When Charles F. Murphy, however, did realize that the insurrection among the people against his legislature and rule at Albany was a genuine one, he directed that the committee headed by " Jim " Frawley, hasten its work of " getting Sulzer."

" Let us have patience," shouted Senator Robert F. Wagner, June 16th, when the senate was called back in extraordinary session, " and the people of the state will be informed on Governor Sulzer."

There was no attempt to discuss the merits of the primary bill which the legislature was called back to consider. It was all a scream of anger that the governor should dare to call an extraordinary session at which to pass a direct primary bill.

It became evident from the outset that some of the state committeemen and county chairmen attended the meetings called by the governor to discuss direct primaries, quietly acquiesced in the proceedings, but continued to be bitter enemies of direct nominations. They were on the side of Murphy and were said to have been advised to pretend sympathy with the governor for the sake of their districts.

Among the state committeemen of this character was William H. Kelley of Onondaga county. Mr. Kelley attended one of the direct primary meetings in the executive chamber and the two democratic assemblymen from his county voted for the primary bill. This was done to save Duncan W.

NOTE—See index for Buffalo and Rochester speeches.

From the Albany Knickerbocker Press, 1913

Peck, state superintendent of public works, whose home is in that county, as much as it was to prevent defeat of the assemblymen should they seek renomination.

The insincerity of the assemblymen—Stephen G. Daley and Patrick J. Kelly—so far as upholding the governor is concerned, was demonstrated when they both voted to impeach him.

Although Duncan W. Peck, superintendent of public works, who had charge of the Erie canal patronage, always pretended to be in sympathy with Governor Sulzer, it was suspected from the time of his re-appointment in January that he held first allegiance to Murphy. His slowness and sometimes refusal to remove Tammany officeholders confirmed the truth of this suspicion.

One of the things for which Governor Sulzer has been criticised by his friends was his retention of Peck, who has been condemned from Buffalo to New York in all the counties affected by the canal, for his activity in behalf of Charles F. Murphy. That the two assemblymen from his home county at last voted with Murphy's men to impeach the governor, was additional proof of his disloyalty, according to the rules of the political game.

William H. Fitzpatrick of Buffalo, the Erie county boss, was another illustration of the deception practiced by the upstate bosses upon the governor. Following the election in November Fitzpatrick professed great friendship for Sulzer, and the governor apparently believed that Fitzpatrick could afford to be independent of Murphy. He praised the Buffalo man in interviews with the newspaper men, and on one occasion said that he was willing to appoint him public service commissioner. He permitted him to distribute the state's patronage in Erie county as Governor Dix had before him. Devoe P. Hodson, recommended by Fitzpatrick, was appointed and confirmed public service commissioner at $15,000 a year.

When the break came with Murphy it also came with Fitzpatrick, because the latter refused to stand with the governor in the legislature. Two of the three Erie county senators, Ramsperger and Malone, voted to exonerate Stilwell and to otherwise uphold Murphy's side in the senate. It was such experiences as these which convinced the governor that no matter what patronage these up-state Murphy men received, they would take it all and then turn against him at the first opportunity should the Tammany boss give the word. Murphy's policy was the same as it had been in the Dix administration—grab all the patronage and give little or no legislation desired by the governor in return.

Governor Sulzer's friends found fault with him because he did not profit from the experience of Governor Dix. They assert that had he begun war upon the tiger from the beginning of his term, instead of trying to dicker with it, he would have laid for himself surer foundation from which to fight.

As an example of how insatiable Charles F. Murphy was in reaching out for patronage, the bill passed by the regular session of the legislature concerning the janitor service of the new state Education building is cited. There were about seventy employes to care for the building, with a payroll of about $4,300 to $4,500 a month under control of the state commissioner of education.

The Tammany men passed a bill during the session of 1913 taking this from the control of the commissioner, and giving it to the superintendent of buildings, who was a political follower of Patrick E. McCabe, clerk of the senate, and Charles F. Murphy's man in Albany county. Governor Sulzer promptly vetoed the grab. With the expectation that the governor would sign the bill, the Murphy legislators had inserted $60,000 for taking care of the building. The education department is keeping the building clean and in good condition for $43,000 to $45,000.

Veto of the bill, a characteristic Tammany measure, brought down on his head the anathema of every job hunter in the Tammany ring, from Charles F. Murphy down. He was denounced as traitor to the party and a wrecker of democracy.

"WHAT ARE YOU GOING TO DO ABOUT IT?"

From the Albany Knickerbocker Press

CHAPTER XV

NORMAN E. MACK ACCEPTS AND THEN DECLINES PLACE ON SULZER PRIMARY COMMITTEE

One of the first things Governor Sulzer did after his return from his last conference with Charles F. Murphy was to advise Senator Stephen J. Stilwell to resign from the senate, warning him if he did not he would submit the charges made against him to district attorney Charles S. Whitman. Stilwell was defiant and in effect informed the governor that he did not care what he did with the charges as he was going to remain a member of the senate.

The next thing the governor did following his interview with the boss was to invite prominent men all over the state to accept membership on a committee of one hundred to promote the cause of a genuine direct primary law. Among the prominent democrats he invited was Norman E. Mack, of Buffalo, long the New York state member of the democratic national committee. Mr. Mack promptly replied by telegraph on April 17th that he would be glad to serve on such a committee. But before the committee assembled on the 26th at Albany, a change came over the spirit of Mr. Mack's dreams. He declined to serve, giving as his reason that he was opposed to any primary law which would permit the voters to nominate directly their candidates for governor and other state officers.

This sudden change of front on the part of Mr. Mack, assuming that he had been well informed of the character of the Sulzer bill discussed in the newspapers for several weeks, indicated to the advocates of the measure that the Buffalo man had gone over to the Tammany side of the bitter controversy then raging.

On April 22nd, Senator John W. McKnight, of Rensselaer county, and Assemblyman Mark Eisner, of New York, introduced in the legislature the Sulzer primary bill, the result of the work of the committee appointed by the governor.

Meanwhile the Blauvelt primary bill had been repassed

and   governor on April 24th once more vetoed it. In that
veto   sage he said:

"W. have been given leadership dishonorable to the various
politi partie of the state and we have been given party
ticket which reflect this dishonorable leadership in disgraceful
secret alliance between big business interests and crooked
and c rupt politics."

Go rnor Slzer's speech to the assembled county chairmen— ifty-on of the sixty-one of the state being present—
the s te comitteemen and friends of state-wide primaries,
delive d in te executive chamber, was pronounced by many
of th newspaers as the most remarkable ever delivered by
a go nor of le state.

It is estimated that more than 500 people were crowded
into   e execive chamber to listen to the governor.

" ere wi be no compromise," said he, " between me
and e boss-ontrolled legislature. I venture to predict that
when he hisry of our state is written this day will be set
dow as one f the historic in its annals. Every democratic
chai an in le state must decide now whether he is for me
or a inst me If he is against me—mark well what I say—I
will agains him.

" *) man ars direct primaries except the man whose charac*
ter l whoseability, and whose mentality and whose democracy
wil ot bear e searchlight of publicity.

o man ars direct primaries unless he would rather be a
aure of iisible government than the servant of the people.
you think will not fight then you have another think coming.
(Laughter a applause.) If you imagine I don't know the
ules of the me remember I have been in the game all my life.
They beat Cvernor Hughes but I am determined they will not
veat Willia Sulzer."

The spee breathed defiance to the bosses and the boss-
ow d legis ure in every line and caused a sensation throughout le sta for never up to that time had Governor Sulzer
d such orous language against the bosses. Following
e meetin i the executive chamber, a public hearing on the
was h before the assembly and senate judiciary com-
assembly chamber.

On April 30th, the primary bill was de eaed in the senate by a vote of 42 to 8.

Opponents of the bill attacked Governor Slzer rather than the measure itself. Tammany senators rid culd and denounced the governor. Leader Wagner declaring thatıe was insincere in professing to be for direct primaries at al Senator John F. Healy of Westchester county was sure thatɩnly a few people in the state wanted the right to nominate their candidates and he was indignant that he should be askd to waste time in considering a proposition so absurd.

The following day, May 1st, the assembly after a stormy session, in which the Tammany leaders xcriated Governor Sulzer, defeated the bill by a vote of 93 t 47

The week previous Governor Sulzer had sat to the senate the nominations of John Mitchell for state ommissioner of labor; John H. Delaney for commissioner f efficiency and economy; John N. Carlisle for commissioner f highways and John B. Riley for superintendent of prison .

By agreement, the nominations of C rlie and Delaney were confirmed by the senate. Governor Swzer had refused to nominate Mr. Delaney unless the Tammny leaders first agreed to confirm Mr. Carlisle's nominatia for the state highway department. The senate refused, bwever, to confirm the appointment of Mitchell or Ri ey. The ostensible reason for the rejection of Mitchell was tht he was not a democrat. The real reason, however, wa tht Mitchell was too independent and would insist upon be ɳg ead of the labor department.

No reason was given for the rejection (Judge Riley's nomination. Privately, the Tammany leacrs admitted it was because he came from Clinton county nd belonged to the democratic organization there, which hadalways asserted its independence of Tammany.

Governor Sulzer sent in Mitchell's name twce to the senate and it was rejected each time. He appointd both men as recess appointees after the legislature a jotned. Attorney General Carmody held that Mitchell's appoirment was illegal but that Riley could hold his office until h successor was appointed and confirmed by the senate. Canody's decision was afterwards upheld by the courts.

NOTE—How the senators and assemblymen voted on the   ɾimary bill see index.

and the governor on April 24th once more vetoed it. In that veto message he said:

"We have been given leadership dishonorable to the various political parties of the state and we have been given party tickets which reflect this dishonorable leadership in disgraceful secret alliances between big business interests and crooked and corrupt politics."

Governor Sulzer's speech to the assembled county chairmen—fifty-one of the sixty-one of the state being present—the state committeemen and friends of state-wide primaries, delivered in the executive chamber, was pronounced by many of the newspapers as the most remarkable ever delivered by a governor of the state.

It was estimated that more than 500 people were crowded into the executive chamber to listen to the governor.

"There will be no compromise," said he, "between me and the boss-controlled legislature. I venture to predict that when the history of our state is written this day will be set down as one of the historic in its annals. Every democratic chairman in the state must decide now whether he is for me or against me. If he is against me—mark well what I say—I will be against him.

"*No man fears direct primaries except the man whose character and whose ability, and whose mentality and whose democracy will not bear the searchlight of publicity.*

"*No man fears direct primaries unless he would rather be a creature of invisible government than the servant of the people. If you think I will not fight then you have another think coming. (Laughter and applause.) If you imagine I don't know the rules of the game remember I have been in the game all my life. They beat Governor Hughes but I am determined they will not beat William Sulzer.*"

The speech breathed defiance to the bosses and the boss-owned legislature in every line and caused a sensation throughout the state, for never up to that time had Governor Sulzer used such vigorous language against the bosses. Following the meeting in the executive chamber, a public hearing on the bill was held before the assembly and senate judiciary committees in the assembly chamber.

On April 30th, the primary bill was defeated in the senate by a vote of 42 to 8.

Opponents of the bill attacked Governor Sulzer rather than the measure itself. Tammany senators ridiculed and denounced the governor. Leader Wagner declaring that he was insincere in professing to be for direct primaries at all. Senator John F. Healy of Westchester county was sure that only a few people in the state wanted the right to nominate their candidates and he was indignant that he should be asked to waste time in considering a proposition so absurd.

The following day, May 1st, the assembly, after a stormy session, in which the Tammany leaders excoriated Governor Sulzer, defeated the bill by a vote of 93 to 47.

The week previous Governor Sulzer had sent to the senate the nominations of John Mitchell for state commissioner of labor; John H. Delaney for commissioner of efficiency and economy; John N. Carlisle for commissioner of highways and John B. Riley for superintendent of prisons.

By agreement, the nominations of Carlisle and Delaney were confirmed by the senate. Governor Sulzer had refused to nominate Mr. Delaney unless the Tammany leaders first agreed to confirm Mr. Carlisle's nomination for the state highway department. The senate refused, however, to confirm the appointment of Mitchell or Riley. The ostensible reason for the rejection of Mitchell was that he was not a democrat. The real reason, however, was that Mitchell was too independent and would insist upon being head of the labor department.

No reason was given for the rejection of Judge Riley's nomination. Privately, the Tammany leaders admitted it was because he came from Clinton county and belonged to the democratic organization there, which had always asserted its independence of Tammany.

Governor Sulzer sent in Mitchell's name twice to the senate and it was rejected each time. He appointed both men as recess appointees after the legislature adjourned. Attorney General Carmody held that Mitchell's appointment was illegal but that Riley could hold his office until his successor was appointed and confirmed by the senate. Carmody's decision was afterwards upheld by the courts.

NOTE—How the senators and assemblymen voted on the direct primary bill see index.

CHAPTER XVI

THE FRAWLEY COMMITTEE AND ITS WORK

Among the bodies which won a malodorous reputation in connection with the impeachment of Governor Sulzer was the Frawley committee. It was composed of Senator James J. Frawley, of New York county; Senator Felix J. Sanner, of Kings county; Senator Samuel J. Ramsperger, Erie county; Senator Elon R. Brown, Jefferson county; Assemblyman Myron Smith, Dutchess county; Assemblyman LaVerne and P. Butts, Otsego county; and Assemblyman Wilson R. Yard, Westchester county.

All three assemblymen, as indeed were sixty-two of the seventy-nine assemblymen who voted for impeachment, were defeated either for renomination or re-election a few weeks or months later.

Myron Smith was the only Republican among the assemblymen on the committee. He was a relic of the Old Guard of notorious memory which flourished in republican politics prior to and during the administration of Governor Hughes. He was always ready to help Tammany in the assembly.

Assemblyman Butts came from the independent county of Otsego, but from the moment he entered upon his duties at Albany he placed himself as the disposal of Charles F. Murphy. He was therefore considered a " safe " man to place on the Frawley committee.

Assemblyman Yard came from Westchester county, which, bordering on New York, has usually been the prey of Tammany. Yard professed in his ante-election proclamations to be a militant independent and reformer, but he, too, rushed into the arms of the boss when he arrived in Albany and remained a servile ever after.

Senator Frawley, the chairman, a fine specimen of the Tammany politician, as contemptuous of principle in politics as he was devoted to the commercial god in public affairs, dominated the committee.

Senator Felix J. Sanner of Brooklyn and Senator Samuel J. Ramsperger of Buffalo were perfect models of Tammany

MATTHEW T. HORGAN
Secretary to the Frawley Committee denounced by Gov. Sulzer as a
Tammany Spy.

WILLIAM H. FITZPATRICK
Tammany's Leader in Erie County.

"statesmen" who "stand without hitching." No matter how risky the job Tammany had in hand these two men, upon orders, could be depended on to help.

Senator Elon R. Brown was leader of the republican minority in the senate at the time of his appointment on the Frawley committee. He was an excellent example of the old Tory republican, distrustful of the people and clinging with religious zeal to the political forms and substance of the monarchical past. He had had some personal differences with Governor Sulzer and his chief delight was in ridiculing the executive at every opportunity in the senate chamber.

Such were the seven members of the Frawley committee sent abroad by the legislature to "get something" on Sulzer.

The four senators were appointed by Lieutenant Governor Martin H. Glynn, presiding officer of the senate, and the three assemblymen by Speaker Alfred E. Smith of the assembly, upon authority of a resolution adopted by both houses May 2nd, 1913, the day previous to the adjournment of the regular session.

Little or no attention was paid to the resolution at the time as upon its face it contained nothing to reveal the real purpose of the committee, the resolution reading in part:

"To examine into the methods of financial administration and conduct of all institutions, societies or associations of the state, which are supported either wholly or in part by state moneys."

This was presumed to mean investigation particularly of the prisons of the state to offset or discredit the work of George W. Blake, Governor Sulzer's investigator, who was then engaged on the inquiry. The committee did, in fact, subpoena Blake and did what it could to discredit his work relating to the examination of affairs at Sing Sing, Great Meadows and other prisons.

The committee engaged Eugene Lamb Richards, Tammany state committeeman from Richmond and Rockland counties, as counsel, and Matthew T. Horgan as secretary. Richards at the time of his appointment was counsel for the state conservation commission at a salary of $7,000 a year. Horgan had been intimately connected with Governor Sulzer during his campaign for governor in 1912; had access to his home

"statesmen" who "stand without hitching." No matter how risky the job Tammany had in hand these two men, upon orders, could be depended on to help.

Senator Elon R. Brown was leader of the republican minority in the senate at the time of his appointment on the Frawley committee. He was an excellent example of the old Tory republican, distrustful of the people and clinging with religious zeal to the political forms and substance of the monarchical past. He had had some personal differences with Governor Sulzer and his chief delight was in ridiculing the executive at every opportunity in the senate chamber.

Such were the seven members of the Frawley committee sent abroad by the legislature to "get something" on Sulzer.

The four senators were appointed by Lieutenant Governor Martin H. Glynn, presiding officer of the senate, and the three assemblymen by Speaker Alfred E. Smith of the assembly, upon authority of a resolution adopted by both houses May 2nd, 1913, the day previous to the adjournment of the regular session.

Little or no attention was paid to the resolution at the time as upon its face it contained nothing to reveal the real purpose of the committee, the resolution reading in part:

"To examine into the methods of financial administration and conduct of all institutions, societies or associations of the state, which are supported either wholly or in part by state moneys."

This was presumed to mean investigation particularly of the prisons of the state to offset or discredit the work of George W. Blake, Governor Sulzer's investigator, who was then engaged on the inquiry. The committee did, in fact, subpoena Blake and did what it could to discredit his work relating to the examination of affairs at Sing Sing, Great Meadows and other prisons.

The committee engaged Eugene Lamb Richards, Tammany state committeeman from Richmond and Rockland counties, as counsel, and Matthew T. Horgan as secretary. Richards at the time of his appointment was counsel for the state conservation commission at a salary of $7,000 a year. Horgan had been intimately connected with Governor Sulzer during his campaign for governor in 1912; had access to his home and private papers and all who knew of these relations were astonished to hear of his connection with the Frawley committee even at that early time doing its best to find something against the governor. Horgan was afterwards denounced by Governor Sulzer as a Tammany spy. Other men who had · wormed their way into the confidence of the governor suddenly appeared as assistants to the Frawley committee, all of which indicated to the governor and his friends that a deep-laid conspiracy had been afoot long before he was nominated at Syracuse the year previous.

But the committee did not find its attack on the governor's investigators as fruitful a field as it reckoned on. Something else had to be done to stop the deadly work of Hennessy in the highway department and Blake in the prisons. All through May and a part of June the members of the committee worked to bring something serious to the surface, but apparently their efforts were in vain.

, At the extraordinary session of the legislature called by the governor to meet June 16th, the opportunity came. In addition to recommending enactment of a direct primary law, Governor Sulzer in his message recommended legislation amending the corrupt practices act. This was immediately seized on by the Tammany man as sufficient authority to amend the resolution adopted at the regular session creating the Frawley committee and to extend its powers.

Senator George F. Thompson, republican member from Niagara and Orleans counties, was used as the agent of Tammany to accomplish this. He introduced a resolution June 25th in the senate by which it was resolved that the " whole subject of any wrongful or unlawful influence aforesaid, and of receipts and expenditures of candidates for the elective office to be filled by the votes of the electors of the whole state, be referred to a certain joint legislative committee of the senate and assembly to examine into the methods of financial administration."

This Thompson resolution, amending that of Frawley adopted at the regular session, was held to arm the committee to go into the governor's campaign receipts and expenditures.

Instead of adjourning sine die, after defeating the direct primary bill the second time, the Tammany leaders changed

their minds and took a recess from time to time for the purpose
of receiving the report of the Frawley committee.   The committee thereupon began delving into the Sulzer campaign
receipts and expenditures, its meetings for that purpose being
held in Albany and New York.

CHAPTER XVII

CHARGES OF GRAFT MADE AGAINST JUSTICE DANIEL F. COHALAN

Soon after the Frawley committee began its hunt for evidence against Governor Sulzer which could be used to halt his highway and prison investigations, charges were preferred against Daniel F. Cohalan, justice of the supreme court in the first judicial district, former legal and political adviser of Charles F. Murphy.

John A. Connolly, president of the Victor Heating Company, New York city, testified that while Cohalan was influential in Tammany and before he was a supreme court justice he demanded 55 per cent. of the profits on any contracts which he was instrumental in obtaining from the city.

Connolly swore he had paid Cohalan $3,940, always in money, for his influence in obtaining city contracts; that he had afterwards demanded return of the money, after he and his friends had made complaint to Charles F. Murphy, and that Cohalan repaid him the amount.

Subsequently Connolly wanted to get a public job and sought Cohalan's aid. The latter was accused of offering to get Connolly a job provided the latter gave Cohalan his note for $4,000. Judge Cohalan defended this transaction by claiming he had submitted to blackmail when he returned the $3,940 to Connolly and that the note was to repay what was honestly due him.

The Association of the Bar of the city of New York asked Justice Cohalan to appear before the grievance committee of the association and answer the charges. Instead of availing himself of that privilege he asked Governor Sulzer to submit the case to the legislature, then in extraordinary session, which the governor did.

The evidence was heard by the judiciary committees of the two houses of the legislature, presided over by Senator John F. Murtaugh, of Elmira. After taking testimony for three or four days a sub-committee consisting of Senator James A. Foley of New York, Senator Herbert P. Coats of Franklin

ISODOR KRESEL, WILLIAM T. JEROME AND JUDGE COHALAN

This picture was taken while Judge Cohalan was on trial.

county; Assemblyman Aaron J. Levy of New York; Assemblyman John L. Sullivan, Chautauqua county, and Assemblyman Michael J. Schaap, New York, prepared a report in which it was held that the charges preferred against Justice Cohalan should be dismissed because they had not been proved.

Justice Cohalan was represented at his trial by John B. Stanchfield, William T. Jerome and I. J. Kresel, all of whom, two months later, represented the board of managers in the impeachment proceedings against Governor Sulzer.

The judiciary committees were represented by Joseph A. Kellogg, first deputy attorney general, and William D. Guthrie appeared in behalf of the association of the bar of the city of New York.

In summing up against Justice Cohalan, Mr. Guthrie, in part, said:

" Judge Cohalan committed more than a mistake when he submitted to the blackmail of Connolly and paid him $3,940 in bills in order to stop the exposure as hush money. These transactions covered two years, $500 and $1,000 at a time invariably in bills, invariably without any record whatever kept, except the rceord that happens to have been produced out of the books of the Victor Heating Company which are fully corroborated today by the admissions of Judge Cohalan.

" Is it conceivable that this highly educated and trained and skilled lawyer did not appreciate the seriousness of what he was doing, and are you satisfied that the only reason why he did it was to serve his party, and that he was willing to put this thing upon himself and his profession in order that he might insure the success of Tammany hall during the campaign of 1909 ?

" The inference to be drawn from these facts is to be drawn by you and not by us. Again, how extraordinary the substitution of the perjured amended complaint for money loaned, the statement by Cohalan of the agreement in the presence of Cruikshank that they would agree that the money had been loaned in order that this bogus, fictitious complaint or pleading might be drawn; the false records then made; the delivery of that false and perjured affidavit to Judge Cohalan himself, and the writing on the back of that rotten, manufactured, fabricated evidence of the receipt for the bills paid on the 27th of May by Mr. Justice Cohalan himself to Mr. Cruikshank.

" We ask you to take the evidence of Mr. Cruikshank and Judge Cohalan and determine yourselves whether or not the transaction was extremely suspicious, and whether it does not tend, admitted as it is on the stand by Judge Cohalan, to shatter the confidence of the community, I will not say in the character, but in the mental and moral poise of Mr. Justice Cohalan.

" Now, jumping to the next significant fact, the note of $4,000. You will read the testimony in that regard and you will conclude whether you are willing to accept the story that this note and this affidavit, which we insist was nothing but a perjured affidavit, were given solely as evidence of the retraction of false charges, of the withdrawal of charges which had been previously made. If that had been the purpose, of course, a brief statement, sworn to by Connolly, could have been prepared.

" We submit that if you will read that note, and the accompanying so-called estoppel affidavit, that it is almost preposterous to suggest that this clever lawyer accepted this note and this affidavit, at that time, for no other purpose than as evidence of the withdrawal of the previous charges. But if that were in doubt, let us come to what happened this year.

" Mr. Justice Cohalan is on the bench as a member of the supreme court of the state. He receives the most insulting letter that any justice of the supreme court ever received. The letter was contemptible. The letter practically charged a criminal offense against Mr. Justice Cohalan, that he took this note as a consideration for a promise to procure this individual, Connolly, a public office.

" What ought Mr. Justice Cohalan have done for himself, for his profession? He ought to have defied Connolly's attorney, Mr. Warren. He ought, if he hadn't been afraid that something might be exposed, to have turned the letter over to somebody, such as the Bar association, for its consideration, instead of surrendering the note and affidavit.

" I venture to submit that the conceded and undisputed features of this whole distressing case establish not only grave mistakes and acts on the part of Mr. Justice Cohalan, which are blameworthy, but such as to shatter the confidence which the people of the state of New York ought to repose unreservedly in the honor, in the spotless honor of their judges."

Justice Cohalan was exonerated in the senate by a vote of 31 to 8, and in the assembly by a vote of 112 to 18.

CHAPTER XVIII

FRAWLEY COMMITTEE DELVES INTO SULZER'S CAMPAIGN ACCOUNTS

Justice Cohalan had just been exonerated by the Tammany legislature when the Frawley committee began to dig into Governor Sulzer's campaign accounts. As already pointed out, this was made possible by the resolution introduced by Senator George F. Thompson of Niagara county, prompted undoubtedly by Tammany leaders, extending the power of the committee to deal with that section of the primary law relating to campaign contributions.

And thus by the irony of fate Governor Sulzer's earnest plea to the extraordinary session of the legislature on June 16th for a genuine direct primary law was made the legal agency by his enemies to attack his honor and bring about his removal.

For nearly two months the members of the committee had been casting about for something which could be used to obstruct the governor's investigators and to embarrass his primary campaign. It had done what it could to harass Hennessy and Blake and now suddenly it saw an opportunity to make trouble for Sulzer in a new direction. The secretary of the committee, Matthew T. Horgan, who had been appointed by John H. Delaney, commissioner of efficiency and economy, a deputy in that department at $5,000 a year, was "loaned" by Delaney to the committee. He had pretended to be an intimate friend of Sulzer during the campaign for governor and knew all about the candidate's campaign finances.

The first meeting of the committee to hear testimony on the governor's campaign receipts and expenditures was held at the Capitol in Albany, July 30th, and continued there and in the City hall, New York, until August 8th. During those hearings it developed that while Governor Sulzer had made affidavit to the secretary of state that he had received contributions aggregating $5,640 from sixty-eight persons, he had received $12,405.93 from ninety-four contributors.

Louis A. Sarecky, who had been an employe of Mr. Sulzer for ten years while he was a member of congress, had been

"And He Used Campaign Funds to Gamble in Wall Street, and ——"

From the Saturday Evening Post

authorized during the campaign to endorse his name to any checks donated to the campaign fund. Mr. Sarecky was a witness before the committee but refused to answer most of the questions by advice of his counsel, Louis Marshall. Mr. Sarecky's usual reply was that he would not answer questions relating to the governor's bank affairs and amounts contributed to his campaign unless allowed counsel at the hearing so that " the whole story could be told." He contended that without counsel being present the committee's lawyer, Eugene Lamb Richards, would bring out only one side of the story.

At the proceedings of August 6th, Mr. Richards read the following letter received from Charles F. Murphy:

" C. F. MURPHY, 305 East 17th Street,
         " New York, July 31, 1913
" The Hon. JAMES J. FRAWLEY,
       Senate Chamber, Albany, N. Y.:
   " DEAR SIR.—This morning's statements report Governor Sulzer as saying that ' large contributions from contractors, the office holders, the special interests, and prominent democrats interested in the campaign were made through the bagman · direct to Mr. Murphy.'

   " These insinuations are untrue. If Governor Sulzer has any information as to misconduct on my part relating to campaign contributions I request him to furnish it to your committee, and I will appear for examination at any time.
                " Yours truly,
         "(Signed)   CHARLES F. MURPHY."

Chairman Frawley enclosed a copy of this letter to Governor Sulzer and invited him to appear before the committee and " furnish it at once with any such information in your possession, together with the names and addresses of any witnesses, who can give us sworn testimony, in support of your charge."

The information which the committee appeared to be so eager to obtain concerning campaign contributions paid to Mr. Murphy through his " bagmen " was at that time in possession of John A. Hennessy and much of it made public during the ensuing municipal campaign in New York city, as well as

in the John Doe proceedings begun by district attorney
Charles S. Whitman of New York county.

In concluding its report to the senate and assembly the Frawley committee drew the following inferences from the testimony
it had taken:

" Governor Sulzer made a false public statement, when on
July 30, 1913, he said that he was away campaigning and that
he did not know of the campaign contributions omitted from
his sworn statement. The Elkus check was endorsed by
Sulzer personally and he acknowledged the letter of Elkus
transmitting it as a campaign contribution.

" We submit to the legislature that it was false when William
Sulzer swore that he had received only $5,460 of campaign
contributions and that he did so with full knowledge that he
had received an amount many times that sum and had converted
the same to his private uses; that he used contributions given
to aid in his election for the purchase of stocks in Wall street
which he or his agents still hold; that he has been engaged in
stock market speculations at the time that he, as governor,
was earnestly pressing legislation against the New York Stock
Exchange which would affect the business and prices of the
Exchange; and that there was evidence before this committee to sustain a finding that as governor he has punished
legislators who opposed him by vetoing legislation enacted
for the public welfare, and has traded executive approval of
bills for support of his direct primary and other measures.

" We submit to the senate and assembly that the facts
above stated are sufficiently serious in character and are so
violative of the laws of this state and the rules of fitness for
and conduct in high office, that the public interests demand
some action in reference thereto whether through the exercise
of powers of the legislature, or by referring the facts and
evidence to other duly constituted officers charged with duties
in respect thereof.

" There is in the possession of this committee further au-
thentic information of other similar evidence in respect to the
subject of this report, as strong in quality and in the large
amounts involved as that on which sworn testimony has
already been given.

" This committee, therefore, has not completed its investigation either on this subject or others covered by the resolutions under which it is acting, but it has felt that the revelations set forth in this report and the testimony accompanying it should be brought to the attention of the legislature at once without awaiting a final report either on this or other subjects.

" The questions here involved are vital to clean government. They are above party or partisanship. They are vital to the citizens of the state and call for prompt and well-considered action. They call for an answer from Governor Sulzer, because both his obstructive tactics and his silence warrants the conclusion that the charges can neither be answered nor explained.

" We recommend the punishment for contempt of Louis A. Sarecky and Frederick L. Colwell, hereinbefore referred to and we transmit herewith the record of the hearings with the testimony and exhibits.

"Albany, N. Y., August 11, 1913

" Respectfully submitted by order of the committee,

" THE JOINT LEGISLATIVE INVESTIGATING COMMITTEE,"

JAMES J. FRAWLEY,
Chairman.

" EUGENE LAMB RICHARDS,
Counsel.

" MATTHEW T. HORGAN,
Secretary."

CHAPTER XIX

GOVERNOR SULZER'S LAST SPEECH IN THE EXECUTIVE
CHAMBER

While the Frawley committee was hastening its work of collecting facts on which to base the articles of impeachment the Sulzer campaign committee, or " war board," as it came to be known, was enthusiastically carrying on the propaganda for direct primaries.

On August 4th, only nine days before the assembly voted to impeach the governor, another big meeting of county chairmen and advocates of the reform was held in the executive chamber to organize for the election of an assembly pledged to a real primary law. At that time Governor Sulzer seemed to foresee what so soon was to be his fate, for he said:

"*My friends, I am carrying a heavy burden. You know something about it, but you do not know all about it. I am doing so simply because I made up my mind when I took the oath of office that I would be the governor in fact as well as in name. Because I made up my mind that no influence should control me while I was the governor, but the dictates of my own conscience, and my determination to do my duty, day in and day out, come what may. For these reasons, and others, I have been hounded, traduced, vilified and threatened as no other man has ever been, who occupied this office, in all the history of the state.*"

Those who saw and heard the governor on this occasion will agree that his appearance and manner indicated that he was sorely troubled but resolute to go through with the fight to the bitter end. He was applauded at nearly every sentence. Brief addresses were made by many of the men present. The speakers included: Assemblyman Verne M. Bovie, Westchester county; Eugene D. Scribner, Gloversville; M. Z. Havens, Syracuse; Jay W. Forrest, Albany; former Congressman Theron Akin, Montgomery county; George F. Ketchum, chairman of the Orange county democratic committee; John T. Cronin, Beacon; Mayor Roscoe Irwin, Kingston; Rev. Canon William S. Chase, Brooklyn; and Daniel J. Dugan, Albany.

"HIS MASTER'S VOICE."

From the Albany Knickerbocker Press

Nearly all of the speeches were militant in their defiance of
Murphy and in pleading for non-partisan action at the election
to insure a direct primary and unbossed assembly.

General Amasa J. Parker, of Albany, presided and resolutions authorizing the appointment of campaign committees
in every assembly district to labor for a direct primary assembly
were adopted.

Former Congressman Akin urged the governor to vigorously
swing the axe and said if he were governor, when so many
heads of state departments were with Murphy and opposing
direct primaries, he would order the heads of such disloyal
employes brought into him on a pike pole.

" I voted for William Sulzer for governor and not for Charles
F. Murphy or Packy McCabe," declared Mr. Forrest as his
listeners applauded. Referring to Mr. Glynn, Mr. Forrest
said:

" One man who ought to be standing with Governor Sulzer
today, and who a few years ago advised Governor Hughes to
use the axe on the ' vampire ' bosses, is with Charles F. Murphy. When I went into the Times-Union office to copy the
editorial advising Governor Hughes to use the axe on the bosses,
Martin H. Glynn refused to permit me to do it. The only
reason he gave was that he didn't want to get mixed up in this
direct primary fight because it would hurt his political future.
Well, any man who thinks he can stand in the way of progress,
that man's future is gone before he starts."

Assemblyman Verne M. Bovie of the second district of
Westchester county offered resolutions endorsing the stand the
governor had taken and calling for the election of assemblymen
who will carry out the platform promises.

" I like to stand by Governor Sulzer," said he, " because he
has met opposition from the machine when he dared to stand
by the pledges of the platform not only before but after election. We ought to support him and see to it that the next
legislature will carry out these promises for direct primaries."

At the suggestion of M. Z. Havens of Syracuse, the resolution was amended pledging the conference not to support any
candidate not in favor of the direct primary bill.

Eugene D. Scribner of Gloversville also had resolutions
adopted, expressing unwavering confidence in Governor Sulzer

and offering support for his endeavor to carry out the promises of the party.

"I do this because I believe the governor is trying to carry out the party promises in good faith," said Mr. Scribner. "If the time ever comes that he does not do this I shall oppose him. I want to say that any assaults made on him because of his position on this question will be utterly futile and of no force and effect." (Applause.)

George F. Ketchum, chairman of the Orange county committee, called attention to the fact that both the assemblymen from his county, Caleb H. Baumes, a republican, and William T. Doty, a democrat, had voted for the bill.

"There is no criticism of either of these men for doing so," said Mr. Ketchum, "because it is well known that they represent public sentiment in both of the dominant parties in our county.

"This is a fight to the death between two men—one here in Albany, who has been elected governor, and another man in New York city, who thinks he is governor. The people will stand by their fighting governor and he will surely win the victory." (Applause.)

John T. Cronin, who in June had been elected commissioner of public safety of the new city of Beacon in Dutchess county, in the first commission government in this state, told the story of how the independents had defeated by two to one a combination of the two old machines.

"The people of that assembly district," said he, "will retire assemblyman Myron Smith to the political scrap heap next November because he voted against the direct primary bill. I don't care under what party name the assemblyman is sent to Albany, as long as he is for a real direct primary bill.

"I used to be a democrat, but under the reign of Murphy in New York city I was driven from the party."

"And there are 100,000 democrats like you in New York city who have been driven out of the democratic party," interrupted a New Yorker from Manhattan.

Resuming, Mr. Cronin said that the only way to get a direct primary assembly is for all who believe in it to unite on a candidate in each district whether they are democrats, republicans or progressives.

Mayor Roscoe Irwin of Kingston denounced as cowardly and contemptible the assailants of Governor Sulzer, declaring that their methods were worse than those of the cuttle fish.

"They are trying," said he, "to blind the people of the state by these slanderous stories to the real issue. Governor Sulzer, it should be borne in mind, is not fighting his own battle but the cause of the people."

County Chairman George E. Noeth of Monroe county said that the most important thing to do at once was to find candidates for the assembly known to be absolutely for direct primaries.

"We know," said he, "that there are organizations in this state professing to be for direct primaries, which are owned by the two political bosses."

A New York city democrat told Governor Sulzer that the sooner he began to drive out of state office the men not loyal to him in his effort to live up to the party platform, the sooner the stampede to this cause. He urged the governor to stand by John Purroy Mitchel, the fusion candidate for mayor in New York, whereupon there was general applause.

"Invisible government now rules New York," said he, "but with the election of John Purroy Mitchel all that condition will disappear and Governor Sulzer will be honored for supporting him."

The Rev. Canon William S. Chase of Brooklyn at this point offered his resolution for the appointment of an executive committee to conduct the assembly campaign.

Daniel J. Dugan, state committeeman for Albany county, said that as state committeeman he was making a fight at the primaries for a county committee in favor of carrying out the pledges of the party. He said that in the event the enrolled voters refused to do this on primary day, the large number of direct primary voters in other parties and not enrolled, probably could elect assemblymen committed to that reform.

Robert E. Gregg, former assemblyman from Lewis county, reported that the sentiment in that section of the state was strong for the Sulzer bill, although the assemblyman had voted against it.

The governor spoke as follows:

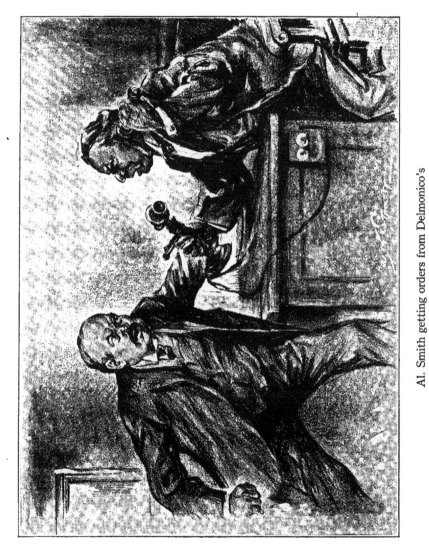

Al. Smith getting orders from Delmonico's

" It is a great pleasure to me to greet you and to welcome you today in the executive chamber.

" This conference was called by the friends of direct primaries to counsel as to the best way to nominate and elect members of assembly who will stand by the people and vote for state-wide direct primaries in the next legislature.

" I have always been of the opinion that a member of the legislature, state or national, should be true to the principles of his party; should be anxious at all times to carry out the promises of his party, and should always be responsive to the will of the people.

" However, in our legislature at present that idea seems to be reversed. Its members apparently are more anxious to carry out the will of the bosses than the will of the voters.

" Conscious of the rectitude of our intentions, and with the knowledge of public sentiment, we feel that it is the duty now of the men charged with the responsibility, who have within their grasp the machinery of the party, to see to it that the men who have been false are held accountable; to see to it that men who will be responsive to the will of the voters are nominated for member of assembly in each assembly district of the state. In that way we will make progress. In that way we will get a very different kind of assembly next year. In that way only can we succeed.

" No one has a higher opinion of the legislature of our state than the man who is now addressing you. I use the expression generally. I served in the popular branch of the legislature for five years, nearly a quarter of a century ago, and through my own efforts and by my own exertions, I rose, as a young man, step by step, until I became its speaker—one of the youngest speakers in the history of the state.

" I know something about the legislative history of our state. I could name many great men who have served with honor and distinction in the popular branch of our legislature. It is a great forum. It is the agency of the people of the state to express their will.

" The office of assemblyman is most important, and is great enough for the ambition of any man. In the years gone by we had many great men in the assembly of our state.

" Today I regret to say that cannot be said concerning the

present assembly. I want to be charitable. You know, and I know, and the people know, that the present legislature is controlled by influence adverse to the best interests of the people of the state. It is a matter that now challenges the sober judgment of the people. It is a matter that is now an affront to the intelligence of the citizens, and it is humiliating, not only to me, in my efforts to do right; in my desire to keep the faith; and in my determination to do my duty; but to the due administration of public affairs.

"Another election is approaching—a very important election to the taxpayers of New York. We meet here in council to take some action in order that the next assembly shall be different from the present assembly. In order to make that a living fact it is necessary for you to see to it that the right kind of men are designated in each assembly district for members of assembly.

" What do I mean by that ? Simply this: In the present crisis in the state of New York, where one man challenges the whole people, and because he cannot have his way, he says to the people that they shall not have their way. So we say now, that in each of these assembly districts, in the first instance, we shall appeal to that public spirit, and to that patriotism, which has never failed to respond, when it was necessary to respond, we ask you to aid us so that the ablest and the best men can be designated for members of assembly, regardless of party affiliations, shall be elected to carry out the will of the people, and to see to it that the administration of state affairs is not longer paralyzed.

"As I have said, many great men have been assemblymen in New York. We want great men in the assembly next year; men who dare to do right; men who are free and independent; men who believe in truth and dare to maintain it; men who will see to it that the right shall prevail—regardless of political or personal consequences.

" In each assembly district there are worthy men, eloquent men, brave men, honest men, who will respond to the call; who will allow their names to be used in this struggle for good government, and who will consent to be candidates for assembly. They will be elected. They will come here the first of the year, take the oath of office, and be true to it—true to the general welfare, true to the commonwealth of New York—true to party promises, and true to all that is good and honest and decent in public affairs.

"As the governor, through you, representing what you do, and having it in your power to accomplish results, I now appeal to the intelligent, to the patriotic, and to the public spirited citizens of New York to come forward in this campaign and aid us to elect an assembly that will be beyond the influence of any man, and responsive only to the will of the people.

"My friends, I am carrying a heavy burden. You know something about it, but you do not know all about it. I am doing so simply because I made up my mind when I took the oath of office that I would be governor in fact as well as in name. Because I made up my mind that no influence should control me while I was the governor, but the dictates of my own conscience, and my determination to do my duty, day in and day out, come what may. For these reasons, and others, I have been hounded, traduced, villified and threatened as no other man has ever been who occupied this office, in all the history of the state.

"However, I have no fear of the ultimate result. I know by experience, by the truths of history, by that intuition which is unerring, that justice will prevail, and that right makes might.

"If the honest folk, and the patriotic people of New York will stand up together in this campaign we will win on election day, a victory that will clarify the political atmosphere and go far for years to come to give the state of New York what the state of New York needs—an honest government, and an efficient government, and an economical government—a government in the interests not of the few but for the benefit of all.

"I could say much that I will at present refrain from saying. Let us trust that in the wisdom of your counsel much good will come. You can count on me in the future as in the past to go forward in the work of reform. I shall count on you to aid me. Let us all work together for the good of the state, and certainly that should be the highest ambition in the estimation of every good citizen."

This was the last speech of Governor Sulzer in the executive chamber and the last he made as governor.

CHAPTER XX

MURPHY'S ASSEMBLY ORDERED TO IMPEACH THE GOVERNOR

Edward Croker, former fire chief of New York city, met Senator James J. Frawley during the summer and asked:

"Do you really intend to impeach Sulzer; do you intend to go through with this business?"

And Frawley's reported reply was:

"Of course we do. If we don't he will send us all to jail. It is his life or ours."

That conversation was first made public during the New York city campaign in October by John A. Hennessy, and its truth was afterwards confirmed by Mr. Croker in a newspaper interview, who said: "Every word of that is true. The conversation between Frawley and me took place at the Long Beach railroad station where we happened to meet."

That the fear of jail was the impelling Tammany motive in the attack on Sulzer was manifest from the outset. It was evident all through the Frawley committee activities and at every session of the assembly and high court of impeachment until the vote for removal was recorded.

The moment the Frawley committee on August 8th concluded taking testimony, the report on its findings was hastily prepared and rushed to the printer for presentation to the assembly Monday evening, August 11th. The members were summoned by telegraph and every artifice and trick employed to get them to Albany in a hurry.

For a week there had been talk in the air to the effect that Murphy had at last obtained "something on Sulzer," and that the governor was to be impeached. The haste with which the assembly was summoned and especially the feverish anxiety betrayed by Speaker Alfred E. Smith, Majority Leader Aaron J. Levy and all the other Tammanyites in the assembly to adopt the Frawley report and articles of impeachment brought denunciation from the people all over the state.

Following adjournment of the Frawley committee in New York, Chairman Frawley, Assemblyman Aaron J. Levy, Senator Wagner, Speaker Alfred E. Smith and Eugene Lamb

BREAKING THE PENAL LAW

From the Albany Knickerbocker Press

"IMPEACHING SULZER"

From the Albany Knickerbocker Press.

Richards went to Saratoga Springs, where they remained over Sunday and prepared the committee's report and resolutions to be passed by the assembly Monday night. It was stated that even at that time communication was had with Edgar T. Brackett, whose home is in Saratoga Springs, by the Tammany men on the question of his employment to assist in the prosecution of the charges against Governor Sulzer before the court of impeachment.

Monday night's session of the assembly was a memorable one for excitements and disorder. The program was to jam through the Frawley report and present the resolution of impeachment introduced by Assemblyman Aaron J. Levy. The vote to receive the Frawley report was 65 to 35, and to receive the Levy resolution to impeach, 65 to 30.

In vain did Assemblyman Harold J. Hinman, republican minority leader, Albany county; Louis D. Gibbs, democrat, Bronx county, and Michael Schaap, progressive, New York county, plead for more deliberation in the procedure. They asked for at least enough time to enable the members to read and understand the report which at the last moment had been placed on the desks of the assemblymen. But all these pleadings fell on deaf ears.

Assemblyman Hinman moved that the subject be referred to the judiciary committee for a week so that there might be time to study and discuss one of the most serious questions ever presented to an assembly. His motion was voted down by 62 to 39.

Had there been enough votes—a majority of 150—Tammany would undoubtedly have adopted even the resolution of impeachment the same night without further deliberation. But, in spite of liberal use of the telegraph and telephone all Monday, Charles F. Murphy apparently was unable to get the necessary seventy-six assemblymen that night and so an adjournment was taken to Tuesday forenoon at 11 o'clock.

All next day the struggle continued for more votes and it was not until nearly midnight of August 12th that the assembly was called to order by Speaker Smith. Word went out to the Tammany men to talk against time, as a few votes were still needed to put through the resolution of impeachment. Speaker Smith, Leader Levy, Patrick E. McCabe

and other leaders had been busy all day in the speaker's room
at the rear of the assembly calling in doubtful assemblymen
as they arrived and questioning them where they stood on the
subject of impeaching the governor.

The arguments used were of a widely varied character and
included all that politicians of that type are accustomed to
employ when in desperate straits. At 6 p. m., Tuesday,
Speaker Smith is said to have jubilantly telephoned Charles
F. Murphy that he had seventy-five votes besides his own,
making the bare majority necessary to carry the impeachment
resolution. The boss is reported to have demanded that they
get at least eighty before calling the assembly to order. And
so the telephone, the telegraph and all other means of communication were again brought into play to cajole, threaten
and persuade absent members to come to the rescue of the
boss.

Those who had to wait in the assembly chamber all through
the weary hours will never forget the feeling of depression
that the surroundings created. It was vaguely known to all
that something unusual and dreadful was impending; that
conspirators behind closed doors nearby were preparing for
the degradation of a high official, whose alleged offenses even
then were but little known to the public.

Tammany assemblymen, those of them who were not asleep
in their seats, were as flippant as if the occasion were a political
holiday. All they knew or cared to know was that the boss
" wanted this job done," and it was not for them to ask the
reason.

The constitution contemplated that the assembly in impeachment cases was to act as the grand jury; that all of its members
were to be deliberate and judicial, careful to know the facts
before blackening a man even by accusation.

But had any grand jury acted in the treatment of any petty
case in the inconsiderate manner in which this Tammany
assembly did in the impeachment of a governor, it would have
constituted a scandal in any normal community. There was
no semblance of seriousness or dignity among assemblymen
who knew beforehand what they were going to do.

Tammany leaders, despairing of getting the necessary
seventy-six votes from the democratic side to adopt the im-

HOW MURPHY "IMPEACHED" SULZER

From the Albany Knickerbocker Press

HOW MURPHY "IMPEACHED" SULZER

From the Albany Knickerbocker Press

peachment resolution, appealed to the republicans and enough were quickly forthcoming. Of the seventy-nine who finally voted for the Levy resolution, seven were republican assemblymen. All seven were defeated either for renomination or re-election a few months later.

"Even the lowest criminal at the bar of justice," declared Assemblyman Gibbs, a democrat from Bronx county, in pleading for a little time for deliberation, "is entitled to that much of a square deal, and yet tonight the assembly of the great state of New York is attempting to rush through this resolution before the members have had an opportunity to study the contents of the report upon which it is based. The hour is near when there will be a demonstration throughout this state that will overwhelm the party responsible for this political crucifixion."

"It is an insult to the assembly," said Assemblyman Michael Schaap, progressive leader, "to offer such a resolution here tonight. I appeal to you not to drag the honor of the state in the dust."

Some of the assemblymen needed to make up the majority did not arrive from New York until after midnight and when the Tammany leaders knew they had enough votes the proceedings were expedited. Assemblyman Levy began to speak at 3 o'clock in the morning and spoke for two hours. His speech will not live in history. It was a bold but not an ingenious attempt to support a bad cause.

While he spoke many of the members slept or were heedless of what was going on. Half an hour before he closed and moved that a vote be taken the first rays of the rising sun came in through the assembly chamber windows, only to accentuate the scene made ghastly by the many prostrate assemblymen and general disorder of the room.

√ At 5:13 a. m., August 13th, the vote of 79 to 45 was announced by Speaker Smith and Governor Sulzer had been impeached. v √

There was a rush of the newspaper men to the telegraph offices and of the legislators either to their lodging places for rest or to the railroad stations to take trains home.

THE LEGISLATURE IN SESSION

Between three and five o'clock Wednesday morning, August 13, 1913
Aaron J. Levy's Speech at sunrise.

Here is the vote on the impeachment resolution:

The following democratic assemblymen voted to impeach Governor Sulzer:

Frederick S. Burr, Kings.
LaVerne P. Butts, Otsego.
James C. Campbell, New York.
Charles J. Carroll, New York.
Raymond B. Carver, New York.
Thomas B. Caughlan, New York.
Marc W. Cole, Orleans.
Salvatore A. Cottillo, New York.
Cornelius J. Cronin, Kings.
Louis A. Cuvillier, New York.
Stephen G. Daley, Onondaga.
Karl S. Deitz, Kings.
George E. Dennen, Kings.
Thomas F. Denny, New York.
Charles D. Donohue, New York.
John Dorst, Jr., Erie.
Joseph H. Esquirol, Kings.
Stephen A. Fallon, Suffolk.
Daniel F. Farrell, Kings.
Joseph V. Fitzgerald, Erie.
James H. Finnigan, Kings.
James J. Garvey, Kings.
George Geoghan, Erie.
William J. Gillen, Kings.
Mark Goldberg, New York.
Abram Greenberg, New York.
Wm. Pinkney Hamilton, Jr., Kings.
Ernest E. L. Hammer, New York.
Harry Heyman, Kings.
Thomas L. Ingram, Kings.
Edward D. Jackson, Erie.
Thomas Kane, New York.
John A. Kelly, Dutchess.
John J. Kelly, Kings.
Joseph D. Kelly, New York.
Patrick J. Kelly, Onondaga.

John Kerrigan, New York.
Owen M. Kiernan, New York.
David H. Knott, New York.
Thomas J. Lane, New York.
Jesse P. Larrimer, Kings.
Aaron J. Levy, New York.
David C. Lewis, New York.
Tracy P. Madden, Westchester.
Thomas B. Maloney, Nassau.
Martin G. McCue, New York.
Eugene L. McCollum, Niagara.
Minor McDaniels, Tompkins.
Peter P. McElligott, New York.
Patrick J. McGrath, New York.
Ralph R. McKee, Richmond.
John J. McKeon, Kings.
Patrick J. McMahon, New York.
Joseph J. Monohan, Kings.
Mortimer C. O'Brien, Westchester.
Vincent A. O'Connor, Kings.
Harry E. Oxford, New York.
E. Burt Pullman, Herkimer.
John J. Robinson, Suffolk.
James M. Rozan, Erie.
Jacob Schifferdecker, Kings.
Jacob Silverstein, New York.
George F. Small, Erie.
Frank J. Taylor, Kings.
Robert L. Tudor, New York.
James B. Van Woert, Lewis.
James J. Walker, New York.
Theodore Hackett Ward, New York.
Edward Weil, New York.
Frederick Ulrich, Kings.
Wilson R. Yard, Westchester.
Alfred E. Smith, Speaker, New York.

Republican assemblymen who voted to impeach Governor Sulzer:

Frank M. Bradley, Niagara.
Clarence Bryant, Genesee.
Eugene R. Norton, Washington.
Herman Schnirel, Ontario.

Myron Smith, Dutchess.
Thomas K. Smith, Onondaga.
John R. Yale, Putnam.

Democratic assemblymen who voted against impeachment:

Albert C. Benninger, Queens.
Verne M. Bovie, Westchester.
Samuel J. Burden, Queens.
Dr. Robert P. Bush, Chemung.
William T. Doty, Orange.
Edward A. Dox, Schoharie.
Mark Eisner, New York.
Fred. F. Emden, Oneida.
John K. Evans, Sullivan.
Charles H. Gallup, Monroe.
Eldridge M. Gathright, Ulster.
Albert F. Geyer, Erie.
Louis D. Gibbs, New York.
Frederick G. Grimme, Rockland.
John W. Gurnett, Schuyler.

Alexander W. Hover, Columbia.
Augustus S. Hughes, Seneca.
Lawrence M. Kenney, Ulster.
J. Lewis Patrie, Greene. (Mr. Patrie waited until the last before voting, to be sure that his vote was not needed to impeach the governor).
C. Fred Schwartz, Rensselaer.
James L. Seeley, Steuben.
Arthur P. Squire, Schenectady.
Howard Sutphin, Queens.
John W. Telford, Delaware.
Tracy D. Taylor, Rensselaer.
Clare Willard, Cattaraugus.

Republican assemblymen who voted against impeachment:

Caleb H. Baumes, Orange.
William C. Baxter, Albany.
Mortimer B. Edwards, Broome.
Brayton J. Fuller, Oneida.
Walter A. Gage, Montgomery.
Michael Grace, Cayuga .
Harold J. Hinman, Albany.
Edward M. McGee, Livingston .
John G. Malone, Albany.

Spencer G. Prime, Essex.
Frank L. Seaker, St. Lawrence.
Gilbert T. Seelye, Saratoga.
Walter A. Shepardson, Chenango.
Morrell E. Tallett, Madison.
Niles F. Webb, Cortland.
James H. Wood, Fulton and Hamilton.

Progressives who voted against impeachment:

Birnkrant, New York.
Michael Schaap, New York.

Solomon Sufrin, New York.

OF THE SEVENTY-TWO DEMOCRATIC ASSEMBLYMEN WHO VOTED TO IMPEACH GOVERNOR SULZER ONLY SEVENTEEN, ALL TAMMANY MEN, WERE RE-ELECTED AT THE ENSUING NOVEMBER ELECTION. ALL SEVEN REPUBLICANS WHO VOTED TO IMPEACH WERE DEFEATED EITHER FOR RENOMINATION OR RE-ELECTION. NEVER BEFORE IN THE HISTORY OF THE NEW YORK STATE ASSEMBLY HAD THERE BEEN SO COMPLETE A SWEEP BY THE VOTERS AS THE RESULT OF A VOTE ON ANY ONE SUBJECT.

CHAPTER XXI

" GOVERNMENT BY INVESTIGATION SHOULD NOW CEASE "—*Glynn*

One of the first announcements made by Lieutenant Governor Glynn upon laying claim to the acting governorship was that government by investigation should now cease.

In view of what Senator Frawley had declared concerning the importance of stopping Governor Sulzer from pursuing his graft investigations, the Glynn announcement was regarded as a particularly brazen one. As a matter of fact, the Hennessy investigation did stop soon after the impeachment on account of lack of money and the refusal of Tammany witnesses to appear before Mr. Hennessy. Norman E. Mack was asked to appear and give evidence relating to his participation in the collection of campaign funds. Mr. Mack at first said he would appear in Albany and subject himself to examination, but at the last minute hired Daniel J. Kenefick, a Buffalo lawyer, to write that he had discovered that Mr. Hennessy had no authority, since the governor had been impeached. Mack's reply was accompanied by a suit against Hennessy for slander.

Duncan W. Peck, state superintendent of public works, was also summoned by Mr. Hennessy to tell what he knew about canal employees being held up for contributions to the campaign. Peck, doubtless taking his cue from Mr. Glynn's pronunciamento, likewise declined to appear.

All over the state indignation of the public over the impeachment of Governor Sulzer was expressed in mass meetings and through the newspapers. In fact, resentment of the people was made plain throughout the country, the brazen and contemptuous act of a political boss in ordering an assembly to impeach a chief executive being without precedent in the history of the United States.

Although the probability of impeachment had been discussed in the newspapers for several weeks, the actual carrying out of the threat at Albany came as a thunderbolt out of a clear sky.

" Bold and unprincipled as Murphy has proved himself to

be, I don't believe he will go so far as to impeach Governor Sulzer," was a common remark heard among the people in their daily talk.

The first protest meeting was held in Rochester August 15th, two days after the impeachment, and was attended by more than 5,000 people. Among the speakers were members of all political parties. Resolutions were adopted condemning the assembly for what it had done and speeches were delivered by George Herbert Smith, former republican assemblyman; George P. Decker, former counsel to the state conservation commission; and Thomas H. Armstrong, progressive.

Similar meetings quickly followed in Schenectady, New York, Albany, Ticonderoga and other places. The New York meeting was held in historic Cooper Union. Rev. Canon William S. Chase of Brooklyn presided. The speakers were: Thomas M. Osborne, William S. Bennet, former congressman, Rev. Dr. Charles H. Parkhurst, Samuel Bell Thomas, L. B. Miller, editor of "Warheit," a Jewish daily newspaper; Rev. Dr. Madison C. Peters, Alexander Bacon and General Horatio King.

Dr. Parkhurst, known as a valiant opponent of political vice in New York city during all his life, said:

"We have reached a crisis in the history of our state. If the evil influences operating at Albany can throw out a legally elected governor because he is a barrier to their ambitions, they can throw out his successor if he should happen not to suit them. Made more than ever conscious of their power, they will go on using it with ever increasing arbitrariness of purpose and method. This is not a fight in the interests of the governor, but a fight against the polluted ambitions of the man who is trying to crush him. Profound as may be our respect and warm as may be our regard for Mr. Sulzer, and intense as may be our appreciation of what he means to the people and of what the people mean to him, the governor, nevertheless, is merely an incident, whatever he may have done or may not have done. The question is a bigger one. The question is whether this state is to be ruled by one man, and he a man that is bad from away back, a graduate from the bar room, with no stock in trade but his immoral audacity and his ill gotten gains? That is the question that is up to

IMPEACHING SULZER

FROM THE ALBANY KNICKERBOCKER PRESS

be, I don't believe he will go so far as to impeach Governor
Sulzer," was a common remark heard among the people in
their daily talk.

The first protest meeting was held in Rochester August 15th,
two days after the impeachment, and was attended by more
than 5,000 people. Among the speakers were members of all
political parties. Resolutions were adopted condemning the
assembly for what it had done and speeches were delivered by
George Herbert Smith, former republican assemblyman;
George P. Decker, former counsel to the state conservation
commission; and Thomas H. Armstrong, progressive.

Similar meetings quickly followed in Schenectady, New
York, Albany, Ticonderoga and other places. The New York
meeting was held in historic Cooper Union. Rev. Canon
William S. Chase of Brooklyn presided. The speakers were:
Thomas M. Osborne, William S. Bennet, former congressman,
Rev. Dr. Charles H. Parkhurst, Samuel Bell Thomas, L. B.
Miller, editor of " Warheit," a Jewish daily newspaper; Rev.
Dr. Madison C. Peters, Alexander Bacon and General Horatio
King.

Dr. Parkhurst, known as a valiant opponent of political
vice in New York city during all his life, said:

" We have reached a crisis in the history of our state. If
the evil influences operating at Albany can throw out a legally
elected governor because he is a barrier to their ambitions,
they can throw out his successor if he should happen not to
suit them. Made more than ever conscious of their power,
they will go on using it with ever increasing arbitrariness of
purpose and method. This is not a fight in the interests of
the governor, but a fight against the polluted ambitions of
the man who is trying to crush him. Profound as may be our
respect and warm as may be our regard for Mr. Sulzer, and
intense as may be our appreciation of what he means to the
people and of what the people mean to him, the governor,
nevertheless, is merely an incident, whatever he may have
done or may not have done. The question is a bigger one.
The question is whether this state is to be ruled by one man,
and he a man that is bad from away back, a graduate from the
bar-room, with no stock in trade but his immoral audacity
and his ill-gotten gains ? That is the question that is up to

IMPEACHING SULZER

From the Albany Knickerbocker Press

... .

....

.. .

... . under the con-
.... governor. It
... .r's advisers that the
... impeached executive
.... of governor until he
.... from office

... . of counsel, to submit
... . This offer was

THE GOVERNOR AND THE PRETENDER

From the Albany Knickerbock Pre

the state and to us as its true and loyal citizens." (Prolonged applause and cheers.)

Rev. Dr. Peters also stirred the great audience when he said:

" Whatever may be Governor Sulzer's mistakes, all men, throughout the whole country, who are not professional politicians, feel that no public official has ever shown higher courage and greater virtue than Mr. Sulzer has proved during the brief period of his incumbency, and everybody knows that the bitterness of the attacks upon him which have led to the impeachment proceedings have been in proportion to his political honesty and public virtue in the discharge of his duties.

" William Sulzer has been an ' impossible governor,' to use Tammany's own words, because it has been impossible to use Sulzer as a rubber stamp and allow Murphy and his gang to longer loot the state of New York, and when the governor determined to destroy Tammany the boss saw no escape except to destroy the governor. And what is the high crime —he failed to return to a few admiring friends a small sum of money which had been privately sent to him for his personal use during the campaign.

" Surely that must seem like a high crime and a misdemeanor to a leader of an assembly who can pull off five thousand dollars to get a bill through the legislature to pay eleven thousand dollars."

From the date of the impeachment Governor Sulzer was placed under a vow by his lawyers not to speak for publication. For a man who was accustomed to discuss through the newspapers his public affairs day after day, this pledge was an onerous one for him to make, especially when he knew he was being misrepresented and maligned.

From the moment the impeachment articles had been delivered to the senate on August 13th, the legal advisers of lieutenant governor Martin H. Glynn held that under the constitution he automatically became the acting governor. It was as stoutly held by Governor Sulzer's advisers that the constitution contemplated that an impeached executive should continue to perform the functions of governor until he had been convicted and removed from office.

Governor Sulzer offered, under advice of counsel, to submit the question to the courts for adjudication. This offer was

THE GOVERNOR AND THE PRETENDER

From the Albany Knickerbocker Press

rejected by the lieutenant governor, who contended that there was nothing for the courts to pass upon, the constitution, according to his view, being clear on that point.

"The entire matter," wrote Mr. Glynn, "is now in the highest court of the state—the court of impeachment—the most august body known to our system."

To his intimate friends, Governor Sulzer frequently stated after his impeachment and before the trial that he knew enough of the character of Charles F. Murphy to feel sure that he would be removed.

"Tammany controls two-thirds of the court," he said, "and it has already been decreed that I am to be ousted from office."

Referring to the members of the court of appeals, the governor remarked that three of the ten members were dominated by Murphy and three by William Barnes, the republican boss. He believed that these six members were as incapable of doing him justice as the average Tammany senator.

CHAPTER XXII

THE HIGH COURT OF IMPEACHMENT CONVENES

During the month which intervened between impeachment by the assembly and the opening of the court of impeachment, the state senate chamber was transformed at an expense of about $2,500 to the state. The platform of the presiding officer was changed from the south to the west wall of the chamber and the seats moved to conform to the shift. Additional seats were placed in front of the chamber to accommodate the judges of the court of appeals and on the southern side for the board of managers.

Rigid rules were adopted to prevent easy access to the senate galleries and to the lobby. The force of doorkeepers and other employes adequately conformed to Tammany's idea of expending public money.

It being the first time that a governor had been impeached in New York state, the forms of procedure caused considerable discussion before adoption. The court of appeals was made up of seven judges elected by the people. Under the constitution the governor could appoint four justices from the supreme court to serve as associate judges when the amount of work warranted the addition. In 1913 there were three of these associate judges, making a total of ten members of the court.

For a time one of the questions in controversy was whether these associate judges were eligible to sit in the court of impeachment. It finally was decided by the court that they were eligible although there are constitutional lawyers who continue to contend that the contrary is true.

One of the seven elected judges, John Clinton Gray, was absent in Europe at the time of the trial, hence nine judges were members of the court.

Fifty-one senators composed the state senate, but at the time of Governor Sulzer's impeachment there were two vacancies. One was in the twenty-first district caused by the conviction for extortion of Senator Stephen J. Stilwell. The other was in the twenty-sixth district due to the resignation of

Senator Franklin D. Roosevelt to accept the office of assistant secretary of the navy.

Senator John C. Fitzgerald of the twelfth district was ill during the trial and could not attend. This left forty-eight senators and nine judges to participate in the trial, making a total of fifty-seven members in the court.‸ Two-thirds of that number, or thirty-eight, were necessary to convict the governor on any of the charges preferred against him by the assembly.

When it is remembered that twenty-four of the twenty-nine democratic senators sitting in the court were controlled by Tammany, all of them following orders of the boss, the hopelessness of the governor's friends that he had any chance of acquittal may be understood. Added to these were the machine republican senators who were in the habit of acting with Tammany men when their votes were needed. There were sixteen republicans in the senate and at least ten of these were known to be bitterly and blindly partisan in their attitude toward Sulzer.

The counsel on each side before the court were: for the board of managers: chief counsel, Alton B. Parker, former chief judge of the court of appeals; democratic candidate for president in 1904 against Theodore Roosevelt; law partner of William F. Sheehan, former lieutenant governor; permanent chairman of the state convention in 1912 which nominated Sulzer.

John B. Stanchfield, democratic candidate for governor in 1900; corporation lawyer and eminent reactionary in politics; distinguished himself as the Tammany orator at the democratic national convention of 1912 at Baltimore, in a bitter attack on William J. Bryan.

Edgar Truman Brackett, former state senator and republican leader in the senate; counsel for William Barnes in the senate investigation of Albany city and county affairs in 1911.

Eugene Lamb Richards, Tammany state committeeman; counsel for the Frawley committee in digging up charges against Governor Sulzer.

Isodor J. Kresel, former assistant district attorney in New York county under William T. Jerome, and given the name of the " ferret."

LAWYERS FOR IMPEACHMENT MANAGERS

From left to right   Eugene Lamb Richards, Isodor J. Kresel,
Edgar Truman Brackett, John B. Stanchfield

Hiram J. Todd, law partner of Senator Brackett; and Henderson Peck, Troy.

For Governor Sulzer: chief counsel, D-Cady Herrick, former justice of the supreme court, democratic candidate for governor in 1904; former district attorney of Albany county.

Irving G. Vann, former associate judge of the court of appeals.

Harvey D. Hinman, former state senator from Binghamton district; supporter of Governor Charles E. Hughes in his fight for direct primaries.

Austin G. Fox, New York, special district attorney in the Lexow investigation of New York city affairs.

Louis Marshall, New York, eminent constitutional lawyer.

Judge James Gay Gordon, Philadelphia, Pa.

Roger P. Clark, former district attorney of Broome county.

Elihu Root, Jr., son of United States Senator Root.

One of the first objections raised by Judge Herrick in behalf of Governor Sulzer was to the eligibility of certain members of the court.   He specifically objected to members of the Frawley committee, Frawley, Ramsperger and Sanner, who had been engaged in collecting evidence against the governor, sitting as jurors in the case, as they had publicly expressed opinions on the subject.   He also objected to Senator Wagner sitting in judgment on the ground that in case of the governor's removal he would succeed lieutenant governor Glynn to that office, a fact which would make him personally interested in the outcome of the trial.

The court ruled that there was nothing in the constitution to prevent these senators from sitting and voting in the court. Presiding Judge Cullen, however, apparently believed that while there was no legal reason for the withdrawal of the senators, who had so often betrayed bias against the governor, there was a moral reason for their retirement, for he said:

"If any member of the court feels that such action as he has previously taken in regard to the matters which are now to be tried, or his personal feelings towards the respondent, are such as to disqualify him, or to impair his ability to render a just and fair verdict, according to the oath which he has taken, he may now appeal to the court to be excused from sitting."

This announcement by the presiding judge was intended to place the notoriously prejudiced members of the court or jury on honor, but it did not result in the withdrawal of a single member. Had the protested members been disqualified Governor Sulzer could not have been convicted. There would not have been the necessary thirty-eight votes to convict and remove him.

Each of the fifty-seven members of the court had to take a solemn oath to try the accused governor without prejudice. It was when Senator Frawley stood up and raised his hand to swear he could do this that Judge Herrick raised the objection. While Judge Herrick was setting forth his reasons Frawley continued to hold his hand up and there was a buzz of excitement and interest throughout the chamber. The chairman of the investigating committee plainly showed nervousness as he waited for the ruling of the court. Remarks could be heard in the galleries: " That's the man we have heard so much about," and " He's the Tammany man so much opposed to the governor."

Louis Marshall delivered an exhaustive and scholarly argument to show that all precedent was against the legislature acting at an extraordinary session on any subject not recommended by the governor in his message. He contended, therefore, that the assembly had no authority to impeach the governor. Mr. Marshall spoke for more than two hours. One part of his speech which attracted general attention was:

" If such a procedure should be declared to be within the spirit of the constitution, the time may come when, as a result of momentary excitement, the rhetoric of a demagogue, or headlong passion, a bare majority of the assembly may be brought together by malign influences, for the very purpose of impeaching every member of the Court of Appeals and every justice of the Supreme court.

" Under such circumstances chaos and anarchy would reign, and grim revolution would stalk throughout the state. This is not a mere figment of the imagination.

" If the contentions of the managers in the present case were upheld, would it not, at such periods of storm and stress as are apt to arise in every decade of our history, seal the fountains of justice and paralyze the arm of the judiciary ?

" This is not a novel position from the standpoint of history. It is as old as tyranny; as ancient as lawlessness. Those who

SENATORS WAGNER AND FRAWLEY

Senator Robert Wagner as a result of the removal of Sulzer became
Lieutenant-Governor. Senator James J. Frawley asked for and received as a
souvenir the pen that wrote the decision of the court that removed Sulzer.

controlled the machinery of the star chamber in the days of the Tudors; those who issued letters to cachet in the reign of Louis XV; the mobs which in our own land have resorted to lynching have been actuated by a common abhorrence of legal procedure according to established principles, and have viewed the restraints of the written law and of elemental justice as technicalities.

"And we have now, in our day, come to the task when an appeal to the supreme law—the constitution—which. enshrouds the self-imposed restraints of a free people, is likewise treated as a technicality whenever it is believed that it may wrest from immolation the victim of partisan fury or from confiscation the property of those against whom popular prejudice has been aroused.

"To dismiss the articles of impeachment which have been presented to this tribunal for lack of jurisdiction would not be a triumph of technicality.   It would be the victory of the constitution and of the law.   It would be a vindication of that sacred instrument to which we all owe fealty."

Judge Parker and Senator Brackett replied to Mr. Marshall their claim being that the prohibition of the constitution on the legislature at extraordinary sessions referred only to matters of legislation, and that as an impeaching body the assembly could meet at any time or place.

By a vote of 51 to 1 the court decided that the assembly had the constitutional power to impeach at an extraordinary session even when not authorized by the governor to consider the subject.   The dissenting vote was by Senator Gottfried H. Wende, of Buffalo, who, in casting his vote, said:

"As I read the constitution, the assembly at some time had an absolute right of framing these articles of impeachment. That right existed up to the time that they took an adjournment sine die; and when they adopted the resolutions adjourning sine die they foreclosed their right to any question of impeachment or to act upon anything else, if they were to be called together in extraordinary session, only such subjects as the governor would present.   I therefore vote aye."

CHAPTER XXIII

ASSEMBLY DENOUNCED FOR USURPATION

The second vital question which the court of impeachment was asked to dispose of before hearing testimony was whether the constitution permitted it to try the governor on offenses alleged to have been committed prior to his inauguration.

His counsel asked the court to dismiss the first, second and sixth articles of impeachment, which were:

That he violated the penal statutes by the filing of a false statement of campaign expenses.

That in swearing to this alleged false statement of campaign expenses he committed perjury, a specific violation of the penal statutes.

That he committed grand larceny by misappropriating to his own purposes checks meant for campaign contributions.

For hours the lawyers on both sides talked while most of the members of the court either lounged half asleep in their seats or walked up and down the lobby of the senate chamber paying no attention to the contentions of counsel on a subject so important to the accused governor.

Those citizens of New York state who assume that the proceedings of the court were as " dignified " and " solemn " as they frequently had them pictured should be disillusioned. Most of the members acted as if they did not care to hear any argument or testimony and had made up their minds long before the court assembled to " get that fellow," in the parlance of Tammany.

Austin G. Fox, of counsel for the governor, in the course of his speech for dismissal of the three charges because they related to acts alleged to have been committed prior to the inauguration of Sulzer, said:

" We do not appear here for William Sulzer. We have not reached that step yet. We are here to denounce the usurpation of power by seventy-nine members of the assembly, and if you do not stop it here who can tell what it will attempt to do next, when a hostile faction has control not only of a majority of the assembly but of this impeachment court ?

From the Albany Knickerbocker Press

"It was to be expected that, sooner or later, the popular branch of the legislature, acting in the heat of political excitement, or in subservience of some popular demand, or possibly, with a desire to gratify the personal enmity of some powerful political leader, might seek to overstep the well settled limitations of their lawful authority.

"May not the time yet come when there will arise some political leader whose ascendancy will be so great and whose rancor will be so bitter that he may not only control a majority of the assembly, but, in some future senate, may find complaisant members in numbers sufficient to register his decrees, if we depart one jot from the fundamental doctrine that where there is no misconduct in office alleged the remedy by impeachment will not lie?

"It has been our experience in times past that political leaders once gained power not only to loot the treasuries of our state, but to invade our courts of justice."

In his characteristically caustic style Senator Brackett replied to these contentions as follows:

"He who deliberately fills out a false statement in November is not fit for public office in January. He who commits larceny in October may not be entrusted with the responsibilities of high office three months later.

"The world hates a liar, but it is not for lying that we ask the conviction of William Sulzer.

"Shall it be said to students of our system of government that securing the highest office in the state purges of loathsome crime; that the way to avoid punishment for perjury is to be elected to high office. and that such election retains the occupant in association with decent men of high place?

"When the members of the high court of last resort, sitting in and a part of this august tribunal, come to the courtesies of the next holiday season, must they feel that they are clasping hands with a perjurer and a thief, because the admitted perjury and larceny were committed fifteen minutes before 12 o'clock noon of January 1, 1913?"

At the suggestion of Judge Cullen the question of whether the three articles should be admitted was deferred until after the testimony had been heard.

Then came the calling of witnesses, Jacob H. Schiff, New York city banker, being the first to testify.

Mr. Schiff said he congratulated Governor Sulzer by letter upon his nomination, and soon after Governor Sulzer called upon him at his office, October 16, 1912. He to'd this story of the meeting:

" Governor Sulzer came into my office and he discussed the general political situation. He said he was gratified that he was going to have my support. I asked him whether there was anything special I could do for him and he said, 'Are you going to contribute to my campaign fund?'

" I said, ' Yes, I shall be willing to do so,' and he said, ' How much will you contribute?' I said, ' $2,500.' He replied, ' Can you make it any more?' I then said to him, ' No, that is about as much as I care to give you.' Then he said, 'All right, please make your check to the order of Louis A. Sarecky.' I believe that is the name. That was the conversation I had with him."

Mr. Kresel produced the canceled check and showed that across the face of it was written, " Mr. Schiff's contribution towards William Sulzer's campaign expenses." Mr. Schiff said he put that on there only to identify the check when he turned it over to the Frawley investigating committee, and meant the term " campaign expenses " to be general.

The cross-examination of Mr. Schiff was conducted by Louis Marshall and was short and to the point, Mr. Marshall smiling at the answer to his question, " Did you intend that this should be used for any specific purpose? " meaning the check for $2,500.

The answer was:

" When I used the expression ' campaign funds ' it was a very general expression. I certainly had no objection whatsoever, and I think it was the general intent and purpose of the conversation that Governor Sulzer could use this $2,500 for whatever he would please."

Henry Morgenthau, another witness, testified that he had contributed $1,000 to the governor without specifying that it was for any particular purpose. Mr. Morgenthau subsequently testified that the governor had called him up by telephone at New York and asked him to be as easy as he could on him, if called as a witness, and Mr. Morgenthau replied that he would tell the truth, refusing to say the $1,000 was a personal gift.

Richard Croker, Jr,. son of the former boss of Tammany, said he gave Sulzer $2,000 to be used as he saw fit.

Duncan W. Peck, re-appointed by Governor Sulzer at the beginning of the year as state superintendent of public works, the salary of which office is $8,000 a year, swore that while Mr. Sulzer was touring the state as a candidate for governor he handed him a $500 bill at Troy. Peck testified that he received a letter from the Frawley committee asking him to appear and testify, whereupon he went to see Governor Sulzer and asked him what he should do.

"He said: 'Do as I shall; deny it,'" Mr. Peck swore.

"But I suppose I will be under oath," Mr. Peck said he told the Governor, declaring that the Governor's answer was: "That's nothing, forget it."

Governor Sulzer afterwards admitted he received the $500 but denied that he had made any such statement attributed to him by Peck.

Allan H. Ryan, son of Thomas F. Ryan, wealthy New York city financier, testified that Governor Sulzer had asked him for money after his nomination and that he had given him, through his secretary, I. V. McGlone, $10,000 in ten $1,000 bills. He also swore that Governor Sulzer had asked him since the impeachment proceedings had begun to see Senator Elihu Root at Washington and endeavor to have him see William Barnes, the Republican state chairman, for the purpose of persuading the latter to request the republican state senators to vote that the impeachment was unconstitutional. Mr. Ryan said he refused to see Senator Root.

Other witnesses were produced, who testified they had contributed money to the Sulzer campaign but the foregoing were considered the most important.

Mr. Ryan, upon being recalled a day later, testified that when he refused to see Mr. Barnes the governor asked him to see Delancey Nicoll, a Tammany lawyer, and ask him to see Murphy and have him stop the impeachment proceedings and that he (the governor) "would do the right thing." Mr. Ryan said he went into the country and forgot all about Governor Sulzer's request.

CHAPTER XXIV

SULZER CHAFES UNDER THE BAN OF SILENCE

Judge D-Cady Herrick, chief counsel for the governor, found it increasingly difficult during the progress of the trial to keep Governor Sulzer under restraint. From the beginning of the proceedings the governor contended that his lawyers should keep in mind that there were two courts before which he was being tried—" Murphy's court," as he styled it, and the court of public opinion.

" The only chance I have to obtain justice," he argued, " is to let the people of the state know all about the motives and character of my accusers; why these impeachment proceedings were started and what these accusers hope to accomplish by my removal from office. Mr. Murphy's plan is to so narrow the taking of evidence that but little more than one side will be heard and nothing about the diabolical plot to conceal the crimes of men high in his organization."

Consultations were held every night at the People's house by counsel for the governor and by his friends not connected with his legal advisers. The lawyers were divided as to the policy which should be pursued in the defense before the court. Judge Herrick enjoined strict silence upon the governor so far as the giving out of public statements was concerned.

Among those who met at the mansion every night, in addition to the counsel, to discuss and advise, were: Alexander S. Bacon, Nathan B. Chadsey, Samuel Bell Thomas, Charles Henschell, Martin O'Brien, Wallace Hunter and William Liller.

Senator Harvey D. Hinman and other advisers did not see any objection to the governor making public denial of certain assertions of witnesses on the stand and of otherwise appealing to the court of public opinion. Judge Herrick was reminded that the trial, although in a sense a legal proceeding, was also political in its character.

Theodore Roosevelt wrote a letter to Governor Sulzer while the trial was in progress, urging him to take the public into his confidence. The governor prepared a statement for that purpose in the form of a reply to Mr. Roosevelt, containing substantially what he gave out after the trial. It set forth his meetings with Charles F. Murphy and the threats that had been made unless he did the bidding of the boss.

When this letter was shown to Judge Herrick for his approval he promptly vetoed the plan to have Mr. Roosevelt make it public upon its receipt. Colonel Roosevelt, therefore, was given the information privately and not permitted to give it out to the newspapers as at first had been contemplated by Governor Sulzer.

This was a sore disappointment to the governor, who agreed heartily with Mr. Roosevelt that he should take the public into his confidence. Judge Herrick, however, had his way, threatening to withdraw from the case if his ideas were not carried out.

There was also a difference of opinion as to whether Governor Sulzer should go on the witness stand and tell his own story. In preparation for that event, Senator Hinman and Roger P. Clark, night after night at the People's house, put Mr. Sulzer through long examinations, just as if he were on the witness stand. All that he said was taken by a stenographer and afterwards transcribed. He was not allowed to use this until after his removal from office. Some of his friends declared that if it had been made public during the trial it might have saved him. The statement is incorporated in full in Chapters IX and X of this book.

As soon as he knew that Charles F. Murphy had decided to order his assembly to impeach him Governor Sulzer had a detectaphone installed at the People's house by the Burns detective agency. It was placed in a revolving bookcase in the first room to the left of the front entrance to the house which was used by Governor Sulzer as his office at the mansion. Close to the bookcase were two large leather chairs in either of which the person to be detectaphoned was placed, while an expert operator in another part of the building took down the conversation. Governor Sulzer, after the trial, made public an alleged conversation thus recorded between himself and John H. Delaney, commissioner of efficiency and economy, on the subject of the $25,000 declared to have been contributed by the late Anthony N. Brady to the campaign fund. The story was that Samuel A. Beardsley, representative of Brady,

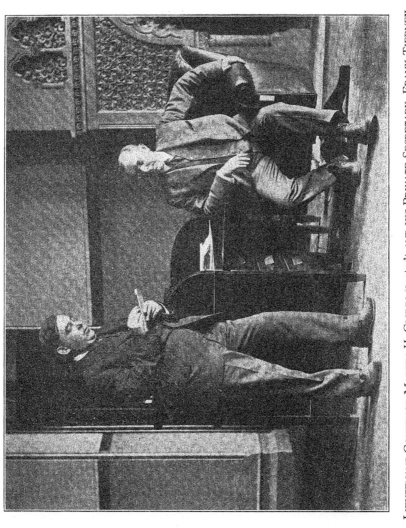

LIEUTENANT-GOVERNOR MARTIN H. GLYNN (seated) AND HIS PRIVATE SECRETARY, FRANK TIERNEY
This picture was taken immediately after the Assembly passed the impeachment articles

offered the money to Mr. Sulzer, who refused it, but said he
would turn it over to Charles F. Murphy for the state campaign fund.   Delaney is declared to have been the intermediary
between Sulzer and Murphy on that occasion.   In the detectaphone report, Sulzer is shown to have informed Delaney
that he would have to go on the stand and tell the truth about
the contribution and that Delaney would probably have to
also testify in court that he received the money and delivered
it to Murphy.   Delaney is quoted as dodging considerably,
but, to the satisfaction of the governor, he admitted that the
money had been delivered to Murphy.

Mr. Murphy, while the New York city campaign was on,
admitted he received the $25,000, but, much to the amuse-
ment of the populace, insisted he had returned it to Mr. Brady.

An effort was made to allow Mr. Beardsley to testify, in
behalf of the governor, that he had been offered and refused
this $25,000 but it was not permitted under the " laws of
evidence."

The same ruling prevented testimony from John A. Hennessy,
Sulzer's special investigator, by whom it was proposed to be
shown the motive of the attack on Governor Sulzer.   Mr.
Hennessy would have testified to what he found in some of the
departments and the relation between his work and the activity of the Frawley committee.

Governor Sulzer also wanted to show in court that he had
been offered and refused amounts for his campaign aggregating
$102,500.   Included in this total was the $25,000 from Beardsley, really from the electric power trust interested in the defeat
of the Capitol district hydro-electric power bill; $25,000 from
the horse racing interests; $10,000 from the United States
Steel Corporation; $10,000 from the New York Telephone
Company; and similar sums from large corporations.   No
evidence of this kind was permitted in spite of the fact that
the court heard daily of the amounts the governor accepted
from friends who were not seeking legislation at Albany.

CHAPTER XXV

Summing Up and Removal

Former Senator Harvey D. Hinman, of Binghamton, N. Y., made the opening address for Governor Sulzer after the board of managers had announced that they rested their case. His speech was the first before the court to refer strongly to the motives behind the attack on the governor and proved to be a refreshing departure from the strictly legal appeals bound to narrow lines by the rules of evidence.

"In determining the questions before it, this court must necessarily take into consideration the question of public good," declared Mr. Hinman. "In case it finds the respondent guilty, it must determine whether he ought to be removed. That involves the motives which led to this impeachment; that is, as to whether or not the proceeding and the result sought to be obtained are in the true interest of the public."

Raising his voice, Mr. Hinman exclaimed dramatically:

"The question must be, and is, was the respondent impeached because of 'mal and corrupt conduct in office,' or was he impeached because of what he refused to do since he took office."

It was the first time the court had to listen to the charge that the governor was being impeached because he insisted upon doing his duty. and every member was brought up at attention, almost breathless to catch the next words as Mr. Hinman went on:

"Was the proceeding instituted because of a desire to accomplish a public good or was it for the purpose of getting rid of a public official who was performing his duty?

"Was he impeached, as they say, for 'stealing' the moneys which his friends gave him, or was it because he was preventing the grafters from stealing the moneys of the taxpayers?

"Was he impeached because, as they say, he made a false oath, or was it because he refused to violate his official oath of office.

"These are some of the questions which the public are expecting this court to answer," he said. "Upon their answer, we believe, depends quite largely the future welfare and interests of the state.

"We are living in strange days. There has never been a time within my recollection when there was such a spirit of unrest and uneasiness on the part of the people generally. The time is surely coming—indeed it may be near at hand—when we as a people must demonstrate whether our form of

AARON J. LEVY
Tammany Leader of the Assembly
This picture was taken the next day after
Boss Murphy "got Sulzer."

government, with an almost unlimited elective franchise, can endure. We cannot escape the feeling that what is done here and now may have a tremendous influence on the determination of that question."

Louis A. Sarecky, secretary to Governor Sulzer when the latter was a congressman and who had charge of his financial affairs during his campaign for governor, was the principal witness for the respondent. Mr. Sarecky, a young man twenty-seven years old, born in Odessa, Russia, assumed all blame for making up the statement of campaign expenses for Governor Sulzer; declared he had signed the governor's name on checks sent him for campaign expenses. In the presence of the court he signed the name " Wm. Sulzer " in a manner that proved his ability to imitate the governor's handwriting so that it could not be distinguished from the real signature except by experts.

Sarecky was subjected to a searching cross-examination by John B. Stanchfield, but he bore up amazingly under it all, admitting that he had used money received during the campaign to settle obligations incurred by the governor without consulting him.

Sarecky's testimony began on October 7 and was concluded on the 8th. On the 9th, Louis Marshall began the summing up in a speech which will be ranked among the great forensic efforts in the history of the American bar.

Those who listened to his powerful appeal will long remember these words:

"And now William Sulzer, who wrought all this, stands before you today, on trial for his very existence, charged with being a common criminal, and for what? Not because while an incumbent of office he has been guilty of official corruption; not because he has taken one dollar of the people's money, or has enriched himself at their expense, or has received a bribe, or has done aught to injure the public weal; not because he has been guilty of treason, of a violation of the constitution, or of his oath of office; not because he has neglected the performance of his official duties, or has absented himself from the seat of government, or indicated, to the slightest degree, a lack of zeal for the public welfare. It is not charged that he was incompetent or ignorant, or incapable of performing the duties of his office, or that he has not been duly watchful of the interests which he has been sworn to guard. It is not charged that he has entered into a conspiracy with those who would loot the public treasury, or who would batten on contracts improvidently or corruptly drawn without safeguards to forestall adequately the possibility of fraud and collusion. The achievements of his administration, as they have passed before the eyes of the people, absolve him from all suspicion of guilt in regard to any of the offenses contained in the category of the usual form of official misconduct.

"And yet the impeachment managers are now seeking to remove William Sulzer from the office which he has thus honorably filled, fifteen months before the expiration of the term for which he was elected. If Macaulay's celebrated New Zealander, or Montesquieu's famous Persian were now among us, we might well ask, why in this land of boasted liberty and freedom one deserving so well at the hands of his fellow men should be subjected to this awful degradation, and why the state which he has served so well should be involved in his ruin and disgrace. The only answer which could be vouchsafed to them is to be found in the articles of impeachment, which, as the record shows, were adopted at dawn on the fatal 13th day of August, 1913, by the assembly of the state of New York, in less than thirty-six hours after the presentation of the reports of an investigating committee which the members of the assembly could not possibly have read or considered when they voted the adoption of these articles."

Alton B. Parker followed in his summing up for the managers in which he held that all of the charges had been proved and he asked for removal of the governor.

Judge Herrick concluded for the governor. It was a dignified and eloquent appeal for justice. One of the striking parts of his address was where he referred to the testimony of Duncan W. Peck and Allan H. Ryan who had accused the governor of attempting to unduly influence the court. Judge Herrick said:

" Imagine yourself in his place. There are some things that a decent, manly man cannot do to save himself. Some things that a man of even low ethical standards cannot shield himself by. Some sacrifices of others that he cannot allow to be made, even at the risk of losing high position and being forever disqualified for political preferment and honors. Which would you do ? Run the risk of losing the empty honor of being governor—empty if held with dishonor—or lose the respect of every decent and honorable man in the whole United States by saving yourself at the expense of the honor and integrity of the one you are bound to love and protect. Imagine yourself, I say, in that position, with his experience, the political surroundings that he had been brought up in, the political ideals

that he possessed, the political education that he had received
in a school where it is supposed that political influence can reach
not only into the courts, but even into the sanctuary of the
church. Is it any wonder that, in desperation, he resorted to
the methods best known to people brought up in such a political
school; with such a political education, and endeavored to
secure the influence of political leaders of both parties to have
the impeachment articles brought by the assembly declared
to be illegal for lack of jurisdiction as he had been informed
and advised by high legal authority they were.

"Is it any wonder that he preferred to risk his high position
and all future political advances rather than subject himself
to the scorn of every honorable man, and should resort to these
methods, which you and I, and all right thinking men, consider dishonorable and regard as an imputation upon our
courts of justice, that it should even be thought for a moment
they could be reached by political or other influence?"

Senator Brackett delivered the last address for the managers. It was characteristically bitter and unrelenting. He
ridiculed the attempt of Senator Hinman to liken Sulzer to
Saul as follows:

"But the first of January comes, and from that moment
he is a converted man; but, my brothers, there are some of
us here to whom through the years the question of conversion
has been very much before our eyes, and yet I cannot fail to
remind you that the great church which stands today, as it
has stood from the beginning, firm in the belief of a conversion
from sin, that it yet demands repentance. Never yet, when you
were standing behind the sacred desk, never yet have you
permitted to join holy church, a man whom you did not believe
in your heart had repented of his sins. Oh, but on the first of
January, like Saul of Tarsus on his way to Damascus, there
came a light, yet before that moment he was in gall of bitterness and bondage of sin, although prior to that time he had done
nothing but serve the forces of evil, yet from the first day of
January, when the light came to him, he became a consecrated
man and devoted himself thenceforth to the service of God
and humanity in the people's house.

"Oh Saul! Oh Saul! Persecutor of the saints, but the
greatest of the Apostles! What foolishness has been attempted

through the years because of that sudden conversion of yours on the way to Damascus! There is many a man that tries to liken himself to Paul when the only likeness is to that of Saul. Saul saw a light, but he respected it. He repented of his sins, Saul, having seen the light, announced that from that moment he renounced the devil and all his works.

"He did not go around trying to suborn perjury. When he got together the few Christians in the upper chamber, wherever he could get them, to preach the word, after his conversion, he did not whisper to one of them that if he was sworn he hoped they would be easy on him. Before he opened the meeting with prayer, he didn't call one of them aside and see if he could send word to tamper with the court that was going to try him, and he finally won a glorious martyrdom by sincerity, and not by posing; by honest work, not by many professions; by doing the work and not being a rank hypocrite.

"Can you imagine Paul telephoning to Gamaliel that he was "the same old Saul. And can't you make it more than $7,500?"

After the speeches by counsel the court went into executive session to discuss the charges. Informal votes were taken on the various articles of impeachment. Notwithstanding the secrecy with which these sessions were supposed to be surrounded the newspaper correspondents were able to predict what the votes were to be in the open session.

The votes in the open session on the eight articles were:

1. Filing a false statement of campaign contributions. Guilty, 39; not guilty, 18.

2. Perjury, swearing this statement was true. Guilty, 39; not guilty, 18.

3. Felony, trying to bribe witnesses to withhold testimony from Frawley legislative committee. Not guilty, unanimous.

4. Misdemeanor, in attempting to suppress testimony by deceit, fraud and threats. Guilty, 43; not guilty, 14.

5. Misdemeanor, in wilfully preventing a witness from appearing before the Frawley legislative committee. Not guilty, unanimous.

6. Larceny, in converting campaign contributions to his private use. Not guilty, unanimous.

7. Corrupt use of office in attempting to influence the vote and actions of public officers. Not guilty, unanimous.

8. Using his authority or influence as governor in affecting the price of securities on the stock exchange. Not guilty, unanimous.

Shall the Governor be removed from office?

Yes, 43; no, 12.

Shall William Sulzer be disqualified from again holding office?

No, unanimous.

It will be observed that the vote on article one was close, 39 to 18. If the governor had two more votes he could have been acquitted on this charge of falsifying his campaign statement regarded as the most serious one of all. The vote on this article was:

GUILTY—39. Judges Frederick Collin, Elmira; William H. Cuddeback, Buffalo; John W. Hogan, Syracuse (democrats); Frank H. Hiscock, Syracuse; Nathan L. Miller, Cortland (republicans).

Senators George A. Blauvelt, Monsey, Rockland county; John J. Boylan, Manhattan; Daniel J. Carroll, Brooklyn; William B. Carswell, Brooklyn; Thomas H. Cullen, Brooklyn; James A. Foley, Manhattan; James J. Frawley, Manhattan; Anthony J. Griffin, Manhattan; John F. Healy, New Rochelle; William J. Heffernan, Brooklyn; James D. McClelland, Manhattan; John F. Malone, Buffalo; John F. Murtaugh, Elmira; Bernard M. Patton, Queens; Henry W. Pollock, Manhattan; Samuel J. Ramsperger, Buffalo; Felix J. Sanner, Kings; George W. Simpson, Manhattan; C. D. Sullivan, Manhattan; Herman H. Torborg, Kings; Henry P. Velte, Brooklyn; Robert F. Wagner, Manhattan; Loren H. White, Delanson, Schenectady county (democrats).

Senators George F. Argetsinger, Rochester; Elon R. Brown, Watertown; Thomas H. Bussey, Perry, Wyoming county; Herbert P. Coats, Saranac Lake; Frank M. Godfrey, Olean; Charles J. Hewitt, Locke, Cayuga county; William L. Ormrod, Churchville, Monroe county; Henry M. Sage, Albany; George F. Thompson, Middleport, Niagara county; Henry J. Walters, Syracuse; Thomas B. Wilson, Hull, Ontario county (republicans).

NOT GUILTY—18. Chief Judge Edgar M. Cullen, Brooklyn, and Judge Willard Bartlett, Brooklyn (democrats); Judge Emory A. Chase, Catskill, and Judge William E. Werner, Rochester (republicans).

Senators James F. Duhamel, Brooklyn (independence league and democrat); Walter R. Herrick, Manhattan; John W. McKnight, Rensselaer; Thomas H. O'Keefe, Oyster Bay; William D. Peckham, Utica; John Seeley, Steuben county; Gottfried H. Wende, Buffalo; Clayton L. Wheeler, Hancock, Delaware county (democrats).

Senators James A. Emerson, Warrensburg; Seth G. Heacock, Ilion; Abraham J. Palmer, Milton, Ulster county; John B. Stivers, Middletown; Ralph W. Thomas, Hamilton, Madison county, and George H. Whitney, Mechanicville, Saratoga county (republicans).

ABSENT—Judge John Clinton Gray, Manhattan (democrat) and Senator John C. Fitzgerald, Manhattan (democrat).

After the court had voted to convict on three of the articles and the other five been dismissed for lack of evidence, the final vote was on the question of whether the governor should be removed from office. It was as follows:

HOW THE HIGH COURT STOOD ON VOTE TO REMOVE SULZER

FOR REMOVAL

JUDGES OF THE COURT OF APPEALS

BARTLETT, JUDGE WILLARD, Democrat; Brooklyn.
CHASE, JUDGE EMORY, Republican; Catskill.
COLLIN, JUDGE FREDERICK, Democrat; Elmira.
CUDDEBACK, JUDGE WILLIAM H., Democrat; Buffalo.
HISCOCK, JUDGE FRANK H., Republican; Syracuse.
HOGAN, JUDGE JOHN W., Democrat; Syracuse.
MILLER, JUDGE NATHAN L., Republican; Cortland.
WERNER, JUDGE WILLIAM E., Republican; Rochester.

SENATORS

ARGETSINGER, GEORGE H., Republican, lawyer; Rochester, Monroe county.

BLAUVELT, GEORGE A., Democrat, lawyer; Monsey, Richmond-Rockland district.

BOYLAN, JOHN J., Democrat, real estate; Manhattan.

BROWN, ELON R., Republican, lawyer; Watertown, Jefferson and Oswego district.

BUSSEY, THOMAS H., Republican, manufacturer; Perry, Allegany-Wyoming-Genesee district.

CARROLL, DANIEL J., Democrat, manufacturer; Brooklyn.

CARSWELL, WILLIAM B., Democrat; lawyer; Brooklyn.

COATS, HERBERT P., Republican, lawyer; [Saranac Lake, Franklin-St. Lawrence district.

CULLEN, THOMAS H., Democrat, insurance; Brooklyn.

FOLEY, JAMES, Democrat, lawyer; Manhattan.

FRAWLEY, JAMES J., Democrat, contractor; Manhattan.

GODFREY, FRANK N., Republican, farmer; Cattaraugus-Chautauqua district.

GRIFFIN, ANTHONY J., Democrat, lawyer; Manhattan.

· HEALY, JOHN F., Democrat, manufacturer; New Rochelle, Westchester county.

HEFFERNAN, WILLIAM J., Democrat, retired; Brooklyn.

HEWITT, CHARLES J., Republican, coal and lumber dealer; Lock No. 40, Cayuga-Seneca-Cortland district.

HERRICK, WALTER R., Democrat, lawyer; Manhattan.

McCLELLAND, JAMES D., Democrat, lawyer; Manhattan.

MALONE, JOHN F., Democrat, casualty agent; Buffalo, Erie district.

MURTAUGH, JOHN F., Democrat, lawyer; Elmira, Chemung-Schuyler-Tompkins-Tioga district.

ORMROD, WILLIAM L., Republican, lawyer; Churchville, Monroe district.

PATTEN, BERNARD M., Democrat, real estate; Queens.

POLLOCK, HENRY W., Democrat, lawyer; Manhattan.

RAMSPERGER, SAMUEL J., Democrat, bookkeeper; Buffalo-Erie district.

SAGE, HENRY M., Republican, real estate; Menands, Albany district.

SANNER, FELIX J., Democrat, real estate; Brooklyn.

SIMPSON, GEORGE W., Democrat, lawyer; Manhattan.

SULLIVAN, C. D., Democrat, real estate; Manhattan.

THOMPSON, GEORGE F., Republican, lawyer; Middleport, Orleans-Niagara district.

TORBORG, HERMAN H., Democrat, lawyer; Brooklyn.

VELTE, HENRY P., Democrat, lawyer; Brooklyn.

WAGNER, ROBERT F., Democrat, lawyer; Manhattan.

WALTERS, J. HENRY, Republican, lawyer; Syracuse, Onondaga district.

WHITE, LOREN H., Democrat, insurance; Delanson, Schenectady district.

WILSON, THOMAS B., farmer; Hull-Wayne-Ontario-Yates district.

AGAINST REMOVAL

SENATORS

DUHAMEL, JAMES F., Independence League, patent lawyer; Brooklyn.

EMERSON, JAMES A., Republican, banker; Warrensburg, Clinton-Essex-Warren district.

HEACOCK, SETH G., Republican, oil producer; Ilion, Fulton-Hamilton-Lewis-Herkimer district.

McKNIGHT, JOHN W., Democrat, railroading; Castleton, Rensselaer district.

O'KEEFE, THOMAS H., Democrat, retired; Oyster Bay, Suffolk-Nassau district.

PALMER, ABRAHAM J., Progressive, fruit dealer; Milton, Ulster-Greene district.

PECKHAM, WILLIAM D., Democrat, physician; Utica, Oneida district.

SEELEY, JOHN, Democrat, physician; Woodhull, Steuben district.

STIVERS, JOHN B., Republican, editor; Middletown, Orange-Sullivan district.

THOMAS, RALPH W., Republican, lawyer; Hamilton, Otsego-Madison-Chenango district.

WHEELER, CLAYTON L., Democrat, plumber; Hancock, Delaware-Broome district.

WHITNEY, GEORGE H., Republican, druggist; Mechanicville, Saratoga district.

Excused from voting—CHIEF JUDGE EDGAR M. CULLEN, Democrat, Brooklyn; SENATOR GOTTFRIED A. WENDE, Democrat, Erie.

Absentees—SENATOR FITZGERALD, Democrat, New York; ill health.

JUDGE JOHN CLINTON GRAY, absent in Europe.

Membership of Senate—Democrats, 30; Republicans, 16; Progressives, 1; Independence League, 1. Total, 48.

Membership of Court of Appeals—Democrats, 5; Republicans, 4. Total, 9.

Grand total vote of court, 57.

When the clerk announced the vote was forty-three to twelve, with two not voting, President Judge Cullen, in a low voice, made this announcement:

" The respondent, William Sulzer, having been convicted by the vote of more than two-thirds of the members of this court on the first, second and fourth articles of impeachment, and the court having resolved that for the offense of which he has been convicted the respondent be removed from office, it is the judgment of the court and it is now the duty of the president to declare that for those offenses the said William Sulzer, governor of the state, be and he hereby is removed from his said office as governor."

The presiding judge's announcement was made at exactly 11:55 o'clock a. m., on Friday, October 17, 1913.

Governor Sulzer's removal came after he had served 290 days of the term of two years for which he had been elected.

There was joy among the senators, especially the Tammany men, as they voted to convict and remove the man whom they so much feared. There was a spirit of levity among these members of the senate noticeable to all beholders.

To Patrick E. McCabe, clerk of the senate, credited with firing the first broadside against the governor in June leading to his impeachment, fell the rare pleasure of writing out, by his own hand, the formal notice of removal to be served on Governor Sulzer. It was brief and was as follows:

" The assembly of the state of New York, having heretofore, to wit, on the 13th day of August, nineteen hundred and thirteen, presented to the senate of said state articles of impeachment against William Sulzer, governor of said state, and the president of the senate having in accordance with law summoned the senators and the judges of the court of appeals of said state to meet as a court for the trial of impeachments on the eighteenth day of September, nineteen hundred and thirteen, and the said court having convened on said day and the said William Sulzer, governor of said state, having ap-

PATRICK EDGAR MCCABE
With the order of the High Court of Impeachment removing William Sulzer
from office

peared thereat by counsel and having filed his answer to said articles of impeachment, and the impeachment having been tried, and the court having by the vote of a majority of more than two-thirds in number, convicted the said respondent of the charges contained in the first, second and fourth articles of impeachment, and the court having resolved that for the offenses of which he had been convicted the said William Sulzer be removed from his office as governor;

"*It is hereby declared and adjudged that the said William*

Sulzer be and hereby is removed from the office of governor of the state of New York."

The scene of vindictiveness was further heightened by the spectacle of Senator James J. Frawley standing by Mr. McCabe and asking with triumph in his voice for the pen with which the document had been written as a souvenir.

Thus ended an impeachment trial which will go down into history as a farce and a tragedy. It was a farce because at least three members of this so-called " high court of impeachment "— JAMES J. FRAWLEY, FELIX J. SANNER and SAMUEL J. RAMSPERGER—sought the evidence, heard the testimony in the notorious Frawley committee, publicly and privately expressed their convictions, and then sat in what was termed the " highest court in the land."

It was a tragedy because of the precedent it established, whereby a partisan assembly, controlled by special interests, may at any time constitute itself a mob and remove high officials, executive or judicial, regularly chosen by the people.

CHAPTER XXVI

SULZER SAYS HIS REMOVAL WAS A POLITICAL LYNCHING

At the People's House Governor Sulzer had been expecting for several days to hear that the court of impeachment had voted to remove him from office. During the trial and for some time prior to the convening of the court he had not been to the executive chamber at the capitol. His intimate friends rallied around him during all the trying period to offer him sympathy and assistance.

Chester C. Platt, his private secretary, was the first to notify the governor of the action of the court. Mr. Sulzer did not show any emotion but merely heard what Mr. Platt had to say and continued to walk up and down the room on the second floor of the mansion with his hands clasped behind his back.

Surprise was expressed by some of the governor's friends that the court, after having gone so far, had not also voted forever to disqualify him from holding office.

Later in the day the deposed governor by appointment met the newspaper correspondents and issued to them a statement.

"By virtue of a power," he said, "beyond the present control of our electorate, I now hand back to the people the commission they gave me, and I hand it back to them untarnished and unsullied."

Referring to the last statement he had made to the public September 14, in which he had expressed a belief he would have a fair trial Mr. Sulzer said:

"I did not think Senator Wagner, Senator Frawley, Senator Ramsperger, Senator Sanner, Senator Brown, Senator Blauvelt, and Senator Thompson would act as my jurors and judges, as they were either interested personally in the outcome of my trial, or had acted as my prosecutors and condemned me before trial, or on account of personal grievances had expressed an opinion as to my guilt. The impropriety of these senators voting for my conviction must be apparent, and vitiates the judgment, because had they refused to vote—as a sense of decency should have induced them to do—I would not have been convicted on any one of the articles of impeachment.

"My trial, from beginning to end, so far as the Tammanyized part of the court was concerned—was a farce; a political lynching; the consummation of a deep-laid political conspiracy to oust me from office. I am glad it is all over. I am tired of being calumniated; tired of being hunted and hounded; tired of trying to do my duty and being traduced.

" The court ruled in everything against me, and ruled out everything in my favor. The well-settled rules of evidence were thrown to the winds. A horse thief, in frontier days, would have received a squarer deal.

" Mr. Murphy controlled the assembly, and ordered the impeachment. He controlled most of the members of the court, and dictated its procedure, and wrote the judgment. He was the judge and the jury; the prosecutor and the bailiff.

" The meetings of the court were in secret, and behind closed doors. It was a star-chamber proceeding, where the enemies of the state could work for my conviction undiscovered.

' They called it the high court of impeachment, but history will call it ' Murphy's High Court of Infamy.' The trial was a human shambles; a libel on law; a flagrant abuse of constitutional rights; a disgrace to our civilization; and the verdict overturned the safeguards of liberty, and the precedents of three centuries. The judgment will not stand the test of time. The future historian will do me justice, and posterity will reverse the findings of the court."

Mr. Sulzer said he had been anxious to take the witness stand in his own behalf to refute the Peck testimony, to explain what Morgenthau had said against him and to disprove the charges made by Allan Ryan, but that his lawyers had advised against it because under the rulings of the court excluding testimony by John A. Hennessy and other witnesses in his behalf it was clear that his own story on the stand would also be ruled out as inadmissible.

Mr. Sulzer said he was heavily in debt and speaking of the charges that he had used his candidacy for governor to make money he said:

" Had I wanted to make money out of my campaign for governor, I certainly would not have rejected, as I did, offers

of donations from several citizens of upwards of $100,000—
and borrowed the money I did from Reilly, and Meany, and
several others.   The court ruled out all testimony concerning
sums of money offered to me by Judge Beardsley and others,
and which I declined, at the time, to accept, for good and
sufficient reasons.

"I want to thank Judge Cullen and the members of the
court who voted for my vindication; the able lawyers who
stood by me and gave me wise counsel, and the friends of good
government throughout the state whose belief in my honesty,
and whose faith in the rectitude of my intentions never
wavered."

*"The three things that led up to my removal were my fight for
direct primaries, the graft investigations and not the least by any
means my signing of the full crew bill which gave me the enmity
of the great railroad corporations."*

NOTE—For memorandum approving full crew bill—the man above the dollar—see index

CHAPTER XXVII

DEPOSED GOVERNOR GREETED AS A HERO

At just 11.55 o'clock Friday morning, October 17th, 1913, by the big, hand carved clock in the senate chamber, presiding Judge Edgar M. Cullen of the high court of impeachment announced that Governor Sulzer "is hereby removed from office."

Five minutes later the impeachment court adjourned sine die, its work having been completed in one month and one day.

The verdict of the court had hardly been pronounced when plans were under way for a public demonstration to be tendered to the deposed governor. At eight o'clock that same night, a meeting was held at the Ten Eyck hotel and the following were chosen as a committee to make arrangements: Jay W. Forrest, chairman; Henry L. Kessler, vice-chairman; John D. Chism, secretary; F. H. Bryant, treasurer; William Hough, Martin O'Brien, William M. Hacker, William J. T. Hogan, Anthony Flanigan, George A. Harrig, Robert S. Ross, M. Lincoln, George Clapham, S. Pearson, Aaron V. Dodge, Charles Schessler, Ben A. Henschel, J. P. McGarrahan, J. H. Haskell, Dr. M. L. Rowe, Andrew Shannon, Michael Gillooly, John J. Evers, Zenas P. Burns, Benjamin Lodge, William S. Kelly, Charles Holle, Patrick J. Powers, Eugene J. Kennedy, Patrick F. Ryan, Charles Grace, William Happ, George R. Happ, George B. Lidsy, John F. Hanify, Frank Graves, Francis Willard, Emil Kovarik and Chester C. Platt.

It was the intention of the committee to meet at the Ten Eyck hotel at eight o'clock the following night (Saturday, October 18th, 1913), and with about two hundred citizens march over to the Executive mansion and present to Governor Sulzer a loving cup with the confidence and esteem of the citizens of Albany.

The next morning it seemed from the numerous inquiries that there would be more than was originally planned who desired to join in the demonstration, so a band was secured. It commenced to rain at about six o'clock and continued to pour all evening, but notwithstanding, when the word was given to start for the mansion, over three thousand men carrying umbrellas fell into line. Through the rain and mud they marched down South Pearl Street and up Madison Avenue toward the mansion, at every corner and all along the line of march men fell in behind and joined the procession so that by the time the Executive Mansion was reached there were between eight and ten thousand people in line. They filled the Executive Mansion, the spacious grounds and the surrounding streets, and amid the lurid flame of red fire, the hissing of fireworks, the air was rent with cheer upon cheer. It seemed as if all Albany was there to pay homage—not to an incoming governor, but to a governor who had been removed because he would not do the bidding of Tammany Hall. Far into the night the line that seemed to be endless crowded forward to shake the hand of the deposed governor. After the presentation of the loving cup, which was inscribed as follows:

PRESENTED

TO

HON. WILLIAM SULZER

BY

THE CITIZENS OF ALBANY

IN LOVING REMEMBRANCE OF DUTIES
WELL PERFORMED

A MARTYR TO THE CAUSE OF HONEST
GOVERNMENT

OCTOBER 18TH, 1913

Governor Sulzer thanked the citizens in a few well chosen words, but this would not do, the air was filled with cries of " speech, speech, we want Sulzer," and in answer to the calls that would not cease Governor Sulzer stepped out on the porch facing the grounds of the mansion. As the tall form appeared in view he was greeted with cheer upon cheer, the downpouring rain had no effect, they were there to let him know that the findings of Murphy's court of infamy did not represent the feelings of the citizens of Albany. When the governor could make himself heard he spoke as follows:

" My friends, this is a stormy night. It is certainly very good of you to come here to bid Mrs. Sulzer and me goodbye. (A voice: ' You will come back, Bill, in one year.')

" You know why we are going away. (A voice: ' Because you were too honest to let them get away with it.')

" You know the people elected me the governor. (A voice: ' You bet your life, and we will do it next fall.') by the largest plurality ever given a candidate for governor in the history of the state. Of course, I appreciated that, and I made up my mind when I took the oath of office I would be true to the people, and show my appreciation of their confidence in me, and what they had done for me, by serving them fearlessly and honestly and faithfully. (Cheers.)

I have done it. My conscience is clear, and tells me truly that I have done no wrong; but my whole duty, bravely and honestly, day in and day out, to all the people of the state, as God gave me the light to see the right. (Cheers.)

"A combination of political conspirators removed me from the office the people gave me, because I was after the grafters, and was sending them to prison for robbing the taxpayers. (Cheers.)

" They say they impeached me for taking my own money. (Laughter.) I impeach the criminal conspirators, these looters and grafters, for stealing the taxpayers money and that is what I never did. (Cheers.)

" It is a long lane that has no turn. My day will come again. From Murphy's high court of infamy, I appeal to that higher court—the court of public opinion. (A voice: ' You have got to do it.')

" Let those who have failed take courage;
    Tho' the enemy seems to have won,
Tho' the ranks are strong, if he be in the wrong
    The battle is not yet done;
For, sure as the morning follows
    The darkest hour of the night,
No question is ever settled
    Until it is settled right."

" I know, just as sure as I am standing here, that the court of public opinion before long will reverse the judgment of

Murphy's court of infamy. (Cheers.) Posterity will do me justice. Time sets all things right. I shall be patient.

"Tammany Hall can take away the office the people gave me, but Tammany Hall cannot take away my manhood (Cheers) my self-respect; my determination to fight on for the rights of the people, and for honest government, in the future just as I have fought for these things in the past.

"I thank you one and all from the bottom of my heart, and assure you that I shall never forget your abiding confidence in me, and your unwavering loyalty to our cause, in coming out on this stormy night to say farewell to Governor Sulzer. (Cheers.)

"Let us say farewell to Governor Sulzer, and never forget that he was not the governor long, but while he was governor he was THE GOVERNOR and not a rubber stamp." (Loud cheers.)

The New York newspapers in commenting upon the demonstration the following Sunday morning, October 19th, 1913, said:

"It was an eye-opener for the machines. It was more like an ovation to a returning war hero." And the Albany Knickerbocker Press on Monday morning, October 20th, said: "The enthusiastic and surprising demonstration of affection accorded Governor Sulzer by thousands of Albany citizens during the rain storm of Saturday night is still being talked of everywhere. All agree that such a popular expression of feeling seldom has been shown."

Sunday afternoon Governor Sulzer and Jay W. Forrest went for an automobile ride. It was during this ride that the question of whether he should accept the nomination which the progressive party of the sixth assembly district of the City of New York, which it had been intimated a committee was to tender to him the following day, was discussed.

Mr. Forrest strongly urged the governor to accept the nomination and while he did not say in so many words that he would do so, he did ask Mr. Forrest to be present at the Executive Mansion the next morning and meet with him the committee which was to tender such nomination.

On Monday morning, October 20th, the committee representing the progressive party arrived at the Executive Mansion, and the following went into conference on the question as to whether the governor should accept the nomination for member of assembly from the sixth district of the City of New York: Governor and Mrs. Sulzer, Jay W. Forrest, Rev. Albert Bruchlos, spokesman for the committee, Max Steindler, progressive candidate for alderman from the sixth district, and Mr. Lawrence, the gentleman who had been nominated for member of assembly by the progressives, and whose withdrawal made way for the nomination by the committee to fill the vacancies of William Sulzer for said office.

After a long discussion, the committee returned to New York to meet at the law office of Governor William Sulzer at 115 Broadway, New York city, at five o'clock that afternoon, to arrange for the nomination of Sulzer that evening.

That evening Governor Sulzer in company with Mr. Forrest received the reports of the convention over the long distance telephone at the Executive Mansion. As the news came over the wire of the wonderful enthusiasm shown over his nomination, the governor walked the floor, seeming to forget his surroundings as he planned the fight to be made in New York. Murphy's high court of infamy had removed him without the law, he was now actively in the fight to remove Murphy within the law.

Arrangements were made for the return to New York on the following day, Tuesday, October 21st. The demonstration of the Saturday evening was potent in the coming fight— it gave to William Sulzer the knowledge that the people were up in arms against the methods used to remove him from office. The eight or ten thousand citizens of Albany gave him the courage to accept the nomination and the fight to dethrone King Murphy was on.

CHAPTER XXVIII

SULZER NOMINATED AND ELECTED TO ASSEMBLY

Tuesday night, October 21st, will long live in the memory of those who were at the Grand Central station when William Sulzer and wife arrived from Albany. Fifty thousand people were there to welcome the man who had been cast out of office by the orders of Tammany Hall. It was a mad scene of waving hats and hands—it was an ovation which few men have accorded them. It was a triumphal procession from the station down through the East Side of New York to the Broadway Central hotel. Napoleon, the conquering hero on his return to Paris was never accorded a more popular demonstration. History in New York has never seen its like. A continuous ovation befitting a monarch tendered to the man who but a few hours before had been removed from the office of governor of the Empire state of the Union.

The man who had been cast out had come back and the people, irrespective of party and not so much for the man as for the principle involved, were ready to vindicate their fitness for self-government by showing to the world their resentment against boss-rule. From the moment William Sulzer arrived in New York city, there was no doubt what the people would do to Tammany Hall the day they had a chance to vote.

Headquarters were opened at the Broadway Central hotel and the active work of the campaign was started. Men flocked there to offer their services. From far away Texas, Judge Moore would come to speak against Tammany. From every state in the Union letters poured in wishing God speed.

Wednesday night the writer, in company with Judge Martin O'Brien, of New York, Anthony Flanigan of Albany, Wallace B. Hunter of Troy, Henry Kessler, Wm. J. T. Hogan and Rabbi Levison of Albany in company with William Sulzer opened the campaign in the sixth assembly district. As the automobiles swung into Avenue C, thousands upon thousands, and then more thousands, fell in behind the machines. It was all the police could do to keep the crowds back to let the ma-

chines creep along.   The cry, " We want Sulzer! We want
Sulzer! Sulzer! Sulzer! We want Sulzer!" became louder and
louder as thousands upon thousands took up the cry.   "Roll
thunder, roll. Ware, Chief! Ware !" that cry was the doom of
Tammany Hall.   It spelled the political death of every man who
had participated in Murphy's court of infamy.   The inspector
of police, who was standing on the running board of the machine
putting his hand on the shoulder of the writer, said, "My
God, turn around and look at that crowd!"   As far as the
eye could see from house to house the street was jammed with
a living mass of humanity.   Just then the machines passed
under a banner inscribed "Aaron J. Levy."   Never to my
dying day shall I forget that noise of bitter contempt.   It
was as if the submerged snarl or growl of the entire beastly
world was let loose at once.   The man does not live who can
take pen in hand and describe that growl.   It seemed to come
from the throats of thousands who had from centuries of
oppression recourse only to the snarl of the lion in captivity.
Bosses may come and bosses may go, but the liberty of this
republic will never perish with the consent of the men of the
East side of New York.   If there are any people in this country
who are more against the tyrannical oppression of the political
system which creates the master class of bosses than the Jew
of the East side, I have yet to meet them.   The Jew knows
what oppression in any form means.   He has had centuries
of experience.   He came to this country to escape the system,
not to help establish one.

    The first meeting was held in Hennington Hall.   Upon
arriving at the hall it was a case of fight your way in, surrounded by policemen to hold back the crowds.   The scene
at this hall was the same as at all other meetings.   If there
were any chairs or seats you could not see them.   If there was
an aisle you would not know it.   If there was a law against
over-capacity it could not be enforced.   As you looked from
the stage all you could see was a packed, jammed humanity,
you might wonder at how you got into the hall, but your
heart would almost stop beating when you thought how you
were going to get out.   We left Sulzer on the outside to make
a speech while we went inside to speak.   How Sulzer was to
get into that hall was the question that was running through

DOOMED!

From the Albany Knickerbocker Press

my mind. Could it be done? While thinking along this lin₁t
of a sudden a yell goes up, " Here comes Sulzer," and over th₁d
sea of heads could be seen policemen pushing their way throug₃ll
that mass of humanity. On they came pushing, crowdin of
clearing foot room for Sulzer. In course of time they reach/ho
the platform and as Sulzer stood up, in the language of t/or
west, " Hell broke loose for twenty minutes." The ki yi oι
the west has nothing on the hurrah of the East side.

Presently you could hear a pin drop as the long arms of
Sulzer waved for silence. William Sulzer, the veteran of many
campaigns, is again speaking in a voice that rings clear and
cold as steel. He is not on the defensive. He is the ag-
gressor. Now he is speaking to his people and they listen.

Mr. Sulzer said: " I am going back to Albany for the good
that I can do."

" In view of the pleadings of life-long friends, and the request in writing from more than half of the registered voters
in the sixth assembly district, regardless of party affiliations,
begging me to accept the nomination for member of assembly,
to further the cause of honest government, I have consented
to accept the nomination and go back to Albany, as a member
of the assembly, for the good that I can do.

" Of course, I appreciate the confidence in me of some of
my old neighbors and constituents, and no words of mine can
tell how grateful I am for their support and unwavering
loyalty.

" I am a non-partisan candidate, having no axe to grind, and
no motive, or purpose, other than to do what I can for the
cause of good government, the struggle for which at Albany
brought about my removal from the governorship by an arrogant boss whose dictates to do wrong I defied.

" I shall go back to the legislature, as the representative of
the plain people, to aid the cause that lacks assistance; to
fight the wrongs that need resistance; for the future in the
distance, and the good that I can do.

MURPHY'S HIGH COURT.

" Mr. Murphy controlled the assembly, and ordered my
impeachment. He controlled most of the members of his

THE DELUGE

From the Albany Knickerbocker Press

high court, and dictated its procedure and the judgment. He was the judge and the jury, the prosecutor and the bailiff.

" They called it the high court of impeachment, but history will call it the Murphy high court of infamy. The trial was a human shambles; a libel on law; a flagrant abuse of constitutional rights; a disgrace to our civilization; and the veridct overturned the safeguards of liberty and the precedents of three centuries.

" The judgment will not stand the test of time. The future historian will do me justice.

THE COURT OF PUBLIC OPINION.

" There is a higher court than Murphy's—the court of public opinion. I have appealed from Murphy's court of political passion to the calmer judgment of posterity, and the sober reflection of public opinion.

" When I refused to obey the orders of the boss to stop the investigations of Blake and Hennessy, and clog the wheels of the machinery of justice, which I set in motion to prevent the further looting of the state, Mr. Murphy threatened me with degradation and removal from office.

" From that day to this, all that money, all that power, all that influence can do to disgrace me and destroy me has been done.

" However, I am in the fight for good government; in the fight to stay to the end; and the forces of righteousness will prevail over the forces of iniquity.

> " However the battle is not ended,
>   Though proudly the victor comes,
> With fluttering flags and prancing nags,
>   And echoing roll of drums;
> Still truth proclaims this motto,
>   On letters of living light,
> No question is ever settled
>   Until it is settled right."

" Now, another thing. The ' chief ' and his wax figures in the Murphy high court said that my campaign statement last year was erroneous. It was testified on the trial, and not contradicted, that I did not make up that campaign statement; that I did not read it; that I asked if it was correct; that I was told it was as correct as it could be made; and that then

I signed it. That is all I had to do with it, and I have not seen the statement from that day to this.

"Mr. Murphy knew more about my campaign statement than I did, because the men he had planted in my office from the time I was nominated until I went to Albany knew everything that was going on and kept Mr. Murphy advised.

"They say Mr. Murphy took a leading part in making up the statement last fall of the democratic state committee. I want to ask him if the statement of the democratic state committee is correct. He knows all about it. Let him tell us if that is correct.

MURPHY OFFERED TO DESTROY CAMPAIGN STATEMENT

"I have notified the secretary of state not to let that campaign statement get out of his office. Mr. Murphy threatened me about my campaign statement, and intimated that it would disappear from the files of the secretary of state, if I would take 'orders.' Of course I refused to be a party to such an iniquity. Knowing what I do I hope the campaign statement of the democratic state committee will not disappear from the official files of the secretary of state. At all events, I have a certified copy, and I hope others interested will get a certified copy. They say Mr. Murphy put the names of a lot of dummies in that statement as contributors who never contributed a dollar. How about that, Mr. Murphy?

"TIGHT WAD PLUNKETT" DUMMY CONTRIBUTOR

"Among those names, as contributors to the democratic state committee is the name of one George W. Plunkett, for the sum of $5,000. This is 'Tight Wad' Plunkett, otherwise known as 'Honest Graft' Plunkett. I am advised he did not contribute a dollar. Why was his name put on the statement of the state committee for $5,000? They tell me 'Tight Wad' Plunkett would not give $5 to save the democratic party from the demnition bow wows. If he did contribute this money let Plunkett say so, and tell where he got it. Has he a receipt for it? Did he pay it in cash or by check? Can he produce the check? Will his bank account show that he drew the money out in cash? Let Plunkett tell about it. I see he is getting his name in the newspapers. Let Murphy tell about it. Plunkett and Murphy know. This is only one case. There are others.

"How preposterous it is for Murphy to remove me from the governorship because the men the boss had around me made up an erroneous statement of my campaign funds, while the statement he and his lieutenants made for the democratic state committee is ten times more incorrect. What a farce it all is! Does boss Murphy expect to get away with it? Does the boss think the people have lost their senses, and will vote for Mr. Murphy's yellow dog ticket when Murphy removed from office the governor the people elected?

REMOVED FROM OFFICE BECAUSE HE WOULD NOT DO WRONG

"The people know that my removal from office by Mr. Murphy was because I would not do wrong; because I would not do what Mr. Murphy wanted me to do; because I would not be a Murphy tool; because I refused to be a party to the looting of the state.

"The voters will answer Mr. Murphy on election day. They will tell the boss what they think of him. The best way the voters can express their indignation of my removal from office, and their desire for honesty in city and state affairs, is to vote against every candidate on the Tammany hall ticket from mayor to alderman in every borough in greater New York. That is the way to beat the 'chief.'

MURPHYISM MUST GO

"Murphyism must go or our free institutions are doomed. No man, and no official, can serve Murphy and the people; the 'chief' and the city; if he is true to Murphy, he must be false to duty; he cannot be loyal to one without betraying the other.

"The way to beat the 'boss' is to beat the ticket of the 'boss.' The Murphy ticket should be defeated in the interest of good government, and for the general welfare.

The Brady $25,000

Mr. Murphy has taken several days to answer my charges about the Brady $25,000 which I refused from Judge Beardsley, and which Judge Beardsley gave to Mr. Murphy, and which the ' chief ' never accounted for.

" Mr. Murphy calls on a dead man to prove that he returned this money. He says he gave it back to Anthony N. Brady, but Brady is dead and he can't corroborate Murphy. Was anybody with them when the money was paid back ? Beardsley took the money to Murphy in bills.

" Why didn't Murphy give the money back to Beardsley ? Were there any witnesses present, so that Judge Beardsley can feel sure that the money he gave Murphy was turned back to Brady ? Will Judge Beardsley take Murphy's word for it ? Why don't you ask Judge Beardsley what he thinks of Murphy's story ? It is to laugh.

" Everybody knows that Brady and Murphy were not on speaking terms. Let Murphy make an affidavit that he paid the money back to Brady, stating the circumstances of the payment in detail.

" Let Murphy make his affidavit, too, that he did not get Allan Ryan's $10,000. If he did not get the Ryan $10,000, who kept it, and where does he think it went ? Has somebody in Murphy's confidence been robbing him ? But I know that Murphy received Allan Ryan's $10,000, because he admitted it. So it is now too late to lie about it.

" Will Mr. Murphy be good enough to give the name of the lawyer who prepared his statement ? Mr. Murphy could not do it. Who did ? The people should know. If you believe what Murphy says you must believe that he is not in politics as a trade.

"Anybody who believes that Murphy is not a broker in public offices may possibly believe that Murphy did not send McCall to me begging for offices.

" Judge McCall, of Tammany Hall, is trying hard to show that he was not a messenger for the chief.

" I would like to tell you a story about this, but I can't tell it because it would violate confidence.

" If Ed McCall will release me and others from the obligation of confidence the whole story will be told, and it will show that when Charles F. Murphy picked McCall for mayor he chose a man he can trust to take his orders and do anything the ' chief ' tells him.

" Mr. Murphy is rattled; he knows his ticket is beaten; his statement is feeble, and it is all too bad for Tammany.

" Mr. Murphy wants us to believe that he was turning away money. That will make the braves laugh. I have asked Mr. Murphy to tell us where he got his fortune, said to be $15,000,000. He dare not answer. How do you suppose he grew rich if he refused money that came his way ? But everybody believes the ' chief' got the Brady and Ryan money.

I know it—and there are others who know it.

" You can rob the people for years; you can fool the people for years; you can outrage the people without letting them know it for years; but when the people find out how they have been plundered; how they have been fooled; how they have been outraged, their wrath is terrible.

" Murphy himself, drunk with power and blind with hate, has engineered his own undoing.

" Now, Mr. Murphy, I ask you again:

" First, Mr. Murphy, they say you made $15,000,000 since you became the leader of Tammany Hall. Where did you get it ?

" Second, Mr. Murphy, what did you do with the $25,000 Mr. Brady offered me through his counsel, Samuel A. Beardsley, which I refused to accept, and which you took ?

" Do not say you returned it to Mr. Brady. He is dead and cannot call you a liar, and besides, you and Brady did not speak. You know why. So do I. Just tell us why you did not give it back to Judge Beardsley, or what you did with it. I know, and if you do not tell the truth about it I will.

" Third, Mr. Murphy, what did you do with the $10,000 Allan Ryan sent me, and which I sent to you, and which you admitted to me you received ?

" Do not lie about it and make it appear that your bagman kept it. I would not do that. It will hurt you with the other bagmen. Look out for your bagmen. If they get rattled like you they may squeal—and what a story of graft they could tell.

Fourth, Mr. Murphy, who put the name of George W. Plunkitt on the campaign statement last fall of the demo-

"FEAR HATH TORMENT"

From the Albany Knickerbocker Press

cratic state committee, as a contributor for $5,000? Did Plunkitt give the money or was he a dummy?

"Fifth, Mr. Murphy, who promised Stilwell, if he would hold his tongue, a light sentence; then a stay of proceedings; then a pardon when I was removed from office, and who did not keep either of these promises?

"Mr. Murphy, when you answer truthfully these five questions it is my purpose to ask you five more—and I know—and you know I know."

And so it was from hall to hall, from park to square, it was all the same, five and six meetings a night.

There was gloom in Tammany Hall. Dark, thick gloom. Defeat stared the chief in the face. By impeaching a governor elected by the people, they are about to lose an empire, the richest in the world.

Tammany Hall, founded by Aaron Burr, and set going upon its mission heavenward or hellward according to the point of view, when it impeached the governor, boxed the compass. And now it is to be impeached by the court of public opinion and removed from office.

It was a mistake to impeach Sulzer. Yes, but it is too late now, the people are about to act, they are about to impeach Tammany Hall, not because of the personality of William Sulzer, not primarily on account of Sulzer, but because they want to demonstrate to the chief of Tammany Hall and all bosses who place their will above that of the people that they, the people of this, the Empire state of the Union, are fit for self-government.

Tammany may plan and scheme. Election day approaches slow but sure, the people's court is about to render judgment. At last here is a court which does not obey the edict of Delmonico's.

The newspapers on that August morning, when the assembly over the telephone had carried out the edict of the Chief, reported Charles F. Murphy as smiling. There is no smile on this morning. "You make me laugh," said Sir Hudson Lowe to the exile on the rocks of St. Helena. But the time came when he did not smile. Charles F. Murphy smiled, the time has come when the smile has disappeared.

Mitchell carries the city of Greater New York by 121,000

majority, electing the entire fusion ticket. There is no smile on the face of the chief. William Sulzer defeats his republican opponent by a vote of three to one. He also defeats Silverstein his democratic opponent, by a vote of three to one. Silverstein voted to impeach Sulzer. Of the seventy-nine assemblymen who voted to impeach Sulzer only seventeen were able to crawl back. A democratic majority of twenty-eight reduced to a minority of forty-six out of one hundred and fifty. Where there were five progressives there are now twenty-four. The chief has lost his smile. William Sulzer goes back to Albany, and the work of investigation will not stop.

The year 1913 will live in the history of New York state. The history of the year 1914 is yet to be written. This book began with William Sulzer's nomination and his inauguration on January 1st, 1913, as governor of the state, the story ends with William Sulzer, assemblyman from the sixth assembly district of the city of New York, January 1st, 1914.

CONCLUSION

The story of William Sulzer has been finished. He was educated and brought up politically under the environment of Tammany hall. He played the game according to the accepted standards. In so far as he stood for the principle involved, ninety per cent. of the people were with him. Sulzer the man might be the greatest egotist the world has ever known. He might have smashed all the finer moral codes in his ambitious scramble for power. He might have been insincere to friend and foe. He might have believed in the end justifying the means. All that has been said about him may be admitted as true and the result is the same. The people of the state have not rallied to the support of Sulzer personally. It has been a far greater issue than the question of Sulzer. The people of the state can forget Sulzer, but they cannot forget that the power that removed Sulzer might be used to remove another Hughes.

The fight for popular government will go on. Sulzer has played his part and his race may be run, but the great living issues pulsating with the life-blood of humanity will go on and on until a brighter, cleaner day arrives in our political life.

Invisible government has had its day, the people at last are awake to the fact that ballots are only respectable when they represent convictions. The day is forever past when men will blindly go to the polls to register the wishes of a political boss under the threat of regularity. The time has arrived when the people demand that every creed and every champion of a creed must halt at the frontier of their intellectual approval before they shall be allowed to advance. Progress is the watchword of humanity and he who would attempt to stop the wheels of progress is doomed to defeat. The night has been long, sometimes it has seemed as if the day would never come, but at last the lances of the morning light shine through the clouds. The ideals of democracy are coming to the front. The old regime is passing away. The people demand social justice, economic freedom and political liberty. Thieves have been rioting in the rich rewards of treason, but by the living God they have gone too far, the sleeping commonwealth leaps to its feet to sleep no more until it has run the rascals out.

Sulzer has played his part.   His future is within his own keeping.   But no matter what point of view may be taken of the man himself, he has acted his part and it has shown the people the dangers with which they are beset.

"God give us men!   A time like this demands
Strong minds, great hearts, true faith, and ready hands.
Men whom the lusts of office do not kill;
Men whom the spoils of office cannot buy;
Men who possess opinions and a will;
Men who have honor—men who will not lie;
Men who can stand before a demagogue,
And face his treacherous flatteries without winking;
Tall men, sun-crowned, who live above the fog,
In public duty, and in private thinking;
For while the rabble, with their thumb-worn creeds,
Their large professions and their little deeds,
Mingle in selfish strife.   Lo!   Goodness weeps,
Wrong rules the land, and waiting JUSTICE sleeps."

THE CAPITOL

THE EXECUTIVE CHAMBER—CAPITOL

APPENDIX

THE GREAT S(T)EAL OF THE EMPIRE STATE

From the Albany Knickerbocker Press

EXTRACT FROM ARGUMENT
OF HON. HARVEY D. HINMAN OF COUNSEL FOR GOVERNOR WILLIAM SULZER

While we have no doubt concerning the correctness of our contention that under all precedents and under the law, the respondent cannot properly or legally be impeached for acts done while a private citizen and outside of his office, as governor, we have no right, of course, to anticipate what the action of this court is to be on that proposition.

If this court were finally to decide against the respondent on the question whether acts done as a private citizen and before entering office are impeachable offenses, and were to find the respondent guilty by a two-thirds' vote on any one of the articles, it would then pass to the second question, which is "Shall the respondent be removed from office ? "

In considering and determining that question, what factors or elements are to be considered ? Our position on that question is that the welfare and best interests of the state and of its people must be the main consideration; that what the respondent was or was not, and what he did or did not do before he became governor, is of minor importance. The great question would then be, what has he done and what has he failed to do, what has he tried to do and what has he tried not to do, as governor ? Did he as a private citizen before he became governor do anything for which he should be removed from office ?

If his administration on the whole has been in the interest

of the people of state—if what he has done and has been attempting to do as governor has been in accordance with the solemn promise which he made when he took his official oath of office—if what he has done and attempted to do is to rid the governmental departments of the state of graft and grafters (if graft and grafters exist)—if the public welfare will be promoted by a continuance of the investigations which he had instituted and which were in progress before his impeachment, and which have been suspended during and because of his impeachment, and which will, in all probability, not be resumed if he be found guilty and be removed—then surely he ought not to be impeached and ought not to be removed from office because of any acts done by him before January 1, 1913, whether they be acts of omission of or commission.

Saul and his friends were engaged for years in the work of persecuting and killing off Christians. On one of his trips to Ephesus he saw the light. From that day on he divorced himself from his former friends and faithfully discharged the duties of discipleship. From that day on his former friends became his enemies and his persecutors, but they did not attempt to impeach him or his epistles because of what he had done while acting with them and while one of them. When, in the nineteenth centuries, has voice been raised to condemn Paul or his epistles for his acts as Saul?

In determining the questions before it, this court must necessarily take into consideration the question of the public good. In case it finds the respondent guilty, it must determine whether he ought to be removed. That involves the motives which led to this impeachment, that is, as to whether or not the proceeding and the result sought to be obtained are in the true interest of the public. .

The question must be, and is, was the respondent impeached because of " mal and corrupt conduct in office," for crimes and misdemeanors; or was he impeached because of what he refused to do since he took office?

Was the proceeding instituted because of a desire to accomplish a public good or was it for the purpose of getting rid of a public official who was performing his duty? Was the respondent impeached because, as they say, for " mal and corrupt conduct in office." or because of honest conduct in office?

Was he impeached, as they say, for "stealing" the moneys which his friends gave him, or was it because he was preventing grafters from stealing the moneys of the taxpayers? Was he impeached because, as they say, he made a false oath, or was it because he refused to violate his official oath of office?

These are some of the questions which the public are expecting this court to answer, and which this court, under the questions to be voted upon, will have to answer. Upon their answer, we believe, depends quite largely the future welfare and interests of the state.

In all that we have done and in all that we shall do in this case, we have endeavored to assist the court to the best of our ability in arriving at a just and right conclusion of this matter.

We are living in strange days. There has never been a time within my recollection when there was such a spirit of unrest and uneasiness on the part of the people generally. The time is surely coming—indeed, it may be near at hand—when we as a people must demonstrate whether our form of government, with an almost unlimited elective franchise, can endure. We cannot escape the feeling that what is done here and now may have a tremendous influence on the determination of that question.

We consider it of the utmost importance that what is done here and now should not only be well and rightly done, but that it should be done in such a manner as to convince the people of the state that it has been so done.

HON. LOUIS MARSHALL, OF COUNSEL FOR GOVERNOR WILIAM SULZER, IN SUMMING UP, SAID:

"Are the impeachment managers in earnest? Are they treating the court with the degree of candor which one may expect in such a case as this? If they are, then it is a demon-

stration that, in their attempt to destroy the governor, they have lost all sense of proportion; that they consider everything grist which comes to their mill; and that they evince a disposition to accomplish their ends by hook or by crook, by pandering to every prejudice, by casting forth a dragnet in the hope that something may be found which will enable them to disable and disarm the governor whom they deliberately set out to make harmless when they discovered that it was his purpose to be the governor of the state, and to assert his independence in that high office."

Mr. Marshall's address was regarded as a brilliant portrayal of the entire case, showing numerous precedents set by high courts by which the impeachment court should be guided. Mr. Marshall took up every one of the eight articles, carefully analyzed the charges, the evidence which had been submitted by the prosecution, and showed on how little fact the prosecution had based its "house of cards," as he termed it.

WINS ATTENTION INSTANTLY

" We are on the threshold of an event which will make a permanent impression upon the history of our beloved state, which will entail consequences far beyond our ken; which will determine whether or not the reign of law has ceased, and that of passion and prejudice begun," asserted Mr. Marshall in opening.

He had the attention of the court instantly. Every eye was upon him; every ear trained to catch his words. Famed as a constitutional lawyer, an effective orator, Mr. Marshall had no difficulty in keeping his hearers at attention during his entire argument.

"While the duty which rests upon counsel cannot be too greatly emphasized, that which rests upon this court is infinitely greater," he asserted. "For while it is given to counsel but to present arguments, it is for the court to decide, to adjudge, to create a precedent which will inevitably and irrevocably declare the policy of this state with regard to the permanency of its institutions and the independence of those who make up the sum total of its official life.

"The picture which is now unfolded before the vision of the civilized world is almost unique in the experience of mankind. The governor of the greatest state in the union, who was elected less than one year ago by an unprecedented majority, is upon trial before a court which is composed of the judges of the court of appeals and the senators, on an impeachment which charges him with the commission of various acts, which, it is asserted, entitle the complainants to a judgment of forfeiture of that office and which will place an everlasting stigma upon his name, and upon the honored office to which he was thus triumphantly chosen by the suffrage of his fellow citizens, amid loud acclaim.

WHO IS THIS RESPONDENT?

"Who is this respondent, who has thus been placed, as it were, in the prisoners 'dock, against whom there is asked to be pronounced the everlasting doom of infamy and shame, who is sought to be driven out of the office to which he was exalted but a few short months ago, and to be forever deprived of the right to hold public office and to serve the state.

"It is William Sulzer, who has just passed his fiftieth birthday, which was celebrated by those who stood highest in the civic and political life of the state, with congratulations and rejoicing, and occasion when even some of those who are now serving as impeachment managers indulged in loud sounding praises of him, and were among the foremost to do him honor."

The political history of Governor Sulzer was related by Mr. Marshall. He told of the good done by Mr. Sulzer while in the New York state legislature, of the progressive legislation he fathered in congress, of the attempt he has made to clean the grafters out of public life in this state since becoming governor, and the reforms he has worked in state departments.

" The eyes of the people were opened, as they never had been before, to abuses and evils which cried to heaven for correction and redress," declared Mr. Marshall.

"And now," he went on, " William Sulzer, who wrought all this, stands before you today, on trial for his very existence, charged with being a common criminal.

THE CHARGES ANALYZED

" It is not charged that he was incompetent or ignorant, or incapable of performing the duties of his office, or that he has not been duly watchful of the interests which he has been sworn to guard. It is not charged that he has entered into a conspiracy with those who would loot the public treasury, or who would fatten on contracts improvidently or corruptly drawn without safeguards to forestall adequately the possibility of fraud and collusion. The achievements of his administration, as they have passed before the eyes of the people, absolve him from all suspicion of guilt in regard to any of the offenses contained in the category of the usual form of official misconduct.

" These charges are eight in number. Six of them practically centre around a report filed by the respondent in the office of the secretary of state shortly after the election of 1912. The remainder, the seventh and eighth, relate to other matters and are practically negligible as has been admirably shown in the opening address of Senator Hinman on behalf of the respondent. Because of this report the impeachment managers have made the state to reverberate with all the volume of vociferation that would have been directed against a Benedict Arnold or an Aaron Burr, against one guilty of ' treasons, stratagems and spoils.'

" The entire penal law has been ransacked for epithets and characterizations. A veritable Newgate calendar has been evolved out of that single act. Article one makes it a violation of the corrupt practices act. The kaleidoscope is shaken, and article two converts it into a charge of perjury. Article three makes it bribery. Article four, the suppression of evidence in violation of section 814 of the penal law. Article fifth, the preventing and dissuading a witness from attending under a subpoena, in violation of section 2441 of the penal law. Article six, larceny, in violation of sections 1290 and 1294 of the penal law. Certainly the ingenuity of trained prosecutors, provided with microscopical eyes that see bad in everything and behold everywhere the microbe of crime, has been strained to the utmost."

THE CASE IN DETAIL

Taking up the first of the impeachment articles, alleging the filing of a false statement of Governor Sulzer's campaign expenses, Mr. Marshall said that no full statement of contributions made to a candidate was required. The statutes provide a remedy for violation of such requirement as the law does make, which remedy is the compulsion to file a true and complete statement of expenditures. Where a statutory remedy is provided for an offense, that remedy is exclusive and no other can be applied.

Of the second article, that relating to perjury in signing the affidavit accompanying the statement of expenses, Mr. Marshall declared that the oath which Governor Sulzer took was a voluntary and extra-judicial oath, not required by law, and that under the law no perjury charge could be based upon a misstatement in such an oath. There was no criminal intent, he said, and he recited Sarecky's story of his preparation of the statement with such data as he could recollect, of taking it to Sulzer with the assurance that it was " as good as he could do," and of Sulzer's signing it upon that assurance without examining it or paying any attention to it. It was a mistake, an inadvertency, perhaps. Mr. Marshall contended, but it was not done with the intent to commit a felony. Further, the legislature never intended to declare the submission of a defective or incomplete statement of this nature perjury, for it

specifically denominated a lapse of the kind a misdemeanor
and provided for it a comparatively trivial punishment.

Turning to article six, charging grand larceny in appropriating money given to Sulzer during his campaign, Mr. Marshall
declared that the money was given to Sulzer, not stolen by
him.   Larceny, he showed, must be an invasion of ownership,
a seizure of property rights belonging to another.   No such
element is charged in regard to the money given to Sulzer.
It cannot be supposed that he held this money in a fiduciary
capacity, because if the status were fiduciary it would necessarily follow that those who gave it must have expected it to
be returned, which is not true.   Neither did he have it in the
capacity of an agent or trustee.   For whom was he trustee,
Mr. Marshall asked.   Further, the same man cannot be both
trustee and beneficiary, under the law and under common
sense.   He was the beneficiary; therefore he was not the trustee, and the money was his.   More important than all, however, on the question of the alleged theft of this money, there
was no felonious intent in regard to his use of it, and Mr.
Marshall quoted at length from a recent decision of the court
of appeals, reading opinions of Chief Judge Cullen, Judge Gray,
Judge Werner and Judge Hiscock, to show that felonious
intent must be proved before a larceny charge can stand.
However ill advised Sulzer might have been, Mr. Marshall
concluded, the suspicion of criminality in connection with his
use of the money given to him during his campaign does
violence to credulity and common sense.   He cited the cases
of Daniel Webster and William McKinley in this connection,
both of whom were improvident and heavily in debt and both
of whom were dependent largely upon gifts of money made to
them by their admirers, unconditionally and for their personal
use and support.

THE BRIBERY CHARGE

Turning to article three, charging the bribery of witnesses
and naming Melville B. Fuller, Frederick Colwell and Louis A.
Sarecky, Mr. Marshall demonstrated that the testimony of
Fuller made it clear that Governor Sulzer had said nothing
whatever to him about not appearing before the investigators.
Of Colwell nothing appears in the evidence save that John

Boyd Gray said he heard Colwell say he was going to Albany to see William Sulzer, a hearsay declaration in no manner binding upon the respondent and unworthy of admission into the record. As to Sarecky, it was clear that his testimony before the Frawley committee showed that he was anxious to testify. He volunteered his testimony, in fact, asking only that he might have counsel present, in order to make sure that all the story should be told. Mr. Marshall paid a warm tribute to Sarecky, defending his qualifications and denouncing bitterly the methods of the prosecution in spreading inuendoes, insinuations, shrugs and whispers for newspaper headline circulation, as he said, reckless of truth and heedless of disproof.

Under the fourth article, alleging the suppression of evidence, the record is entirely barren, Mr. Marshall said. Again, as to the fifth article, charging that Governor Sulzer wilfully prevented and dissuaded Colwell from appearing, the case is absolutely blank, he declared. Not a whisper of evidence has been brought to support either allegation. Counsel then turned to the testimony of Duncan W. Peck that he gave Governor Sulzer $500 last fall and that the governor last July asked him to deny it. Sulzer had no motive to place himself thus in the power of a man whom he considered guilty of frauds, said Mr. Marshall, while Peck had every motive to lie about a man whose continuance in office was likely, as the lawyer asserted Peck to know, to result in the disgrace of Peck and perhaps in his loss of liberty. Mr. Marshall in scathing sarcasm pronounced the testimony of Peck to be intrinsically untrue. He mocked Peck's appeal to the presiding judge against revealing his confidential conversation, and derided the sudden glibness with which the story was then poured forth, declaring the exact detail with which the conversation was repeated under oath after months had elapsed to be a feat which every member of the court knew to be entirely impossible of truth.

Of the testimony of Morgenthau and Ryan Mr. Marshall argued that the governor's appeals to them were honest and justifiable when the state of mind of the respondent was considered. There was not in the testimony of these men, he said, one word showing crime under the articles of impeachment to which the court must confine itself. The testimony was introduced, he asserted, only as foundation for the bruiting of theories and concoction of rumors, designed by the managers of the impeachment through some esoteric force to create a sentiment which should accomplish by indirect appeal that which the evidence did not and could not warrant.

Turning to the seventh article, charging the use of executive power over legislation to influence the votes of Assemblymen Prime and Sweet, Mr. Marshall contended that the law cited in the article has no connection of any sort with the charge made. The statute refers exclusively to the bartering of nominations or offices of public employment or to questions of salary and emoluments. The testimony, he said, was trivial, and the charge absurd.

The eighth article, he continued, charging the manipulation of stock exchange legislation by the governor for his personal profit, was even more contemptible. It was an insult to the intelligence of the court, as it was to the people of the state, he said, and it was unbacked by the slightest suggestion of evidence.

In conclusion, Mr. Marshall declared the impeachment managers to have taken counsel of desperation. Their acts, he said, betokened a state of mind " which, if it ever enters the portals of the temple of justice will portend unspeakable and immeasurable evils to the state." The fate of Sulzer, he said, was not that with which the court was concerned. " Our individual predelictions, our partisan feelings, the satisfaction of our momentary desires," he continued, " are of little moment. They are but baubles, the toys of children of larger growth. But what is of the utmost concern to every patriotic citizen, to every lover of justice and righteousness, to every man who has aspirations for a higher life and for the elimination from the world of tyranny and despotism, is that the law shall not be weakened or undermined, whatever the immediate consequence of its strict application shall be. * * * Upon your decision rests not the future of William Sulzer but the happiness of future generations. Shall ours be a government of laws, or of passion and caprice ? Though life is sweet may I not live to see the day when the law shall cease to be paramount in our daily lives and in our system of government."

HON. ALTON B. PARKER, CHIEF COUNSEL FOR IMPEACHMENT
MANAGERS, IN SUMMING UP, SAID:

THE ISSUES CONDENSED

" The cause for impeachment may be condensed from the constitution and foregoing authorities into three words: Unfitness for office. · And the object of impeachment into four: Security for the state. Let us again summarize the provisions of the constitution upon the cause, first, all state officers are impeachable for mal and misconduct in their respective offices; and, second, for mal and corrupt ·conduct in office, and for high crimes and misdemeanors.

" Then came the third constitution, of '46' with the provision that the assembly shall have the power of impeachment absolutely and unlimited, without specification as to the officers, the cause, or time of the cause of impeachment in that connection, and with the two new provisions to which I have already referred for the removal of judicial officers and also the provision of section 7 of article 10.

" The constitution states it is true, that provision shall be made by law for the removal for misconduct or malfeasance in office of all officers except judicial, but the primary object of the provision was not to specify a cause, but to authorize a concurrent procedure for removal, and without power to disqualify the persons removed from holding office in the future, and probably was not intended to reach the chief executive officer of this state; and I would like to ask your honors, each

and any one of you, to answer for yourselves, is there any
doubt in the minds of any one of you, that if any member of
the supreme court of the state of New York, if against any
member of the supreme court of the state of New York, under
impeachment charges such as these, and with proof such as is
before you, would there be a single vote in this chamber
against his removal and his disqualification.   I say, upon your
consciences, that there can be, as it seems to me, made by any
one of you but one answer to that question; you would vote
to remove him, and to disqualify him.   Besides, who would
be so shameless as to say that if the governor or the lieutenant
governor should secure his election to office by fraud or bribery,
that he should be permitted to hold it for the reason that he
committed the crime or wrong before his term of office began ?
But as a step, and from his standpoint, a necessary step in the
acquisition of that office.   If such were the case then the paper
and words which we call the constitution, the foundation and
palladium of state government, would be nothing but a pitfall
and a snare in the toils of which the people might at any time
be caught and bound hand and foot with no means of relief
or escape, none whatever.   For your honors well know, and all
of you, for it has been referred to before in this trial, that when
the subject was up for discussion before the court of appeals,
in 156 New York, that court said, and as a part of its argument
in reaching the conclusion that the court would not grant
a mandamus against the governor because it was without
power to enforce it, that it had not the power to take the
governor and put him in jail for contempt, he being the chief
executive officer of the nation.

" In reaching that conclusion, the court said, in the opinion
written by Judge Haight:

" ' There is no power of removal of a governor except by
impeachment.   Nor is election to an office a certificate or any
guaranty of fitness to hold that office.   Such is not the nature
of the transaction between the candidate or the voter.'

" There is always a tacit, if not an express understanding—
more often the latter—between them, that the candidate is
honest, capable and fit to discharge the duties of the office.   If
he is not so, and is elected, then he has obtained the office by
false pretenses, fraud and deceit, and nobody should be bound
by his election.

THE QUESTION TO BE DISCUSSED

" Of course, an election is no answer to charges of misconduct committed thereafter.   It has been sometimes urged by writers that it was for misconduct which happened before.   It has been common reading that where offenses were known and the subject of discussion and were passed upon by the people at the polls, that they had the right to condone the offenses; but it never has been suggested before this trial, so far as my reading goes—and I have devoted considerable time to the subject—that the offenses which were committed afterwards, after the people had passed upon it, were within at all the rule which led to the suggestion that an offense which the people have condoned ought not to be passed upon by a court of impeachment, but the people have never condoned these offenses. They were not known to the people.   They were committed in the dark, during the campaign for the office, and some of the offenses, the filing of the statement and the taking of the oath, were committed after the election had taken place.

" There are other matters in that connection that I would like to discuss, but my time is flying, indeed has already passed, and I cannot encroach further upon those who are to come after me.

" The purpose of the trial upon impeachment is to protect the honor of the commonwealth, the liberties of the people and the coffers of the state from the dangers of usurpation, stains and depredation of public officials found to be so unworthy of the people's trust and so unfit to hold the high office with which they have been honored and whose official tenure is a public menace.

" The purpose of the constitution in its provisions for impeachment is not to castigate the wrongdoer but to insure to the people just and honest administration by furnishing a method for the removal of all officials found by its tribunal to be guilty of such offenses as make them plainly the wrong instrument for the administration of good government.   It is the people of a sovereign state, whose liberties, lives and happiness are in the hands of its public officials, who are entitled to the first consideration and the prime protection of this court.

" Therefore, the question to be considered is not, Is this

he action of ı emers of this
ence brought to bar on those
_n view, deemed powerful to

ontempt of th s kgh court, of
.igh crimes anc msdemeanors,
and dishonora ole onduct just
e, and during thcterm of his
be a servant f tis sovereign
any other offi e c post what-

'ful and crimir ıl iolations of
nor; they defv henajesty of a
elligence of a recpeople, and

'ant stands guilt · ofhese offenses
and proven by unontrovertible
the court of pu olicopinion, this
on the evidenc h·e presented,
testimony of h s sifty defenses
·dge, by technic· itiı, the trial of
ırt, in which evası n ublic opinion,
d to judicial op nio, finds direct
..c public opinion tals cognizance
...nt here is suffe inı from such a
· htedness that e emwhen directed
.. he cannot dis rn he dishonest,
ıre of the acts provd.

the

I

IATION OF SULZER

·hrough its severe ey something of
·'ant's frantic effort to cover the
ᴢ. Defiance, de ens justification,
of his accuser atmpts to sup-
and efforts to c st ıe blame else-
been stripped from hı quaking flesh
d before this court, whout a rag of
ın clinging to his defoned and muti-

"That he sought to coerce the action of members of the court on this trial, through influence brought to bear or force he, in his narrow and mistaken view, deemed powerful to accomplish that coercion.

"That he has been guilty of contempt of this high court, of gross misconduct in office, of high crimes and misdemeanors, and of such unlawful, dishonest and dishonorable conduct, both prior to his induction into office, and during the term of his office, as utterly unfits him to be a servant of this sovereign people, in this high office or in any other office or trust whatever.

"These acts constitute wilful and criminal violations of public duty and personal dishonor. They defy the majesty of a sovereign state, insult the intelligence of a free people and outrage every sense of honor.

"Before this bar, the defendant stands guilty of these offenses charged by the impeachment and proven by uncontroverted evidence. Before the bar of the court of public opinion, this defendant stands condemned on the evidence here presented, and on the further damning testimony of his shifty defenses and of his futile efforts to dodge, by technicalities, the trial of the issues before this high court. In which evasion public opinion, with a freedom not permitted to judicial opinion, finds direct evidence of guilt. That same public opinion takes cognizance of the fact that the defendant here is suffering from such a severe attack of moral nearsightedness that even when directed by a myriad scornful fingers, he cannot discern the dishonest, criminal and dishonored nature of the acts proved.

DENUNCIATION OF SULZER

"Even justice must see through its severe eye something of the pathetic in this defendant's frantic efforts to cover the nakedness of his wrongdoing. Defiance, retreat, justification, prevarication, denunciation of his accusers, attempts to suppress and falsify testimony and efforts to cast the blame elsewhere—each in turn has been stripped from his quaking flesh until he stands now naked before this court, without a rag of his attempted vindication clinging to its reformed and much-loved manhood.

defendant guilty and to be punished by deprivation of office, but, rather, Is he guilty and therefore a menace to the state while he holds in his contaminated hand the power conferred upon him by our constitution and laws.

"Whether there was ever a day when William Sulzer was fit for great public office we need not inquire. We may shut out his past with shuddering hope that he may have been, and inquire whether the consideration of his conduct is so closely connected with, so immediately prior and so necessary a condition precedent to his induction into office that it constitutes a part of his gubernatorial career.

PARKER SUMS UP HIS POSITION

"With all defenses in and swallowed whole, and with all the scapegoats cruelly overburdened with his responsibilities and the misdeeds from which he alone benefited, these facts yet stare William Sulzer in the face and defy refutation.

"1. That the defendant collected personally many thousands of dollars for campaign purposes, and appropriated most of the total to his personal use.

"2. That he committed perjury, in swearing to a false report of his collections and expenditures; the former being many times the amount acknowledged; that he swore to a sum as his total collection which was less than the amount of a single contribution paid to him personally in cash, in the same office in which he committed his perjury.

"That he deliberately, with an intent which could by no possibility have been honest, sought to procure the contributions in such form, and to make acknowledgment thereof in such form, as should best elude detection. That even as he took pains to conceal the receipt of campaign contributions, so did he strive, by trick and device, to conceal his dishonest conversion of sums so collected.

"That he sought, by the exercise of the power and prestige of his high office, to prevent the truth, and the full truth, being told by witnesses called to testify before the committee and this court of impeachment.

"That he in effect suggested a barter of appropriations for legislative votes for a bill he sought to pass.

" That he sought to coerce the action of members of this court on this trial, through influence brought to bear on those he, in his narrow and mistaken view, deemed powerful to accomplish that coercion.

" That he has been guilty of contempt of this high court, of gross misconduct in office, of high crimes and misdemeanors, and of such unlawful, dishonest and dishonorable conduct just prior to his induction into office, and during the term of his office, as utterly unfits him to be a servant of this sovereign people, in this high office or in any other office or post whatever.

" These acts constitute wilful and criminal violations of public duty and personal dishonor; they defy the majesty of a sovereign state, insult the intelligence of a free people, and outrage every sense of honor.

" Before this bar, this defendant stands guilty of these offenses charged by the impeachment and proven by uncontrovertible evidence. Before the bar of the court of public opinion, this defendant stands condemned on the evidence here presented, and on the further damning testimony of his shifty defenses and of his futile efforts to dodge, by technicalities, the trial of the issues before this high court, in which evasion public opinion, with a freedom not permitted to judicial opinion, finds direct evidence of guilt. That same public opinion takes cognizance of the fact that the defendant here is suffering from such a severe attack of moral nearsightedness that even when directed by a myriad scornful fingers, he cannot discern the dishonest, criminal and dishonored nature of the acts proved.

DENUNCIATION OF SULZER

" Even justice must see through its severe eye something of the pathetic in this defendant's frantic efforts to cover the nakedness of his wrongdoing. Defiance, defense, justification, prevarication, denunciation of his accusers, attempts to suppress and falsify testimony and efforts to cast the blame elsewhere—each in turn has been stripped from his quaking flesh until he stand now naked before this court, without a rag of his attempted vindication clinging to his deformed and mutilated manhood.

guise h... been torn from his back, the petticoat
...ted f... safety to the armor of defiance in which
to att...k and expose a political leadership to
foun... him suing for a merciful obliteration of
...d off...ng the bribe of submission.

...is sh...s more perfectly the complete baseness
...r, unfit...ng him utterly for any public or private
his ...rt to coerce the members of this court
...s hi... warped intellect mistakenly instructed
...wer o... coercion.

...f the...rigin of these charges, regardless of who
...ds of this man, or who his enemies, regardless
...inf...ion of discomfort, this court must, we
on ... the evidence that this defendant has
...scon...ct so gross as to necessitate his removal
...eace, ...osperity and good government of this

...urt a...ne rests the duty of delivering this state
that...ke the sword of Damocles hangs above
man ...conclusively demonstrated to be guilty
...he...s wrongdoing remains in the executive

court ... shall commit the decision of the case
... Sula... securely confident that the honor,
...are of ...s, the Empire state, are assured of the
...emplat... by the constitution in its creation of

ou for yo...patience."

HON. D-CADY HERRICK, CHIEF OF COUNSEL FOR GOVERNOR
WILLIAM SULZER, IN SUMMING UP, SAID:

"Mr. President and gentlemen of the court: As we had
anticipated, the prosecution have been driven in this case, as
you have seen from the address of the late chief judge of the
court of appeals, to this posi-
tion: That this court is
bound by no law excepting
its own feelings, excepting
its own determination, that
it is not to determine but to
make the law, that it is to
usurp legislative functions.
And you are to set that
precedent for all time to
come unless there is a radical change in our constitution.   Because it necessarily
flows from his argument
that a man can be impeached
for not only any offense but
for no offense.   That if for
any reason, political or otherwise, it is determined that a
public official is no longer
fit for office because he be-

lieves or does not believe in the direct primaries, because
he is a low tariff or a high protective man nay, more—
if there is no limit, then the private citizens may be impeached,
great political leaders, against whom charges are continually
made, as they are today in the public prints, may be impeached by the assembly and brought before a court composed
as this is, and forever disqualified as citizen and ruined in
his political leadership and power.

"That is a boundless sea upon which he asks you to venture;
no rudder, no compass to steer and guide you.

"In the learned brief prepared the managers, and I

" Every disguise has been torn from his back, the petticoat in which he trusted for safety to the armor of defiance in which he threatened to attack and expose a political leadership to which we have found him suing for a merciful obliteration of his misdeeds and offering the bribe of submission.

" No act of his shows more perfectly the complete baseness of his character, unfitting him utterly for any public or private trust, than does his effort to coerce the members of this court through channels his warped intellect mistakenly instructed him held the power of coercion.

"Regardless of the origin of these charges, regardless of who may be the friends of this man, or who his enemies, regardless of any personal infliction of discomfort, this court must, we feel certain, find on all the evidence that this defendant has been guilty of misconduct so gross as to necessitate his removal for the honor, peace, prosperity and good government of this community.

" With this court alone rests the duty of delivering this state from the menace that like the sword of Damocles hangs above it so long as this man so conclusively demonstrated to be guilty of deliberate and heinous wrongdoing remains in the executive chair.

"And to this court we shall commit the decision of the case against William Sulzer, securely confident that the honor, safety and welfare of this, the Empire state, are assured of the protection contemplated by the constitution in its creation of this high court.

" Thank you for your patience."

HON. D-CADY HERRICK, CHIEF OF COUNSEL FOR GOVERNOR
WILLIAM SULZER, IN SUMMING UP, SAID:

"Mr. President and gentlemen of the court: As we had anticipated, the prosecution have been driven in this case, as you have seen from the address of the late chief judge of the court of appeals, to this position: That this court is bound by no law excepting its own feelings, excepting its own determination, that it is not to determine but to make the law, that it is to usurp legislative functions. And you are to set that precedent for all time to come unless there is a radical change in our constitution. Because it necessarily flows from his argument that a man can be impeached for not only any offense but for no offense. That if for any reason, political or otherwise, it is determined that a public official is no longer fit for office because he believes or does not believe in the direct primaries, because he is a low tariff or a high protection man—nay, more—if there is no limit, then the private citizens may be impeached, great political leaders, against whom charges are continually made, as they are today in the public prints, may be impeached by the assembly and brought before a court composed as this is, and forever disqualified as a citizen and ruined in his political leadership and power.

"That is a boundless sea upon which he asks you to venture; no rudder, no compass to steer and guide you.

"In the learned brief prepared by the managers, and I

suspect by the counsel for the managers, and I suspect almost entirely by the learned gentleman who is to follow me, it was practically conceded that there was no power of impeachment for offenses committed before entering upon office, because you will recall the very able effort that was made to demonstrate that the making of this statement of election expenses was official misconduct, that it was so intimately connected with a man's entering upon the discharge of his official duties that it could properly be regarded as being made—I think the word was used—in the ' vestibule ' to office.

" I am amazed, astounded, at an argument from a man who so recently occupied the highest judicial position in this state and who controverts every writer, every public writer, upon the question of impeachment that has ever written, and not a case that he cited sustaining his position was one excepting for official misconduct in office. True, in a prior position, but still official misconduct in public office, not committed as a private citizen. The Barnard case, the Butler case, were both cases of official misconduct, not misconduct as a private citizen, but there has been something said about it, and I might just as well say it in that connection, by a gentleman who was not acting as an advocate, but who was in the discharge of a judicial duty, just as you are, upon the impeachment of Andrew Johnson, as to whether you can remove a man for unfitness for office.

" Lyman J. Trumbull, one of the greatest jurists of his day, speaking upon the same question of the power of removal because of unfitness for office, said:

" ' The question to be decided is not whether Andrew Johnson is a proper citizen to fill the presidential office, nor whether it is fit that he shall remain in it, nor indeed whether he has violated the constitution and laws in other respects than those alleged against him. As well might any other fifty-four persons take upon themselves by violence to rid the country of Andrew Johnson because they believe him to be a bad man, as to call upon fifty-four senators in violation of their sworn duty to convict and impose upon him for any other acts than those alleged in the articles of impeachment. As well might any citizen take the law into his own hands and become an executioner as to ask a senator to convict for acts outside of those prescribed by law. To sanction such principles would be to convict all law worthy of the name since liberty unregulated by law, is anarchy.

" 'Unfit for president as people may deem Andrew Johnson, and much as they might desire his removal in a legal and constitutional way, all save the unprincipled and depraved would brand with infamy and condemn the name of any senator who in violation of sworn conviction would vote to accomplish such a result.'

" He considers, because a man is shown to be unfit in some respects as a private citizen, his reason for his removal, irrespective of what his conduct has been in public office. Let me read you again what Lord Macaulay says in his essay on Lord Clyde, in his trial:

" 'Ordinary criminal justice knows nothing of setoff.' The greatest desert cannot be pleaded in answer to a charge of the slightest transgression. If a man has sold beer on Sunday morning, it makes no difference that he saves the life of a fellow creature at risk of his own. If a man harnessed a little Newfoundland dog to his child's carriage, it is not a defense that he was wounded at Waterloo, but it is not in this way we ought to deal with men who are without ordinary restraint, tried by far more than ordinary temptation and are entitled to more than the ordinary measure of indulgence. Such men should be judged by their contemporaries as they will be by posterity. Their bad acts ought not, indeed, to be condoned, but their good and bad actions ought to be fairly weighed, and if on the whole the good predominates, the sentence ought not to be merely one of acquittal, but of approbation. Not a single great ruler in history can be absolved by a judge who fixes his eye inexorably upon one or two unjustifiable acts. Bruce, the deliverer of Scotland; Moritz, the deliverer of Germany; William, the deliverer of Holland; Henry IV of France, Peter the Great of Russia, how would the best of them pass such a scrutiny. History takes wider views, and the best tribunal for great political cases is the tribunal which anticipates the verdict of history. Reasonable and moderate men of all parties felt this in Clyde's case. They could not pronounce him blameless, but they would not abandon him to the low minded and rancorous pack who would run down and worry him to his death.'

"A man may be unfit in some respects. He may have committed indiscretions or worse in his private life, and yet we are to judge of him, as a public official, by what he does in public office and in no other way.

Intellectual Honesty

" I shall pay but very little further attention in my remarks to the law in regard to impeachable offenses, but refer you to the briefs that have been heretofore submitted upon this subject, which seem to me to uncontradictably establish the law to be, not only now, but as it has been for generations, that no man could be impeached and removed from office except for official misconduct in office.

" I owe a duty to the respondent, to this court and to the state, and, in discharging that duty I am somewhat embarrassed as to how to express some thoughts that have come to me without giving offense. Please believe me that, in what I am about to say, I intend no criticism of any man's conduct, I impugn no man's motives, I intend to cast no reflection upon any man's integrity, but I feel that I must indulge in some reflections as to the nature of this tribunal in some respects.

" In one of my arguments before you—I think the first one— I spoke of the difficulty of being intellectually honest, honest with one's self, and I think I illustrated—if I did not, I will now, by the difficulties a lawyer has when a client comes to him for advice upon some given proposition. It is to the interest of that client to have honest, accurate advice. It is to the interest of the lawyer to give it; and yet, with the insensible proneness of the mind to help out the client, those decisions, those interpretations of the statute that seemed to be beneficial to the client make more of a lodgment and a greater weight in the minds of the attorney than those adverse to his client. So, too, when a question of law is presented to a judge upon the bench, with some preconceived opinion in regard thereto— perhaps obtained years ago, when a lawyer, possibly even when a law student—when he comes to examine that case deliberately for the passing judgment, those decisions, those interpretations of the law and of statutes which are in accord with his preconceived opinion have more effect upon his mind than those that are against that preconceived opinion.

And that is what I mean by the difficulty of being intellectually honest. And hence it is that I feel a sense of embarrassment and difficulty in discussing the cause of this respondent before a tribunal with so many of its members—I say it with all respect—not prejudiced, but predisposed against his case and against him; some by reason of opinions previously formed upon a partial investigation and consideration of the facts.

To such members of this tribunal I say that your bounden duty is to lay aside all previously formed opinions, formed without due consideration, formed without discussion, formed without hearing what was to be said in favor of the respondent, and decide this case as if you had heard it for the first time; and bearing in mind that you have taken your solemn oath to do impartial justice between this assembly who have impeached the respondent, and the respondent himself.

Again, some of you are members of a powerful and imperious political organization, that has kept the respondent in public life for years and has placed him where he now is in more than one respect. Differences have arisen between that organization and this respondent. Many of its members believe him to be ungrateful and disloyal. Who is right and who is wrong I know not; whether the allegiance and loyalty demanded by that organization came in conflict with the allegiance and loyalty that he owed to the state I know not; whatever the causes of these differences may be with that organization, you are bound to disregard them. He is not on trial for disloyalty; he is not on trial for ingratitude; and you have taken a solemn oath to try him impartially upon the charges here brought against him and nothing else.

" Then there is another class of judges, men with whom he has had personal controversies, towards whom he has used abusive and threatening language; some of you he said he would drive from public life. I have no justification for the language used. It was wrong, particularly when addressed by the executive of the state to members of a coordinate branch of the government, but you are to cast aside all personal feelings, disregard all personal controversies, clear your minds of every prejudice, every passion, and every feeling, because he is on trial for none of these things; and you have sworn to pass judgment upon this case impartially.

"Then there is another class of people who think as the late learned chief justice, he is unfit for public office by mental equipment, personal habits, and political ideals. That by reason of all these things he is utterly unfitted to hold the high and dignified position of governor of this great state.

"But he is not on trial for unfitness for office. The people passed on that. Hear what Lyman Trumbull, the one to whom I adverted a moment ago, said when he was giving his reasons for breaking away from the great party that had sent him and placed him in the senate and made it possible for him to be a judge in that great trial in giving his reasons for voting for the acquittal of Johnson:

"'To do impartial justice in all things appertaining to the present trial according to the constitution and laws is the duty imposed on each senator by the position he holds and the oath he has taken; and he who falters in the discharge of that duty, either from personal or party consideration, is unworthy his office and merits the scorn and contempt of all just men.'

"Of all these things that I have referred to, well calculated to predispose you against the respondent, for none of these things, I say, is he on trial. The spirit of fair play that should characterize the conduct of every man in public life towards his political adversary; that requires him to play the game according to the rules; that requires a man, a political leader, when he has made a mistake in putting a man into public office, to smile and bear the weight of his error without wincing, and not attempt to remove him from office by unlawful means to remedy the evil; but not to repeat the mistake again. And the highest sense of honor that should actuate all high-minded men requires that you men free your minds of all preconceived opinions and personal feeling, and determine whether you honestly believe he has been wilfully guilty of the offenses charged against him.

Nay, more—the solemn oath that you have taken before Him to whom you yourself must some time appear for judgment, requires you to cast out all prejudice, all ill feeling, all passion; and judge this man upon the law and upon the facts as applied to the law, and nothing else.

THE PERIL TO THE COURTS

"Again, there is a little sense of embarrassment in what I am about to say.   In my first address I stated that not only was the respondent on trial, but the court itself was on trial in these proceedings.   The presiding judge has stated more than once during the progress of this trial that an impeachment trial is unlike any other, and the strict rules of evidence that are observed in ordinary civil and criminal cases have not been observed.   And it seemed to us that in refusing our last motion to dismiss certain of the articles of impeachment, the rule that requires a prosecutor to establish the guilt of the person prosecuted had been reversed and the burden placed upon us to establish the respondent's innocence.

"What the presiding judge has said with reference to impeachment trials being different from all other trials is true in more than one respect.   They are peculiarly cases where the decision must be in accord with public sentiment.

" If the public sentiment, by a sense of justice, is offended by the composition of the court, or by the decisions it makes, a blow is given to the confidence of the people in the due administration of law, from which it takes a long time to recover.

" Do not misunderstand me.   I am not one of those who believes that our courts of justice, in administering the law, should depart one hair's breadth from what they believe to be the law.   Still the courts, not only for their own preservation and protection, but for the public good, must not only decide right, but it must do it in such a way that the people will believe it to be a right decision.

STATE'S HONOR AT STAKE

"Writers upon impeachment speak of them as being very largely political proceedings against men in public life, where political animosities and partisan feelings are aroused for and against the present judge.   In a tribunal composed entirely of senators, as in the case of the trial of President Johnson, like tribunals existing in almost all the other states in this union, the manner in which they make the decisions, and the decisions themselves, perhaps arouse very little feeling against the administration of justice, because they regard them as political decisions and not judicial decisions. But, in a tribunal like this, composed of the justices of the highest court of this state for the administration of ordinary civil and criminal justice, and composed of senators together with such judges a decision made by such a court, if not in accord with what the people believe to be a right decision, strikes a deadly blow at the confidence of the people in the administration of their laws.

It took many, many years for the supreme court of the United States to recover from the effect of the division upon party lines between the justices of the supreme court who served upon the electoral commission.

"Now, without any disloyalty to William Sulzer, I may say that he is a mere incident in these proceedings; that my effort is very largely in behalf of the dignity and honor of the state, and the preservation, if it can be preserved, of the confidence of the people of this state in the administration of the law. I have got beyond the time when political honor and preferment is for me, but I have a deep respect and affection for the state.

" I have a great respect and affection for the highest tribunals of this state, and for the individual members, and I want to see nothing happen that will impair the confidence of the people in this tribunal, and my interest is that by no decision or by no manner of arriving at the decision should any reflection be cast upon the administration of justice or any new impetus given the feeling which we cannot disguise from ourselves that at present exists against the administration of justice; stirred up, enlarged upon by demagogues and political leaders of singular ability and disingenuousness. With these things in mind, it seems to me that is peculiarly the time and peculiarly the case when the court should not go beyond what is written in the law. It is of the gravest importance that the independence of the three great departments of government should be preserved, the legislative, the judicial and the executive; and before the legislative and judicial departments should combine to overthrow the executive, the law therefor should be clear and plain.

THE COURTS THEMSELVES IN PERIL

" The question of fact will always vary in the different cases, but the law itself should be clear and definite; and no loose or liberal construction should be given to it to accomplish the overthrow of any department of the government or the occupant of any department.

" In the very learned brief prepared by the counsel for the managers, a list of over seventy cases of impeachment is set out. Not one of them but what is for official misconduct. Some two or three for past official misconduct, but still misconduct in office. Not a single one of these cases is an impeachment for acts committed when the person impeached is a private citizen. Not one but where he was an occupant of some public office, when the misconduct occurred. Judge Parker, in his argument, concedes that articles I, II and VI were acts performed out of office, while Governor Sulzer was a private citizen, before he entered upon the discharge of the duties of the office of governor. Now, the public policy of this state, as illustrated by section 7 of article X of the constitution, requiring provision to be made for the removal of public officials for misconduct of malversation in office, section 12 of the code of criminal procedure provides that this court shall have jurisdiction to try impeachments for wilful and corrupt misconduct in office. In 1854 the judiciary committee of the assembly, reported, and the assembly ratified its report, that no one could be impeached except for misconduct in office.

" In 1905 the judiciary committee of the senate reported that impeachments would lie only for misconduct in office and the learned chairman of that committee supported it in a learned and very able opinion.

"In the Guden case, under the power of removal, much broader than that of impeachment, the governor in removing him found he was guilty of official misconduct in taking the oath of office, it being a false oath in entering office, and the appellate division upheld the decision on the ground, among other things, that it was a corrupt agreement while entering into and before becoming a public official, to be performed thereafter, and in the court of appeals the only judge discussing the facts said:

"'There must be a charge of some official misconduct on the part of the officer and that in that case he was shown not only to have made a corrupt agreement before entering his office, but that he carried it out thereafter.'

"Now, with this history of impeachments in this country the past public policy of the state, that this court should go further than has ever before been gone in American history, should go further than had heretofore been written in the law and convict for acts done while a private citizen, upon the extremely slender and tenuous theory that in making a statement of election expenses such statement had some connection with the public office which made it official misconduct, when the defeated candidates have to make a like statement; which statement is not and cannot be made a condition of his entering into office, because the constitution itself provides the only test for entering office; and then to thrust him out after he has entered into office because of this false statement you could not require him to make as a condition for going in, is violating the provisions of the constitution and doing that by indirection which it prohibits doing by direction—I say that with this history of impeachments and the law hitherto related, that before such an extension of the power of impeachment to acts done before taking the office and before becoming a public official, it will be regarded as reaching out for a victim, and that the court did not determine but made the law to fit the case; and it will do more than anything ever done or that can be done in this state to bring about the recall of judges and judicial decisions, or it will at least cause a reconstruction of our whole judicial system.

NOT MERE IDLE DECLAMATION

"This is not mere idle declamation for the purposes of this case, may it please the court, but it is the result of careful investigations. Those people who think there is no feeling of unrest in regard to the courts, the administration of the law and of lawyers are not honest with themselves or are not acquainted with the public condition of affairs. I was charged with investigating this subject nearly a year ago and the conditions that I found existing, the public feeling, I dare not report in full for fear of increasing that public discontent.

Don't blind yourselves! Stop and think the enormous vote cast last year upon a platform attacking our courts and proclaiming belief in the recall and the recall of judicial decisions. So I say that it behooves us that this case shall be so decided in such a manner that the people will believe and understand, and lawyers too, because many of them share in this feeling I speak of, that this court has not gone beyond the law as it has been written for over 200 years in England and this country, and never violated hitherto.

* * * * * * * * * * * * * * * * * * *

PUT YOURSELF IN HIS PLACE

" Imagine yourself in his place. There are some things that a decent, manly man cannot do to save himself. Some things that a man of even low ethical standards cannot shield himself by. Some sacrifices of others that he cannot allow to be made, even at the risk of losing high position and being forever disqualified for political preferment and honors. Which would you do? Run the risk of losing the empty honor of being governor—empty if held with dishonor—or lose the respect of every decent and honorable man in the whole United States by saving yourself at the expense of the honor and 'integrity of the one you are bound to love and protect. Imagine yourself, I say, in that position, with his experience, the political surroundings that he had been brought up in, the political ideals that he possessed, the political education that he had received in a school where it is supposed that political influence can reach not only into the courts, but even into the sanctuary of the church. Is it any wonder that, in desperation, he resorted to the methods best known to people brought up in such a political school; with such a political education, and endeavored to secure the influence of political leaders of both parties to have the impeachment articles brought by the assembly declared to be illegal for lack of jurisdiction as he had been informed and advised by high legal authority they were.

" Is it any wonder that he preferred to risk his high position and all future political advances rather than subject himself to the scorn of every honorable man, and should resort to these methods, which you and I and all right thinking men consider dishonorable and regard as an imputation upon our

courts of justice, that it should even be thought for a moment
they could be reached by political or other influence?

EVILS OF POLITICAL SYSTEM

"One thing, though, further, which Mr. Ryan's testimony
develops, one further thought it brings to my mind, and that
is the evil of our political system of leadership in this country
when great parties in a great state are largely subject to the
control of a single man, who has dominating influence which
can be brought to bear, if he so wills it, to either control the
actions of men in legislative bodies, and even courts, or else
ruin their whole political future; and I congratulate the republican members of this court whose influence it was thus indirectly
sought to obtain the information that came back was that that
great organization would not interfere one way or the other,
that the accredited leader of that organization would not permit any man high or low to even speak to him about the case;
in other words, that the members of this court were not, the
judges of the court of appeals were not to be interfered with
in any way, shape or manner, but permitted to do exactly in
accordance with the views that their consciences compelled.
Still, the information that came back, we do not know from
whom, was not exactly correct. You recollect first that it
was that none but the elected judges of the court of appeals
would sit, would be members of the court; second, that it
would be held that the assembly could come together at any
time, any place, anywhere, at the call of any one private citizen, or anybody else, but so long as a majority of them kept
together they could prefer articles of impeachment; the position that was contended for by the managers; perhaps these
two first replies came from the managers, but this one that I
refer to turned out also to be incorrect, because you have held
that they cannot be convened at any man's whim, upon any
man's call, but being in session, regularly called, that then they
have the right to act.

" I wish that Mr. Ryan had also made inquiry of the leaders
of the other parties. It would have been extremely interesting to know what the response to that inquiry would be.
I trust that it would have been equally frank. If any inquiry
has been made I hope the same statement comes back to those

senators not of the republican faith that they are not to be interfered with, that no instructions are to be given them, that the accredited leader of that party will not permit any one, high or low, to speak to him in regard to this case, but leave those who are his followers to obey the dictates of their own consciences, untrammeled by even a suggestion or request which may involve their political future if that suggestion or request is not obediently complied with.

* * * * * * * * * * * * * * * * * *

NOW FIRST ACCUSED

" In reaching your verdict and determination as to whether the respondent has wilfully done wrong, you must take into consideration the nature and the history of the man and the nature of the offenses.   As I just said, some members of this court have known him for years; know his lack of business habits and business methods; of his carelessness in money matters; of his overweening ambition; know of his egotism; know of his proneness to consider those things which are the creatures of his imagination actual facts; but none of you, none of you in the past have ever regarded him as a dishonest man, a perjurer or a thief—and that is what these charges come down to.

" He has been in public life now for nearly twenty-five years; five years, as I recall it, in the legislature of this state, one year serving as speaker, eighteen years in congress; rising step by step, until by long service and presumed ability, becoming chairman of one of the most important committees in the house.

"At the time he was in the legislature, from common report, and these are things of which men situated as you are can take public notice and judicial notice, money was flowing freely in the legislative halls for those who wanted it, but never the breath of suspicion was cast upon him in those days.   In the days of the Huckleberry grab and other bills of like character, when he was in the legislature, no one accused him of being a party to any corrupt legislation or receiving a penny for his influence, or for his vote.

"Now, after over a quarter of a century of public service he is, for the first time, charged with being a dishonest man, charged with stealing money, charged with plundering his friends, charged with seeking contributions for one purpose, using them for another, and committing perjury to conceal the fact.

"These things, it is said, bring shame and disgrace upon the state. They do! They do! The fact that a great party nominated and the people of the state of New York elected a man to be governor of this great state of the ethical standards of this respondent, must be conceded to be a shame and disgrace to the state of New York, but it is not for those things that you are to remove him from office.

"Another thing that is a shame and disgrace to the state of New York. These things were unknown to the state of New York until the impeachment managers, for some purpose, God only knows what, brought them to light and brought shame and disgrace upon the state of New York.

"I recollect—I am not very familiar in these days with the scriptures, but I recollect there is some passage in the scriptures where the mantle is cast over the naked body of a person to shield him from shame and disgrace.

"When these things became known, those people who had the good name and fame of the state of New York, should have withheld them for the honor and dignity of the state, instead of bringing them forth for the purpose of removing from their path the man who seems to have been an obstacle in doing things that are a great deal worse than anything that is charged up to the governor.

IMPEACHMENT A MISTAKE

"Gentlemen of the managers, these impeachment proceedings are a mistake, a great mistake from any point of view; and I believe that no one now realizes that more than those who were instrumental in bringing them.

"No object in removing him from office because of those things. The term is short. The people can eject him in a short time. The legislature is adverse to him. He can do no harm excepting to investigate, excepting to expose wrong-doing, excepting to stop graft and corruption; but he can do no harm to any honest well meaning people in the state of New York because here is the legislature in both branches hostile to him. Why, then, bring these impeachment proceedings excepting to halt these investigations which Mr. Hennessy says were under way—

The President: " I do not think the evidence goes—"

Mr. Herrick: " I said, ' under way.' I am going no further because you stop us there."

The President: " Very good."

Mr. Herrick: " I had in mind the ruling of the court. The bringing of these impeachment proceedings is lamentable because of the object lesson of what may occur to any man in public life who dares stand and oppose the wishes of those who may know something about his private life and history not known to the general public."

" Now, in conclusion, in rendering your verdict, let it be such a one as will demonstrate to the people of the state that, regardless of any personal feeling toward the accused, or any preconceived opinions, or any political or personal differences with him, they may be convinced that the respondent has had a fair and impartial trial; such a verdict as will sustain the proud reputation of the highest court of this state for learning, impartiality and freedom from political bias; a verdict and decision that will serve as a precedent in years to come, and be a mark of honor to every one who has participated in its rendition.

" Sir, you are approaching the end of your public career. During the time you have received great honors from the state, honors well merited and amply repaid by distinguished services. from boyhood until nearly three score years and ten, upon the battle field, in the councils of a great party, and in the highest tribunals of justice in this state. God forbid that in the closing days of an illustrious career you aid in any way in placing an indelible stain upon the splendid history of the state you have loved and nobly served.

HON. EDGAR T. BRACKETT, OF COUNSEL FOR IMPEACHMENT,
MANAGERS, IN SUMMING UP, SAID:

"With the permission of the court, I think myself happy,
members of the court, that it is given to me to speak to you
at this time. The time, the place, the cause, conspire to
high thought and mighty en-
deavor. 'The blood more
stirs to rouse the lion than
to start the hare.' The pulse
runs higher, the heart beats
stronger in defense of the
honor of the commonwealth,
here fearfully assailed from
within, than in a cause less
sacred. He to whom is given
the opportunity to aid in
shielding the mother who
bore him, the father who
begot, or the state which
has nurtured him, is thrice
happy and blessed among
men.

"No one, even slightly
acquainted with the history
of this greatest of the states,
and of the names that make
that history a glorious one, can avoid a prideful satisfaction
that, in the performance of duty, it is given to him to plead in
behalf of her good name. It is with that pride and that satisfaction, that the managers of this impeachment come before
you in this final stage of this historic trial, to press upon you
that you cast from her service one who has forgotten her honor
and been faithless to the trust she reposed in him. We have here
no feeling akin to professional exaltation in having been able ·
to develop the facts requiring the conviction of the defendant,
but rather, only a feeling of performing a solemn duty to the
people of the state.

"At the time of the commencement of this proceeding a few weeks ago, it was something over forty-one years since the assembly of the state, the representatives of all the people, more truly than any other officer or body known to the law, in the performance of a solemn duty, exercised the functions laid upon it by the constitution and the laws, in the impeachment of a high official of the state. In our freedom from high crime in public place, we had almost forgotten the machinery for its degrees. In a revision of our organic law made during that period, the provisions for the impeachment of a public official were regarded as so little likely to require use, that they received scant attention at the hands of the learned men reviewing them, and left open for high discussion questions that could have been speedily and definitely settled here.

" Through the mists of the years that last state trial rises before us with singular distinctness. In the course of our proceedings here it has been looked to with profoundest respect for precedent and for argument. And as I have studied its record, I have prayed that it would be given to us here, each in his own place, members of the court, counsel, the officials who have served us, to take high courage from the examples there set us, and to meet our duty here as they met theirs there.

"And yet I do not remind you of this high occasion, nor of the exemplars who have gone before, to render you timid in the performance of your work. The intelligence that has been given to us is for use in the doing of great as well as of small duties. We must take the final steps in this proceeding in precisely the same spirit that we do our daily round of petty duties through the years. Unawed by responsibility, unafraid of the consequences of any result, unafraid of any result itself, except a wrong one, with appreciation of the great opportunity to do a lasting service for the right, laying aside any baser motives, let us here highly resolve to proceed, as it is given to us to see the light, and with manly hearts.

" Not speaking now to the members of the court accustomed daily to render judgment, to whom the ascertainment of right is a study and justice a habit, but only to those others, unacquainted with judicial work, let me, as one familiar with every temptation that can come to you in the performance of such duty, address myself to you a moment.

Alleges Terrorism

" From the beginning of the impeachment proceedings brought against William Sulzer, nay, from the time that his crimes were first whispered around these halls, on behalf of the defendant there has been a persistent and studied attempt to terrorize the members of this court and every person associated with the prosecution. Every means known to the demagogue has been attempted to accomplish it—the press, a few of its members venal, many of them thoughtless of the grave situation presented, have daily paraded much hopelessly bad law and have direfully threatened those who were so singular as to say that they doubted the wisdom of allowing a criminal to remain in the executive chair. Political extinction has been threatened to those bold enough to urge that it might be well to have an orderly investigation of the matters charged against this man. Counsel have been warned that their appearance for the people here would result in savage attacks upon them. We have witnessed the indecency—for I think it can be called nothing less—of public meetings called to overawe your judgment and to give you instructions how to decide this cause, before a single word of sworn testimony had been given to you. In season and out, it has been preached that justice would not be done here, when justice was the last thing desired by the preachers. No such campaign has ever been devised as the one that has thus attempted to influence and to terrify you from the performance of your duty.

"Against all this I hold up to you the simple oath you took at the beginning of this trial. Its solemn words are fresh with you, and I know that in their presence the least thoughtful will be sobered to the fullest sense of his duty. as I know that this wave of clamor will never rise in its influence to the level of the soles of your feet.

" So to all those who have professed doubts as to whether justice would here dominate, who have sought to discredit in advance the patient fairness by which every right of the defendant has been here conserved throughout the days, to all right reverends and " wrong reverends," everywhere, who profess to find here not the solemn performance of a public duty laid on you by the law, but only an opportunity to scourge and strike the political enemy, I send greetings and invite them to learn from the great apostle of moderation of speech and ask them to come and see how, under the strictest forms of law, divesting themselves of every unworthy motive or thought the representatives of a free people come together and give judgment.

CHARGES A FALSE ANSWER

" What answer has the defendant made to these charges ? And the answer which he brought here, signed with his own name, and filed with this court to stand on the records to the end of recorded time, is typical of the man and typical of his effort, and every act that has been proved in the case.

" He came into this court, having exhausted every dilatory motion and every point of law which the ingenuity of the most learned counsel in the state could discover to raise here. Having exhausted all that in an effort to secure the dismissal of these charges without being called upon to meet the great, crucial fact as to whether or not he was guilty, and without being called upon to put any evidence in—having thus exhausted all means of delay, he comes here and he files an answer signed with his own name.   And what is that answer, in the light of the testimony that is here, unanswered in the slightest degree, uncontradicted to the extent of a syllable, what answer is that ?   He comes here and admitting the mere formal facts that he was a candidate for governor and is now governor, and that he did file a statement, every one of which, of course, was susceptible of proof here within ten minutes from the time the court convened, he thereupon solemnly, in the face of all the people of the state, filed with this great court an answer which is itself an infamous lie, when he says that he denies each and every one of the facts set up in article I.   And if you will consider from now to the end of the chapter that it is typical of this defendant, that wherever he thinks the proof cannot be found, he submits a denial, you will find the key to the answer of many a question that will be put to you in the consideration and final decision of this case.

"What is the proof? And when I come here on the question of proof, I confess to you that I am embarrassed beyond measure. Ordinarily, it is given to counsel, where there has been evidence submitted on the trial of the case to see where reason and experience point the line of truth between the two statements.

"But here, what was there? If I commenced to argue before this court as to the truth of the evidence submitted on behalf of these managers, I would be justly called by the presiding officer, who might say, ' why do you argue to some things as to which there is no possible contradiction '?

"And so it is like arguing with the east wind, or it is similar to wrestling with the ague. You cannot get ahead with anything that can be said, because the simple statement of a proposition demonstrates that the evidence given on our behalf here is true, and that there is not a single word of contradiction with respect to any part of it.

THE CAMPAIGN STATEMENT

" In the statement that was filed by this defendant made out on the 13th of November, and filed in the secretary of state's office on the next day, he certified to the secretary of state and to all the people of the state by whose grace and favor he had received a majority of the votes at the previous election that he had received during his campaign but the sum of $5,460, the donors of which were named and were sixty-eight in number. He certified that the expenses which he had incurred during that campaign were $7,724.09, and thereby he meant to have the people of the state and anyone who would come and read to believe that he had been elected by the contributions of sixty-eight small contributors who altogether had given him during his campaign less than $100 apiece as an average. And the thought was in his little mind as he did that was posing as he had posed during the years as one who was still in the congress a poor man, fighting the people's battle, that the great common people were the ones who were his friends and the only ones who had contributed anything to his election. All of the great interests that cluster around

Broad and Wall streets, all of the interests that might come here and want legislation; all of those interested in politics, were carefully left off from the statement, and it was only the little men contributing, as I say, less than one hundred dollars apiece that had risen in their might and made William Sulzer the governor of the state. It was only they who had contributed as he certifies to the secretary of state.

"What is the uncontradicted proof with respect to it? What answer does my friend make here, do either of the learned counsel make who have argued here? What answer is there? The uncontradicted proof stands here, you will find the details of it in the sheets that have been passed around, and which while one of the learned counsel says it is incorrect, has not lhad its incorrectness pointed out in the slightest degree. It stands that every entry made in this sheet is proven and proven beyond fact and without contradiction by the evidence in the case, and the reference is made in the paper itself to where the evidence will be found.

"By that paper it is shown and by the evidence therein referred to it is shown that during the time of his campaign, although he had reported receipts of but $5,460, there had been paid to him in the way of contribution checks that had been actually traced to him, and upon which there are marks which he could not avoid or escape, $12,700, or more than twice as much unreported as he had reported. It is demonstrated that there was of cash that has been traced to him unreported in this statement which he thus filed, the sum of $24,700, or nearly five times as much as the amount which he admitted in his statement he received. And it has been demonstrated, the shameful act has been demonstrated, that during the time of the campaign he paid to brokers in Wall street securities $40,462, much of which was the very checks which were handed to him for the campaign purposes. Ah, but, says the defendant, these people were so enraptured with my previous personal history, they were so in love with the situation that made it possible for me to be governor, that knowing the necessities with which I was afflicted, they made a purse for my personal comfort and to relieve me from the slough of debt in which I have been wallowing for years.

SULZER'S SITUATION

" I want to stand for the proposition, first, that he who is nominated a candidate for a public office, who receives contributions during that campaign, if nothing is said on the subject, receives them with the implied understanding and obligation that they are for the purposes of his campaign. There shall be no opportunity for hair splitting on this. The man who so far refines that he can claim to himself or to another, let alone to this high court, that having been nominated for an office by a great party in the state when contributions are made to him, whether by personal friends or by persons interested in the success of the party, who can so far refine that to claim he can out of his own grace, if I use the language of the catechism right, out of his own grace and favor only think he can say ' This check is mine; this large check is mine; that little one is for the purposes of a personal campaign; this one I will not report; that one I must and will '—the man who makes any such claim as that stands in a position for the first time of making it, for no other human being from the time we have had popular elections until the present moment has ever had the hardihood to come and make any such claim.

" What is the actual situation in which a candidate for place who receives contributions stands? He is not nominated for his own glory, however, this defendant may have thought that was so, it was not for the glorification of William Sulzer that he was nominated as the candidate of the democratic party on the morning of the 3rd of October, 1912, at Syracuse. He was nominated as a representative of a party; he was nominated to be supported by the party, and when the contributions from that moment came in, any man who had any conception whatever, not simply of ethic but of decency, knew and recognized, and must have known and recognized to the full, were contributions because the contributor desired the candidate of the party should be elected for which he had been nominated and because the contributor had an interest in the success of that party. * * *

DECLARES SULZER A LIAR

" Do you think—and Mr. Presiding Judge, I hesitate to ask the question as an insult to your intelligence. What do you think, can any rational man think for a single minute that when on the 13th day of November, 1912, William Sulzer affixed his signature to the statement that he had received during the campaign $5,460, that there was not running in his mind at the very instant that he did it, 'And I have got $10,000 of Thomas F. Ryan's money in my pocket this minute as clear gain ? ' * * *

" Let us get away from the sham and the pretense that the Schiff check was anything else than a contribution made for campaign purposes. Do you think when he came to make his false certificate and to certify to the secretary of state and to all the world that he, the apostle of the plain people, had been elected with contributions of only $5,460, that he did not know alongside of the fact of Mr. Ryan's $10,000 check, in his brain, that there was the $2,500 check of Jacob H. Schiff as to which he was fully the gainer. So the certificate was false. 'And so the affidavit that was made to it was false.

" I am not now discussing the question of perjury. I am not going over the law as my associate, skilled on the criminal side of the law, gave it to you here earlier in the trial. We stand here on every line and every word of the brief which he has thus filed here, and I shall not go over it here again.

" The certificate was false. The affidavit which he made there was false; whether or not he can escape on the claim that because it was not required by the statute that he should swear to it all, as to whether he can escape the penitentiary or the state's prison on that plea is not here at all. When he put his name to the affidavit and swore to it before Abraham J. Wolff, he swore to a lie; and whether or not he was guilty of legal perjury that would justly land him in the state prison he was guilty of the moral perjury, he was guilty of all the blackness of intention of all the guilty heart that he would or could have been had he sworn as required by the statute and he believed he was.

SULZER AND SAUL

" But the first of January comes, and from that moment he is a converted man; but, my brothers, there are some of us here to whom through the years the question of conversion has been very much before our eyes, and yet I cannot fail to

remind you that the great church which stands today, as it
has stood from the beginning, firm in the belief of a conversion
from sin, that it yet demands repentance.   Never yet, when
you were standing behind the sacred desk, never yet have you
permitted to join holy church, a man whom you did not believe
in your heart had repented of his sins.   Oh, but on the first of
January, like Saul of Tarsus on his way to Damascus, there
came a light, yet before that moment he was in gall of bitterness and bondage of sin, although prior to that time he had
done nothing but serve the forces of evil, yet from the first
day of January when the light came to him he became a consecrated man and devoted himself thenceforth to the service
of God and humanity in the people's house.

   "Oh, Saul! Oh, Saul! Persecutor of the saints, but the
greatest of the Apostles!   What foolishness has been attempted
through the years because of that sudden conversion of yours
on the way to Damascus!   There is many a man that tries to
liken himself to Paul when the only likeness is to that of Saul.
Saul saw a light, but he respected it.   He repented of his
sins.   Saul, having seen the light, announced that from that
moment he renounced the devil and all his works.

   "He did not go around trying to suborn perjury.   When
he got together the few Christians in the upper chamber,
wherever he could get them, to preach the word, after his
conversion, he did not whisper to one of them that if he was
sworn he hoped they would be easy on him.   Before he opened
the meeting with prayer, he didn't call one of them aside and
see if he could send word to tamper with the court that was
going to try him, and he finally won a glorious martyrdom by
sincerity, and not by posing; by honest work, not by many
professions; by doing the work and not being a rank hypocrite.

   "Can you imagine Paul telephoning to Gamaliel that he
was 'the same old Saul.   And can't you make it more than
$7,500 ? '

THE ELECTION LAW

   "These are facts.   The certificate was false.   The affidavit
was made with all the blackness of heart that could cause a
man to be guilty of rank perjury anywhere.

"And then he took every dollar that was thus contributed
to him, of which I have given you a list, and went to play in
Wall street, and bought Big Four stock. Oh, well, our friends
say, that is all true; that is all true, and it may not have been
ethical; it was not quite ethical. Perhaps it was unmoral, a
little unmoral, but still he has been elected by the people. Is
the election law a joke? Is the statute, for the passage of
which, and the perfection of which high-minded men and
women during the years have come here year after year for
the purpose of getting it into some kind of shape where, if the
use of money in elections could not be prevented, it could at
least be exposed? A law which never yet has taken any step
backward. Where every step that has been taken at all has
been in the direction of making it tighter, of making it more
perfect, so that no one should be able to slip through its meshes.
Is this law still discovered to be a joke? That it is only a
question of the lighter ethics as to whether it shall be obeyed
or not? * * *

My friends have waxed earnest, to say nothing of the elo-
quence. They have waxed earnest in the proposition that,
in all the years there has been every effort made to make this
law so that it would require to be done just what was intended
by it, that the wisdom of the legislature and the executive
who have concurred in the passage of this law has been so at
fault that today it means nothing. If you hold this man
guiltless of crime in this connection, at least members of the
senate, have the decency to introduce a bill to repeal it, and
have it done quickly and thoroughly.

On this 19th day of July or soon thereafter, this defendant
the governor of the state of New York, sitting in the chair that
has been occupied by men of the highest character—and praise
God that from the beginning none of them have ever been
suspected before of personal dishonesty—the chair that within
the time of my own official life and recollection was occupied
by Levi P. Morton, a man who would no more do a dishonorable
act that he would put his right arm in the fire and let it wither;
it was the chair in which next sat the brilliant Frank S. Black,
than whom no more knightly soul ever sat or came to the city
of Albany or came to that high office. From the beginning it
has been rendered sacred by great names of great men, men

who would have scorned a dishonorable thing as they would have shunned a wound. And it was left to this year of grace one thousand nine hundred and thirteen, this year of wrath, it was left to have in the executive chamber a governor who could so far forget not only decency and official honor, but who so forgot pride of honor, so far forgot the limitations not only of the criminal but the moral law as to ask this great officer of the state under him to go on the stand and commit rank perjury to save his miserable soul from the punishment that it deserved. Did Peck tell the truth? Why, there is the easiest way in the world to raise an issue; the easiest way in the world if Peck did not tell the truth, some witness can come here and testify that he did not. In all the attack on Peck the learned counsel forgot to have the testimony contradicted. Why, I recall one time in the trial of an action how tremendous energies were bent to the impeachment of a witness who had testified to a fact and the learned counsel who impeached it so devoted their energies to that single fact that they forgot entirely to contradict him. If Peck did not tell the truth here no one knows better than the learned counsel who sit at the table of this defendant how to meet it and how to beat it and they know, too, that it does not come by a vociferous denunciation of the witness who is entirely uncontradicted and if at any time, in representing Mr. Peck at all, I take the liberty of saying—if at any time Mr. Sulzer, this defendant, sees fit to join issue as to any question of fact with Mr. Peck on the witness stand in any county of the state, Mr. Peck will submit it to the following grand jury to say which one has committed perjury, he or this defendant, and if there was no corroboration whatever, there is not a member of this court here that would have the slightest justification for disbelieving Peck, but when you add to Peck's testimony the fact that he is corroborated in the strongest degree by Morgenthau, whom they do not dare to contradict or claim is untruthful; by Morgenthau to whom he made a similar dishonorable request; you have the testimony of Peck utterly uncontradicted and utterly irrefragable.

BRACKETT'S PERORATION

" Oh, members of the court, an acquittal to this man upon this evidence, would be a wretched gift indeed. Think of the

position in which he would be placed by such a verdict. Dead
forever among honorable men; cut off already by the unanswered evidence in this record from ever again striking
hands in friensdhip with those who devote their lives to lofty
purposes. And yet, an outcast among men, compelled for a
brief time to represent the honor and dignity of the Empire
state, to meet in official contact those, the latchets of whose
shoes he is unworthy to loose, by whom hence he is abhorred;
charged with the great duty to see that the laws which he himself has flagrantly violated are faithfully executed against
others; charged by the constitution to see that the laws
which he himself has flagrantly violated are faithfully executed
against others. Think of him—if your imagination can
carry you to such lengths, solemnly considering an application for a pardon for one who had been convicted of a violation
of the election law as to corrupt practices. Think of him in
all the multifarious situations requiring not only actual freedom from things criminal, but even from any suspicion thereof.
Knowing full well, appreciating to the utmost the degradation
that must come and the disgrace that must come upon this
unhappy man by your verdict of guilty, I still beg you not to
think that you will mitigate his punishment by a judgment of
acquittal of the charges here proved. It will not be your action
that will render him infamous for all the future. That future
is already his before you speak. If he takes the wings of the
morning and flies to the uttermost parts of the earth, the
record of his disgrace is there before him, to meet and greet
and abide with him. If he call upon the mountains and the
rocks to fall upon and hide him, he will still know no respite
from the disgrace that henceforth must walk by his side.

" Do not believe that you can lessen his punishment, whatever your decision here. All that you can do is to pronounce,
in form of law, in performance of your solemn duty, the judgment that will free the state from the contaminating touch of
this man from this time forth.

" It is to you alone that the people look for relief. Much
has been said on the part of the defendant that he derives his
title to his great office by election by the people and that you
may not rightly set aside the choice. Let me remind you that
the same people who elected him governor of the state have

placed in your hands, not simply the authority but the mandate, if two-thirds of your number find him guilty of crime unfitting him for the exercise of the duties of his office, to remove him. And there rests no heavier duty upon this body than that of convicting upon impeachment any official proved guilty. Forced upon you by no act or wish of your own, the situation requires you to do justice and fear not.

"The pen that writes the judgment of this court will be mightier for weal or for woe of this state and for all the people thereof, than any implement of war ever wielded by the arm of man—mightier to us awaiting its record—mightier to all the coming ages. If this last and best attempt at self-government, under which we have rested in security in all the century and a third of our national life, under which the state has been the leader of all the sisterhood that compose the republic—if this shall fail at the point that we may not remove from high office men confessedly guilty of crime, then, indeed, are we of all men the most miserable. We can transmit our trust as guardians of the present, 'as the heirs of all the ages in the foremost files of time,' to no successor save the coming generation. If that generation come to its inheritance blinded by the example of corrupt officials unpunished and unrebuked, we are near the fall, as we well deserve to be.

"You alone can deliver us from the body of this death, oh, wretched men that we are; you alone can deliver us from the body of this death.

"And so we leave this case with all its vast interests, the interests of all who love the state and are jealous for its honor and good fame in your hands; leave it with all that it means to the people and the future. Words fail me in the contemplation of all that your decision means. If it ever pleases the Father of us all to guide with his own hand those engaged in the performance of a great public duty, may that guidance be yours this day, and may the decision here rendered bear sure impress that it comes from a wisdom that maketh judgments far above the twilight judgments of this world."

The President: " I have prepared an opinion which I am
sorry to say is at some considerable length on the questions
involved in this issue that we are now disposing of.   It is not
my purpose to read all of it, but some part of it I think it is
proper I should read on this occasion.   Other parts of it I shall
merely abbreviate by stating the conclusions which I have
reached.

" The first article of impeachment, and the second article
of impeachment, and the sixth article of impeachment are
intimately connected, and in the opinion which I have written
they are treated together, and possibly it will be more convenient for me to treat them so now.   It will avoid repetition
when the vote is taken on the other two articles which I have
named.

" First, as to the facts, I regret to say that I am constrained
to find the facts as follows:

" I find that the respondent did take advantage of his nomination and candidacy for office to seek to personally enrich
himself by diverting the contributions which he might receive
for campaign purposes.

" I find that he did verify that by his oath, knowing it
to be false.   At the same time, I shall vote not guilty of these
articles for reasons which seem to me to dictate such a course,
whatever may be my personal opinion of the acts done and committed by this respondent.

" First, a moment as to the character of the acts.   The use
of this money for his own purposes other than political work
was not an offense.   On the contrary, it is very doubtful
whether it was not within his legal right to use it for any purpose
for which he saw fit.   I have pleaded that at length in my
opinion.   I have given the authorities which assert the proposition.

"As to his filing a false certificate, in my opinion, it is matter
of law that the corrupt practices act, now a part of the election
law, did require him to state the amounts and sources of all

election contributions, and in my judgment, nearly all, possibly with two or three exceptions, of the moneys paid to him, were such contributions.

".I find, however, this: That his oath to the truth of this statement was extra-judicial, so far as it related to his receipts. The election law does not require a verified statement while the penal law, which does require a verified statement, does not require that that statement should contain the receipts of the party making the statement.

NOT GUILTY OF LEGAL PERJURY

" It, therefore, is plainly extra-judicial to the oath, and it is elementary law. However, he was not guilty of legal. So much for that. But I am frank to say that if those acts had been committed during his incumbency in office I should have regarded his moral offense great enough to require his removal. But I am of the opinion that it cannot be considered as ground for impeachment, and that it would be an eminently dangerous doctrine to treat them as such.

" The question, however, whether these acts of the respondent constituted crimes is not decisive of the issue before us. They displayed such turpitude and delinquency that, if they had been committed during the respondent's incumbency of office, I think they would require his removal.

" This brings me to what I consider the serious question in the case: Can a public officer be impeached for acts committed when he was not an officer of this state? The question is not one of power, but one of right. Doubtless, if the assembly impeaches and the court convicts and removes from office, that judgment cannot be attacked, no matter what the reasons assigned for the removal may be, but the questions remain: Are such acts rightly ground for impeachment? Should this court so decide?

" Never before the present case has it been attempted to impeach a public officer for acts committed when he was not an officer of the state. No suggestion to that effect can be found in any opinion of courts of impeachment, in the arguments of counsel on such trials, or in the text writers. In several cases where it has been sought to remove the officers for such acts by judicial proceedings, the right has been expressly denied.

" In the year 1853, the judiciary committee of the assembly of this state reported that no person can be impeached who was not at the time of the commission of the alleged offenses, and at the time of the impeachment, holding some office under the laws of this state.

" In 1905 the assembly committee reported that Justice Warren B. Hooker was not subject to impeachment, because the acts did not constitute wilful and corrupt misconduct in office, but that the justice was subject to removal under the provisions of article II of section 6 of the constitution, which authorizes judges—mark, judges alone—judges to be removed by the joint action of two-thirds of both houses of the legislature.

" In this view, apparently, though not in express terms, the judiciary committee of the senate concurred and the justice was proceeded against, but not by impeachment.

" It is contended, however, that by the change made in the phraseology of the constitution of 1846 from that of the preceding constitution, a court of impeachment has been granted the right to remove a public officer on any ground that it may deem sufficient to disqualify. It seems to me it would be most unfortunate if such a doctrine were to prevail. The condition would be then that characterized by Judge Story as ' truly alarming.'

BARNARD CASE ONLY PRECEDENT

" I shall not now read the argument by which I seek to establish that the true interpretation of the constitution confers no such power. The only precedent cited by the learned managers for the assembly to support their claim is the impeachment of Judge Barnard in 1872. Some of the offenses charged had been committed in a previous term. The contention of the respondent in that case was that he was not liable to impeachment during one term for acts done in a previous term. This was overruled, and probably the weight of precedent throughout the country is in accord with that decision. I am at a loss, however, to see how that is an authority for the proposition when an officer can be impeached for acts done when he was not in office at all. In fact, the two cases in which that ruling has been followed, that is, the case of Nebraska, the impeachment of Governor Butler, and in Wisconsin, the impeachment of Judge Hubbel, the constitution expressly limited the power to impeach to misconduct in office. Therefore, in those cases it must have been decided that liability for offenses during a previous term, and liability for offenses when not in office, were entirely distinct propositions.

" It is urged that the offenses charged against the respondent were part of the means by which he obtained his office. A slight reference will show that this argument cannot be sustained. The respondent's dishonesty in diverting the money contributed to him could in no way help him to get the office. On the contrary, this failure to properly expend the money had, if any effect, a reverse one. The falsification of the statement filed by him could have no effect on his election, because that had already occurred, though doubtless the public was properly interested in knowing what had been contributed and in what amounts. The statement was not required of all persons elected to office, but of all those who had been candidates for office, and on elected and on defeated was equally imposed the duty of making the statement. The falsification was made by the respondent, not for any matter connected with his election, but to conceal the misappropriation of the money. The statute is directed solely to securing purity of politics and enacted for that purpose. The suggestion that it was intended also to insure publicity of the names of those who had assisted the successful candidates, so that people might judge of his subsequent conduct in office, and might know whether it was dictated by subservience to persons or interests who had contributed, I think unsound. A statute enacted for that would be, to say the least, of doubtful constitutionality.

" The constitution prescribes the oath of office to be taken by all public officers and then enacts; and no other oath, declaration or test shall be required as the qualification for any office of public trust. A statute prescribing that any one elected to office should say by whom and to what extent others had aided him as a condition of entry upon his office might well be deemed in conflict with this constitutional provision.

Reference was made there to a decision made by the supreme court. Will it be asserted that a law would or could require an officer, as a condition of his entry upon office, to declare under oath all his dealings during the past, or the property that he may own at the time in specific detail so that the people might judge how far personal interests affected his official actions ? The assertion is erroneous that impeachment proceedings are in no respects punitive and solely preventitive to safeguard the state. If the doctrine contended for is correct, a man guilty of any offense in his past life of sufficient gravity to justify his removal if committed when in office, may be removed from office without an opportunity to show that both his official conduct and private life during his official term have been of the most exemplary character. There is no statute of limitations on impeachment. The rule here contended for amounts in reality to an ex post facto disqualification from office for an offense which had no such penalty when committed, without affording an opportunity for showing either repentance or atonement. Men have committed serious crimes, even felonies and subsequently attained high public position. Instances will occur to all of us. If the legislature may define the grounds of impeachment—and I am not prepared to deny or affirm that proposition, being impressed by the argument of Judge Vann to that effect—it may prescribe for what offenses committed prior to the commencement of his term a candidate—during what period an officer is subject to impeachment. With such legislation an official tenure of office would be safeguarded by law and not dependent on the conflicting views of the various tribunals as to what renders a person unfit for office. For, unless the man is disqualified by law his fitness for office is to be determined solely by the electors. That is their right. The matter is of particular importance in this state because under the constitution the mere presentation of articles of impeachment against a governor or a judge suspends him from the powers and duties of his office. The very fact that we all agree that an officer may be impeached for offenses not amounting to crime so long as it absolutely unfits him on his entry into office makes it true, otherwise one who never violated any law may be removed because as a citizen he failed to conform to our ethical standards. When he enters upon office his conduct is necessarily subject to other restrictions.

" I vote not guilty."

ANARCHY

In voting the governor not guilty on Article IV, Presiding Chief Judge Cullen said in a firm voice and with emphatic manner:

" There is no evidence of any deceit or fraud, and to construe what passed between the respondent and Peck as a threat to remove the latter is to substitute suspicion for proof, vagaries of imagination for evidence. The point here urged may be criticized as technical, but if so, I hope that technicality will always be respected to the extent of preventing the trial of a man for one offense and convicting him of another. Far better the assembly, if it deem wise, should present new articles of impeachment and the state be put to the expense of another trial rather than a precedent should be set for what seems a violation of the ordinary principles of justice. Forms are often necessary to observe to protect the substance that lies behind them. Where they are not observed in substantial matters, law degenerates into oppression on the one hand, anarchy on the other."

GOVERNOR WILLIAM SULZER

By Edgar L. Murlin

William Sulzer, the forty-first governor of New York state, was born in an old brick house on Liberty Street, Elizabeth, New Jersey, on March 18, 1863. He is the second son of a family of seven children—five boys and two girls.

Lydia Sulzer, his mother, was of Dutch and Scotch-Irish ancestry. Thomas Sulzer, his father, was born in Germany, and while a student at Heidelberg University, in 1848, joined the patriot army and fought to establish constitutional government. He was captured and put in prison, but made his escape to Switzerland—thence emigrating to New York City in 1851. He married there, and the family afterward moved to Elizabeth, N. J., and subsequently bought a farm at Wheatsheaf, a suburb of the former place, where the son, William, aided in the farm work, until he went to New York to study law.

William Sulzer was educated in the country school, and graduated from a grammar school in 1877. His parents desired him to study for the ministry, but he became interested in the legal profession and entered Columbia College Law School. He also studied law with Parrish and Pendleton in New York city. In 1884 at the age of 21 years he was admitted to the practice of law at a general term of the Supreme Court held in New York city. and at once opened a law office and began his life work as a lawyer. Early in his career he became a successful lawyer, and throughout his long public service has been more or less engaged in the practice of his chosen profession.

He first entered political life prominently during the presidential campaign of 1884, which terminated in the election of Grover Cleveland as president. Mr. Sulzer upon this occasion was one of the campaign speakers of the democratic national committee. Ever since 1884 he has participated actively in the speaking campaigns of the democratic party at each successive election.

In 1889 Mr. Sulzer was elected an assemblyman from the fourteenth assembly district on an independent ticket, being then only twenty-six years of age, winning the election by a plurality of about 800 votes, his chief platform being that the Broadway railway franchise should not be granted in perpetuity to a private monopoly. He was re-elected to the assembly in 1890, 1891, 1892 and 1893, and each year by increased majorities.

Soon after Mr. Sulzer's election to the assembly he became widely known as an advocate of social, political and economic reforms, the chief among which were embodied in bills abolishing "sweat shops;" providing free lectures for working people; abolishing imprisonment for debt; providing for a constitutional convention; establishing " freedom of worship;" providing for the state care of the insane; for ballot reform; for the punishment of corrupt election practices; abolishing corporal punishment in the prisons; limiting hours of labor; establishing a Saturday half holiday; providing for a weekly payment of wages; establishing a woman's reformatory; and for an epileptic colony. These bills introduced and advocated by Mr. Sulzer became laws.

The " freedom of worship" bill gave to the inmate of any state institution the right to worship God according to the dictates of his conscience. Up to the passage of the " state care act," a large proportion of the insane people of the state whose relatives were too poor to have them cared for in private hospitals for the insane were in charge of local authorities. The " state care act" placed all the hospitals in charge of the state government and greatly improved the means taken to restore the inmates of these hospitals to health.

The title of the Saturday " half-holiday" act indicates the purpose of the measure—to give a longer period of rest for all workers. The women's reformatory was a much needed institution, and since it was established has finely accomplished the aims of those who suggested it. The law providing for free lectures for workingmen and working women has developed since in New York city into its magnificent lecture and musical entertainment system, where hundreds of lectures and musical entertainments are yearly given.

Mr. Sulzer, as a member of the assembly, also introduced and persuaded the legislature to pass a law for the Columbian celebration in New York city; a law codifying the statutes of

"RING-A-ROUND-THE-ROSY"

From the Philadelphia Ledger

the state; a law codifying the laws relating to the quarantine station; a law opening Stuyvesant Park, New York city, to the use of the people; a law opening New York's greatest art gallery, the Metropolitan Museum of Art, to people on Sunday; a law providing a prevailing rate of wage for working people; a law for a state forest park; the law for the preservation of the Adirondack forests; a law for the protection of the head waters of the Hudson river and the conservation of the natural resources of New York state; a law for the completion of the state Capitol; a constitutional amendment for the enlargement of the state's canals; a law establishing the Aquarium in New York city; a law establishing Bronx and Van Cortlandt parks in New York city; the law establishing the great New York Public library, with funds largely contributed by Ex-Governor Samuel J. Tilden; and the law compelling the New York Central Railroad Company to ventilate and light the Fourth Avenue tunnel.

Entering the assembly as one of its youngest members in 180, he rapidly won fame, and power and influence, and was one of the leaders in 1892, the democrats being in control of the body; Speaker of the assembly in 1893; and leader of the majority in 1894. As speaker of assembly he gave the people one of the cleanest, one of the most economical and one of the shortest sessions of the legislature in years. He was one of the fairest and most impartial presiding officers in the history of the state.

In 1894 Mr. Sulzer declined a renomination to the assembly, and was nominated for congress by the democratic party in the tenth congressional district, which then formed a part of New York county, on the " East Side"—a strong republican bailiwick. That year there was a republican " landslide" and the democratic party carried only five congressional districts north of Mason and Dixon's line. Three of these were in New York city and one was Mr. Sulzer's district. Mr. Sulzer was elected by over 800 majority, although David B. Hill, the democratic candidate for governor lost the district by over 200. Two years later Mr. Sulzer as a candidate for congress was the only democrat elected in his district, which he carried by thr the majority he received the first time This was the year of William J. Bryan's first campaign as a democratic candidate for president, and lthough Mr. Sulzer was a staunch supporter of Mr. Bryan, ie latter lost the tenth congress district by over 17,000 vots while Mr. Sulzer carried it by over 2,400. Four years later Ir. McKinley running against Mr. Bryan the second time cared the tenth congress district by 11,000, while Mr. Sulzer ws elected by over 5,000. In 1906 Mr. Sulzer carried the dirict by over 11,000, receiving 75 per cent. of the entire vot cast. He is the only democrat who has ever been able to carry the old tenth district since Cleveland carried it for predent in 1892.

For eighteen years Mr. Sulzer was a membe of congress. In that period he was the author of more tha twenty-five distinct bills embodying progressive legislatin. One law passed, provided for the raising of the battlesip Maine; a second law provided a light for the Statue of Lberty in New York harbor; a third law increased the pay of thletter carriers of the country. One of the chief laws framed ad pressed by him, created the Bureau of Corporations—by nich the anti-trust laws have since been enforced. He vasche author of and succeeded in passing a pension law for th orphans and widows of the deceased soldiers and sailors o' tr Union army. He introduced the bill to regulate the intersate commerce railroads; the bill in behalf of victims of tae isaster to the steamboat "General Slocum"; a bill to restorehe merchant marine by giving preferential duties to America ships; a bill for federal aid in the construction of good natnal roads; a bill to reduce the tariff, especially on goods, ares and merchandise manufactured in the United States ad sold cheaper in foreign countries than here; a bill placing n the free list meat, wood pulp, coal, lumber and white print aper; a bill to establish postal savings banks; a bill to establis a department of transportation; a bill to improve the foreig consular and diplomatic service; and a bill prohibiting the saing of any ship from the United States unless equipped with siety devices.

He introduced and secured the passage of (resolution expressing sympathy with the Cuban patriots; te resolution of sympathy for the Boers in their heroic struge to maintain their independence; the resolution of s-mpthy with oppressed Russian Jews; and the resolution a   ting the treaty with Russia, because that government refu to accept pass-the state; a law codifying the laws relating to the quarantine station; a law opening Stuyvesant Park, New York city, to the use of the people; a law opening New York's greatest art gallery, the Metropolitan Museum of Art, to people on Sunday; a law providing a prevailing rate of wage for working people; a law for a state forest park; the law for the preservation of the Adirondack forests; a law for the protection of the head waters of the Hudson river and the conservation of the natural resources of New York state; a law for the completion of the state Capitol; a constitutional amendment for the enlargement of the state's canals; a law establishing the Aquarium in New York city; a law establishing Bronx and Van Cortlandt parks in New York city; the law establishing the great New York Public library, with funds largely contributed by Ex-Governor Samuel J. Tilden; and the law compelling the New York Central Railroad Company to ventilate and light the Fourth Avenue tunnel.

Entering the assembly as one of its youngest members in 1890, he rapidly won fame, and power and influence, and was one of the leaders in 1892, the democrats being in control of the body; Speaker of the assembly in 1893; and leader of the minority in 1894. As speaker of assembly he gave the people one of the cleanest, one of the most economical and one of the shortest sessions of the legislature in years. He was one of the fairest and most impartial presiding officers in the history of the state.

In 1894 Mr. Sulzer declined a renomination to the assembly, and was nominated for congress by the democratic party in the tenth congressional district, which then formed a part of New York county, on the "East Side"—a strong republican bailiwick. That year there was a republican "landslide" and the democratic party carried only five congressional districts north of Mason and Dixon's line. Three of these were in New York city and one was Mr. Sulzer's district. Mr. Sulzer was elected by over 800 majority, although David B. Hill, the democratic candidate for governor lost the district by over 11,000. Two years later Mr. Sulzer as a candidate for congressman was the only democrat elected in his district, which he carried by three times the majority he received the first time he ran. This was the year of William J. Bryan's first campaign as a democratic candidate for president, and although Mr. Sulzer was a staunch supporter of Mr. Bryan, the latter lost the tenth congress district by over 17,000 votes while Mr. Sulzer carried it by over 2,400.   Four years later Mr. McKinley running against Mr. Bryan the second time carried the tenth congress district by 11,000, while Mr. Sulzer was elected by over 5,000.   In 1906 Mr. Sulzer carried the district by over 11,000, receiving 75 per cent. of the entire vote cast.   He is the only democrat who has ever been able to carry the old tenth district since Cleveland carried it for president in 1892.

For eighteen years Mr. Sulzer was a member of congress. In that period he was the author of more than twenty-five distinct bills embodying progressive legislation.   One law passed, provided for the raising of the battleship Maine; a second law provided a light for the Statue of Liberty in New York harbor; a third law increased the pay of the letter carriers of the country.   One of the chief laws framed and pressed by him, created the Bureau of Corporations—by which the anti-trust laws have since been enforced.   He was the author of and succeeded in passing a pension law for the orphans and widows of the deceased soldiers and sailors of the Union army. He introduced the bill to regulate the interstate commerce railroads; the bill in behalf of victims of the disaster to the steamboat "General Slocum"; a bill to restore the merchant marine by giving preferential duties to American ships; a bill for federal aid in the construction of good national roads; a bill to reduce the tariff, especially on goods, wares and merchandise manufactured in the United States and sold cheaper in foreign countries than here; a bill placing on the free list meat, wood pulp, coal, lumber and white print paper; a bill to establish postal savings banks; a bill to establish a department of transportation; a bill to improve the foreign consular and diplomatic service; and a bill prohibiting the sailing of any ship from the United States unless equipped with safety devices.

He introduced and secured the passage of a resolution expressing sympathy with the Cuban patriots; the resolution of sympathy for the Boers in their heroic struggle to maintain their independence; the resolution of sympathy with oppressed Russian Jews; and the resolution abrogating the treaty with Russia, because that government refused to accept pass-

ports issued to Jewish citizens of this country. He also introduced a resolution to make October 12th a legal holiday, to
be called "Columbus Day;" and he introduced and secured
the passage of a resolution congratulating the people of China
on the establishment of a republic.

Mr. Sulzer wielded a large influence in congress, especially
when he became chairman of the House Committee on Foreign
Affairs. He steadily opposed any intervention in the affairs
of Mexico. He stood firmly for peace, and became the eloquent
champion of the rights of Latin America. He was the author
of the resolution to abrogate the Russian treaty of 1832,
already referred to. It was passed by a vote of 300 to 1—a
memorable victory for the rights of American citizens.

Resolutions, of which he was the author, provided for an
investigation of the corrupt sale of the New York Custom
House; started the movement for the election of United
States senators by the direct vote of the people; originated
the income tax amendment to the United States constitution;
brought about the abrogation of the Russian Treaty; and the
establishment of the parcels post.

Foremost among the achievements of Mr. Sulzer's career in
congress was the passage in the House during the session of
1912 of his bill establishing a Department of Labor with a secretary in the cabinet. Smiled at as a preposterous idea ten years
ago, this bill finally passed the lower house unanimously. Its
passage in the senate followed.

The signing of this Department of Labor bill was the last
official act of President Taft, and he did so on the personal
appeal of Mr. Sulzer. The bill was first introduced by Mr.
Sulzer in 1904, and was reintroduced and advocated by him
in every Congress since that time. In support of the measure,
on one occasion, he thus addressed the House of Representatives:

" My bill for a department of labor is a meritorious measure
and it should be a law. It is the first bill ever introduced in
congress to create a department of labor. It is the first
attempt to systematically classify labor in an intelligent way
that has ever been presented in a bill in Congress, and its
enactment into law will evidence a disposition on the part of
the government to see to it that labor gets full recognition, the
dignity of having a voice in the councils of state, and the oppor-

tunity to have its claims dispassionately discussed. Give
labor this boon and the 'labor question' will be reduced to
the minimum.

"The expense of maintenance of the department of labor
will practically be but little more than the expense for the
maintenance of the various bureaus at the present time.
These bureaus will all be in the department of labor. I do
not think anyone will take exception to the bill on the ground
that it is going to increase the expenses of the government.
A few thousand dollars in a matter of so much moment will be
of little consequence. I believe that if this bill were on the
statute books today it would be a long step toward better social,
economical and commercial conditions; a progressive advance along the avenues of industrial peace; that it would go
far to allay jealousy, establish harmony, promote the general
welfare, make the employer and employee better friends,
prevent strikes, lockouts, blacklists, boycotts, and business
paralysis, and every year save millions and millions of dollars
of losses which result necessarily therefrom.

"Capital as well as labor should favor this department of
labor, because it will go far to solve the labor problem and
bring about industrial peace. For years this legislation has
been advocated by the wage-earners of the country. The bill
meets with their approbation and has the approval of the best
thought in our land. It has been indorsed by some of the
ablest thinkers, some of the wisest political economists, and
many of our leading newspapers. The time is ripe, it seems to
me, for the creation of a department of labor with a secretary
having a seat in the cabinet, with all the rights and powers
conferred by this bill. It will bring labor and capital closer
together, and one is dependent on the other. They should be
friends—not enemies—and walk hand in hand in the march
along the paths of mutual prosperity. This bill, if it becomes
a law, will go far to prevent serious labor troubles in the future,
do much to solve existing labor problems, and every friend of
industrial peace should aid in its enactment. The employers of
labor, as well as the employees themselves, whether they belong
to trades unions or not, are all, so far as I have been able to
ascertain, in accord with the principles of this progressive
legislation and heartily approve of this bill."

It was not until 1912, however, that Mr. Sulzer succeeded in having the bill favorably reported, and when it came before the house it passed without a dissenting vote.

After Mr. Sulzer's election as governor he returned to Washington and spent about three weeks in congress—partly for the purpose of urging the passage in the senate of his bill creating a department of labor. It passed the senate the latter part of February, 1913.

For two weeks prior to its passage friends of the measure were in frequent communication with Governor Sulzer reporting its progress. On its passage the governor exchanged several telegrams and letters with President Taft, urging him to give the measure his official approval. In the senate the bill was slightly amended, which made necessary its re-passage in the house, where it was in charge of Mr. Sulzer's friend, Congressman William B. Wilson, who has been made secretary of labor by President Wilson.

Mr. Sulzer's bill provides for three assistant secretaries of labor, the work of the department being divided as follows: manufacturing and agricultural industries; building of highways and transportation industries, including the telephone and telegraph business; and the building and mercantile industries.

Each of the principal divisions of the department of labor will have a bureau of statistics to collect and report at least once each year as to the conditions of labor in each of the different industries. Special attention will also be given to the collection and publication of statistics regarding the unemployed.

One prime object of the new department of labor will be the establishment of boards of arbitration and conciliation to prevent strikes, as well as to prevent labor disturbances among employees or corporations doing an interstate commerce business.

Mr. Sulzer's record in congress is a monument to his indefatigable industry, and the enactment of progressive legislation along constructive lines.

In January, 1908, Mr. Sulzer married Miss Clara Rodelheim, of Philadelphia, Pa., and Mrs. Sulzer is as democratic and as popular with the people as her distinguished husband.

Mr. Sulzer was elected governor on November 5, 1912, by a plurality of 205,454, which was the largest plurality ever given in the state of New York for any candidate for governor. He received 649,559 votes as the democratic candidate, while Job E. Hedges, republican, received 444,105, and Oscar S. Straus, progressive, 393,183. Mr. Sulzer's large plurality was the more remarkable since Mr. Straus in his campaign declared for the reforms of which Mr. Sulzer for many years had been one of the leading advocates.

It will add to the interest of this character sketch of William Sulzer to describe some of his habits and recount some cf his sayings which reveal him as a governor different in many respects from any who have held office before him. During the campaign which preceded his election he made few promises as to his future policies. One of his oft repeated epigrams was "An ounce of performance is worth a ton of promise." And he pointed out that his record of legislative achievement during five years at Albany and eighteen years at Washington gave the best forecast of what principles would certainly guide him in administering the office of governor. " The record of the past," he said over and over again, "is the best guarantee for the future."

In many of his speeches he said "when I am elected governor the latch-string of the door of the executive office at Albany will always be on the outside, and it will not be so high but that the lowliest can reach it, and the humblest citizen of the state may come to Albany and see the governor and be treated with as much consideration as the richest and most powerful."

. This promise which caused smiles of incredulity with some who did not know the man who made the promise has been carried out with a faithfulness that has resulted in practices which have destroyed many official precedents and rules of official procedure; precedents and rules which have prevailed for many years. It has been in some administrations the rule that few could see the governor except through an appointment made with the secretary and to make such an appointment was often difficult. Only persons of distinction could get an appointment without first stating the object of their visit and many who wished to make such engagements were unable to show satisfactory evidence that they them-

selves or the subject of their visit, were of sufficient importance
to merit a personal interview with the chief executive.

Since Mr. Sulzer has been governor all this is changed.
Man, woman or child, black or white, rich or poor, high or
low, everyone who wants to see the governor sees him and the
richest and most powerful must wait and take their turn.
This has caused some remonstrances to which the governor
only replies " I am a democrat and must treat all alike."

So the governor sees all his visitors in the large reception
room of the executive chamber. Many have private conversations with him, seated by the side of his big desk. But
there are no secret interviews in the so-called " back office."
This is the governor's workshop where he needs only his
stenographer.

There was considerable comment when on Inauguration
Day the customary military parade was omitted and the governor walked from the " People's House" to the Capitol to take
the oath of office and deliver his inaugural address. " I wish,"
wrote Governor Sulzer to the secretary of state, " that all the
arrangements for my inauguration to be as simple, and as
economical, and as democratic as possible." The simplicity
which characterized the inaugural ceremonies has been paral-
leled in many ways in connection with the governor's daily
life. The executive mansion has been rechristened the
" People's House." The public was invited to the legislative
reception and the attendance was the largest ever known.
Albany newspapers declared that 10,000 persons were in
attendance.

The rule that the governor must be attended when receiving
visitors at the executive chamber by either his military secretary or his private secretary is ignored. So is the rule that on
the street and at public functions one of his secretaries shall
always accompany him. Sometimes the governor is accompanied and sometimes he is not. He prefers to go and come
alone. Several times he has attended public dinners in the
evening and afterward walked from the hotel where they were
given to his home. The governor always walks to and from
the Capitol. His life and habits are simple in every way and
democratic to the extreme.

Not only does the governor show his democratic impulses

and his disposition to keep closely in touch with the common man by meeting personally as many of his constituents as possible, but he keeps up a large daily correspondence with persons from all parts of the state, which makes his mail five times as voluminous as that of any of his predecessors, and he prizes highly not only letters of commendation, but also letters which contain words of counsel or criticism regarding public policies, appointments made, and legislative measures advocated.

Mr. Sulzer is progressive in his ideas; takes a broad view of every question; has few prejudices, and those only against intrenched wrongs he wants to see remedied. In his efforts for a common humanity he knows no race, no creed, and no previous condition. He is for man—that is all.

In his speech of acceptance, Governor Sulzer said: " I will go into office without a promise except my promise to all the people to serve them faithfully and honestly and to the best of my ability. I am free, without entanglements and shall remain free. If elected I shall follow the street called straight and the executive office will be in the Capitol. When I take the oath as governor I shall enforce the laws fearlessly and impartially, but with malice toward none. Those who know me best know that I stand firmly for certain fundamental principles—for liberty under law; for civil and religious freedom; for constitutional government; for the old integrities and the new humanities; for equality before the law; for equal rights to all and special privileges for none; for the cause that lacks assistance; against the wrongs that needs resistance; and for unshackled opportunity as the beacon-light of individual hope and the best guarantee for the perpetuity of our free institutions. No influence will control me but the influence of my conscience, and my determination to do my full duty to all the people, as God gives me the light."

In his first annual message to the legislature of 1913, Mr. Sulzer said:

" In view of the increasing expenditures in the administration of state affairs, mounting higher and higher each succeeding year, and necessarily imposing onerous burdens on our taxpayers, I recommend genuine retrenchment in every department of the state, to the end that expenditures be kept down to the minimum and taxation materially reduced.

" Unless this is done in a systematic way additional methods must be devised to raise greater revenue. I am in sympathy with the oppressed taxpayers of our state and to the best of my abili y will aid you in your efforts to lighten their burden. Nothing will gratify me more than to be able to say to the people when you adjourn that this legislature was one of the most economical in the history of the state, and by its wisdom and economies wiped out every vestige of direct tax.

" The way to stop waste and extravagance is to retrench and economize. A cursory examination into state affairs convinces me that many expenditures can be stopped and efficiency promoted if every state officer will clean house, stop waste, and practice every economy consistent with good government and the orderly administration of public affairs.

" Let us do our best, day in and day out, to save wherever it is possible, and make honesty and simplicity, economy and efficiency, the watchwords of our administration of the people's business."

The governor also said in his annual message that many worthy citizens had suggested to him the advisability of examining, through a committee of inquiry, into every department of the state government to ascertain where expenditures could be checked and the money of the taxpayers saved. A few days later he appointed John N. Carlisle, of Watertown; John H. Delaney, of the Borough of Brooklyn, New York; and H. Gordon Lynn, of the Borough of Manhattan, New York, a committee of inquiry, to examine and investigate the management and affairs of any and all departments, boards, bureaus or commissions in the state. Thus for the first time in the history of the state a committee of inquiry was established. The committee in its initial work recommended a decrease in the proposed appropriations for certain departments. It followed up this action by an exhaustive consideration of the sinking funds of the state, reaching the conclusion that there had been an excess of the necessary accumulations for the support of the sinking funds to the amount of $18,773,045.97. Commenting upon the report, Governor Sulzer said:

" This huge accumulation of unnecessary moneys by the imposition of an inequitable tax year after year is the result of poor business administration of state affairs and would ultimately amount to a sum of money in excess of the requirements of the whole amount of authorized bond issues of $234,000,000."

Still later the committee of inquiry stated that at every turn in their examination of state affairs they had noticed a lack of system and method in the administration of the business of the state, a wide departure from anything like uniformity and an unscientific and wasteful absence of appropriate provisions for the promotion of ecenomy. With the view of remedying these evils the committee of inquiry proposed the creation of a department of efficiency and economy; of a state board of est mate; of a state board of contract and supply; and the passage of a bill giving the state comptroller ample powers of auditing the accounts of all state departments.

Commenting upon the bills to carry out these reforms Governor Sulzer said: " These bills meet my approval and will now be introduced in the legislature. They will put the administration of state affairs on a business basis, I want to do that, and these bills will do it. I trust they will promptly be passed. When they become laws it will mean the saving to the taxpayers of millions of dollars every year."

In a message addressed to the legislature early in his administration, Governor Sulzer called attention to the necessity of remedial legislation regarding stock exchanges, treating of " manipulation," " concerted movements to deceive," " short sales," " hypothecation of securities," " trading against customers' orders," " usury," etc. Eleven bills were prepared by the governor and introduced in both houses of the legislature to carry his recommendations into effect.

The second week of his administration Governor Sulzer appointed a special commission to collect facts, receive suggestions and make recommendations as to changes in the public health laws and their administration. This special commission of eminent citizens consisted of Hermann M. Biggs, M. D., chairman; Homer Folks, secretary; John A. Kingsbury, assistant secretary; E. R. Baldwin, M. D., W. E. Milbank, M. D., Mary Adelaide Nutting, John C. Otis, M. D., and Ansley Wilcox.

" In five weeks," as Governor Sulzer said in a message to the legislature, "the commission collected a surprisingly large amount of authoritative information with regard to public health work in the various parts of the state, and submitted findings and recommendations of great interest for the improvement of the laws relating to health."

At a complimentary dinner given in his honor at the celebrated Lotos Club, New York city, Saturday night, February 8, 1913, Mr. Sulzer spoke in part, as follows:

"As many of you know, from reading the newspapers, I have been a very busy man ever since I took the oath of office as the governor of the state To tell the truth I have been working on an average about eighteen hours out of the twenty-four, and this is the first public dinner, or reception, or entertainment, I have been able to attend since the first day of January. Being governor of New York is no easy job—that is if you want to be the governor.

" The members of the Lotos Club are famous for their knowledge of literature, and are familiar, therefore, with the advice Don Quixote gave his faithful follower on 'How to be a Governor;' and the subtle reply of that diplomatic individual when he said: 'He would rather be Sancho Panza and go to Heaven, than be a governor and go to Hell.' Many people, I am reminded daily, take the same view concerning the ultimate dest'ny of the governor of the Empire state. All of which goes to prove that although we live in a progressive period, human nature is much the same now as it was in the days of the gallant Knight of de la Mancha.

" Before I was elected I made up my mind, if successful, to be the governor of all the people. I am going to be. I intend to do the best I can, in my own way, according to my own light, regardless of the political future, or of personal consequences, because I know that the political future is uncertain and that consequences are unpitying.

" Long ago I made a vow to the people that if I became governor no influence would control me but the dictates of my conscience and my determination to do my duty day in and day out, as I see the right. Have no fear. I shall stick to that.

"I stand now where I always have stood, and where I always

will stand—for certain fundamental principles—for freedom of speech; for the right of lawful assembly; for the freedom of the press; for liberty under `aw; for civil and religious freedom; for constitutional government; for equality and justice to all; for home rule; for the reserved rights of the state; for equal rights to every one, and special privileges to no one; and for unshackled opportunity as the beacon light of individual hope, and the best guarantee for the perpetuity of our free institutions.

"New York is the greatest state in the Union. It should always be an exemplar of economical and efficient and progressive administration. As its governor I shall, in so far as I can, give the people of the state an honest, an efficient, an economical and a business-like administration of public affairs. I say businesslike advisedly, because I assure the business men in every part of our state that they can rely on me at all times to do my utmost to promote the commercial interests of our commonwealth. I realize how important they are, and shall always be exceedingly careful to take no step that will jeopardize the financial and the commercial supremacy of the first state in the Republic.

"Suffice it to say that I am a friend of every business whether big or little, so long as it is legitimate, and will always have its welfare in view in the administration of state affairs. To this end I shall continue to work unceasingly for quicker and bet er transportation agencies, and for improved and larger terminal facilities, in order that New York shall continue to receive her just share of the trade and the commerce of the country.

"Whenever in doubt, it is my purpose to confide in the people, and I indulge the hope that when my official term comes to an end I shall have accomplished something to merit their approval, and to justify the confidence they have reposed in the rectitude of my intentions.

"That is all there is to it, and that is all there is to say just now. I have little vanity. I want no glory—no credit for doing my duty—no future preferment—and when the office the people gave me goes back to the people—to whom it belongs —to give to some other man—I say again, and I say advisedly —I want to retire from the misrepresentat`ons and the disappointments of political life—to a little farm, by the side of the road, and be the friend of man."

Mr. Sulzer is a hard worker—and puts in about sixteen hours a day toiling for the state. He resorts to no political arts or personal pretenses. He is just a plain, common, every-day plodding good-natured citizen, sincere, square, and loyal in every fiber of his manhood. He does not command support by subtle influences, trickery, hypocrisy, self-advertising and the command of wealth, like some others, but succeeds solely through his brains, his intrepidity and his fidelity to friends and to princ ples. He never had a press agent. He never financed a publicity bureau. He never paid for puffs. He does his work day in and day out, year after year, quietly, modestly, confident the results will ultimately speak for themselves, and conscious of the fact that the knowledge of duty well done, for duty's sake, and in the cause of freedom and righteousness and humanity, is after all the best reward and the most lasting recompense a public servant can have.

Mr. Sulzer has always been a very modest man concerning his own achievements. And yet the more the people know about Mr. Sulzer the better they like him. As the record of his achievements is unfolded the greater and the grander stands out the man—the plain man of the plain people—and they know him and they love him—this man who does things for the people for the intense love of doing them, and goes his way day after day happy in the consciou ness that there is work to do, and that he is doing his share in his day and generation to make the world better and happier as the Master intended.

Governor Sulzer is a "commoner" through and through. The more you know about him—the more you see of him—the more you study him at close range—the more you like him and the more you will appreciate what he has done, and glory in his trials and his triumphs. He needs no eulogy His career of struggle for higher and better things from a. poor farm boy to the governorship of the greatest state in the Union is an epic poem.

Mr. Sulzer is of large stature, standing over six feet in height with a weight of 185 pounds, which he carries with the grace of a trained athlete. He is abstemious; has sandy hair and steel blue eyes that look straight into yours, and read your innermost thoughts. During the war with Spain he organized a regiment of volunteers and was elected colonel, but for political reasons it was not called into active service. Two of his younger brothers—a captain and a lieutenant— died in the service of their country.

At a recent banquet of the Home Rule Conference and Municipal Government Association of New York State and the legislative committee of the New York State Conference of Mayors, at the Hotel Ten Eyck, Albany, N. Y., Thursday evening, March 13, 1913, Mr. Sulzer said in part:

" The sentiment back of the demand for home rule is the same sentiment that animated the patriotic fathers in their heroic struggle for independence. It breathes the spirit of the Declaration, and it voices the aspirations of every lover of liberty.

" No man is more in favor of home rule than I am. It is a part of my political religion. I believe in local-self-govern- ment for village, and for town, and for city, and for county; and I know that the people are capable of self-government. A denial of this proposition is an indictment of American intelligence and patriotism.

" In my message to the legislature I said: ' Let us stand squarely for home rule and local self-government—home rule for the state—for the reserved rights of the state—against encroachments by the central government at Washington. Home rule for the counties, and the cities, and the towns, and the villages of the state, against legislative tinkering and invasion.' I stand for that. There will be no step backward.

" I believe in local autonomy as a fundamental right. The experience of years has taught us that many of the evils the people want remedied; that most of the things the people want done; can be remedied, and can be done, through local agencies, without interference by the national and state legis- latures.

" Let me urge the people to be firm at all times for home rule; and for the rights of the people in their respective communi- ties to govern themselves politically, without legislative inter- ference except when absolutely necessary. In the future as in the past I shall adhere to that without deviation. The

people can count on me, as the governor of the state, not to
interfere with home rule in any locality if I can possibly avoid
it.   If I do interfere, directly, it must be for the general welfare, and then only in a case that rises superior to local con-
siderations and for the good of the common weal.

"I am now, and ever have been, in accord with that fundamental principle of American statesmanship which asserts
that the states in themselves are sovereigns, and I stand un-
equivocally for their reserved rights against the tendencies of
centralization of the federal government.   We know that the
states are divided into counties, and that each county, in so
far as possible, should have the right to govern itself in civil
and political matters.   For that reason, as the governor, I am
determined to recognise the rights of the counties in every
part of the state through their duly constituted officials and
their electoral machinery.

"Then again, the counties have within their confines, the
villages, the towns, and the cities; and I want to see the greatest amount of local authority concentrated in the hands of
the officials of these constituent parts of the counties of the
state.

"As Thomas Jefferson well said, 'If we are directed from
Washington when to sow and when to reap we shall soon want
bread.'   If that applies to the seat of the federal government
in connection with the rights of the states, it applies with
greater force to the seat of the state government in connection
with the rights of the counties, the cities, the towns, and the
villages of the state.

"We know that in the diversification of power lies the safety
of the state.   We cannot deny the proposition that one generation is as capable as another of taking care of its own local
affairs and solving its own local problems.   Ralph Waldo
Emerson said: 'All forms of government are ridiculous except
those which men make for themselves.'

"You remember Mark Twain once said, 'when in doubt
take a drink.'   My policy as governor is a little different—
when in doubt I shall confide in the people.   I enunciated that
idea in my inaugural address, and have been practising it now
and then as occasion arises.   I know the power of public
opinion.   I believe that all the people are wiser than a few of

the people. Public opinion is the safest guide for legislation
as well as political conduct. As the Bible says: ' In a multitude of counsel there is much wisdom.'

" Cities should be as free from interference from the state as
the states should be free from interference by the federal
government. Municipalities should be independent in matters
of purely local concern, and they should have the right to adopt
their own charter, just as the people of the state have the
right to adopt their own constitution. Municipalities should
have the right to call a city charter convention the same as
the people of the state have the right to call a constitutional
convention.

" The trouble with the cities is not too much democracy
but too little democracy. There is too much state control.
We need home rule to create city democracies, like those of
Athens and Rome. It was *freedom* that inspired in these
cities local *patriotism* such as seldom has been equalled in all
the annals of the world.

" Home rule is the demand on the part of the people to be
trusted—trusted to govern themselves. Democracy rather
than class interest is becoming intelligently organized. With
the growth of cities they are becoming political units of great
importance to the state. The opponents of home rule distrust
democracy, but I do not fear the people. I fear special privileges. Home rulers trust the people, their opponents fear
popular control.

" It is because of the survival of old monarchial ideas that
our cities are not more independent. We proceed on the theory
that the sovereignty which grants a city charter is a power
similar to that formerly wielded by kings and emperors. It is
a concession apparently that we grant to cities power to do
this or that. But in a republic such as ours the sovereignty
resides in the people. The electors are the sovereigns. All
just governments obtain their powers from the consent of the
people.

"We have the highest authority for home rule. Thomas
Jefferson believed that the permanency of our nation depended
upon distribution of the powers of government.

" The diversification of power is necessary for the safety of
the state. Home rule is the aspiration of the progressive

spirit of our times, which demands that affairs of government shall be placed close to the people and kept there. When legislation for a community is carried on at a distance remote public opinion fails to properly influence that legislation.

"Public hearings are efforts to overcome this evil. It is better to have our legislative body close to the community than to take representatives of a community long distances to meet the legislature.

"Let our cities be kept as free from state invasion as the state is kept free from national interference. As states adopt their own constitutions so should cities adopt their own charters. The cure for the evils of democracy is more democracy."

Mr. Sulzer, without doubt, is the best vote getter today in the state of New York. He has always run thousands of votes ahead of his ticket. He has never been defeated. He is a man of the people and for the people.

He is a 32nd degree Mason, has held all the honors in the craft, and years ago became a life member. He is a member of Lloyd Aspinall Post, G. A. R.; the Army and Navy Union; the Eagles; the Pioneers of Alaska; the Arctic Brotherhood; the National-Democratic Club; Manhattan Club; Press Club; Masonic Club; and other social clubs in Washington and New York city. His church affiliations are with the Presbyterian denomination. His most profitable reading has been history, philosophy and political economy; and his advice to young men is to work hard, cultivate good habits, have a motive in life and a positive determination to succeed.

Mr. Sulzer is making good as the governor of the people, and is courageously meeting the expectations and the sanguine predictions of his true friends. He is a very busy man, but his spare hours are spent in writing a book on "Political Economy," which his friends believe will be a standard textbook on economic principles. His rugged honesty, his loyalty to his friends, his fearless devotion to every duty, his fidelity to principle, his ability as a champion of the oppressed in every land and in every clime have made his name a household word among the people of America, and as an apostle of freedom forever enshrined him in the hearts of humanity.

REPORT IN RELATION TO CAPITOL CONTRACTS

By John A. Hennessy

Supervising Auditor to the Trustees of Public Buildings

(William Sulzer, Governor, Martin H Glynn, Lieutenant Governor, Alfred
E Smith, Speaker of the Assembly)

April 8, 1913

On the assignment of the governor, the supervising auditor
to the trustees made án investigation of the state architect's
office in respect to certain contracts in the Capitol. This
investigation was made after a committee of architects representing the American Institute of Architects in the state of
New York had reported to the governor that the state architect,
H. W. Hoefer, and the deputy state architect, J. P. Powers,
were not "by training, experience, or ability competent to
fulfill the duties which inhere in their offices. We regret to
find ourselves under the necessity of recommending the acceptance of the resignations of the state architect and his
deputy, or, wanting the resignations, their summary and
immediate removal."

The supervising auditor found that the state architect had
two companies on percentage contracts wiring the Capitol.
The state architect had made a private contract with the New
York Construction Company, and, at the request of Governor
Dix, had put on the Tucker Electrical Construction Company.
Conditions revealed that the state architect was paying
double overhead charges for supervisors and foremen on the
two jobs and for double timekeepers.

My investigation disclosed that the state architect against
the protest of R. A. Sanders, superintendent of construction,
had removed the state inspectors who took the time on these
two electrical jobs, and had designated two men and put them
on the payroll of the contractors. The state architect had
also requested the Tucker Electrical Construction Company
to remove its foreman "as a personal favor," and appoint one
J. F. Hogan foreman of the job.

THE CLIMBERS

From the Albany Knickerbocker Press

The timekeeper on the Tucker contract was J. J. Gaffney, a sufferer from pulmonary tuberculosis. He checked up the material for his company and at the same time for the state— both material and labor.

The timekeeper for the New York Construction Company was Michael J. Rooney, a marble polisher, who certified to the value of electrical materials, lumber, etc., and who checked up the amount of labor on the job. Further investigation showed that these two electrical contracts were really run by W. S. Costa, secretary to the state architect.

Rooney, who was put on the payroll of the New York Construction Company and checked up the materials and labor for the state, was designated by a political leader. This is also true of Gaffney.

PADDED PAYROLL

An examination of the bills of the two companies showed that the charges for labor were entirely out of proportion to the cost of material, and an analysis made of the bills disclosed that many of the men drawing per diem wages had only a pay-roll connection with the work. The manager for the New York Construction Company in defending the bills for December, January and February admitted that men had been put to work on the order of Mr. Costa and the state architect; that many of the men were unnecessary, but that the company was directly under the instructions of the state architect and his secretary—it being a percentage proposition—and therefore had nothing to do except to carry out the instructions from the state architect's office. It was admitted that the labor in large part was wholly unnecessary, but the contractors held that it was not any of their business to go beyond the instructions of the state architect and his secretary.

The bills of the New York Construction Company when checked up showed a larger percentage of material to labor by more than 50 per cent. than the bills of the Tucker Electrical Construction Company. An analysis of the work done by the Tucker Electrical Construction Company, which had the percentage job under state architect Ware from April, 1911, to June, 1912, shows that under Mr. Ware the percentage of labor was $1.89 to $1.00 of material. The Tucker people were off

the job from June until September, when at the request of
Governor Dix they were given part of the rewiring of the Capitol,
and then they came under the direction of state architect
Hoefer, who selected their foreman for them—Hogan—and the
timekeeper, who checked up their materials and also checked
for the state. Up to the first of February, the percentage of
labor was $10.94 of labor to $1.00 of material, as against $1.89
of labor to $1.00 of material under Mr. Ware. From the middle
of October until the 27th of November the labor was $3,002.06
against $138.21 of material. From the 28th of November to
the 24th of December, there was $8,502.02 of labor to $915.49
of material, and in January there was $8,590.58 of labor to
$782.51 of material. In the fourteen months under architect
Ware, the Tucker Electrical Construction Company showed
$7,188.82 for labor against $3,947.44 for material. In the four
months under Hoefer, the bills showed $25,911.11 for labor as
against $2,255.39 for material.

PROVED TO BE FRAUDULENT

It was clear that the payrolls had been padded, not only as
to actual time worked, but also as to men actually on the job.
When asked to identify eight men down at $5.50 per day, the
supervising auditor was informed that they were masons who
had worked overtime in the secretary of state's office. The
president and treasurer of the Mason's Union of Albany,
summoned to testify as to these masons, said that only two of
the eight were known to him and that only two of the eight
had worked on the job. The two men who did work on the
job, D. McKeon and J. Murphy, testified that they had seen
no other masons at work. The president of the Tucker
Electrical Construction Company, when asked to give the names
and addresses of men on the payroll for amounts varying
from $500 down to $304.44 for 27 days' work done, and down to
$100 for the same period, could not give the addresses and said
that they were picked up here and there and no record kept
of them, although this is a construction company which does
work throughout the country and especially east of Pittsburgh.
An effort to obtain the names and addresses of men who were
charged up with the work was fruitless. When the president
of the corporation and the superintendent were asked to

identify the men as to trades, the identification was proved to be fraudulent.   One of the men, personally well-known to the supervising auditor, was put down as an electrician, when as a matter of fact he is not and did not work on the job.   When summoned to testify he admitted that he had done no work of that kind.   Just how many fraudulent names were on the rolls of the Tucker Electrical Construction Company, it is impossible to say, inasmuch as the addresses of the men cannot be obtained.   The total bill of the Tucker Electrical Company submitted up to the first of February amounts to $41,212.65, and with the February and March work will total close to $50,000.

The work of the New York Construction Company on the same contract for rewiring the Capitol amounted on the percentage contract up to the first of February to $30,486.22, and including the February and March bills will be close to $38,000. This company also has a lump sum contract on the west side of the Capitol building amounting to a trifle more than $46,000; so that the total of the rewiring up to date is about $125,000.

It should be said for the New York Construction Company, that while it employed too many men, its work shows up splendidly in comparison with that of the Tucker people. The percentage of labor is $48.45 to $36.70 for material in December.   In January it was $53.84 for labor to $32.05 for material.   In November it was $46.75 of labor to $38.16 of material.   Thus it will be seen that it was about $1.50 of labor to $1.00 of material, as against more than $10.00 of labor to $1.00 of material under a similar contract by the Tucker people.

James R. Strong, president of the Tucker Company, was asked to give a complete analysis of the work showing the actual material put in, where it was put in, and the labor upon it.   And this in turn was analyzed by Charles G. Armstrong, consulting engineer and architect, in the Singer Building, 149 Broadway, New York City.

SOME SAMPLE CHARGES

This analysis disclosed that the electrical workers were paid $1,000 for relaying tarpaulins, moving furniture and taking up and relaying carpets in the office of the secretary of state, and

$1,000 more for extra overtime on the job, making $2,000 for doing something which does not belong to the electrical business at all and which could have been done by three or four laborers on the Capitol. The company says they moved the furniture in and out every day, getting it ready for the clerks at 9.00 a. m., and took up the carpets and relaid them.

The overseer on the job, that is the superintendent over the foreman, charged $600 for his work and then $600 for his overtime, together with $130 for railroad fares and expenses and $150 for his board, and then the company charged their percentage on the superintendent's time, his overtime, and their percentage on his railroad fares and his meals.

It would be burdensome to continue itemizing these bills, about every third item is extra for overtime. There is one item of $1,147.40 for overtime, and several items of an even $200 a piece for overtime. The temporary lighting in four rooms included $120 for overtime, $90 for general labor; $200 additional for temporary light in rooms for the wiremen, $200 extra cost for overtime; $200 for cutting granite and tile in the secretary of state's office, and $200 extra for overtime. The bill runs along in this same way.

There was no authority from the state architect's office to work overtime, except an order to do so in the secretary of state's office, if necessary. And the contract of the Tucker people provided that where there was any such work, there should be a separate shift of men at the regular rate of wages. It was not within the authority of the state architect to destroy this contract without the assent of the trustees, but he did so, or the contractors say he did so, with the result that men alleged that they worked 20 consecutive hours a day for 27 days in November, for 26 days in December, and for 27 days in January. The foreman on the Tucker job, who was placed there at the personal request of the state architect, worked 24 hours out of 24 hours in many instances, according to the payroll. The payroll is checked up by Gaffney, an admitted consumptive, who when called to give testimony was found to be in a hospital in New York.

LIBERAL WITH STATE MONEY

The consulting engineer, Mr. Armstrong, has gone over the itemized bill of the Tucker Company, and his report to the trustees of public buildings shows that under the percentage contract the cost for each light outlet is $100, and that a fair and reasonable cost—including 10 per cent. profit—should not exceed $39.50 per outlet. The overcharge on each light outlet is $60.50, or an entire overcharge in 139 outlets of $8,288.50. He also finds that there are 40 other light outlets charged for which he cannot find in the plans, or the rooms to which the bills refer. He also finds that the contractors gave no return to the state for 49 floor outlet boxes which were removed. He finds that skilled electricians' labor was charged for cutting woodwork and plaster. He finds that the sum of $1,050 is charged for cutting and patching walls to install 760 feet of conduit worth $27.05. This equals $1.25 a running foot. He finds a charge of $4,600 for cutting and patching to install 3,910 feet of conduit work, or $1.17 a foot. The most liberal price for such cutting and patching would not exceed 50 cents a foot.

He finds also that the bills were improper, inasmuch as a charge of $2,159.93 was improperly made in the figuring out of the percentage on the total of the job. This analysis of the consulting engineer, together with the report of the Tucker Company, is submitted herewith and marked Exhibit "A," to be filed in the minutes.

The special electrical expert engaged finds that the plans for rewiring the building are incomplete, extravagant in design to the last degree, and indefinite as to the number of lights. The supervision of the work has been practically by irresponsible persons, and he recommends that either a blanket contract be made for the remaining work, or the contract be given to some reputable concern on time and material, plus a percentage with an up-set price, which he estimates will not exceed $40,000. The engineer on the job representing the state, and who was assigned to the job by the late architect, Mr. Hoefer, testifies that the remaining work would cost at least $110,000, in his judgment, but Mr. Armstrong says he can now get reputable contractors who will give a bond to do it inside of $45,000.

SHOULD NOT PAY BILLS

The supervising auditor recommends that in view of all the facts, the bills of the New York Construction Company be paid, and that the Tucker Electrical Company be forced to go to the Court of Claims and prove the value of their work and the actual money expended.

In the investigation of the architect's office, it was disclosed that Christian Ashmusen, of Albany, who had been employed in the architect's office until the first of January, had received a contract on the recommendation of Mr. Hoefer, from Governor Dix, to supervise all the electrical work on the Capitol, beginning January 1, on a five per cent. basis. On the work done during January and February, this would give him about $1,500 a month, or a little more. His salary in the architect's office was $2,400 a year, and it was he who attempted to design the costly plans for lighting the capitol. The contract was without the authority of the trustees of public buildings, and Mr. Ashmusen himself has testified that he did not attempt to check up the labor, nor did he attempt to check up the materials received, but he charges five per cent. on all the materials and all the labor. He is willing to compromise with the state and would like to know from the trustees whether he is on or off the job. The electrical engineer engaged by the trustees of public buildings, regards Mr. Ashmusen as incompetent and inefficient, and he himself admits that he did not properly look after the work to which he was assigned on this percentage contract just before the present administration came into office.

An investigation of the plumbing contract held by L. F. Bannon, of Kingston, N. Y., disclosed that the specifications had been departed from radically; that the change had been made without the knowledge of the trustees of public buildings, but had been consented to by the state architect.

The original specifications called for Carrara glass in the toilets in the west wing of the Capitol. The glass for the wainscoting was to be three-fourths of an inch thick, and for the partitions one inch thick. The lintels and jambs of the water-closets were to be two-inch marble. The contractor substituted an Argentine glass for the wainscoting three-eighths of an inch thick, and the partitions are three-fourths of an inch thick, instead of one inch in thickness. The marble for the jambs and lintels was not furnished as required by the specifications, but even the woodwork in the toilets was changed without any authority from the trustees of public buildings and in violation of the contract.

Experts, including one from the Pittsburgh Plate Glass Company, and also the acting state architect, conceded that the glass wainscoting, as well as the partitions in the assembly toilets, the only room yet finished under the contract, are dangerous and should be torn out. The experts also estimate that the contractor made about from 40 to 50 per cent. more on the contract by the changes in specifications. When the late state architect, Mr. Hoefer, was questioned, he said that there was a verbal understanding with the contractor that he was to make the state an allowance, but just what allowance could not be determined at the time. Since Mr. Hoefer has resigned, it has been discovered that instead of an allowance, the contractor was permitted to get an increased sum for the changes which were made, and in fact he received an increase in almost every item in the schedules of his contract. The acting state architect has written the Bannon Company that the contract must be carried out as originally agreed upon, and asks further authority from the trustees of public buildings to submit the matter to the attorney-general, so that, if necessary, the bondsmen may be sued. The total amount of the plumbing contract is $54,488 for the west wing of the Capitol.

WHAT THE ARCHITECT DID

In going over the accounts of the architect, it was found that without any authority from the trustees of public buildings, the late state architect, Mr. Hoefer, let to Callanan & Prescott the work for the marble on the third floor of the Capitol, west wing. Callanan & Prescott sublet this to the Vermont Marble Company, of Proctor, Vermont. The total is $102,900. Callanan & Prescott get 9½ per cent. on this $102,900. The records show that the state architect allowed Callanan & Prescott to select the bidders themselves for the marble, open the bid themselves, so that it may be said in truth that there was

espect of the question whether the west wing of the Capi-
tc sould be finished on a percentage contract by Callanan &
P esott, the supervising auditor to the trustees has taken the
testirony, through a stenographer, of all the gentlemen con-
n cta with the state architect's office who have any super-
v. or work. It is the opinion of the chief draughtsman, the
cf ef engineer and the superintendent of construction—all
tl reenen named by the committee of architects as competent
t pas judgment upon the question—that a continuation of
t e prcentage contract is advisable, if the trustees of public
b ildigs will give the state architect authority to decide just
w iatnen shall be employed on the job, that is the number of
n en 1 relation to the amount of work. These men concede
t at ˙ eight riggers are doing the work of two riggers, and if
fi ty oft-stone cutters are doing work where only fifteen are
n ceary, and that fifty laborers are on a job good for only
t 1 ien, the cost to the state is bound to go far beyond a
p opr contract price.

Th supervising auditor, with the architect and the super-
i tenent of construction, has several times investigated the
w rkoeing done by the contractors, and have found men some-
t ne doing nothing. These men were as many as three or
fcur ogether. And it was also found that there is a regular
a arn signal on each floor when anybody comes along who may
b suoected of a desire to learn whether the men are working.
T ie ontractors, of course, are not to blame to a very large
e. ter as they are urged by county leaders and by some
n emers of the legislature, to put men to work. Where the
a tin state architect has taken men off the job, and in one case
a paiicular man for violating the rule against smoking, the
n en ave been put back through the influence of certain gen-
t ema in the Capitol not in any way connected with the trustees
c pulic buildings.

Th architects who investigated the building for the governor,
a ree that the work done by Callanan & Prescott is first-
ass 1 every respect, that the material is exactly as provided
for ii the specifications, and that no fault can be found with
their 'ork, beyond the question of an over-plus of labor, which,
of corse, fattens the percentage contract.

In 1e week ending February 14th, there were 493 persons on

no real contract on behalf of the state, and no effort whatever made by the state architect's office to obtain proper bidding for the marble.

The contract is of course invalid, not being made according to statute, but as the Vermont Marble Company has proceeded in the belief that the work was properly ordered, the supervising auditor recommends that the contract be properly approved by the trustees of public buildings, inasmuch as the marble will be necessary pretty soon, after the adjournment of the legislature. and probably little money would be saved at this period by a proper letting of the contract. Under this, the state, of course, is practically bound to let the Callanan & Prescott subcontractors lay the marble in the corridors and in the rooms on the west wing of the Capitol building on the third floor, so Callanan & Prescott will receive $9\frac{1}{2}$ per cent. on the cost of the marble and then $9\frac{1}{2}$ per cent. for labor in installing the marble, with which labor they have nothing to do.

GIFT OF 94 PER CENT

It also appears that the former state architect permitted Callanan & Prescott to enter into contracts with the Architectural Plaster Company in the sum of $30,410 for plastering and artificial stone work in connection with the third floor rooms and corridors in which the marble is to be set and with the New York & Batavia Woodworking Company for furnishing woodwork and finish, $35,102, on the third floor. Callanan & Prescott sublet this work and received under the agreement with the architect $9\frac{1}{2}$ per cent. commission on the total of both contracts. This was done without any authorization by the trustees of buildings and without their knowledge. It was a clear gift of $9\frac{1}{2}$ per cent. on $102,900, on $30,410 and on $35,102. The state architect simply gave up his duties, turned his authority over to the contractors and paid them $9\frac{1}{2}$ per cent. on the total of three contracts.

It is suggested to the trustees that direct instructions be given to the state architect that no further work of this sort be done, except under a contract as submitted to the trustees of public buildings, as was done by all architects until Mr. Hoefer came into office.

In respect of the question whether the west wing of the Capitol should be finished on a percentage contract by Callanan & Prescott, the supervising auditor to the trustees has taken the testimony, through a stenographer, of all the gentlemen connected with the state architect's office who have any supervisory work. It is the opinion of the chief draughtsman, the chief engineer and the superintendent of construction—all three men named by the committee of architects as competent to pass judgment upon the question—that a continuation of the percentage contract is advisable, if the trustees of public buildings will give the state architect authority to decide just what men shall be employed on the job, that is the number of men in relation to the amount of work. These men concede that if eight riggers are doing the work of two riggers, and if fifty soft-stone cutters are doing work where only fifteen are necessary, and that fifty laborers are on a job good for only ten men, the cost to the state is bound to go far beyond a proper contract price.

The supervising auditor, with the architect and the superintendent of construction, has several times investigated the work being done by the contractors, and have found men sometimes doing nothing. These men were as many as three or four together. And it was also found that there is a regular alarm signal on each floor when anybody comes along who may be suspected of a desire to learn whether the men are working. The contractors, of course, are not to blame to a very large extent, as they are urged by county leaders and by some members of the legislature, to put men to work. Where the acting state architect has taken men off the job, and in one case a particular man for violating the rule against smoking, the men have been put back through the influence of certain gentlemen in the Capitol not in any way connected with the trustees of public buildings.

The architects who investigated the building for the governor, agreed that the work done by Callanan & Prescott is first-class in every respect, that the material is exactly as provided for in the specifications, and that no fault can be found with their work, beyond the question of an over-plus of labor, which, of course, fattens the percentage contract.

In the week ending February 14th, there were 493 persons on

no real contract on behalf of the state, and no effort whatever made by the state architect's office to obtain proper bidding for the marble.

The contract is of course invalid, not being made according to statute, but as the Vermont Marble Company has proceeded in the belief that the work was properly ordered, the supervising auditor recommends that the contract be properly approved by the trustees of public buildings, inasmuch as the marble will be necessary pretty soon, after the adjournment of the legislature. and probably little money would be saved at this period by a proper letting of the contract.   Under this, the state, of course, is practically bound to let the Callanan & Prescott subcontractors lay the marble in the corridors and in the rooms on the west wing of the Capitol building on the third floor, so Callanan & Prescott will receive $9\frac{1}{2}$ per cent. on the cost of the marble and then $9\frac{1}{2}$ per cent. for labor in installing the marble, with which labor they have nothing to do.

GIFT OF 94 PER CENT

It also appears that the former state architect permitted Callanan & Prescott to enter into contracts with the Architectural Plaster Company in the sum of $30,410 for plastering and artificial stone work in connection with the third floor rooms and corridors in which the marble is to be set and with the New York & Batavia Woodworking Company for furnishing woodwork and finish, $35,102, on the third floor. Callanan & Prescott sublet this work and received under the agreement with the architect $9\frac{1}{2}$ per cent. commission on the total of both contracts.   This was done without any authorization by the trustees of buildings and without their knowledge.   It was a clear gift of $9\frac{1}{2}$ per cent. on $102,900, on $30,410 and on $35,102.   The state architect simply gave up his duties, turned his authority over to the contractors and paid them $9\frac{1}{2}$ per cent. on the total of three contracts.

It is suggested to the trustees that direct instructions be given to the state architect that no further work of this sort be done, except under a contract as submitted to the trustees of public buildings, as was done by all architects until Mr. Hoefer came into office.

In respect of the question whether the west wing of the Capitol should be finished on a percentage contract by Callanan & Prescott, the supervising auditor to the trustees has taken the testimony, through a stenographer, of all the gentlemen connected with the state architect's office who have any supervisory work. It is the opinion of the chief draughtsman, the chief engineer and the superintendent of construction—all three men named by the committee of architects as competent to pass judgment upon the question—that a continuation of the percentage contract is advisable, if the trustees of public buildings will give the state architect authority to decide just what men shall be employed on the job, that is the number of men in relation to the amount of work. These men concede that if eight riggers are doing the work of two riggers, and if fifty soft-stone cutters are doing work where only fifteen are necessary, and that fifty laborers are on a job good for only ten men, the cost to the state is bound to go far beyond a proper contract price.

The supervising auditor, with the architect and the superintendent of construction, has several times investigated the work being done by the contractors, and have found men sometimes doing nothing. These men were as many as three or four together. And it was also found that there is a regular alarm signal on each floor when anybody comes along who may be suspected of a desire to learn whether the men are working. The contractors, of course, are not to blame to a very large extent, as they are urged by county leaders and by some members of the legislature, to put men to work. Where the acting state architect has taken men off the job, and in one case a particular man for violating the rule against smoking, the men have been put back through the influence of certain gentlemen in the Capitol not in any way connected with the trustees of public buildings.

The architects who investigated the building for the governor, agreed that the work done by Callanan & Prescott is first-class in every respect, that the material is exactly as provided for in the specifications, and that no fault can be found with their work, beyond the question of an over-plus of labor, which, of course, fattens the percentage contract.

In the week ending February 14th, there were 493 persons on

the Callanan & Prescott payroll.   On March 26th, through the
efforts of the acting state architect, this number was reduced
to 427, and a further reduction has brought the number under
400. This, however, means a weekly payroll of more than
$8,000, and it is respectfully suggested that if a percentage
contract is to be carried on, a resolution be adopted providing
that all men shall be employed on the job through the state
architect, and that the state architect have authority to say
how many carpenters, how many riggers, how many foremen
of carpenters, how many stone-cutting foremen, and granite
cutters, et cetera, shall be employed on any given amount of
work.   Should this be done, the percentage contract could be
carried out with success for the state, and with speed which
would permit the finishing of the building before the first of
next January.

CONTRACT WITHOUT AUTHORITY

The supervising auditor finds that aside from the marble
architectural and woodwork contracts, which, in a peculiar
way, were let to Callanan & Prescott without any authority
from the trustees of public buildings, a most unusual contract
was let to them without any authority in law.   This was to
purchase furniture from January 1st up to and including
March 11th for various rooms in the senate and assembly
committees.   It seems that the orders came from legislative
officials.   The total purchases amounted to $11,097.85 for
furniture and carpets, the furniture comprising desks, chairs,
tables, et cetera.   This furniture was purchased at the highest
retail prices, through the superintendent of public buildings.
Mr. Callanan cheerfully admits that he had nothing to do
with the purchases, but that he was informed by some one
that there was no money to buy furniture, and that he lent his
credit to the state, for which he charges 9½ per cent. on the
bill, his profit being $1,054.30, making the total purchase of
furniture amounting to $12,152.15.

The proper way, of course, was to have this done through the
state architect's office, and have estimates made and bids obtained from furniture dealers and carpet dealers direct.   An
investigation shows that various typewriter desks, mahogany
divans, mahogany chairs, sectional book cases, et cetera, were

bought at prices at which any person could purchase one desk or one chair, and that there was no attempt made by anyone to conserve the interests of the state.

The purchases were made without any authority in law and the supervising auditor requests that he be instructed as to whether he audit the bill as presented.

On February 14th, 1913, William W. Armstrong, of Rochester, a lawyer, presented to the trustees of public buildings a claim of the R. T. Ford Company amounting to $93,397.95 for work on extras alleged to have been necessary on the educational building. The demand of the Ford Company was referred by the trustees of public buildings to the supervising auditor, to transmit the claim to the architects of the educational building, and they reported specifically on each item. They say that the Ford Company has grossly misrepresented the situation and that they are not entitled to a dollar of the amount claimed.

ATTORNEY-GENERAL'S OPINION

After receiving the report of Palmer, Hornbostel & Jones, the architects, the supervising auditor sent the claim of the Ford Company, together with the communication of the architects, to the attorney-general, and the attorney-general has returned an opinion in which he advises the trustees of public buildings that the Ford Company has no claim of any sort against the state.

The correspondence between the counsel for the Ford Company, the architects and the opinion of the attorney-general, is herewith submitted and marked Exhibit " B."

Palmer, Hornbostel & Jones, architects for the state educational building, submitted to the trustees of public buildings on February 8th, a schedule of items which they believed ought to be approved by the trustees, and amounting in all to $194,503. The matter was referred to the supervising auditor and the acting state architect, who went to the state educational building and saw all the persons in interest and investigated each item. The acting state architect recommends items which with the architects' commissions and expenses will total $52,575.90, as against the items asked for by the educational building architects of $194,503.

The items disallowed included $25,000 for a bronze alle-
gorical sculptured clock; $15,000 for metal vases on the Wash-
ington avenue front to complete pedestals along the Washington avenue front; $3,500 for additional cost of a bronze
candelabra; $4,000 for drives about the north wing; $15,000
for new pedestals for Washington avenue, for the candelabras,
and lesser items relating to plastering, mouldings, ventilation
and painting.

The entire list asked for by the architects, together with the
report of the State architect, and supervising architect, will be
marked Exhibit "C."

It should be said in relation to the $25,000 clock, that in the
report to Governor Dix it was proposed to put this clock in at
$15,000, but that afterwards the architects wrote saying that
the amount was a typewritten error, and it should have been
$25,000. The contract for this clock was signed by Governor
Dix, but never was formally approved by the trustees of
public buildings, nor by the attorney-general or the state
architect.

The consulting engineer employed by the trustees of public
buildings has devised a plan for electrical wiring of the remainder of the building which will reduce the cost very much
by avoiding much cutting of stone. Also he has discussed with
several electrical contractors the question whether their men
would not agree to waive their rights in the premises and let
the Albany Bricklayers, Masons and Plasterers' Union have
its way. The contractors were thoroughly willing to go ahead
with the work and supply men, if necessary, from New York,
who will do it. This seems to be the only way of averting
more delay on the building.

A compilation of the money paid so far on the Capitol shows
that there has been expended directly or indirectly in payments,
or on contracts which have been let that are yet unfinished, a
total of $1,967,574.92, in addition to $100,000 appropriated
immediately after the fire for emergency work. The appropriation in 1911–1912 was $1,500,000 for general rebuilding.
There is a deficit now of $467,574.92. The state architect and
Callanan & Prescott estimate that it will cost $1,000,000 more
to finish the building, and $100,000 for equipment, mainly
filing cases and furniture. It is agreed that the Capitol can be

finished by the first of January if the strike can be immediately settled. The appropriation therefore which must be made by the legislature would have to be $1,100,000, and an additional appropriation of $467,574.92 to make up the deficiency. The state is now indebted to Callanan & Prescott in the sum of $225,000. They have gone along with their payroll, which averages $9,000 a week, and have, they say, borrowed money from the banks in order that the work should be continued pending an appropriation by the state. On March 13th the state owed Callanan & Prescott $214,292.56. The total to Callanan & Prescott, including their sub-contract, amounted up to March 8 to the sum of $1,444,272.75.

The state architect had made a complete report on all the work done and it will be filed in the minutes, and marked Exhibit " D." He has also made for the trustees a complete report of what he believes will be necessary for the completion of the Capitol, and this itemized report is herewith submitted and marked Exhibit " E."

The supervising auditor has had prepared a list of men employed by Callanan & Prescott on the Capitol, together with the persons whose influence put them to work. This list covered all employees on March 26th and another list covers all employees on February 14th. In the list of March 26th, it will be noticed that very many of the men put to work as carpenters, riggers, granite cutters, soft-stone cutters, banker-men, rubbers, and laborers, were certified to and employed by Costa, the discharged secretary of the state architect's office.

An entire list of the men employed, together with their recommendations for appointment, is herewith submitted and marked Exhibit " F."

"IT IS TO LAUGH!"

From the Albany Knickerbocker Press

REPORT BY JOHN A. HENNESSY

Commissioner under the Moreland Act to Investigate the Several Departments of the State Government, August 18, 1913

The indictment of Bart Dunn, Tammany Hall member of the democratic state committee, and of William H. Whyard, the real democratic boss of Rockland county, marks the beginning in the courts of the work which Governor Sulzer set out to do four months ago.

The other men indicted were tools of bigger men in the democratic administration under Governor Dix. All the men, big and little, in the state can be brought to trial, and all the highway frauds, big and little, uncovered.

The cases in Rockland county differ in no material respect from those in other counties. The work was about 70 per cent. fraudulent and the state got 30 cents on the dollar.

The Rockland county cases were presented to the district attorney there seven weeks ago, but one legal knot after another came in the way to delay a grand jury investigation. Similar difficulties in legal procedure and the necessity for a certain line of proof have delayed the presentation of cases in other counties. Several of these cases are now ready for grand juries.

As these cases develop the electors of New York state will learn that the political organization, so-called democratic, captained by Charles F. Murphy in New York city, by William H. Fitzpatrick in Buffalo and by William H. Kelley in Syracuse, is organized to loot the treasury and regards every honest man as its enemy.

It is for the people of the state now to say whether the highway frauds shall be laid bare up to the point of getting all the criminals. It is a big job for big men and it needs money.

Three months ago when Mr. Murphy's legislature found the governor was in earnest in his promise to uproot all frauds, Mr. Sulzer's contingent account for investigation was cut off and he was left without a penny. I was asked by him to investigate highway contracts in a state nine times the size of Massachusetts and to do it without a force of trained investigators and road engineers. A private appeal to a dozen men brought small

"IT IS TO LAUGH!"

From the Albany Knickerbocker Press

REPORT BY JOHN A. HENNESSY

Commissioner under the Moreland Act to Investigate the Several Departments of the State Government, August 18, 1913

The indictment of Bart Dunn, Tammany Hall member of the democratic state committee, and of William H. Whyard, the real democratic boss of Rockland county, marks the beginning in the courts of the work which Governor Sulzer set out to do four months ago.

The other men indicted were tools of bigger men in the democratic administration under Governor Dix. All the men, big and little, in the state can be brought to trial, and all the highway frauds, big and little, uncovered.

The cases in Rockland county differ in no material respect from those in other counties. The work was about 70 per cent. fraudulent and the state got 30 cents on the dollar.

The Rockland county cases were presented to the district attorney there seven weeks ago, but one legal knot after another came in the way to delay a grand jury investigation. Similar difficulties in legal procedure and the necessity for a certain line of proof have delayed the presentation of cases in other counties. Several of these cases are now ready for grand juries.

As these cases develop the electors of New York state will learn that the political organization, so-called democratic, captained by Charles F. Murphy in New York city, by William H. Fitzpatrick in Buffalo and by William H. Kelley in Syracuse, is organized to loot the treasury and regards every honest man as its enemy.

It is for the people of the state now to say whether the highway frauds shall be laid bare up to the point of getting all the criminals. It is a big job for big men and it needs money.

Three months ago when Mr. Murphy's legislature found the governor was in earnest in his promise to uproot all frauds, Mr. Sulzer's contingent account for investigation was cut off and he was left without a penny. I was asked by him to investigate highway contracts in a state nine times the size of Massachusetts and to do it without a force of trained investigators and road engineers. A private appeal to a dozen men brought small results in money. It seemed impossible to interest them in a situation that involved millions of the public funds. The work as it slowly progressed pointed unerringly to a sinister story of graft in almost every state department. My commission under the Moreland act was broadened by the Governor, so that I might take up all the strings as we found them.

There is enough of proof today outside the highway department to make it vital that the good citizenship of the state shall free the government from existing conditions, uncover all the grafters and lay bare the state comptroller's office.

I have had three road engineers, and, until I could no longer pay him, an accountant in the work of disclosing the highway frauds. I have been assisted by special investigators from time to time, whenever I could afford to pay for this form of work. The small staff under my direction has had to confine itself to one county at a time, and embarrassed by lack of information owing to the theft of necessary records from the highway department.

I have complete cases now in seven counties, splendid testimony to the unselfish work of these road engineers who in the beginning paid their own maintenance and other expenses, as I had no funds. Had the legislature not cut from the supply bill the governor's item of $30,000 for investigations, I could have enlarged my force so as to cover all the counties and obtained evidence sufficient to lay bare the entire conspiracy to rob the state of its highways for the enrichment of politicians and contractors.

Even with what we already have accomplished I believe it is now possible to get at the top, and at the top are several high state officials whose enmity to Governor Sulzer began when he appointed me to run down graft.

At the top, too, are men whose members of assembly voted to sustain the governor on direct primaries, but who joined the impeachment crew when it became evident four weeks ago that nothing but lack of money could stop complete graft exposures in this state.

A concise story of the Rockland county frauds will do to illustrate the conditions in the remainder of the state. The conditions are not better but may be worse in other counties. Bart Dunn, Tammany hall chieftain on the East Side, got a "contract" to lay a concrete road four inches deep and less than three miles long on top of a fine old macadam road in Rockland county. The concrete was to be screened washed gravel, approved sand and cement. The road was to cost $31,000. Instead of buying gravel for use in making the concrete, Dunn took the old stone belonging to the state out of the macadam road, mixed it with poor sand and an insufficient amount of cement, and called it a concrete road.

This did not satisfy his appetite for graft. For a distance of nearly a mile he did not lay any concrete. He simply mixed some sand with the old stone, placed it in the road and and then covered it with a cement grout about one-quarter of an inch thick. Even this robbery of the state was not sufficient. The concrete road was to be four inches thick. The depth of the loose stone and concrete found averaged two inches in depth for more than two-thirds of the road. Of course this road went to pieces before it was finished, but notwithstanding the protests of property owners, the department of highways, through its various officials, accepted the road, and paid the contractors in full.

Perhaps more interesting, as a bit of deviltry in road building, is the contract for resurfacing another Rockland county road for which William H. Whyard, local Democratic boss, and others have been indicted. This road was to have a new top three inches deep on a surface a little more than four miles long. It was one of those "contracts" handed over night. Sometimes over the telephone. Notwithstanding the state supplied the asphaltic oil for the bituminous top, the cost was to be $26,000. After the "contract" was signed, it was decided to make the surface four inches deep and an additional $10,000 was allowed in a "supplementary agreement."

Investigations directed by me, after I had twice visited the highway, disclosed that the top surface of the road instead of being built four inches deep averaged less than two inches in more than one-half of the road. For four-fifths of a mile the contractor did not put in a new surface at all, but covered the old macadam road with a light asphaltic oil. He thus robbed the state of all new stone he charged for and was paid also for the placing and rolling of this stone as well as

for the manipulation of asphalt never used in the penetration
and binding of the " phantom " stone.

*Even with this fraud there was not enough of clear profit to
go around for everybody. The contract called for a road sixteen
feet wide. In some places the road is only eleven feet wide and
generally thirteen and one-half feet wide, which means a steal
of at least 30,000 running feet in a road four miles long, each
foot four inches deep. This missing stone was charged and the
contractor paid for penetrating it with asphalt oil.*

The remarkable condition here is that the defendant, Whyard, otherwise the Aetna Contracting company, built a road
half as deep as the specifications demanded, a much narrower
road and was paid in $10,000 excess of the original contract
price.

Let it be understood that these are not the only crooked
roads in Rockland. Each road takes a week of expert investigation and analysis; then another week of careful preparation for the district attorney. With my little staff of three
men it was necessary to pull up stakes at Rockland if the
conspiracy which has made a sham of our highway system
was to be uncovered.

*In more than forty roads examined in twenty-two counties, we
have found only three that pass muster, and only one that is
clean all the way. There are men now congratulating themselves
that they are immune from discovery and prosecution. They
assume this because we have not been in their counties. We have,
however, analyzed their contracts, the time in which the work was
done, and the reports as to material, etc. Fraud stands out as
clearly as a mountain peak from a valley. All we need is the
men and the time to get the legal evidence.*

Facts cannot be destroyed in a road less than a year old,
and many of these roads are not nine months old. As we
want no indictments where we cannot be equally sure of
convictions, we have not busied ourselves with openly fraudulent roads finished in the first year of the Dix administration.
No petit jury probably would convict on the conflicting testimony which would be produced. The frauds of 1911, 1910
and 1909 in road building will have to go unfinished unless
some genius as a lawyer proves able to piece certain circumstances together and strong enough to overcome the volume
of defensive testimony.

When this road investigation began, democratic leaders warned Governor Sulzer that he would not be able to get back to the highways of Governor Hughes' time, and that the net result would be an attack on the previous democratic administration, which, they said, was no worse than under republican auspices.

I rather think they were correct in their general statement. Roads built in 1910 were resurfaced last year at great cost. This, of course, proved the 1910 roads, so repaired, to be badly constructed. The repairs wiped out all the original evidence that would be good in law. More startling, however, is the fact that the repairs of most of these roads last year was a mere sham.

I cannot specify them now as to location, as some are already singled out for grand juries, and others will be reached, if we get the financial assistance necessary in a big job of this kind. I predict, the "good roads" of this state built in the last four years will need within 24 months at least $6,000,000 for repairs. The best roads in the state, bar a few, are those built prior to 1908. Some of them are almost as good as new today. The men who built them were crowded out of business by the contractors' ring. These contractors stood in with crooked division engineers, and honest road builders couldn't make enough to feed their horses and maintain their plants. The story of this, however, is for another day.

As to present conditions, let me say that a new road accepted on February 26 of this year is now advertised for repairs; that another road finished this year is also on the list for repairs despite a cost of $15,000 a mile; that roads finished in December of last year are already full of ruts; that roads not yet completed but let under the Dix administration are a joke upon state government; that the road inspectors and engineers are almost as a whole incompetent or dishonest, or merely automatons for political bosses.

The men put upon the roads by the democratic state administration last year were more than two-thirds in number O-K'd by Thomas F. Smith for Tammany, by John F. McCooey, by Fitzpatrick of Buffalo, and by Kelley of Syracuse. Some of them were barbers, some of them were liquor dealers. Some of them had no known vocation. The remainder were appointed by members of the state committee in their respective districts. They were ward heelers pure and simple. These men named to watch contractors were largely nominated in the first place by the contractors interested. Some of these fellows rarely saw the roads, but cheerfully signed estimates every month upon which bills were paid. They certified to the arrival of material that never was delivered.

I am making only a surface review of the conditions. In the main office in Albany things are worse than on the road. Contracts, as I shall prove, were approved when most of the work was done. So-called bidding was the broadest sort of farce. The man who gave up readily and freely was the best thought of. Such a man could put gravel and sand upon a road instead of the imported stone his contract called for. Such a man could put decayed stone in a roadbed instead of material from a quarry. Such a man could take stone fences, bury them in the road, charge for rock excavation and then for sub-base. Such a man could steal oil from one road and have it delivered on another job. The game of give and take was reduced to a well-handled if crude proposition.

The first deputy commissioner of highways told the contractors when to pay their campaign contributions, how they should execute their bonds with C. F. Murphy, Jr.'s, Bonding Company, how they could get along best in the new road combination brought to its highest criminal efficiency in the last year of the Dix administration.

All the things I say, and much I cannot reveal, can be made clear to all the people if the newspapers and public opinion will force the fight on graft. The fight will be one of magnitude, and one which will be won only by resolute men amply equipped against resourceful enemies. The fight properly begun cannot be lost, and is bound to purify public life for a period of years.

It is a much bigger struggle than the fight against Tweed and Samuel J. Tilden's fight against the canal ring. In the entrenchments of the thieves will be found men who have been elevated to high and supposedly virtuous office, and men who have today the confidence of their fellow citizens.

The trail of graft will run from the Comptroller's office into the banks and out again. The misuse of the excise department

will leave, when exposed, a trail of shame, and blacken some of the men now loudly crying for the life of the governor.

When the story of the canal system is told, the highway thefts won't look so big. When the state election department is fully investigated the people will stand aghast in contemplation of the men selected to give them pure elections. In my commission from Governor Sulzer I have gone into the departments named just enough to cut the surface. I had a few personally selected volunteers and one or two investigators to assist me from time to time. I have lacked the money to sink the probe, but as I begun the work the "system" soon took notice. A complete detective service trailed me and several volunteer workers. I shall not now recite the obstacles but will say that the grafters never go to sleep at the switch. Lest something might be overlooked they shadowed my wife and my daughter.

Alleged friends have been thrown up against me in the hope of making situations that would force me into unenviable positions. Twice I have escaped by sheer good fortune from incidents that any innocent man would have found himself in, however hard to explain to enemies; and once w thin ten days a well-considered "plant," known now and proved to a dozen of my friends, was made fruitless by straightforward action wh ch at the time looked like criticism of the governor's judgment.

I am simply a small agent in the fight against graft, yet Tammany senators whisper in confidence to other men that I am or have been an embezzler and am or have been a taker of graft. The head of one department tells in confidence how he will make Stilwell appear not half the crook I am. These political grafters and character assassins pay their attention to me, a simple agent of Governor Sulzer—an agent bent upon revealing what can be discovered without adequate organizat on. Is it any wonder, therefore, that they so fiercely attack their own governor, who four times declined to revoke my commission and who declined to stop investigations which would lead to state-wide exposure?

It is not my place to defend Governor Sulzer from recent charges nor would it be proper, but I would be untrue to myself were I to pass without comment the most vital point in these graft investigations. I offered to efface myself two months ago and again six weeks ago when men who call themselves leaders in the party warned the governor that his investigations would wreck the organization. All their enmity was aimed first at me and then blazed with fury at Mr. Sulzer when he sent for the district attorney of several counties and outlined the testimony I was gathering.

No one better than I knows that had the governor agreed not to execute his oath of office he would be today unchallenged in his place as the Executive, no matter what other bitterness might be displayed against his independence of boss control. His inflexible determination to go after all the looters and his purpose to begin with the indictment of Bart Dunn, a member of the state committee from Tammany Hall, ended all relations. Then the savagery of recent events took life in a conference held by Charles F. Murphy.

"It's his life, not ours," was the way one Murphy leader put it to a group of newspapermen.

For grand jury reasons this narrative is lacking in some essential statements now probable. There are two things to be done at once.

First. Money and men should be forthwith provided for the further exposure of the highway frauds and the graft allied with them. This is the most important question at the moment. The conditions I have unearthed in Rockland are state-wide. They reveal a conspiracy against honest government. They call for resolute action and for swift punishment. They reveal an extraordinary condition of blackmail which it is not wise for me to specify by detail, at this time.

Second. Every earnest effort of every good citizen and every good newspaper, regardless of politics, should be put forth night and day for the election of an assembly independent of the bipartisan bosses, one that will be able to probe all the way into every department of state government and uncover the silent partners outside who have made honest administration a joke.

I shall supplement this highway story with another, giving a flash of the graft in this and other departments and defining the issue which has made Murphy of New York, Fitzpatrick of Buffalo and Kelley of Syracuse decree political death to those in their own party who care to be honest in office.

REPORT ON AUBURN PRISON

By George W. Blake

A special commissioner appointed to investigate prisons and reformatories of this state

Hon. William Sulzer,

Governor State of New York, Executive Chamber, Albany, N. Y.

Sir.—Herewith is a report of the investigation made by me of Auburn Prison, under authority vested in me by your commission of the 14th inst. Included in this report you have a summary of the report made by an accountant who examined the books of the prison, all of which is respectfully submitted together with the testimony.

Introduction

I have found in Auburn Prison brutality, violation of the law, waste and general incompetency. Twenty-eight prisoners have become insane during the last twelve months. The testimony of trustworthy witnesses indicates that cruel punishment deprived some of these prisoners of their reason, that the prison doctor is careless and unfeeling, and that he has repeatedly refused to attend upon women during confinement.

More than three thousand pounds of food is thrown into the swill barrel every week. This refuse was weighed as it came from the tables. Sworn testimony proved that the waste had been going on for two years, at least.

The current report of Warden Denham recommends an appropriation of $75,000 for centralizing the boilers and $4,000 for a filtration plant. The testimony also shows that the expenditure of any money for these purposes would be useless, that nothing would be gained by relocating the boilers, and that a filtration plant is not needed.

A careful examination of the workshops reveals a cash investment by the state of $535,492.05 and shows that the

DARBY AND JONAH!

From the Albany Knickerbocker Press

proceeds from the sale of manufactured goods are decreasing. A comparison of the first five months of the fiscal year with the same period a year ago, exhibits a falling off in production of more than $20,000, and a decrease in gross profits of $8,400. The entire industrial plant has been conducted in opposition to the public interest, and solely in the interest of individuals.

It is my opinion that the whole industrial matter should be the subject of a special investigation.   I do not believe that the gross mismanagement of the industrial part of the prison has been due solely to carelessness or incompetency.

The state has been supporting a number of fine horses and vehicles for the pleasure of the warden.   The annual cost of maintaining this luxury is an unnecessary burden upon the people.   The value of the horses and vehicles is at present $2,500.

It is difficult to imagine a worse condition of affairs.   Later, if you please, I will supplement this report by suggestions tending to reduce the cost of maintenance and production and for the improvement of the general condition.   I recommend now as speedy a change as possible in the wardenship, and the creation of a bureau for the purchase of all the supplies used by the prisons and reformatories.

I would also recommend that these prisons be kept as units, so that each one may have its own appropriation, its own allotment of supplies, and be compelled to stand upon its own feet.   The present method seems to have been adopted because it was a good method to cover up defects; in other words, so that there would be a general average in bad management and extravagance, and no one prison could make a better record than another.

It is my opinion, based upon facts gathered from the testimony, and by personal investigation into the various departments of the prison, that it would be possible to reduce the cost of maintaining this prison $75,000 a year, and at the same time to improve its general condition.

The legislature of 1912 appropriated $6,000 for a new industrial office.   This office is not needed.   The appropriation runs out in two years.   I suggest that it be permitted to run out.

GENERAL ADMINISTRATION

*Lack of Efficiency and Culpable Carelessness in handling state's
money and materials*

The entire administration of the prison is lacking in almost
every essential for efficiency. There is no real supervision,
every one of the officials appearing to do as he pleases. If the
warden or superintendent Scott wanted information concerning
any special department the man in charge of that department
was called to the warden's office. Neither the superintendent
nor the warden, nor any other official, having the right to
suggest better methods, or to command them, ever paid
adequate attention to the prison management. Mr. Mills, the
sales agent, was permitted full control over the shops. He
appointed himself state superintendent of industries, and gave
orders to the employees. In every case these orders were
obeyed. He was recognized as the master in all industrial
matters. Why he was permitted to exercise this authority
must remain for a time a matter of conjecture. Under his
control the shops were kept busy making articles that were not
saleable. Complaint has been made of the lack of storage
room. There are about 18,000 Warren desks stored in the
prison grounds now, and 12,000 more in course of manufacture,
and yet the cry is for more money to increase the operating
space. The desks which they make are those on which a royalty
has to be paid. Any other kind of desk would be just as satisfactory.

I cite the two following instances to show how bad the
industrial management is:

Baskets weighing about thirty pounds that were made in
Auburn prison were shipped to the Riverside Hospital in New
York. The charge for the baskets was $15. The cartage from
the Grand Central freight yard in New York City to the hospital was $12 and the bill was O. K'd by F. H. Mills. It
appearing certain that the hospital would object to this charge
the amount for cartage was reduced to $3, and the remaining
$9 was charged up against the cost of manufacture. It did
not seem to occur to anybody here that the bill of the truckman
should be disputed. He is allied with a strong political faction
in New York.

A stool was made in Auburn prison at a cost of seventy cents and shipped to Dannemora. The carrying charges were seventy-eight cents.

It frequently happens that goods made here and shipped to New York had to be renovated at something like two-thirds of what it costs to make them. Bills for renovating and repairing newly made articles are from $400 to $600 a month. The man having this contract is also allied with some strong influence in New York city. If the men in charge of this prison did not share in this graft they certainly permitted its creation and continuance.

One glaring feature of the wrongs inflicted upon prisoners is that of fines, and this will be elaborated when a report making suggestions is made.

The pro rata cost of feeding the prisoners, as it appears in the records, is a false pro rata, because it includes food consumed by others than the convicts.

The man in charge of the boilers and machinery says that he spends over $300 and $400 a month for incidentals. These charges were outside of the estimate for maintenance.

There are three boilers for heating, and nine for power. Any sort of proper management would recognize the advisability of using electric power and individual motors for the running of the various shops. But, instead of that, an expenditure of $75,000 has been recommended to take all of these boilers up and concentrate them in one spot. . This is an outrageous suggestion, because such a concentration would be useless, and would result in the abandonment of many of the boilers that are perfectly good where they are. There is testimony to the effect that even if it were necessary to concentrate these boilers, it could be done for about half of the appropriation asked for.

There is a wide difference in the testimony concerning the consumption of coal. I did not have time to give this particular matter as much attention as it deserved, but I think it would bear close inspection under a new prison administration.

The man in charge of the boilers for the women's prison swore they consumed 1,200 to 1,500 tons of coal a year, while the same service ought to be procured at a consumption of not more than 780 tons.

The total amount of money expended from "special appropriations" from January 1, 1911, to April 1, 1913, was $52,034.12. The monthly average was $1,927.19. The prison has been carrying a shortage on its books of $2,895.51, which occurred under B. Frank Weinegar while he was a clerk in the prison. This shortage has never been made good although Mr. Weinegar and the assistant clerk were under bonds. One of these bondsmen was Arthur M. Ward, of Jamestown, N. Y.

The law gives the agent and warden the power to collect this debt but he failed to take any steps in this transaction. Weinegar is still employed in the prison as correspondence censor.

The method of having all the supplies bought for the male prison and certain portions transferred over to the female prison, makes it possible to juggle the accounts, and to show unwarranted charges for supplies for the women's prison. This alone shows the necessity of adopting the suggestion that each prison be treated as a unit. You will see ample and corroborative reasons for this suggestion in the testimony which accompanies this report.

I want to say once more, that there has never been any inspection or supervision, or useful suggestions, either by Colonel Scott or Warden Benham, toward more efficient management of this prison, better control of the institution, or its conservation in the public interest, so far as I have been able to learn.

The Prison Doctor

Charged with the neglect of the sick and brutality toward prisoners

The physician of the prison has held that place since May 8, 1898. He is an autocrat. Abundance of evidence shows that he is brutal in his treatment of the sick, neglectful of their needs and that he flagrantly violates that section of the prison law which defines his duties. No effort has ever been made by any of his superiors to compel him to moderate his severity or stop him from compelling sick men to expose their persons for examination before their associates or to curb his intolerant and incompetent administration. I realize the fact that these are severe charges—so severe that I did not call the doctor as a witness, because I feel that his administration of the hospital should be the subject of a thorough investigation by a grand jury.

The bulk of the evidence gathered against this physician comes from persons other than convicts. I was careful in this matter.

SEVERITY CAUSES INSANITY

You will find attached to this report the statement of a man whom you will recognize as being entirely trustworthy and who declares that during the past year a number of persons have gone insane after punishment inflicted by orders of this physician.

You will read of men that have been confined in cells for long periods, and that they come out of these cells with shattered nerves, and with every reason to believe that they will never recover their health.

This doctor has absolute control over the sick. At a time when men should receive humane treatment they go under the control of this physician who treats them in a more brutal manner than they are ever treated when they are well.

Every nook and cranny of the prison reeks with tales of the cruelty of this man. I was not able to discover that either the warden or Colonel Scott or any of their subordinates ever made any attempt to protect the defenseless sick from this treatment. Once under this doctor's care the men are in a desperate plight.

If he desires, he has the power of ordering into an isolation cell any sick man he pleases and the unfortunate prisoner immediately falls under the suspicion that his mind is unbalanced. Here is some of the testimony:

Q. What would happen if a man became insane? A. Why, there are so many men that are put in that condition we have to send them up to Dannemora for being insane.

Q. When the men came here were they apparently sane? A. Yes, sir.

Q. Were they long term prisoners? A. Not all of them.

Q. How long had the men been here on an average? A. Some had not been here over a year.

Q. Quite long enough to have this system affect their minds? A. Yes. Some of the men really grew insane from evil habits. This, of course, hastened their insanity. But I have had them appeal to me for relief, and when I tried to do something for

them I was told I was interfering with the doctor's prerogatives. Nothing would be done, and the men would lose their minds, and we would ship them off to Dannemora.

Q. Did you ever notice the condition of any of the men after leaving these cells. A. I have.

Q. What was it? A. They were exceedingly nervous. I have often gone down to visit the men while they were in the cells, and looked through the little openings, and it was so dark in there that I could not see them. A great many of them have broken down; some of them are affected for life.

Q. So far as you know, a man is punished that way without any regard as to whether he is a strong man or a weak man? A. I have never known of any distinction being made.

Q. Do you think punishment of this character is necessary? A. I would say that it was not; I should say they should have enough water to drink, and enough bread to eat; and I think they should have bedding to lie on.

Q. They are punished in a three-fold manner; by depriving them of water, light, and by creating physical discomfort? A. I consider it a more crying shame to have them square-chalked, which leads to insanity. I have seen boys break down completely, and beg to me to get them relief.

Q. Is it your opinion that a man might remain normal throughout his life, and become insane through this treatment? A. Yes, through being square-chalked. Yes, I know it to be so.

Q. How often was the superintendent here? A. Well, I do not know; he was here three months ago.

Further testimony was to the effect that one man is now confined in one of these cells who is on the verge of insanity.

CRUELTY TO REFRACTORIES

Refractory prisoners put in cells for punishment have only two gills of water every twenty-four hours. The doctor fixes this amount and declared it was sufficient to maintain life. I weighed the measure used in supplying the prisoners with water and found that its weight was eight and one-half ounces. If these punishment cells were light and sanitary the punishment would be very heavy; but the fact is, that these cells are only eight feet two and one-half inches long, four feet seven inches wide and eight feet high. They are perfectly dark and the only ventilation comes through the iron doors. There is no furniture whatever in the cells, except a quart can into which the scanty supply of water is poured. The floor has four rows of iron rivet heads that make a recumbent position practically impossible so that a man is deprived of his sleep and rest as well as his food, drink, air and light. This punishment is worse than the old stringing-up machine and other modes of physical torture that have been abandoned by the state, because it affects the victims nerves as well as his brain and body.

NEGLECT TO INVALID WOMEN PRISONERS

The treatment by the doctor of some of the unfortunate women prisoners confined in the women's prison is even worse. In some respects it is horrible. During the last twelve or fifteen years there has been an average of one child-birth a year, and sworn testimony, amply corroborated, proves that in these cases the unfortunate women have been left entirely to the care and mercy of convict nurses, some of whom were convicted for abortion. One of the women who served in the capacity of nurse and physician was Augusta Nack, who was convicted of complicity in the brutal murder of Guldensuppe. Although the women prisoners are bad women, no man with an humane feeling or imagination can fail to realize the terror of a woman lying in child-bed and being attended in the dim watches of the night by such a woman as Mrs. Nack.

Here is part of the testimony given by a woman who was matron of the women's prison for eighteen years:

Q. Were any children born in the women's prison. A. Yes, during my time about eighteen.

Q. How many during Warden Benham's administration? A. Approximately, five or six.

Q. What kind of attendance did the inmates receive when in childbirth? A. Not any, only from midwives.

Q. Do you mean to say from women who were in prison through their criminal practicing of medicine? A. No, from practicing abortion.

Q. Was it not the physician's duty to attend to these unfortunate women? A. It was, but he never would come when I called him.

Q. Did you ever fail to notify him when his services were needed? A. No, sir.

Q. Did you ever notify him and have him refuse to come? A. Yes, sir.

Q. What did he say? A. He told me to let Augusta attend to the case.

Q. Who is Augusta? A. Augusta Nack.

Q. What was she in prison for? A. For the murder of Guldensuppe. She acted as the attendant in delivering five or six children while she was there.

Q. Do you mean to tell me that the prison physician turned these women over to the care of Augusta Nack, the woman in prison for complicity in a murder crime? A. Yes, sir.

Q. Did you ever know of a case where the doctor responded when called to attend a woman in this condition? A. Never; during my entire time there he never was at a birth.

Q. Can you tell me of any specific case where the prison physician refused to attend an inmate at your request? A. Certainly, he refused in not coming to a confinement, and the child was delivered by one of the inmates who had been convicted of abortion.

Another woman, at present employed in the prison, testified to this effect: A convict has charge of the hospital. There have been a dozen or more children born here within my knowledge. I think some of the women nurses were convicted of abortion. I know of one child having died. I do not think Colonel Scott made any investigation into the child's death. I knew the child was ill, and asked the convict nurse if I should call the doctor, but she told me that everything possible had been done.

Then this testimony appears:

Q. Then, as a matter of fact, the child died without medical attention? A. The doctor is the best judge of that.

Q. Did the prison physician ever attend any women who became mothers here? A. Not to my knowledge. I think there have been three or four times, maybe five times, when the doctor has not been in attendance.

Q. It would make no difference, then, whether or not a child was born in the daytime or the nighttime, the doctor would leave it to the nurses? A. So far as I know.

The general condition of the prison brought about by the

physician's administration is so bad and of such long duration
that it requires immediate attention and correction. No
official who paid any attention to the situation could have
failed to discover it.

STEAM APPARATUS AND WATER SUPPLY

The last report made by Warden Benham contains recommendations for the concentration of the twelve boilers used in
the prison and an additional appropriation of $4,000 for filtering
the water supplied by the city of Auburn.

Testimony from experienced engineers and mechanics employed in the prison is to the effect that nothing whatever
would be gained by placing all of the boilers in one spot, but
that it was certain that a great deal would be lost. Such a
change would necessitate the discarding of some of the boilers
that are perfectly good, and which would serve the purpose for
a dozen years to come. It was suggested by these witnesses
that electric power should be installed for the use of the shops
which would greatly reduce the cost and be more efficient in
every way.

While $75,000 has been asked to move all the boilers to one
place, the man in charge of them said that some of the estimates
for doing this work were from $25,000 to $30,000.

Another employee, familiar with the work done in the shops,
was asked:

Q. Would it not be a better idea to use electricity for all
power?   A. I am very much in favor of that.

Q. So if you had individual motors you would not have to
run the whole plant if you wanted to use one motor?   A. Yes,
sir.

Q. Then you would be in favor of installing electrical power
as fast as possible?   A. I certainly would.

Q. Any expenditure of a large amount of money for steam
power would be a waste of money?   A. I think it would; I
think so.

Another practical engineer and mechanic employed in the
prison was asked:

Q. Don't you think it would be better and cheaper in every
way to bore artesian wells for water for prison use inasmuch as

water is costing the prison so much now?   A. I should think it would.   There is certainly a lot of water here.

The water supply of the prison comes from Owasco lake, which is owned by the state, and reaches Auburn by gravity. The prison pays from $2,500 to $2,800 a year in water bills. Two artesian wells could be driven that would supply the prison with pure and wholesome water at a less cost than is now paid in two years for the city water.   It is difficult to imagine why recommendations for the expenditure of $97,000 should be made to continue a system that is unwise and prodigal.

Waste in the Commissary Department

It is with some hesitation that I report on the condition of the commissary department of the prison.   Conditions there almost exceed belief.   More than 3,000 pounds of perfectly good food, prepared for the prisoners, goes into the swill barrels every week, and is carted away to be fed to pigs and chickens.

I had this refuse weighed as it came from the tables, and later proved by witnesses under oath that the great waste has been going on for nearly two years at least.   This was the last of the waste and extravagance in the matter of food and was the final act.   But leading up to it were many acts that plainly displayed a criminal disregard of the public money.   Staple articles have been purchased in the highest markets, in the most expensive and inconvenient forms, and with a total disregard of any kind of method or system.   There has been an entire lack of any kind of supervision on the part of the managers of the prison, or of any proper management whatever.   Employees in the various parts of the prison, competent to advise better business methods, have been ignored completely and made to understand that their help in any administrative capacity was not wanted.

In every branch of the commissary department there has been a riot of wanton waste and extravagance and a flaunting display of gross ignorance concerning even the most ordinary business knowledge.

It is difficult to believe that any man of conscience, having control of the work of providing for the daily needs of the prisoners, could permit such a condition of affairs to continue without at least making some effort at correction.   I have tried diligently to learn whether any such effort was ever made, but without result.   I have asked the men employed in this branch of the prison work whether the warden, the recent superintendent of prisons, or any of their subordinates had ever made an investigation of prisons, or into the way the commissary end of the prison was conducted, and was told that no such inquiry had ever been made to their knowledge.

I have asked them if they thought the system in practice was good or bad and they replied that it was bad.   When I asked them why they did not suggest better ways of doing the work, they replied that they did not believe any advice or suggestion from them would have been welcome.

Here is a sample of one day's waste, as it came from the tables on Friday, March 1, 1913.

From the breakfast table, 194 pounds of hash and bread.

From the dinner tables came 145 pounds of solid food, consisting of salmon, boiled potatoes, sweet mixed pickles and bread, and in addition 502 pounds of soup.   Soup is served twice a week, so that of this food alone there has been wasted every week more than half a ton.

Here is part of the sworn testimony of a witness, who declared that the figures given above are accurate:

Q. What is done with the refuse from the tables?   A. It goes to the swill barrel.

Q. What is done with the swill barrel when it is full?   A. A fellow comes and carts it away.

Q. This refuse is made up from the refuse from the tables? A. Yes, sir. ˙ The man who carries away the swill said he fed it to his pigs.

Another employee of the Commissary department testified that no effort had ever been made before to discover what the waste was.

PURCHASING METHODS UNBUSINESSLIKE

This witness replied to other questions as follows:

Q. Is it not a fact that some of the goods were purchased when the market was highest?   A. Yes, sir.

Q. Then it is your opinion that the method of buying these upplies is an expensive and unnecessary method?   A. Yes, sir.

son
t for
hat

n of

Q. Were the methods better under the previous superintendent than under Colonal Scott? A. I would say they were, looking at it from an economical view.

Q. Did the prices increase under Colonel Scott? Yes, sir. They increased independently of the fluctuations of the market.

Witnesses testified that many of the supplies used were bought in small packages, and that no effort was ever made to have them put up in bulk by large manufacturers. They said that if this were done the cost would be much less, and that much labor and time would be saved in preparing the food for the table. Asked if they knew whether they received the quality of supplies the contracts called for, they replied they had no means of knowing, because the contracts were made in Albany, where all the samples were kept. They merely received what came to them without question.

One of the witnesses was asked:

Q. The samples are kept a few hundred miles away from the institution? A. Yes, sir.

Q. Do you think that is a good method? A. No, I do not.

Q. If you had the samples here, you and the man who prepares the food would be able to see if the state was getting what it paid for? A. Yes, sir.

Q. From whom do you buy eggs? A. From a wholesale grocer in this city.

Q. He gets the eggs from the farmers around here? A. I think so.

Q. So there were no transportation charges? A. I do not think there were.

Q. You paid twenty-five cents a dozen for eggs on Easter, while the market price was twenty-one cents? Why did you pay so much? A. Bids for eggs were opened on February 15th.

Q. Do you find that you pay more when you buy from local dealers? A. Sometimes.

This, a fair sample of the business administration of the prison. Bids for eggs were opened in February, when eggs were high. The same condition exists in nearly every line of produce. It was said in extenuation of this absurd method that the law was responsible for it; if this is true, the law should be amended.

STATE PAYS FOR WARDEN'S PLEASURE RIDING

The people of the state of New York maintain for the pleasure of the warden of this prison, and the matron of the women's prison, a handsome stable, equipped with horses and vehicles representing an investment of more than $2,000 and a coachman at a salary of $1,020 a year, besides a cost of nearly $1,500 annually for feed and repairs. In addition to this cost, there has been the incidental cost of cutting a carriage-way through the massive prison walls.

This expensive establishment has been one of the conspicuous public features of the prison management, which has been clamoring for more room and new buildings while this large stable building has been used and maintained for private purposes.

There are in the stable four horses—a magnificent team for the warden, and two other horses—one of which is for the use of the matron of the woman's prison. The value of the team, estimated by the coachman, is $1,000.

Here is some of the testimony from the coachman:

Q. What kind of driving do you do; pleasure driving, is it not? A. Oh, yes, mostly that.

Q. Where do you drive? A. Out in the country.

Q. Where for instance? A. Well, I drive to Sennett—Mrs. Benham has a farm down there—I have driven down there many times.

Q. Do you ever drive out to Owasco lake? A. Lots of times.

Q. The horses are maintained by the state, aren't they? A. Yes.

Q. So far as you know, this equipment, this private prison stable, has never been used for any other purpose except for the pleasure of the warden, his family and his friends? A. That is just the right answer; that is right.

Q. Then the same thing is true in regard to the matron of the women's prison? A. Just the same thing.

Q. Then this equipment has been used by the warden for his own pleasure and not for the prison's use? A. Yes, sir.

GEO. W. BLAKE,
Commissioner.

"THE STATE GOVERNMENT."

From the Albany Knickerbocker Press

LIST OF MEN AT DIRECT PRIMARY CONFERENCE CALLED BY
GOVERNOR SULZER AT THE EXECUTIVE CHAMBER

Senator Thomas H. O'Keefe, Oyster Bay, N. Y.
Henry S. Orr, Chairman, Town Comm., Hempstead, N. Y.
Lawrence E. Kirwin, Commissioner Elections, Nassau City.
Chas. H. Perry, Port Washington, N. Y.
Matthew Hutchinson, Port Washington, N. Y.
William Scully, Westbury, N. Y.
Alva R. Smith, Bellmore, N. Y.
William O'Keefe, Oyster Bay, N. Y.
Henry P. Keith, State Committeeman, Nassau City.
D. Henry Brown, Sheriff, Suffolk County.
Rowland Miles, Northport, N. Y.
Rev. W. A. Byrne, 274 Wellington Ave., Rochester, N. Y.
E. D. Sanborn, Gloversville, N. Y.
H. W. Borst, Amsterdam, N. Y.
A. J. Elias, Buffalo, N. Y.
Willard M. Phillips, 43 High St., Newburgh, N. Y.
Rev. Wm. Sheafe Chase, 481 Bedford Ave., Brooklyn, N. Y.
Peter Cedar, Pelham, N. Y.
Joseph J. McNally, Albany, N. Y.
Henry L. Stoddard, Evening Mail, New York City.
James F. Quigley, 51 Linden St., Brooklyn, N. Y.
Charles S. Aronstrom, 199 8th Ave., Brooklyn, N. Y.
G. F. Ketchum, Warwick, N. Y.
Albert S. Manning, Otisville, N. Y.
A. G. M. Thompson, Middletown, N. Y.
W. J. Cregan, Monroe, N. Y.
S. V. Casey, Canaseraga, N. Y.
Daniel Sheehan, Mayor of Elmira, Elmira, N. Y.
D. F. Sullivan, Newport, N. Y.
Wm. E. Leffingwell, Watkins, N. Y.
John Mitchell, Mount Vernon, N. Y.
James Olive, Lemontville, N. Y.
Daniel D. Frisbie, Troy, N. Y.
C. Fred Schwarz, Troy, N. Y.
A. J. Warner, 209 Partridge St., Albany, N. Y.
Chas. Oberlander, 120 Northland Ave., Buffalo, N. Y.
John Fitzgibbons, 164 East Bridge St., Oswego, N. Y.
James E. Tierney, 137 Eagle St., Albany, N. Y.
John L. Mager, Utica, N. Y.
Thos. J. Torpy, Peekskill, N. Y.
Daniel B. Thomas, 203 Broadway, Albany, N. Y.
Chas. Ward, Livonia, N. Y.
Daniel T. Lawlor, 171 Livingston Ave., Albany, N. Y.
Dr. A. D. Youngs, Amsterdam, N. Y.
Arthur J. Ruland, Binghamton, N. Y.
W. W. Farley, Binghamton, N. Y.
Chandler Oakes, 27 Cedar St., New York City.
James R. Price, State Athletic Comm., 41 Park Row, New York City.
Wm. H. Hecox, 137 Chenango St., Binghamton, N. Y.
Geo. P. Decker, Rochester, N. Y.
R. A. Davis, 65 N. Pearl St., Albany, N. Y.
Eugene M. Earle, White Plains, N. Y.
John Gill, 1520 Roselle St., New York City.
Edward T. McCarthy, Whitehall, N. Y.

Franklin J. Johnson, 2229 Adams Place, New York City.
F. Reichmann, Albany, N. Y.
Rev. O. E. Miller, 61 State St., Albany, N. Y.
James L. Gernon, 411 Albermarle Road, Brooklyn, N. Y.
Edward F. Roache, Editor, Whitehall Times, Whitehall, N. Y.
J. J. McGarrahan, 539 Hamilton St., Albany, N. Y.
John D. McMahon, Rome, N. Y.
William Moyland, Elmira, N. Y.
D. G. Donnelly, Elmira, N. Y.
S. J. Tilden, New Lebanon, N. Y.
I. Van Ness Phillips, Claverack, N. Y.
Leroy R. Smith, Herkimer, N. Y.
John H. Burke, Ballston Spa, N. Y.
T. W. McAnamey, Watkins, N. Y.
J. B. Macreery, Watkins, N. Y.
Mortimer S. Kelly, Elmira, N. Y.
Fred B. King, "Morning Herald," Gloversville, N. Y.
Wm. T. Jenkins, Castleton Apartments, St. George, S. I.
Fred H. Hopkins, Gloversville, N. Y.
Stephen Ryan, Norwich, N. Y.
Irving Russell, Saugerties, N. Y.
John N. Bogart, Saugerties, N. Y.
E. F. Hunting, Albany, N. Y.
John Zwack, Albany, N. Y.
Frederick Oschoff, Amsterdam, N. Y.
John T. Little, 20 Vesey St., New York City.
Nathan B. Chadsey, 20 Vesey St., New York City.
J. J. Barrett, 411 Union Bldg., Syracuse, N. Y.
Eugene Terry, Ithaca, N. Y.
Eldridge M. Gathright, Marlboro, N. Y.
John S. Wolf, 1614 First St., Rensselaer, N. Y.
John A. Butler, 66 West 53rd St., New York City.
John C. McGee, 353 Amsterdam Ave., New York City.
Chas. A. Duell, Jr., 2 Rector St., New York City.
William Grant Brown, 160 Broadway, New York City.
M. F. Collins, Troy, N. Y.
John J. Walligan, 361 West 56th St., New York City.
A. P. Squire, Schenectady, N. Y.
Thereon Akin, Fort Johnson, N. Y.
F. E. Wadhams, Albany, N. Y.
Rev. E. W. Miller, Albany, N. Y.
W. A. Niver, Schenectady, N. Y.
Mark Eisner, 170 Broadway, New York City.
Frederick W. Smith, Rochester, N. Y.
George E. Noeth, 28 Main St., Rochester, N. Y.
Eugene M. Strauss, Powns Building, Rochester, N. Y.
W. J. O'Brien, 151 Selye Terrace, Rochester, N. Y.
William A. Buckley, 31 Cameron St., Rochester, N. Y.
John J. Cummins, 441 South Salina St., Syracuse, N. Y.
Frederick Anthridge, Poughkeepsie, N. Y.
Simeon Holroyd, 299½ Lark St., Albany, N. Y.
Joseph McDonough, 73 Hudson Ave., Albany, N. Y.
James L. Dempsey, Clinton, N. Y.
Fred H. Wilson, 130 Wadsworth Ave., New York City.
John J. O'Connell, 697 West End Ave., New York City.
P. J. Baker, 610 Riverside Drive, New York City.
Isaac Dalrymple, Esq., Otselic, N. Y.
Lauros G. McConachie, 110 N. Allen St., Albany, N. Y.
A. A. White, 609 Myrtle Ave., Albany, N. Y.

Henry F. Toohey, Schuylerville, N. Y.
John J. Hopper, 215 West 125th St., New York City.
Edmund O'Connor, 7416 6th Ave., Brooklyn, N. Y.
Patrick J. Blute, 440 West 44th St., New York City.
Alex Silberg, 192 So. Pearl St., Albany; N. Y.
Robert Abraham, M. D., 257 West 88th St., New York City.
L. M. Josephthal, 26 East 73rd St., New York City.
Bainbridge Colby, 32 Nassau St., New York City.
Isaac Norton, Johnsonville, N. Y.
John Kennedy, Batavia, N. Y.
Arthur J. O'Keefe, 141 Fiske Place, Brooklyn, N. Y.
John N. Harman, 553 Lincoln Place, Brooklyn, N. Y.
John McGarvey, Bristol Hotel, Rochester, N. Y.
William Geiger, Wyandauch, Suffolk County, N. Y.
A. R. Smith, Bellmore, L. I.
James H. Graf, 106 Orange St., Albany, N. Y.
Michael M. O'Sullivan, 26 Bassett St., Albany, N. Y.
Robert Little, Latham Corners, N. Y.—Cohoes, R. F. D.
M. V. Dolan, 279 Hudson Ave., Albany, N. Y.
J. A. Buckley, Penn Yan, N. Y.
Alexander Karlin, 320 Broadway, New York City.
James A. Lavery, 30 North Clover St., Poughkeepsie, N. Y.
Elizabeth Evans, 56 East 55th St., New York City.
A. C. Baggerly, Savannah, N. Y.
A. S. Hughes, Seneca Falls, N. Y.
Harriett Stanton Blatch, 15 West 91st St., New York City.
John J. Ryan, Medina, N. Y.
Edmund C. Viemeister, 36 3rd Ave., Rockaway Park, New York City.
Calvin E. Keach, Troy, N. Y.
P. H. Wallace, Editor, " Evening Dispatch," Cohoes, N. Y.
Nathan F. Barrett, New Rochelle, N. Y.
Homer D. Call, Secretary, A. M. C. & B. W. of N. A., Syracuse, N. Y.
Maurice De Young, 194 Schaeffer St., Brooklyn, N. Y.
Alexander W. Hover, Germantown, N. Y.
August F. Biesel, Niverville, N. Y.
Frank E. Xavier, 10 Warburton Ave.,Yonkers, N. Y.
Carl G. Clarke, Perry, N. Y.
M. S. Decker, Albany, N. Y.
John J. Malone, 181 N. Main St., Gloversville, N. Y.
Horatio M. Pollock, 447 Manning Boulevard, Albany, N. Y.
James F. Swanck, 302 Broadway, New York City.
Herman A. Rappolt, 879 Morris Ave., Bronx, New York City.
John E. McGeehan, 1731 Weeks Ave., Bronx, New York City.
Norbert Blank, 2319 Creston Ave., Bronx, New York City.
Andrew J. Carson, Cor. Field Place and Creston Ave., New York City.
Thomas J. Torby, Peekskill, N. Y.
Henry H. Childers, 677 Broadway, New York City.
Walter E. Ward, 78 State St., Albany, N. Y.
Fred M. Eames, 794 Myrtle Ave., Albany, N. Y.
Eugene B. Patton, 65 Lancaster St., Albany, N. Y.
Sumner H. Lark, 898 Gates Ave., Brooklyn, N. Y.
George L. Pryor, 90 West 134th St., New York City.
John J. Teahan, 78 Clinton Ave., Brooklyn, N. Y.
Joseph P. Powers, 253 Anistel Boulevard, Arverne, N. Y.
Daniel McCoy, 334 West 47th St., New York City.
J. H. Danforth, Gloversville, N. Y.
Grover C. Layner, Cobleskill, N. Y.
Hon. John Seeley, Woodhull, N. Y.
J. L. Ten Eyck, 180 Washington Ave., Albany, N. Y.
John Eddy, Glenmont, N. Y.

John J. Sheehan, 88 Waverly Ave., Brooklyn, N. Y.
George M. Colville, Binghamton, N. Y.
Justin V. Purcell, Corning, N. Y.
Stephen H. Murray, 2184 Fulton St., Brooklyn, N. Y.
Anthony Planigan, 15 Van Woert St., Albany, N. Y.
Wm. J. T. Hogan, 731 Broadway, Albany, N. Y.
W. M. Cameron, Glens Falls, N. Y.
Thos. J. Dunn, Glens Falls, N. Y.
Frank L. Ryan, Norwich, N. Y.
Z. A. Steigmuller, Editor, "Binghamton Press," Binghamton, N. Y.
Martin F. Dillon, Skaneateles, N. Y.
Hon. Chas. H. Gallup, Rochester, N. Y.
Louis Duncan, Pelham Manor, N. Y.
Frank Jerome Houle, Pelham Manor, N. Y.
S. Marsh Young, 220 West 59th St., New York City.
James Devine, Schenectady, N. Y.
Thomas Devine, Schenectady, N. Y.
John Bulman, 480 Clinton Ave., Albany, N. Y.
Chas. E. Brennan, 86 State St., Albany, N. Y.
David E. Eichenbroner, 344 Manning Boulevard, Albany, N. Y.
Wm. L. Terry, Waterford, N. Y.
P. H. McGoldrick, 292 Hamilton St., Albany, N. Y.
George E. Becker, Gallupville, N. Y.
C. H. Rogers, 77 Van Woert St., Albany, N. Y.
Wm. H. Faxon, Chestertown, N. Y.
Louis Hart, 10 Benson St., Albany, N. Y.
James V. May, Albany, N. Y.
Henry J. Crawford, 391 Madison Ave., Albany, N. Y.
H. W. Olmstead, Dannemora, N. Y.
Ralph B. Tompkins, 14 Grand St., Albany, N. Y.
J. Richard Kevin, M. D., 252 Gates Ave., Brooklyn, N. Y.
Maurice E. Connolly, Corona, New York City.
Peter J. Collins, 135 Westminster Road, Brooklyn, N. Y.
Walter H. Burn, 259 Hillside Ave., Jamaica, N. Y.
Charles Jerome Edwards, 399-A Grand Ave., Brooklyn, N. Y.
Daniel B. Cushman, Norwich, N. Y.
William H. Moore, Hotel Empire, New York City (% N. Y. World).
Vito Cantessa, 311 East 119th St., New York City.
Dr. W. A. Cummings, Ticonderoga, N. Y.
Frederick W. Hinrichs, 367 Henry St., Brooklyn, N. Y.
Hamilton Holt, 130 Fulton St., New York City.
Dr. Francis E. Franczak, Health Dept., Albany, N. Y.
John H. Brandow, 59 Manning Boulevard, Albany, N. Y.
D. Henry Brown, Riverhead, N. Y.
Wm. R. Fanning, Riverhead, N. Y.
Rowland Miles, Northport, N. Y.
Otis F. Lewis, Barge Canal Office, Albany, N. Y.
J. J. Cahill, 197 Congress St., Brooklyn, N. Y.
Edwin Corning, 103 Washington Ave., Albany, N. Y.
E. J. Wyer, 399 Western Ave., Albany, N. Y.
Jerry F. Connor, Oneida, N. Y.
Francis X. Disney, Elmira, N. Y.
Daniel Sheehan, Elmira, N. Y.
John W. Gurnett, Watkins, N. Y.
William Leffingwell, Watkins, N. Y.
Daniel J. Dugan, Albany, N. Y.
Albert J. Danaher, Watervliet, N. Y.
Frank M. Baucus, 7 Bridge Ave., Troy, N. Y.
M. H. Hoover, 3 North Main Ave., Albany, N. Y.
O. W. Cutler, Niagara Falls, N. Y.

John Wm. Kelly, 650 9th Ave., New York City.
Matthew J. Dobson, 360 West 45th St., New York City.
Frederick Reyher, 658 10th Ave., New York City.
Michael J. Hickey, 304 West 46th St., New York City.
Philip Fouldman, 512 West 46th St., New York City.
Frank C. Kunkel, 504 West 46th St., New York City.
Daniel J. Cosgro, Cohoes, N. Y.
William P. McEwing, Albany, N. Y.
Jos. Cassidy, Far Rockaway, N. Y.
Martin Mager, Middle Village, L. I.
George N. Webster, Flushing L. I.
Ira H. Le Veen, 60 Union Place, Richmond Hill, N. Y.
Edwin Vlimenter, Butler Blvd., Jamaica, N. Y.
Luke Keenan, 475 Albert St., Long Island City.
Andrew Zorn, Long Island City.
Daniel S. Quigley, 155 North 7th St., Brooklyn, N. Y.
Fremont Wilson, 672 St. Nicholas Ave., New York City.
Geo. B. Wende, 120 Erie County Bank Bldg., Buffalo, N. Y.
Louis Schan, 178 Hudson Ave., Albany, N. Y.
John T. Gorman, Cohoes, N. Y.
J. W. Griggs, Albany, N. Y.
Edw. E. Perkins, State Committeeman.
T. D. Fitzgerald, Albany, N. Y.
Daniel Harris, Brooklyn, N. Y.
Thomas Martin, 50 Ida St., Troy, N. Y.
Patrick J. Prendergast, 15 Harrison Place, Troy, N. Y.
John McClan, 606 West 137th St., New York City.
M. C. Padden, 158 Bowery, New York City.
F. A. Palladino, Albany, N. Y.
H. Gordon Lynn.
Arthur J. Smith.
Martin Van Tannell, 453 State St., Albany, N. Y.
Wm. V. Tassell, 4 Central Ave., White Plains, N. Y.
Vigil H. Kellogg, Watertown, N. Y.
Amasa Houton, 203 Broadway, New York City.
Dr. Louis Gluckman, 69 Ave. B., New York City.
Matthew L. Horgen, Brooklyn, N. Y.
D. W. Rich, Syracuse.
Henry G. Adams.
James A. Parsons, Hornell.
E. E. McGarr.
W. W. Thomas.
Thomas Gilleran, 48 E. Kingsbridge Road, New York City.
George E. Mayer, 3104 6th Avenue, Troy, N. Y.
John Sayles, Mayor's Office, Buffalo, N. Y.
Clarence J. Shearn, 140 Nassau St., New York City.
Thomas E. Ryan, 11 Delaware Street, Albany, N. Y.
John Ward, 84 N. Allen St., Albany, N. Y.
Arthur Johns, 6 West 33rd St., New York City.
Albert E. Henschel, 53 West 130th St., New York City.
Richard W. Sherman, Conservation Comm., Albany, N. Y.
Thos. H. Lee, Stony Point, N. Y.
J. G. Liebfred, 48 Charles St., New Rochelle, N. Y.
Joseph B. Handy, Staten Island, N. Y.
William R. Murray, 326 Livingston Ave., Albany, N. Y.
Alex. E. Oberlander, " Oberlander Press," Syracuse, N. Y.
Fred H. Wilson, 130 Wadsworth Ave., New York City.
Albert Dulin, 854 W. 180th St., New York City.
John J. O'Connell, 31 Nassau St., New York City.
Lucien Knapp, Long Island City, N. Y.

Peter Nelson, Albany, N. Y.
Chas. F. Rattigan, State Committeeman, Albany.
Frank D. Bailey, Sidney, N. Y.
Stephen Whitbeck, Coeymans Hollow, N. Y.
Millard J. Bloomer, 381 E. 149th St., New York City. Representing
    Francis W. Bird, Chairman, N. Y. County Progressive Committee.
      Progressive Party,
        and
    Augustus F. Schwarzler, Chairman, Bronx County Committee, National
      Progressive Party.

Warner M. Sweet, Fillmore, N. Y.
H. S. Bacon, Capitol, Albany, N. Y.
Henry D. Hamilton.
Col. W. D. G. Washington, 39 West 32nd St., New York City.
A. G. Reymond, Greenwich, Conn.
J. A. Costman, 239 West 68th St., New York City.
Louis Schnitzer, Albany, N. Y.
George H. McGuire, Syracuse, N. Y.
Luke A. Keenan, Long Island City, L. I.
E. H. Strong, Millbrook, N. Y.
A. R. Smith, Bellmore, L. I.
James F. Murray, Johnstown, N. Y.
Stephen Vincent, 147 Congress St., Troy, N. Y.
W. B. Hunter, 14 8th St., North Troy, N. Y.
C. E. Akin, Patterson, N. Y.
Alex. Rosenthal, 234 Mary St., Utica, N. Y.
Patrick Doris, 256 Flushing Ave., Brooklyn, N. Y.
Harry B. Winter, 61 So. Lake Ave., Albany, N. Y.
H. E. Cole, 59 Chestnut St., Rensselaer, N. Y.
Calvin J. Huson, Dresden, N. Y.
Jay W. Forrest, 89 So. Manning Boulevard, Albany, N. Y.
John P. Kelly, 253 Broadway, Troy, N. Y.
Jason P. Merrill, Ithaca, N. Y.
Parmer Slingerland, Cobleskill, N. Y.
Anthony Giblin, 15 Second St., Albany, N. Y.
B. B. Haile, Herkimer, N. Y.
S. B. Decker, Ithaca. N. Y.
Philip J. Klem, Herkimer, N. Y.
Joseph Borandess, New York City.
Frank E. Munson, Herkimer, N. Y.
John Williams, Deputy of Labor, Albany, N. Y.
Chas. H. Trask, Little Falls, N. Y.
Hugh Reilly, West Lawrence St., Albany, N. Y.
Nathaniel B. Spalding, Schodack, N. Y.
John Fields, Middleville, N. Y.
H. M. Golden, Mohawk, N. Y.
J. E. Rafton, Mohawk, N. Y.
Capt. H. P. Whiterstine, Bay Shore, N. Y.
Geo. P. Fox, Philmont, N. Y.
Dr. George E. Beilby, 247 State St., Albany, N. Y.
A. T. Blessing, Schenectady, N. Y.
James F. Hennessey, Watervliet, N. Y.
John J. McLaughlin, 1621 Broadway, Watervliet, N. Y.
Meyer Wolfuout, 61 2nd Ave., New York City.
Jacob New, 26 Court St., Brooklyn, N. Y.
John Scally, Westbury, L. I.
Francis L. Ganley, Fort Edward, N. Y.
Edward F. Hale, Schenectady, N. Y.
Lyman S. Holmes, Schoharie, N. Y.
Lester T. Hubbard, Albany, N. Y.
Clinton Beckwith, Herkimer, N. Y.
James H. Mooney, Ilion, N. Y.
Frank E. Munson, Herkimer, N. Y.
Dennis Spellman, New York City.
A. E. Cowles, Wellsville, N. Y.
Albert E. Hoyt, 410 Western Ave., Albany, N. Y.
M. Z. Havens, Syracuse, N. Y.
Stephen V. Lewis, Cohoes, N. Y.
Anthony G. Oliver, Fulton, N. Y.
John T. Norton, Troy, N. Y.

Peter Nelson, Albany, N. Y.
Chas. F. Rattigan, State Committeeman, Albany, N. Y.
Frank D. Bailey, Sidney, N. Y.
Stephen Whitbeck, Coeymans Hollows, N. Y.
Millard J. Bloomer, 381 E. 149th St., New York City.   Representing:
    Francis W. Bird, Chairman, N. Y. County Progressive Committee,
    Progressive Party,
        and
    Augustus F. Schwarzler, Chairman, Bronx County Committee, National
    Progressive Party.

"HE'S GOOD ENOUGH FOR **ME**"

From the Albany Knickerbocker Press

HOW THEY VOTED ON THE FIRST PRIMARY BILL

The Sulzer bill for state-wide direct primaries and electoral reform which was introduced in the legislature on April 21, 1913, provides for the nomination by the people of all State offices, it does away with all committee designations, it prohibits the use of party funds at primary elections, it prohibits the use of all emblems and straight voting circles on the primary ballots, and it provides for the election of United States senators by the people in accordance with the recent constitutional amendment, nominations to be made at an official primary in the same manner as for the office of governor.

This bill was defeated in the state senate because both parties caucused against it—the first time such a thing was done in the history of the state—by a vote of 42 to 8; and in the assembly by a vote of 47 to 93; the division of the vote by political parties was as follows:

Ayes—Senate, 6 Democrats, 1 Republican, 1 Republican-Progressive.

Nays—Senate, 27 Democrats, 15 Republicans.

Ayes—Assembly, 30 Democrats, 12 Republicans, 5 National-Progressives.

Nays—Assembly, 67 Democrats, 26 Republicans.

THE FOLLOWING SENATORS VOTED IN FAVOR OF THE BILL:

Thomas H. O'Keefe, Democrat, Oyster Bay, N. Y., representing first district, comprising Suffolk and Nassau counties.

James H. Duhamel, Democrat, Brooklyn, N. Y., representing eighth district, comprising part of Kings county.

Abraham J. Palmer, National Progressive and Republican, Milton, N. Y., representing twenty-seventh district, comprising Ulster and Greene counties.

George H. Whitney, Republican, Mechanicville, N. Y., representing thirtieth district, comprising Washington and Saratoga counties.

John W. McKnight, Democrat, Castleton, N. Y., representing twenty-ninth district, comprising Rensselaer county.

Clayton L. Wheeler, Democrat, Hancock, N. Y., representing thirty-ninth district, comprising Delaware and Broome counties.

John Seeley, Democrat, Woodhull, N. Y., representing forty-third district, comprising Steuben and Livingston counties.

Gottfried H. Wende, Democrat, Buffalo, N. Y., representing fiftieth district, comprising portion of city of Buffalo, and portions of the county of Erie outside of the city of Buffalo.

THE FOLLOWING ASSEMBLYMEN VOTED IN FAVOR OF THE BILL:

Albert C. Benninger, Democrat, representing third district of Queens county.

Verne M. Bovie, Democrat, New Rochelle, N. Y., representing second district of Westchester county.

Robert P. Bush, Democrat, of Horseheads, representing Chemung county.

Samuel J. Burden, Democrat, Long Island City, representing first district of Queens county.

Charles J. Carroll, Democrat, New York City, representing twenty-ninth district of New York county.

Marc W. Cole, Democrat, of Albion, representing Orleans county.

Stephen G. Daley, Democrat, of Syracuse, representing the second district of Onondaga county.

William T. Doty, Democrat, of Circleville, representing the second district of Orange county.

Edward A. Dox, Democrat, of Richmondville, representing Schoharie county.

Mark Eisner, Democrat, New York, of the seventeenth district of New York county.

John K. Evans, of Bloomingburgh, representing Sullivan county.

Charles H. Gallup, Democrat, of Adams Basin, representing the fifth district of Monroe county.

Eldridge M. Gathright, Democrat, of Marlborough, representing the second district, Ulster county.

Albert F. Geyer, Democrat, of Buffalo, representing the third district of Erie county.

Louis D. Gibbs, Democrat, representing the thirty-second district of New York county.

Frederick G. Grimme, Democrat, of Sparkill, representing Rockland county.

John W. Gurnett, Democrat, of Watkins, representing Schuyler county.

Alexander W. Hover, Democrat, of Germantown, representing Columbia county.

Augustus S. Hughes, Democrat, Seneca Falls, representing Seneca county.

Lawrence M. Kenny, Democrat, Saugerties, representing first district of Ulster county.

Alfred J. Kennedy, Democrat, Whitestone, representing second district of Queens county.

Eugene A. McCollum, Democrat, Lockport, representing the first district of Niagara county.

Minor McDaniels, Democrat, Ithaca, representing Tompkins county..

C. Fred Schwarz, Democrat, of Troy, representing first district of Rensselaer county.

S. L. Seely, Jr., Democrat, Canisteo, representing the second district of Steuben county.

Arthur P. Squire, Democrat, Rotterdam Junction, representing Schenectady county.

Howard Sutphin, Democrat, Jamaica, representing the fourth district of Queens county.

John W. Telford, Democrat, Margaretville, representing Delaware county.

Tracey D. Taylor, Democrat, Berlin, representing second district of Rensselaer county.

Clare Willard, Democrat, Allegany, representing Cattaraugus county.

REPUBLICANS

Caleb H. Baumes, Newburgh, representing first district of Orange county.

John D. Fuller, Marcy, representing third district of Oneida county.

Walter A. Gage, Canajoharie, representing Montgomery county.

Edward C. Gillette, Pen Yan, representing Yates county.

Clinton T. Horton, Buffalo, representing second district of Erie county.

John Knight, Arcade, representing Wyoming county.

Frank L. Seaker, Gouverneur, representing first district of St. Lawrence county.

Gilbert T. Seelye, Burnt Hills, representing Saratoga county.

John L. Sullivan, Dunkirk, representing second district, Chautauqua county.

Morell E. Pallett, DeRuyter, representing Madison county.

Charles J. Vert, Plattsburg, representing Clinton county.

James H. Wood, Gloversville, representing Fulton and Hamilton counties.

NATIONAL PROGRESSIVE

Maxim Birnkrant, New York city, representing tenth district, New York county.

George W. Jude, Jamestown, representing first district of Chautauqua county.

Michael Schaap, New York city, representing thirty-first district of New York county.

Solomon Sufrin, of New York city. representing the eighth district of New York county.

Lester D. Volk, Brooklyn, representing the sixth district of Kings county.

SENATORS WHO VOTED IN THE NEGATIVE WHEN THE SULZER STATE-WIDE PRIMARY ACT WAS VOTED UPON:

REPUBLICANS

George F. Argetsinger, of Rochester, representing the forty-fifth district which consists of wards of the city of Rochester and certain towns of Monroe county.

Elon R. Brown, of Watertown, representing the thirty-fifth district comprising the counties of Jefferson and Oswego.

Thomas H. Bussey, of Perry, representing the forty-fifth district composed of the counties of Genesee, Wyoming and Allegany.

Herbert Coats, of Saranac Lake, representing the thirty-fourth district, composed of the counties of St. Lawrence and Franklin.

James A. Emerson, of Warrensburg, representing the thirty-third district, composed of the counties of Clinton and Essex and Warren.

Frank N. Godfrey, of Olean, representing the fifty-first district, comprising Cattaraugus and Chautauqua counties.

Seth G. Heacock, of Ilion, representing the thirty-second district, composed of the counties of Lewis, Fulton, Hamilton, and Herkimer.

Charles J. Hewitt, of Locke, representing the fortieth district, composed of the counties of Cayuga, Seneca and Cortland.

William L. Ormrod, of Churchville, representing the forty-sixth district, composed of wards of Rochester and towns of Monroe county.

Henry W. Sage, of Menands, representing the twenty-eighth district, composed of Albany county.

John D. Stivers, of Middletown, representing the twenty-fifth district, composed of the counties of Orange and Sullivan.

Ralph W. Thomas, of Hamilton, representing the thirty-seventh district, composed of the counties of Otego, Madison, and Chenango.

George H. Thompson, Middleport, representing the forty-seventh district, composed of Orleans and Niagara counties.

J. Henry Walters, of Syracuse, representing the thirty-eighth district, composed of the county of Onondaga.

Thomas B. Wilson, of Hall, representing the forty-second district, composed of the counties of Wayne, Ontario and Yates.

DEMOCRATS

George A. Blauvelt, of Monsey, representing the twenty-third district, composed of Richmond and Rockland counties.

John J. Boylan, of the fifteenth district, composed of part of the county of New York.

Daniel J. Carroll, of Brooklyn, representing the seventh district, composed of part of the county of Kings.

William B. Carswell, of Brooklyn, representing the sixth district, composed of part of the county of Kings.

Thomas H. Cullen, of Brooklyn, representing the third district, composed of part of Kings county.

John C. Fitzgerald, of New York, representing the twelfth district, composed of part of New York county.

James A. Foley, of New York, representing the fourteenth district, composed of part of New York county.

James J. Frawley, of New York, representing the twentieth district, composed of part of New York county.

Anthony J. Griffin, of New York, representing the twenty-second district, composed of part of New York county.

John J. Healy, of New Rochelle, representing the twenty-fourth district, composed of Westchester county.

William J. Heffernan, of Brooklyn, representing the fifth district, composed of part of Kings county.

Walter R. Herrick, of New York, representing the seventeenth district, composed of part of New York county.

James D. McClelland, of New York, representing the thirteenth district, composed of part of New York county.

John F. Malone, of Buffalo, representing the forty-eighth district, composed of part of the city of Buffalo.

John F. Murtaugh, of Elmira, representing the forty-first district, composed of the counties of Tompkins, Chemung, Tioga and Schuyler.

Bernard M. Patten, of Long Island City, representing the second district, composed of the county of Queens.

William D. Peckham, M. D., of Utica, representing the thirty-sixth district, composed of the county of Oneida.

Henry W. Pollock, of New York, representing the eighteenth district composed of part of New York county.

Samuel J. Ramsperger, of Buffalo, representing the forty-ninth district, composed of part of the city of Buffalo.

Felix J. Sanner, of Brooklyn, representing the ninth district, part of Kings county.

George W. Simpson, of New York, representing the nineteenth district, part of New York county.

Stephen J. Stilwell, of New York, representing the twenty-first district, composed of part of New York county.

Christopher D. Sullivan, of New York, representing the eleventh district, composed of part of New York county.

Herman H. Torberg, of Brooklyn, representing the tenth district, composed of part of Kings county.

Henry P. Velte, of Brooklyn, representing the fourth district, composed of parts of Kings county.

Robert F. Wagner, of New York, representing the sixteenth district, composed of part of New York county.

Loren H. White, of Delanson, representing the thirty-first district, composed of the counties of Schenectady, Montgomery and Schoharie.

ASSEMBLYMEN WHO VOTED IN THE NEGATIVE:

REPUBLICANS

Simon I. Adler, of Rochester, representing the second district of Monroe county.

William C. Baxter, of Watervliet, representing the third district of Albany county.

Frank M. Bradley, of Barker, representing the second district of Niagara county.

Clarence Bryant, of LeRoy, representing Genesee county.

Mortimer B. Edwards, of Lisle, representing Broome county.

Michael Grace, of Weedsport, representing Cayuga county.

Harold J. Hinman, of Albany, representing the first district of Albany county.

Jared W. Hopkins, of Pittsford, representing the first district of Monroe county.

John G. Jones, of Carthage, representing the second district of Jefferson county.

Alexander MacDonald, of St. Regis Falls, representing Franklin county.

H. Edmund Machold, of Ellisburg, representing the first district of Jefferson county.

Edward M. Magee, of Groveland Station, representing Livingston county.

John G. Malone, of Albany, representing the second district of Albany county.

Eugene R. Norton, of Granville, representing Washington county.

August V. Pappert, of Rochester, representing the third district of Monroe county.

John C. Fitz erald, o New York, representing the twel
district, compo d of par of New York county.

James A. Foley, of Nw York, representing the fourteer
istrict, compo d of par of New York county.

James J. Frawl y, of ew York, representing the twentie
istrict, compo d of par of New York county.

Anthony J. Griffin, o New York, representing the twen
second district, composeof part of New York county.

John J. Heal of Ne Rochelle, representing the twent
composedof Westchester county.

William J. H fernan of Brooklyn, representing the fif
district, comp d of par of Kings county.

Walter R. H ick, o New York, representing the seve
teenth district, composeof part of New York county.

James D. M(lland, of New York, representing the thi
teenth district, composeof part of New York county.

John F. Mal of iffalo, representing the forty-eight
district, compo of par of the city of Buffalo.

John F. Mur gh, o Elmira, representing the forty-firs
tl counties of Tompkins, Chemung

o Long Island City, representing the
second district, composed f the county of Queens.

William D. P kham, M. D., of Utica, representing the
comp sed of the county of Oneida.

k, of Nw York, representing the eighteenth
district comp d f part f New York county.

Samuel J Ramsperge of Buffalo, representing the forty-
part of the city of Buffalo.

Felix J. Sumer, of Bro lyn, representing the ninth district,

New York, representing the nineteenth district, part of N York county.

Stephen J. Se ell, of ew York, representing the tw
first district, comp sed c art of New York county.

Christopher D. Sulli of New York, representi
compos of part of New York county.

Herman H rberg, Brooklyn, representing the
district, comp f Kings county.

John C. Fitzgerald, of New York, representing the twelfth district, composed of part of New York county.

James A. Foley, of New York, representing the fourteenth district, composed of part of New York county.

James J. Frawley, of New York, representing the twentieth district, composed of part of New York county.

Anthony J. Griffin, of New York, representing the twenty-second district, composed of part of New York county.

John J. Healy, of New Rochelle, representing the twenty-fourth district, composed of Westchester county.

William J. Heffernan, of Brooklyn, representing the fifth district, composed of part of Kings county.

Walter R. Herrick, of New York, representing the seventeenth district, composed of part of New York county.

James D. McClelland, of New York, representing the thirteenth district, composed of part of New York county.

John F. Malone, of Buffalo, representing the forty-eighth district, composed of part of the city of Buffalo.

John F. Murtaugh, of Elmira, representing the forty-first district, composed of the counties of Tompkins, Chemung, Tioga and Schuyler.

Bernard M. Patten, of Long Island City, representing the second district, composed of the county of Queens.

William D. Peckham, M. D,. of Utica, representing the thirty-sixth district, composed of the county of Oneida.

Henry W. Pollock, of New York, representing the eighteenth district composed of part of New York county.

Samuel J. Ramsperger, of Buffalo, representing the forty-ninth district, composed of part of the city of Buffalo.

Felix J. Sanner, of Brooklyn, representing the ninth district, part of Kings county.

George W. Simpson, of New York, representing the nineteenth district, part of New York county.

Stephen J. Stilwell, of New York, representing the twenty-first district, composed of part of New York county.

Christopher D. Sullivan, of New York, representing the eleventh district, composed of part of New York county.

Herman H. Torberg, of Brooklyn, representing the tenth district, composed of part of Kings county.

Henry P. Velte, of Brooklyn, representing the fourth district, composed of parts of Kings county.

Robert F. Wagner, of New York, representing the sixteenth district, composed of part of New York county.

Loren H. White, of Delanson, representing the thirty-first district, composed of the counties of Schenectady, Montgomery and Schoharie.

ASSEMBLYMEN WHO VOTED IN THE NEGATIVE:

REPUBLICANS

Simon I. Adler, of Rochester, representing the second district of Monroe county.

William C. Baxter, of Watervliet, representing the third district of Albany county.

Frank M. Bradley, of Barker, representing the second district of Niagara county.

Clarence Bryant, of LeRoy, representing Genesee county.

Mortimer B. Edwards, of Lisle, representing Broome county.

Michael Grace, of Weedsport, representing Cayuga county.

Harold J. Hinman, of Albany, representing the first district of Albany county.

Jared W. Hopkins, of Pittsford, representing the first district of Monroe county.

John G. Jones, of Carthage, representing the second district of Jefferson county.

Alexander MacDonald, of St. Regis Falls, representing Franklin county.

H. Edmund Machold, of Ellisburg, representing the first district of Jefferson county.

Edward M. Magee, of Groveland Station, representing Livingston county.

John G. Malone, of Albany, representing the second district of Albany county.

Eugene R. Norton, of Granville, representing Washington county.

August V. Pappert, of Rochester, representing the third district of Monroe county.

Cyrus W. Phillips, of Rochester, representing the fourth district of Monroe county.

Ranson L. Richards, of Fillmore, representing Allegany county.

Herman L. Schnirel, of Geneva, representing Ontario county.

Walter L. Shepardson, of Norwich, representing Chenango county.

John A. Smith, of North Lawrence, representing the second district of St. Lawrence county.

Myron Smith, of Millbrook, representing the first district of Dutchess county.

Thomas K. Smith, of Syracuse, representing the third district of Onondaga county.

Thaddeus C. Sweet, of Phoenix, representing Oswego county.

Niles F. Webb, of Cortland, representing Cortland county.

John R. Yale, of Brewster, representing Putnam county.

Albert Yeomans, of Walworth, representing Wayne county.

DEMOCRATS

Frederick S. Burr, of Brooklyn, representing the ninth district of Kings county.

James C. Campbell, of New York, representing the thirteenth district of New York county.

Raymond R. Carver, of New York, representing the twenty-seventh district of New York county.

Thomas B. Caughlan, of New York, representing the first district of New York county.

Salvatore A. Cotillo, of New York, representing the twenty-eighth district of New York county.

Cornelius J. Cronin, of Brooklyn, representing the twenty-eighth district of Kings county.

Louis A. Cuvillier, of New York, representing the thirtieth district of New York county.

Karl S. Dietz, of Brooklyn, representing the tenth district of Kings county.

George E. Dennen, of Brooklyn, representing the tenth district of Kings county.

Thos. F. Denny, of New York, representing the tenth district of New York county.

Charles S. Donahue, of New York, representing the ninth district of New York county.

John Dorst, Jr., of Akron, representing the ninth district of Erie county.

Joseph H. Esquirol, of Brooklyn, representing the eighteenth district of Kings county.

Stephen C. Fallon, of Setauket, representing the first district of Suffolk county.

Daniel J. Farrell, of Brooklyn, representing the seventh district of Kings county.

Joseph V. Fitzgerald, of Lancaster, representing the seven district of Erie county.

James J. Garvey, of Brooklyn, representing the fourteenth district of Kings county.

George Geoghan, of Buffalo, representing the eighth district of Erie county.

William J. Gillen, of Brooklyn, representing the second district of Kings county.

Mark Goldberg, of New York, representing the eighteenth district of New York county.

Abraham Greenburg, of New York, representing the twenty-sixth district of New York county.

Wm. P. Hamilton, Jr., of Brooklyn, representing the twelfth district of Kings county.

Ernest E. L. Hammer, of New York, representing the thirty-fifth district of New York county.

Richard F. Hearn, of Buffalo, representing the fifth district of Erie county.

Henry Heyman, of Brooklyn, representing the twenty-first district of Kings county.

Thomas L. Ingram, of Brooklyn, representing the twenty-third district of Kings county.

Edward D. Jackson, of Buffalo, representing the fourth district of Erie county.

Thomas Kane, of New York, representing the twenty-first district of New York county.

John A. Kelly, of Poughkeepsie, representing the second district of Dutchess county.

John J. Kelly, of Brooklyn, representing the first district of Kings county.

Joseph D. Kelly, of New York, representing the twelfth district of New York county.

David C. Lewis, of New York, representing the twenty-third district, New York city.

John Kerrigan, of New York, representing the eleventh district of New York county.

Owen M. Kiernan, of New York, representing the twenty-fourth district of New York county.

David H. Knott, of New York, representing the twenty-fifth district of New York county.

Harry W. Kornobis, of Brooklyn, representing the fourth district of Kings county.

Jesse P. Larrimer, of Brooklyn, representing the sixteenth district of Kings county.

Aaron J. Levy, of New York, representing the fourth district of New York county.

Tracey J. Madden, of Yonkers, representing the first district of Westchester county.

Thomas B. Mahoney, of Great Neck Station, representing Nassau county.

Martin G. McCue, of New York, representing the sixteenth district of New York county.

Peter P. McElligott, of New York, representing the seventh district of New York county.

Patrick J. McGrath, of New York, representing the twentieth district of New York county.

Ralph R. McKee, of Tompkinsville, representing Richmond county.

John J. McKeon, of Brooklyn, representing the eighth district of Kings county.

Patrick J. McMahon, of New York, representing the thirty-fourth district of New York county.

Joseph J. Monahan, of Brooklyn, representing the twenty-second district of Kings county.

Mortimer C. O'Brien, of White Plains, representing the fourth district of Westchester county.

Vincent C. O'Connor, of Brooklyn, representing the fifth district of Kings county.

Harry E. Oxford, of New York, representing the third district of New York county.

J. L. Patrie, of Catskill, representing Greene county.

E. Bert Pullman, of Fulton Chain, representing Herkimer county.

John J. Robinson, of Centerport, representing the second district of Suffolk county.

James Rosen, of Buffalo, representing the sixth district of Erie county.

Jacob Schifferdecker, of Brooklyn, representing the nineteenth district of Kings county.

Jacob Silverstein, of New York, representing the sixth district of New York county.

George F. Small, of Buffalo, representing the first district of Erie county.

Frank J. Taylor, of Brooklyn, representing the third district of Kings county.

Robert L. Tudor, of New York, representing the fourteenth district of New York county.

Frederick Ulrich, of Brooklyn, representing the seventeenth district of Kings county.

James B. Van Woert of Greig, representing Lewis county.

James J. Walker, of New York city, representing the fifth district of New York county.

Theodore Hackett Ward, of New York city, representing fifteenth district of New York county.

Edward Weil, of New York city, representing twenty-second district of New York county.

Thomas E. Wilmott, of Brooklyn, representing fifteenth district of Kings county.

Wilson R. Yard, of Pleasantville, representing third district of Westchester county.

Alfred E. Smith, of New York, representing second district of New York county.

KING CANNOT

From the Albany Knickerbocker Press

WHY I AM FOR DIRECT PRIMARIES

Speech of Governor Sulzer at the Auditorium in Buffalo, N. Y.,
Monday night, May 19, 1913

Mr. Sulzer said:

" It is self-evident to me that if the people are competent to directly elect their public officials they are also competent to directly nominate these officials.

" If it is important for minor officers to be nominated by the people, it is still more important that the people be given the power to nominate candidates for United States senator and for governor. That if public service corporations and special interests seek to control public affairs for the promotion of their selfish ends through the manipulation of party conventions, the plain people should seek to do the same thing by taking in their own hands the right to nominate directly these important officials.

" The truth is that the delegate system of nominating officers has completely broken down and proven itself not only inadequate to carry out the wishes of the people, but it has become an instrumentality through which the powers of government are prostituted and brought under the dominion of unscrupulous men seeking special privileges.

" In this campaign for direct primaries, I am appealing now directly to the people, and they are responding as they always will respond when their rights are jeopardized and their liberties are subverted, and they hear the call of duty and see the opportunity to assert effectually their inherent power and inalienable rights.

" From every farm, and hamlet, and town, and city come voices declaring that the time has arrived to dissolve the political bonds by which the few have enthralled the many by skillful, secret and disgraceful manipulations of party conventions, and to establish state-wide direct primaries, abolishing state conventions, as they already have been abolished in two-thirds of the states which form this Union.

" Every day I see accumulating evidence of the truth, which I stated in my recent direct-primary message to the legislature, that those who would subvert the powers of government to personal advantage and to special privilege find their greatest opportunities to carry on this nefarious work through the skillful manipulations of political conventions.

"Political conventions must go. Disgraceful secret alliances between special privilege and crooked politics must cease. That is all there is to it.

"The power of special privilage is greater in New York than in any other state, because in New York is centered the great financial interests of the nation. Most of these interests are sound, legitimate and honest, but some of these interests are illegitimate, and it is the last mentioned kind which are fighting the salutory reforms which I am advocating—reforms which will faithfully carry out the letter and spirit of the political platforms of every party in this state.

"The spirit of true democracy is summed up in the slogan 'Let the people rule.' They cannot rule until they obtain a successful method of nominating the candidates of all political parties.

"New York state is one of the last states in the Union to capitulate to the present-day demand for popular rule in the nomination of candidates for all public offices. It is bound to come in New York. The fight is on, and the people are in earnest.

"The power of special privilege is making its last stand in our state, but will be overthrown, and overthrown speedily, by a righteous public sentiment.

"Every day I am hearing from senators and assemblymen who voted against our direct primary bill, and who now assure me they will give it their support at the coming special session of the legislature, because they have learned since they returned home that by voting against the direct primaries, they misrepresented the sentiment of their constituents.

"From others I hear that they will support the bill if it be amended so that state conventions may be continued. The play of 'Hamlet' with Hamlet left out would not be more of an abortion than a direct primaries law with the state convention retained.

"To have direct primaries and to have state conventions is impossible. Direct primaries have been devised to permit the

people to nominate their officers directly without the intermediary of delegates, and as, of course, you cannot have state
conventions without delegates, it follows that state conventions
must go and honest direct primaries must come.   There is no
middle ground.   There can be no compromise.   Those who
want to straddle are against us.   You cannot straddle a
principle.

" The widespread demand for direct primaries originated
mainly from the scandalous failure of state conventions to
faithfully reflect the sentiment of the voters.   Again and
again candidates having strong support in state conventions
have been set aside and the bosses have brought forward at the
last moment a dark-horse candidate and secured his nomination through skillful political manipulations.

" There are only two kinds of primaries—direct and indirect.
The latter constitutes the reactionary delegate system;   the
former constitutes the present progressive system.   There are
no two ways about it.   The principle admits of no compromise.
I am for the direct system.   I want the people to nominate
because I want the people to rule.

" The democratic party, in the state of New York, in its last
state convention, declared in emphatic terms for direct primaries
and state-wide at that.

" I believe it is my duty, as the governor, elected on that
platform, to do everything in my power to carry out this solemn
pledge.   Every democrat in the state elected on that platform
should uphold my efforts to redeem the pledge and keep faith
with the voters.

" So far as I am concerned there will be no step backward.
I am in the fight to stay and to the end.   Hence I urge every
honest democrat in the state who believes in fair play, who
wants to keep good faith, and who favors redeeming solemn
party promises to aid me in the struggle.

"We will win in the end.   The leading newspapers of the
state; seven-tenths of the voters of the state, regardless of
party affiliations; and the overwhelming popular sentiment of
the people, are behind the cause for direct primaries, and are
with me in the fight for the legislation.

" Let me tell you briefly just what our direct primary bill
accomplishes:

" 1. All party candidates for public offices, except town, village and school district offices, are to be nominated directly by the enrolled party voters at an official primary.

" 2. A state committee of 150 members, one from each assembly district, and a county committee for each county, to be elected directly by the enrolled party voters at the official primary. All other committees to consist of the members of the state committee and the members of the county committee or committees residing in the political subdivision.

" 3. All party candidates for public office to be voted for in the official primary to be by petition only, the same as independent candidates.

" 4. Every designating petition to contain the appointment of a committee for filling vacancies on the primary ballot.

" 5. Candidates to be arranged on the ballot under the title of the office. Order of arrangement to be determined in each group by lot by the commissioners of election in the presence of the candidates or their representatives. All emblems on the primary ballot abolished. Names of candidates to be numbered from one upward. Voter to indicate his choice by making a separate mark before the name of each candidate.

" 6. The number of enrolled party voters required to sign a designating petition is fixed at one per cent. of the party vote for governor at the last preceding election, except that for state-wide offices the number need not exceed 3,000 enrolled voters of which fifty shall be from each of twenty counties. The number in the city of New York need not exceed 1,000 enrolled party voters, with other maximum limits for smaller subdivisions.

" 7. The primary district is made identical with the election district and primaries of all parties to be held at the same polling place, conducted by the election officers.

" 8. The chairman of a county committee may be elected from outside the committee membership.

" 9· Each party to have a party council to frame a platform; such council to consist of the party candidates for office to be voted for by the state at large; party congressmen, and party United States senators; candidates for the senate and assembly and members of the state committee.

" 10. A special enrollment each year in the month of June

for a new party created by the vote at the last preceding general election.

" 11. The time for filing independent nominations subsequent to the filing of party nominations increased from five days to fourteen days. The number of signers of an independent certificate of nomination reduced to conform substantially to the number of signers of a party designation.

" 12. Election of United States senators by the people provided for in accordance with the recent constitutional amendment. Nominations to be made at official primary in the same manner as for the office of governor.

" 13. Registration days in the country reduced from four to two, and registration in the country by affidavit required where voter does not appear personally.

" 14. Boards of election in counties having less than one hundred and twenty thousand inhabitants reduced from four members to two.

" 15. The use of party funds at primary election prohibited.

" 16. The penal law to be amended limiting the amount that may be expended by a candidate for the purpose of seeking a nomination to public office or election to a party position.

" 17. Delegates and alternates from the state at large, and from congressional districts, to the national convention to be chosen by the direct vote of enrolled party voters at the official primary.

"Any proposition less than this begs the whole question, and violates the pledged faith of the democratic party to every voter in the state. I am now, and always have been, and always will be in favor of carrying out our platform pledges to the letter. The best way to strengthen a political party is to keep the faith. I want to restore to the people of the state the complete control of their state government; to afford the voters of the state the freest expression of their choice of candidates for public office; and I believe that our 'state-wide' direct primary bill embraces an honest, a sincere, a comprehensive and a practical plan for these accomplishments.

" Besides, I consider that our 'state-wide' direct primary bill is an absolutely nonpartisan measure, which faithfully reproduces, and will substantially carry into practice, the pledges of the three great political parties concerned in the last state election; and that, on its merits, it will meet the approval and have the support and the backing of a large majority of all the citizens of this state.

" I am convinced that every member of the legislature is solemnly bound in honor, and by the highest moral and political obligations, to vote for its enactment; and those who fail to do so will be forced to yield to public opinion and be replaced by others who will vote to give the state an efficient and just state-wide direct primary law, that will embrace every office, from governor down to constable.

" Is it necessary for me, or any other man, to say that in continuing the delegate system in nominating state officers, electors are not allowed to nominate directly?   In continuing the delegate system, we are therefore ignoring and repudiating our platform pledges and betraying the people with false pretenses. I shall not be a party to such repudiation. I shall not endorse such a betrayal of the people. No political party can make me a political hypocrite.

" The democratic candidates promised the people in the last campaign that if we were successful, we would give them— among other things—a state-wide direct primary law.

" I ran for the governorship on the platform of the Syracuse convention. I helped to write that platform, and after I was nominated I stood on it throughout the campaign—squarely and honestly.

"At the request of my party I made a campaign through the state. They tell me I spoke to more people during the contest than any other candidate in all the history of the state. I told the people that if I were elected I would do everything in my power to carry out the pledges of my party as enunciated in the Syracuse platform. Many doubted the sincerity of these campaign speeches; but there was one man who never doubted their sincerity, and that is the man who is now governor of the state.

"When I cannot be honest in politics, I shall get out of politics. I believe honesty in politics will succeed, just the same as I believe honesty in business will succeed. If anyone doubts that, all he has to do is to think of what has been accomplished in this country during the past quarter of a century by the men who have dared to be true, and have been honest in politics.

"When I make a promise to the people I keep it, or I frankly tell the people why I cannot keep it. When my party makes a promise to the people, I want my party to keep the promise, or I want the people to know the reason why.

" Let us keep the faith. That is where I stand, and I will stand there to the end. If any democrat is against me in my determination to keep democratic faith, I must of necessity be against him.

" It is all very simple to me. If any democrat in this state is against the democratic state platform that man is no true democrat; and as the democratic governor of the state I shall do everything in my power to drive that recreant democrat out of the councils of the democratic party.

" The record will show that for years I have been a consistent advocate of genuine direct primaries, and I firmly believe that the enactment into law of a state-wide direct primary bill, along the lines of the measure we have caused to be prepared, and which was introduced in the legislature, will accomplish what the voters desire, and reflect greater credit on the members of the present legislature than the passage of any other act that can, or will be presented, for the consideration of its members this year.

" Let us be honest with the voters and keep our pledges to the people. At all events, as the governor, I shall, and if the legislature does not, I want the voters to know the reason why.

"When we consider the waste, the extravagance, the inefficiency, and the corruption, which have recently been brought to light in connection with the administration of public affairs in our state, and which are the cause of painful humiliation to every thoughtful and patriotic citizen, all due, in no small degree, to the fact that in recent years political power has been gradually slipping away from the people who should always control it and wield it, there can be no doubt as to the necessity of this legislation and as to our duty in this all important matter.

" Every intelligent citizen is aware that those who subvert the government to their personal advantage have found their greatest opportunities to do so through the adroit and skillful manipulation of our system of party caucuses and political conventions. It must cease or our free institutions are doomed."

DIRECT PRIMARIES

Address delivered by Jay W. Forrest, of Albany, N. Y., at Van Curler
Opera House, Schenectady, N. Y., May 21st, 1913

Governor William Sulzer insists that the legislature keeps
its promise, and appeals to the people to see to it that the
faith is kept.

Jefferson smashed the semi-royalism of the Federalist with
an appeal to the people.

Jackson dethroned King Caucus and the rule of the Bank
Ring by organizing a break-away appeal to the masses.

Governor William Sulzer states his position as follows: " I
helped write the Democratic platform at Syracuse; I ran on
that platform, and I am here today because of the pledges of
that platform. No man, no faction, no party, can make me
a political hypocrite, and, when I read in that platform the
pledge for a direct primary law, I say that when I make a
promise I will keep it."

The movement is a democratic one, and is animated by a
desire for a wider popular participation in the government by
the people. The direct primary is the organic part of a general growth of democratic sentiment demanding methods by
which more direct responsibility of the governor to the governed can be secured. Startling disclosures respecting the
betrayal of public trust by party leaders has aroused the
people to a crusade for responsible party government.

The convention no longer expresses the popular will. Delegates have become the main shafts of political machines. Corporate wealth and influence dictate the policies of the dominant parties, while candidates and office-holders, instead of
being responsible to the voters, are responsible to the boss and
the ring which nominate them.

The government must be brought back to the people. They
must be given the power to directly nominate their party candidates. If they are sufficiently intelligent to directly elect
them by means of the Australian ballot, they are sufficiently
intelligent to directly nominate them.

Jay W. Forrest

Those who oppose the direct primary deny the right or the ability of the party voters to choose their own candidates directly. Their position is untenable, as it is opposed to the fundamental principles of self-government upon which this republic rests.

It was Boss Tweed who said: " Let me name the candidates and you can vote for them."

It was Daniel Webster who said: " It is time to do away with caucuses; they make great men little and little men great. The true source of power is the people."

The statesman, John C. Calhoun, in a speech in the United States senate, said: " When it comes to be once understood that politics are a game; that those who are engaged in it but act a part; that they make this or that profession, not from honest conviction or an intent to fulfil them, but as the means of deluding the people, and through that delusion to acquire power,—when such professions are to be entirely forgotten, the people will lose all confidence in public men; all will be regarded as mere jugglers,—the honest and the patriotic as well as the cunning and the profligate; and the people will become indifferent and passive to the grossest abuses of power on the ground that those whom they may elevate, under whatever pledges, instead of reforming, will but imitate the example of those whom they have expelled."

Woodrow Wilson said in his speech accepting the Democratic nomination for the presidency: " The rule of the people is no idle phrase, those who believe in it, as who does not that has caught the real spirit of America? believe that there can be no rule of right without it; that right in politics is made up of the interests of everybody, and everybody should take part in the action that is to determine it. We are working towards a very definite object, the universal partnership in public affairs upon which the purity of politics and its aim and spirit depend.

If the American people desire better government they must reform it; not simply by voting for the party of their fathers on election day, not necessarily or primarily by forming new parties, not in the main by being independent of party, but by becoming better members of each and every party with which they are or may be affiliated, by taking hold and run-

ning the party machine for righteous living and good government, instead of permitting the party machine to run them
for graft and vicious government.

We must arouse ourselves to the duty of the hour, to the
necessity of looking after the essentials of our political life,
instead of confining our efforts to mere incidentals; to seeing
to it not merely that we do not vote for the very bad men
our party nominates, but in personally taking hold of affairs
within our own party, and that we, ourselves, nominate men
to whom the custody of public affairs may be safely confided.

Independent voting at the general election, as a method of
reforming government, is like attempting to change the direction of a railroad train by putting on the brakes. If going
the wrong way, you may succeed by this action, in tempo-
rarily slowing down, but the only means through which to
control the direction is through the operation of the engine.
If the American voter desires to return toward the goal contemplated by the Declaration of Independence and provided
for by the Constitution, of a government of, for and by the
people, he cannot effect this result by merely putting on the
brakes of his party train when he conceives that it is going
too fast in the wrong direction. He must get hold of the lever
that guides the party machine or he can never do more than
regulate the speed, he can never alter the course.

If it requires the people other than the politicians to carry
general elections, why cannot the same people, too, carry
primary elections? At primary as well as at general elections
votes count, and the people have the votes.

The politicians, while apparently giving to the people an
important reform which they have demanded, really withhold
to themselves all the real power for evil of the old stand and
deliver system, by leaving it in full sway over the party primaries. And through this system, which permits the ballot-
box to become an auction block for the purchase and sale of
votes, the sellers, with the additional strength of those voted
through coercion, become a force almost invncible.

Governor LaFollette, after rousing the people of Wisconsin
to action toward the overthrow of the government of corporate
greed, struck at the root of the system by his direct nominations
law, which did away with delegate conventions and provided

that the candidates of all parties should be nominated by direct vote of the people entitled to vote at the primaries through the agency of a secret ballot. Such a system is the legal essential to the restoration of popular government, and self-government cannot be assured to the people of this state until we shall have secured nominations by direct vote and a secret ballot to minimize the power of intimidation and the possibility of corruption.

This direct-nomination secret-ballot system places the opportunity for direct and absolute control of government within easy grasp of the people. After the reformation of the system bad government can be ascribed only to depraved public morals. Continued vicious government in a republic may be so ascribed, to a large degree, in any event; but with an enlightened people it becomes the first duty of those interested in the establishment of good government to labor for the removal of all hurdles from the course-way of popular sovereignty.

Why there should be any opposition to the principles of direct primaries it is hard to understand. In truth there is no open opposition, for it would take a courage that is not possessed by the average politician to get up and tell the people that they are not fitted to govern themselves; that they must delegate to politicians the art of choosing the men who are to represent them. In order that the masses of our people may be governed for the benefit of the few, it is necessary that the many have no direct hand in their own governing. It is necessary that the many delegate to representatives the art of governing, and that such representatives should be influenced so as to become the representatives of the few, in order that governing may be carried on for the advantage of rulers, not of ruled.

So the opposition to direct primaries among those who design to make of our government an instrument for the oppression of the many and the enrichment of the few is an opposition that is covert, for to avow it would make it ineffective.

I do not want to be harsh, but he who, understanding, opposes direct primaries is no better than a monarchist, for he holds that the people are not fitted to govern themselves, that the few are fitted by divine law to rule; that the many are condemned to be ruled for the benefit of the few by a law equally divine. This is the law of kings; it is not the law of democracy. It does not breathe the spirit of our Declaration of Independence; he who holds it is false to our theory of government, a worthy monarchist, but an unworthy republican.

No one who believes the people are fitted to govern themselves, capable of discerning what laws are good and what bad, can honestly oppose direct primaries, which means nothing less than government by and for the people.

Direct primaries, or the rule of the people, is only democracy applied, and its growth demonstrates that at the core our people are still democratic—not in a partisan sense, but in the true meaning of that noble word—and they are determined by using direct primaries to change this from a government of the people, by the politicians and for the corporations, to one that, while it is of the people, is actually by the people, and hence is really and truly for the people.

The night has been long, and the darkness deep. Sometimes we were full of despair. It seemed as though the revel of the evil spirits of invisible government would last forever. The public mind seemed strangely dull. The public conscience seemed strangely seared. The public heart seemed strangely cold.

But all the apathy, the discouragement, the tame submission, the cowardly inertia, is passing away. Day is breaking, and the foul creatures of invisible government are slinking to their holes.

At last the people have a governor who stands firm on the rock of Democracy. William Sulzer is making good. He insists on keeping the faith. Let the people insist on the members of the legislature doing the same.

THE POWER TO NOMINATE IS THE POWER TO CONTROL

Speech of Governor Sulzer in Rochester, N. Y., on Wednesday night, June 11, 1913

Mr. Sulzer said in part:

"All I am trying to do, as the governor of the state, is to keep the pledges of my party—to do right—to keep the faith. —and to give the people of the state an honest, an efficient, and an economical administration of public affairs.

" The average citizen would naturally believe that was the easiest thing to do, but I assure him it has been the hardest thing for me to do.

" Ever since I have been the governor every obstacle has been placed in my way by men high in the counsels of my party, because I wanted to do what I believed was right, and what my party promised to do.

" The democratic platform of 1910 declared for 'state-wide' direct primaries, but those who drew the platform of 1912, realizing that the expectations of the rank and file of party voters were not met by the legislation of 1911 pledged the party to ' adopt such amendments to the existing law as will perfect the direct primary system.'

" The electors of the state understood the words 'state-wide direct primaries' to mean direct primaries applied to all state nominations. Democratic campaign speeches and the newspapers which supported our ticket so interpreted these words.

" In my first message to the legislature I said:

" ' We are pledged to direct primaries, state-wide in their scope and character and I urge the adoption of such amendments to our primary laws as will make *complete* and *perfect* the direct primary system of the state.'

" The people expected nothing less from us when we declared for state-wide direct primaries, than the nomination by the voters of all state officers, because it has been demonstrated that under the convention system the will of the people was not faithfully carried out in the state conventions.

" Delegates to the state convention, when assembled for action, have been found not properly responsive to the sentiment of their constituents. They have been found more anx'ous to carry out the wishes of party leaders than to carry out the wishes of the mass of individual party voters. Controlling political power has not passed from the individual unit, in which it should originate, up to the state convention. On the contrary, controlling political power has originated with certain political bosses who have usurped the rights of party voters, and brought about nominations which were desired by the bosses, but not demanded by the voters.

" Do I need to cite that at the assembling of each state convention the interesting questions have been, how many delegates does this leader control, and how many delegates does that leader control, and can such and such groups of delegates be combined by backroom manipulations to bring about certain desired nominations?

" Do I need to cite that state conventions have often been known to nominate candidates who have never been mentioned, nor even thought of, by the rank and file of party voters? Do I need to say that in such cases delegates are not the representatives of the voters, but the representatives of party leaders who deserve the stigma of being called ' party bosses? ' Do I need to say that boss-ruled conventions have become a reproach to any political party?

" The adoption of state-wide direct primaries, and the abolition of state conventions, is in no sense an abandonment of the principle of *representative government*, but on the contrary it is a protest against the *perversion* of representative government.

" Under direct primaries the people will govern themselves, through representatives, but through representatives *selected* by themselves. That is why we want the voters to nominate. Representative government is only made actual when the power to name candidates is taken away from political bosses, or from groups of party leaders, and placed in the hands of the voters of the political party.

" That the voters are determined to have no intermediary between themselves and their public servants has been shown by the adoption of the seventeenth amendment to the Federal

Constitution, under which the people have taken from the legislature powers previously delegated to them to elect United States senators.

" The people believe themselves more competent than their legislators to elect senators in congress, because they so often found members of the legislature were not the faithful agents of the people, but were subject both to boss control and systematic bribery. All the arguments now used against the abolition of state conventions have been used in opposition to the direct election of United States senators, but these arguments have been vain against the rising tide of progressive democracy.

" Let us not deceive ourselves; let us not try to deceive the people; the plain fact is, that in our primary reform legislation we, in New York state, have left off our work just where the people expected us to begin. By not making our direct primary law apply directly to the nomination of state officers we have continued the delegate system in the particular field in which it has proven the most unsatisfactory to the people.

" The sentiment in the state in favor of direct primaries found its origin and growth principally in the fact that under the established primary law the rank and file of party voters were not able to control their delegates when they assembled in the state conventions.

" I am now, always have been, and always will be in favor of carrying out, in letter and in spirit, our platform pledges.

" The best way to strengthen a political party is to keep the faith. I want to restore to the people of the state the complete control of their state government; to afford the voters of the state the freest expression of their choice of candidates for public office; and I believe that our ' state-wide ' direct primary bill embraces an honest, a sincere, a comprehensive and a practical plan for these accomplishments.

" Besides, I consider that our ' state-wide ' direct primary bill is an absolutely nonpartisan measure, which faithfully reproduces, and will substantially carry into practice, the pledges of the three great political parties concerned in the last state election.

" There are only two kinds of primaries—direct and indirect.

The latter constitutes the reactionary delegate system; the former constitutes the present progressive system. I am for the direct system. I want the people to nominate because I want the people to rule. The power to nominate is the power to control. Do not forget that.

" To have direct primaries and to have state conventions is impossible. Direct primaries have been devised by the friends of good government to permit the people to nominate their officers directly without the intermediary of delegates, and as, of course, you cannot have state conventions without delegates, it follows that state conventions must go and honest direct nominations must come. There is no middle ground. There can be no compromise. Those who want to compromise are against us. The principle admits of no legitimate debate. You cannot compromise a principle.

" It is self-evident to me that if the people are competent to directly elect their public officials they are just as competent to directly nominate these officials.

" If it is important for minor officers to be nominated by the people, it is still more important that the people be given the power to nominate candidates for United States senator and for governor. That if special interests seek to control public affairs for the promotion of their selfish ends through the manipulation of party conventions, the plain people should seek to do the same thing by taking in their own hands the right to nominate directly these more important officials.

" The changes which we advocate in our primary law are in harmony with the spirit of the times, and will make for the perpetuation of our free institutions. They aim to restore to the people the rights of the many which have been usurped by the few, for the benefit of invisible powers which aim to control governmental officials, to pass laws, to prevent the passage of other laws, and to violate laws with impunity. To these invisible powers I am now, always have been, and always will be opposed.

" No government can be free that does not allow all its citizens to participate in the formation and the execution of its laws. Every other government is a mere form of despotism. The political history of the world illustrates the truth that under the forms of democratic government popular control may be destroyed, and corrupt influences, through invisible political power, establish a veritable despotism.

" Tweed used to say that he cared not who elected the officials so long as he could nominate them. Do you know why? Because the power to nominate officials is the power to control these officials when they go into office. That is all there is to it—and that is the reason the bosses want to keep this power to nominate. The power to nominate makes the boss. That is the reason why every political boss in the state is against direct nominations. Do not forget that.

" Tweed was a boss. You remember he challenged the power of the people. With brazen audacity he defied the voters and said: ' What are you going to do about it? ' You know the answer. Have the little Boss Tweeds so soon forgotten the tragic fate of Big Boss Tweed? It is an old saying that history repeats itself.

" If it is wise to trust the people with the power to nominate some public officers, I am sure it is just as wise to trust them with the power to nominate all public officers. I believe it is as wise to trust them to nominate a governor as to trust them to nominate a constable, and as wise to trust them to nominate a judge of the Court of Appeals as to trust them to nominate a justice of the peace.

" The people have been trusted with this power in many other states, and they have used it to bring about good government and greatly improved conditions. Let the Empire state put itself in line with the foremost states in the Union, by favoring nominations by the people, for thus only can we secure a government of the people.

" So if any one tells you that a direct nominations law is not a good thing, you deny it, and point to what other states have done through the agency of this beneficent reform.

" No man fears direct primaries, except a man whose character, and whose ability, and whose mentality cannot bear the searchlight of publicity. No man fears direct primaries, unless he wants to be the creature of invisible government rather than the servant of popular government.

" Our state-wide direct primary bill is a good measure. I am for it. My friends are for it. The platform of nearly every party is for it. On this issue there is no middle ground.

The democrats of the state must stand with their governor for direct primaries, or they have got to be against the democratic platform. Let every democrat decide. All my life I have fought for the right; for the truth; for simple justice, and for humanity. I shall not change now.

"What democrat in our state is going to be false to the platform, to be a traitor to the party, and to desert me in the performance of my duty? In this cause for direct primaries I have no fear of the ultimate result. The people will win.

" I say deliberately to the party leaders of the state that you have got to line up the representatives in the legislature, whom you control, to pass this honest, this just, this fair, this non-partisan state-wide direct primary bill, to keep your pledges, or I will line up the people against your representatives for their failure to be true to their pledges.

"When I make a promise to the people I keep it, or I frankly tell the people why I cannot keep it. When my party makes a promise to the people, I want my party to keep the promise, cr I want the people to know the reason why.

" Let us keep the faith. That is where I stand, and I will s'and there to the end. If any man is against me in my determination to keep the faith, I must of necessity be against that man.

" It is all very simple to me. If any democrat in this state is against the democratic platform, that man is no true democrat; and as the democratic governor of the state I shall do everything in my power to drive that recreant democrat out of the councils of the democratic party.

" The record will show that for years I have been a consistent advocate of geniune direct primaries, and I firmly believe that the enactment into law of a state-wide direct primary bill, along the lines of the measure we prepared, and introduced in the legislature, will accomplish what the voters desire, and reflect greater credit on the members of the present legislature than the passage of any other act that can be presented for the consideration of its members this year.

" Let us be honest with the voters and keep our pledges to the people. At all events, as the governor, I shall, and if the legislature does not, I want the voters to know the reason why.

"When we consider the waste, the extravagance, the inefficiency, and the corruption, which have recently been brought to light in connection with the administration of public affairs in our state, all due, in no small degree, to the fact that in recent years political power has been gradually slipping away from the people, who should always control it and wield it, there can be no doubt as to the necessity of this legislation and the duty of every voter in this all-important matter.

" Every intelligent citizen is aware that those who subvert the government to their personal advantage have found their greatest opportunities to do so through the adroit and skillful manipulation of our system of political conventions. It must cease or our free institutions are doomed.

" This is a struggle for good government—a fight to restore the government to the people. The cause is their cause. In this battle for direct nominations I will lead where any man will follow, and I will follow where any man will lead.

" The voters of the state, however, must now see to it that the men they have sent to the senate, and the assembly, keep their promises, and in the extra session vote for our direct primary bill, or never hope again for political preferment.

" In the recent session of the legislature the bosses told the people's representatives to beat our direct primary bill. In the extra session of the legislature, called by me, and soon to convene, I want the voters who elected the senators, and the assemblymen, to tell them to vote for our primary bill. Tell them that, and tell them if they disobey your mandate for the wishes of the bosses you will never vote for them again.

" Instruct your representatives in the legislature what your wishes are in this matter. Tell them what you want them to do about our bill for direct primaries, and rest assured they will not dare to cheat you again.

" If the voters in each assembly and senatorial district will do their duty for the next few days the direct primary bill will be passed in the extra session of the legislature and success will crown our efforts—but every voter must do his duty, and do it now."

respective parties, and are, therefore, in duty bound by the highest political obligations, to vote for a state-wide direct primary measure.

In my message to the legislature at the beginning of the year I said: ' We are pledged to the principle of direct primaries, state-wide in their scope and character, and I urge the adoption of such amendments as will simplify the procedure, and make complete and more effective the direct primary system of the state."

As nothing was done, of material moment, in connection with this recommendation, and to carry out in good faith the pledges above mentioned, I again, in the early part of April, in a special message, urged the legislature, in the interest of the general welfare, to hearken to the insistent demands of the people throughout the state for a direct state-wide primary law. Much to my disappointment, however, the legislature adjourned without, in this respect, meeting the just expectations of the voters.

So a sense of public obligation made it my duty, in the interest of the common weal, to reconvene the legislature in extraordinary session, to the end that the recommendations I have made to the legislature for direct primaries can be considered, without further delay, and a bill passed for direct nominations which will fulfill party pledges. In response to the overwhelming sentiment of the state. I am convinced, we should do this as a matter of duty to our constituents.

The record will show that for years I have been a consistent advocate of direct nominations. I am now, always have been, and always will be in favor of carrying out, in letter and in spirit, the platform pledges of a political party. The best way to strengthen a political party is to keep good faith with the voters.

Hence, in view of all the circumstances, in connection with the struggle in our state for a law to give the voters the right to nominate, it is my candid opinion that the legislature in this extraordinary session, without unnecessary delay, should give heed to its promises, and immediately consider, and, with due deliberation, aid me to write upon our statute books a practicable and a comprehensive state-wide direct primary law that will faithfully carry out our pledges to the people.

STATE OF NEW YORK—EXECUTIVE CHAMBER

Albany, June 16, 1913

TO THE LEGISLATURE:

The Republican party, in convention, last year, as a part of its platform, adopted the followimg:

" We favor the short ballot, surrounding primary elections with the same safeguards as regular elections, the direct election of party committees, the direct nomination of party candidates in congressional, senatorial, assembly, county and municipal subdivisions, and the direct election of delegates to state conventions, with the right of party electors to directly express their preference for nominations for state offices if they so desire."

The Progressive party, in convention, last year, as a part of its platform, adopted the following:

" We pledge the enactment of a real direct primary law applicable to every elective office and a presidential preference primary law."

The Democratic party, in convention, last year, as a part of its platform, adopted the following:

" The Democratic party was the first to recognize the demand for a state-wide direct primary and so declared in the Rochester platform of 1910, and the Democratic legislature of 1911, despite Republican opposition, enacted the first state-wide direct primary law in the history of the state. We again declare in favor of the principle of the direct primary and we pledge our legislature to adopt such amendments to the existing laws as will simplify and perfect the direct primary system."

It must be apparent, to the average man, from a careful reading of these platforms, that the leading political parties, in our state, are irrevocably committed, by the most explicit promises, to the enactment of legislation for direct nominations. As a matter of fact, it seems to me, all the members of the present legislature are instructed by these pledges, of their respective parties, and are, therefore, in duty bound by the highest political obligations, to vote for a state-wide direct primary measure.

In my message to the legislature at the beginning of the year I said: ' We are pledged to the principle of direct primaries, state-wide in their scope and character, and I urge the adoption of such amendments as will simplify the procedure, and make complete and more effective the direct primary system of the state."

As nothing was done, of material moment, in connection with this recommendation, and to carry out in good faith the pledges above mentioned, I again, in the early part of April, in a special message, urged the legislature, in the interest of the general welfare, to hearken to the insistent demands of the people throughout the state for a direct state-wide primary law. Much to my disappointment, however, the legislature adjourned without, in this respect, meeting the just expectations of the voters.

So a sense of public obligation made it my duty, in the interest of the common weal, to reconvene the legislature in extraordinary session, to the end that the recommendations I have made to the legislature for direct primaries can be considered, without further delay, and a bill passed for direct nominations which will fulfill party pledges. In response to the overwhelming sentiment of the state, I am convinced, we should do this as a matter of duty to our constituents.

The record will show that for years I have been a consistent advocate of direct nominations. I am now, always have been, and always will be in favor of carrying out, in letter and in spirit, the platform pledges of a political party. The best way to strengthen a political party is to keep good faith with the voters.

Hence, in view of all the circumstances, in connection with the struggle in our state for a law to give the voters the right to nominate, it is my candid opinion that the legislature in this extraordinary session, without unnecessary delay, should give heed to its promises, and immediately consider, and, with due deliberation, aid me to write upon our statute books a practicable and a comprehensive state-wide direct primary law that will faithfully carry out our pledges to the people.

Direct nominations will go far to restore to the people the complete control of their state government; and afford the voters of the state the freest expression of their choice of candidates for public office.

The voters believe themselves just as competent to directly nominate all officials as the delegates they select. They want this right to nominate because they have so often found the delegate system was not a faithful agency of their wishes, and that it not infrequently failed to meet the demands and the expectations of the people.

All the arguments now used against the abolition of the convention, or the delegate system of nominations, have been used in opposition to the direct election of United States senators, but these arguments have been all in vain against the ever rising tide of popular sovereignty and progressive democracy.

Let us be true to ourselves. Let us not try to deceive the people. The plain fact is, that in our primary reform legislation we, in New York state, have left off our work just where the citizens expected us to begin.

By not making our primary law apply directly to the nomination of state officers we have continued the delegate system in the particular field in which it has proven the most unsatisfactory to the people.

That the voters of our state are determined to have no intermediary between themselves and their public servants has been shown by the adoption of the seventeenth amendment to the Federal Constitution, under which the people have taken from the legislatures of the states the right to elect senators in congress.

There are only two kinds of primaries—direct and indirect. The latter kind constitutes the present reactionary delegate system; the former kind constitutes the progressive system which the people of our state now demand. I am for the direct system.

I want the people to nominate their officials because I want the people to rule their government. The people know that the power to nominate is the power to control. That is the reason the voters, regardless of party affiliations, favor direct nominations.

To have direct primaries and to have conventions of delegates is impossible. Direct primaries have been devised by the friends of good government to permit the voters in each political party to nominate their candidates for public office directly without the intermediary of delegates, and as, of course, you cannot have conventions without delegates, it follows, as the night the day, that the convention system must go, and honest direct primaries must come. There is no middle ground. There can be no compromise. Those who want to compromise are against the enrolled voters of their party. You cannot compromise a principle.

It is self-evident to me that if the voters are competent to directly elect all their public officials they are just as competent to directly nominate these same officials. Any assertion to the contrary is an indictment against the intelligence of the electorate of the state.

If it is important for minor officials to be nominated by the people, it is still more important, it seems to me, that the people be given the power to nominate candidates for United States senator and for governor. If selfish interests seek to control public affairs for the promotion of their personal ends, through the manipulation of party conventions, the plain people should seek to do the same thing by taking in their own hands the right to nominate directly every one of these important officials.

The adoption of state-wide direct primaries, and the abolition of delegate conventions, is in no sense an abandonment of the principles of representative government, but on the contrary it is a protest against the perversion of representative government.

Under direct primaries the people will govern themselves, through officials the same as now, but through officials directly nominated and elected by themselves. Representative government is only made actual when the power to name candidates is taken away from the few, and placed in the hands of all the enrolled voters of each political party.

The changes which the friends of direct nominations advocate in our primary law are in harmony with the spirit of the times, and will go far, in the opinion of sagacious men, to perpetuate our free institutions.

These salutary changes in our primary system aim to restore to the voters of each political party the rights which have been usurped by the few, for the benefit of powers invisible, which aim to control governmental officials, to pass laws, to prevent the passage of other laws, and to violate laws with impunity. To these invisible powers I am now, always have been, and always will be opposed.

No government can be free which does not allow all of its citizens to participate in the formation as well as the execution of its laws. Every other government is a mere form of despotism. The political history of the centuries clearly illustrates the truth that, under the forms of democratic government, popular control may be destroyed, and corrupt influences, through invisible political power, establish a veritable despotism.

If it is wise to trust the people with the power to nominate some public officials, I am sure it is just as wise to trust them with the power to nominate all public officials. I believe it is as wise to trust them to nominate a governor, as to trust them to nominate a constable; and as wise to trust them to nominate a supreme court judge, as to trust them to nominate a justice of the peace. The men who trust the average integrity, the men who believe in the average intelligence, of the voter, know not where, consistently, to draw the line as to the officials all should nominate, and the officials the few should nominate. As a believer in popular sovereignty I am opposed to establishing a political dead line regarding this fundamental right of the people to nominate all of their public servants.

The people have been trusted with this power to nominate in many other states, and they have used it to bring about greatly improved conditions. Let the Empire state put itself in line with the foremost states in the Union, by favoring nominations by the people, for thus only can we secure a government of the people and by the people.

As convincing proof of the success, and the popularity, of state-wide direct primaries, in other states, permit me to respectfully submit to the legislature the following testimony of a few of the most distinguished citizens and public officials in our country.

United States senator George E. Chamberlain, of Oregon, says:

" The direct primary of Oregon has so far proved satisfactory to our people."

United States senator Morris Shepherd, of Texas, says:

" Our system of direct primaries in Texas meets with universal approbation."

William Hodges Mann, governor of Virginia, says:

" Our primary law is applicable to all state offices. Indeed, we have been holding a primary for United states senators for some time, and the legislature has always elected the man selected by the people. I can say that the primary has worked well in this state."

Frank L. Houx, secretary of state of Wyoming, says:

" I consider our state-wide direct primary law one of the best laws ever placed upon our statute books. It eliminates ' Boss Rule ' that has heretofore prevailed in the nominating conventions and gives the people at large a voice in who the candidates shall be."

Governor Cox, of Ohio, says:

"Our primary law applies to all state officers. I would feel that the fundamental principle of popular participation in government would be violated if all the state officers from the governor down were not selected by popular choice."

United States Senator Gilbert M. Hitchcock, of Nebraska, says:

"Our direct primary system, as far as it relates to the candidates for senator or governor, is an unqualified success."

United States Senator Henry F. Hollis, of New Hampshire, says:

" The New Hampshire system of direct primaries certa nly meets the expectations of the people. The politicians criticise the plan, but it works well."

United States Senator James E. Martine, of New Jersey, says:

" I feel justified in stating that our New Jersey direct primary system meets with the general approval of the public."

David S. Crater, the Secretary of State of New Jersey, says:

"The direct primary law of this state applies to state, county and municipal offices; also to members of congress. So far as I am able to determine, it seems to be satisfactory in every respect."

Lee Cruce, the Governor of Oklahoma, says:

" Direct primaries are in operation in this state for the nomination of all state, county and municipal officers. It has given better satisfaction than the old convention system and there is no disposition to return to the old way. Oklahoma has been a pioneer in the matter of direct primaries, and has no reason to take backward steps along these lines."

Governor Oswald West, of Oregon, says:

" The direct primary system in this state obtains from constable to the United States senator, including municipal officers. As a result of the law Oregon has abolished the boss and has relegated a political machine to almost forgotten history. It is most satisfactory, and while the law which was enacted by the people was given an overwhelming majority, I am confident that should the question be again submitted to them, they would endorse the law by even a greater majority than the first. I do not believe that the people of this state would revert to the old system of corrupt political machine methods under any consideration."

Elliott W. Major, Governor of Missouri, says:

"Our law requires all candidates for elective offices to be nominated at a State primary. The law has operated well and has given satisfaction, and is the only way to give the people a fair chance to select the men whom they wish to represent them as party nominees. The people elect their public officers at the general election and the people are competent and qualified to elect their nominees, who in turn become their public officers. Of course the would-be political bosses and certain corporate interests which meddle in politics are opposed to state primaries. It interferes with their manipulations and combinations. They wish to act as the guardians of the people and select their nominees for them. Let the people, by direct vote, select their own candidates. That is pure democracy, and in keeping with the ideals of a republican form of government. I am a strong advocate of the State primary law because it more nearly approaches the real rule of the people. I would rather trust the people than trust the men who, because of their selfish interests, think the people are not capable and should not be permitted to say who they wish for candidates. If you permit such fellows and interests to select your entries for you in the political race, you need not expect much in the end.

" I cannot understand upon what principle anyone can oppose the people in exercising their right to select nominees at a state primary election. Let the people do the selecting, and not a coterie who wish to act for the people. Our state has tried the law and has met the test, and has given entire satisfaction, and no man in this state in public life would dare for a moment to advocate its repeal."

Frank J. Donahue, Secretary of State of Massachusetts, says:

"Our law provides that all officers to be voted for at a state election shall be nominated by direct plurality vote in party primaries. This, as you will see, includes the direct nomination of United States senators. It further provides for the direct election of members of the state committees of the political parties—not less than one from each senatorial district. The state-wide direct primary law was adopted in 1911, and under it we have had two direct primaries. That its operation is satisfactory is admitted even by those who had vigorously opposed for years the passage of such a law by the legislature. The fight for state-wide direct primaries in this state extended over several years, but finally so strong did the demand become that in 1911 the house passed the direct primary bill with only fifteen dissenting votes out of the two hundred and forty members, and it was passed in the senate without a division."

Governor Brewer, of Mississippi, says:

"Our law applies to all state officials. Taken on the whole I regard the primary law as satisfactory. There is no question in the world that by this method the wishes of the people are carried out, which cannot be said of the ordinary ' convention ' method."

United States Senator James K. Vardaman, of Mississippi, says:

" In Mississippi the direct primary law has served to put the government in the hands of the people rather than the bosses. It amuses the voter to study all economic and governmental questions and to realize that this is a government which derives all of its just powers from the consent of the governed. It has done more. It has made the voter feel his responsibility for the laws and to appreciate the real function of citizenship. Every state in this republic should provide for the election of every officer from governor down by a direct vote of the people. The nomination by primary is only an application of this universally beneficent system."

W. C. Elliston, clerk to the Secretary of State of Kentucky, says:

" The primary election law of Kentucky applies to all offices and the various officials, both state and county, are elected under its provisions. The law has been a success from every standpoint, and we think it quite a step along progressive principles to elect our various officers under it."

Governor O. B. Colquitt, of Texas, says:

" I was among the first to advocate a general primary election law many years ago. Formerly a few politicians would get together in precinct or mass meetings, elect delegates, and adopt resolutions committing the party to policies and candidates often not approved by the majority of the people. Our state-wide direct primary is infinitely better than the old system which it supplanted."

Governor Francis C. McGovern, of Wisconsin, says:

" In regard to the operation of direct primaries in our state, it has cleaned up the legislature and given us different kind of men than formerly, more independent."

Governor Luther E. Hall, of Louisiana, says:

" There is no prospect that the state of Louisiana will ever return to the Convention plan of making nominations. Old-time politicians are now and then heard to decry the direct primary and to sigh for the convention, but this sentiment is not wide-spread and may be said to be negligible."

Governor James F. Fielder, of New Jersey, says:

" In 1912 by further enactment amending our primary law, presidential electors were included with the result that there is no longer any convention held in the state of New Jersey for nominating purposes. Last year there was a preferential vote for president, and now all presidential electors as well as all state, county and municipal officers are nominated by the direct primary. The manner in which our laws have been amended from time to time until they finally include all elective officers in the state is the best evidence of their popularity."

Governor George W. P. Hunt, of Arizona, says:

" In Arizona the direct primary law is applicable to all elective state officials. I will say without hesitancy that the system of direct primaries applicable to all officers is immeasurably better than the old method of nominating by conventions."

Charles H. Sessions, Secretary of State of Kansas, says:

" The Kansas law applies to all elective officers from United States senator down to township trustee. The law works so well in regard to its application to nominations for all officers that no attempt, or even a serious suggestion, has been made to repeal it. What opposition there was to the enactment of the law has almost disappeared. Now and then a politician protests against it, but on the whole it is very popular with the people and it has come to stay."

Governor Park Trammell, of Florida, says:

" The primary system has been in force for about twelve years, and has given almost universal satisfaction. Some four years ago in our democratic primary a question was put before the voters as to whether or not a state convention was desired, it being the claim of the supporters of the convention that it was merely for the purpose of making a party platform. Many were of the opinion, however, that it was for the purpose of attacking the primary system. The vote was about five to one against the state convention. This expression indicated very conclusively how the people of Florida felt at that time relative to nominating by primary. The primary system has come to stay in this state."

United States Senator Henry S. Ashurst, of Arizona, says:

" It is impossible to exaggerate the civic benefits which flow from a pure, sweeping, state-wide primary election law. The primary nomination which abolishes the convention, eliminates the ' purchase proxy.' It destroys the secret caucus methods, and it guarantees to the plain citizen the same degree of potentiality as each and every other citizen possesses. Now and then, in the past, a legislature, or a political convention, has been found on the bargain counter and purchased as so many oxen in the field, but it is impossible to purchase all the people.

" In Arizona we have a state-wide primary law for the nomination of all candidates, including United States senators, and while it might seem ungracious in me to praise the bridge which carried me over, I cannot refrain from observing that in Arizona, I, a poor man, with absolutely no income whatever except my small law practice, was enabled by means of the direct primary, where the people had the right to express their choice, to defeat the combined influences of the railroads, national banks, the smelter trust and every corrupt politician in the state, all of which interests confederated and combined in the hope of bringing about my defeat and electing a reactionary.

" I mention this circumstance to show that a direct primary does not operate in favor of the rich man and against the poor man, for we frequently find the argument advanced by the opponents of the direct primary, that 'under the direct primary no one but a rich man may enter the political field.' The very reverse is true. A poor man may enter the primary, and if he have ability, facts, courage and energy, he may canvass any of our largest and most populous states by the expenditure of a few hundred dollars, whereas, if he were required to go before a convention to obtain a nomination, a number of sinister private interests would be able to cohere, by means of purchased proxies and by means of secret caucus methods, control the situation."

This unimpeachable testimony—and I could adduce much more—seems quite conclusive, and if any one tells us that a direct nominations law is not a good thing for New York, we can point to what other states have done through the agency of this beneficent reform as a refutation of the reactionary assertion.

No man fears direct primaries, except a man whose character, and whose ability, and whose mentality cannot bear the searchlight of publicity. No man fears direct primaries, unless he wants to be the creature of invisible government rather than the servant of popular government.

Let me, therefore, renew my former recommendations, reiterate all that I have previously said, and again sincerely and earnestly urge the legislature to pass a direct primary bill that shall provide:

1. That all party candidates for public office shall be nominated directly by the enrolled party voters at an official primary—the official primary to be conducted by the state, and surrounded with all the safeguards of an official election—any violation of the official primary law to be a felony.

2. A state committee of 150 members, one from each assembly district, and a county committee for each county, to be elected directly by the enrolled party voters at the official primary.

3. All party candidates for public office to be voted for in the official primary must be designated by petition only, the same as independent candidates.

4. Every designating petition should contain the appointment of a committee for filling vacancies on the primary ballot.

5. Candidates to be arranged on the ballot under the title of the office. Order of arrangement to be determined in each group by lot, by the commissioners of election, in the presence of the candidates or their representatives. All emblems on the official primary ballot must be abolished. Names of candidates to be numbered. The voter to indicate his choice by making a separate mark before the name of each candidate.

6. The number of enrolled party voters required to sign a designating petition should be fixed at a percentage of the party vote for governor at the last preceding election, except

Such a law, in my judgment, will substantially redeem our party pledges and meet the just demands of the enrolled party voters of the state. Any proposition less than this begs the whole question and violates the pledged faith of the several political parties to their voters in the state.

In this connection, I deem it my duty to say to the legislature, that I have no pride of opinion regarding details and nonessentials in the construction and the enactment of this legislation. The assertion that I have said that my bill must pass without the crossing of a "t," or the dotting of an "i" is absurd, and without the slightest foundation in fact. I have had too much experience as a legislator to utter such narrow-minded sentiments. As a matter of fact, the truth is I have no vanity of authorship, and want none. My struggle is for the essential principle of state-wide direct nominations. On that fundamental principle the friends of state-wide direct primaries declare that there can be no honorable compromise.

No one can be deceived as to my contention and as to my attitude. All I am seeking to accomplish is to write on our statute books, an honest, and a simple, and a practicable direct nominations law—state-wide in its scope and application—in order to carry out in good faith party promises. That is all. Can I be more fair and more reasonable?

Let us be honest about direct primaries, and keep our pledges to the people. At all events, as the governor I shall; and if the legislature does not, the people will know the reason why.

WM. SULZER

that for state offices the number should not exceed 5,000 enrolled party voters, of which 100 shall be from each of at least twenty counties.

7. The primary district should be made identical with the election district, and the primaries of all parties should be held at the same polling place, conducted by the regular official election officers, just the same as an official election.

8. Each party to have a party council to frame a platform; such council to consist of the party candidates for office to be voted for by the state at large; party congressmen and party United States senators; candidates for the senate and assembly; members of the state committee; and the chairman of each county committee.

9. The time for filing independent nominations subsequent to the filing of party nominations should be increased from five days, as now provided, to fourteen or more days. The number of signers of an independent certificate of nomination should conform to the number of signers of a party designation.

10. Election of United States senator by the people should be provided for in accordance with the recent constitutional amendment. Nominations for United States senator to be made at the official primary in the same manner as for the office of governor.

11. Registration days in the country should be reduced from four to two, and registration in the country should be by affidavit where voter does not appear personally.

12. Boards of elections in counties having less than one hundred and twenty thousand inhabitants should be reduced from four members to two, in order to decrease the expenses.

13. The use of party funds at primary elections to be absolutely prohibited, and made a felony.

14. The penal law should be amended limiting to a reasonable sum the amount of money that may be expended by a candidate, or anyone on his account, for the purpose of seeking a nomination to public office, any violation of the same to be a felony, and make the nomination, if secured, a nullity.

15. Delegates and alternates from the state at large, and from congressional districts, to the national convention, should be chosen by the direct vote of enrolled party voters at the official primary.

Such a law, in my judgment, will substantially redeem our party pledges amd meet the just demands of the enrolled party voters of the state.   Any proposition less than this begs the whole question and violates the pledged faith of the several political parties to their voters in the state.

In this connection, I deem it my duty, to say to the legislature, that I have no pride of opinion regarding details and non-essentials in the construction and the enactment of this legislation.   The assertion that I have said that my bill must pass without the crossing of a "t," or the dottir of an "i," is absurd, and without the slightest foundation in tact.   I have had too much experience as a legislator to utter such narrow-minded sentiments.   As a matter of fact, the truth is, I have no vanity of authorship, and want none.   My struggle is for the essential principle of state-wide direct nominations.   On that fundamental principle the friends of state-wide direct primaries declare that there can be no honorable compromise.

No one can be deceived as to my contention and as to my attitude. All I am seeking to accomplish is to write on our statute books, an honest, and a simple, and a practicable direct nominations law—state-wide in its scope and application—in order to carry out in good faith party promises.   That is all.   Can I be more fair and more reasonable?

Let us be honest about direct primaries, and keep our pledges to the people.   At all events, as the governor, I shall, and if the legislature does not, the people will know the reason why.

WM. SULZER

MEMORANDUM APPROVING THE FULL CREW BILL

THE MAN ABOVE THE DOLLAR

BY GOVERNOR WILLIAM SULZER

The Full Crew bill, which I signed, is a meritorious measure and provides that the railroad trains running through the state of New York shall hereafter be sufficiently manned to conserve human life and limb.

Identical bill passed the legislature twice before, but did not meet with executive approval because it was believed the public service commission had power to remedy the evils of which complaint is made. However, the railroads heretofore have contended that the public service did not have this power and was without jurisdiction.

The only objection to the measure on the part of the railroads was that it would increase to some extent the cost of operation by reason of the fact that an additional man would have to be employed on some of the long trains. The same objection could be urged with equal force to any improvement in the methods of railroad operation.

In my opinion the conservation of human life and limb is more important to the people than a little additional expense in the operation of the railroads. The state, for its own welfare, has the right to demand the employment upon the railroads of every safety appliance, whether mechanical or human, in the interest of life and limb and greater safety standards.

Every safeguard, it seems to me, should be employed by the railroads to prevent wrecks; to protect the property of shippers; and to save human life and limb, not only of the employees but of the traveling public. The progressive spirit of the times demands it, and the trend of present day legislation is all that way.

The official records of the state of New York show that five times as many passengers were killed in this state last year as were killed five years ago; three times as many were killed last year as were killed four years ago; more than twice as many were killed last year as were killed three years ago; and more than twice as many were killed last year as were killed two years ago. The records also show an increased annual killing and maiming of employees. The people of the state of New York feel outraged that the railroad companies in New York killed last year 280 employees; maimed 6,690 employees; killed 45 passengers; and injured 945 passengers. The people believe the Full Crew law will go far to stop this slaughter.

The Full Crew law is not unjust to the railroads, but simple justice to the railway employees and the much-concerned traveling public. The rights of the people must not be overlooked, especially in view of the appalling fact that during the twenty-four years covered by the statistics of the Interstate Commerce Commission, 188,037 persons have been killed, and 1,395,618 persons injured on the railroads of the United States. This is an average of 7,835 persons killed, 58,150 persons injured each year, or a total of nearly 66,000 persons killed and injured annually. This means that for every day during the past twenty-four years 181 persons have been killed or injured—nearly eight every hour or one every seven minutes with the regularity of clock work.

The ravages of war pale into insignificance before these sad and silent statistics of the destruction of human life and limb accompanying the peaceful operation of the railroads. Any agency that will stop it is an agency for good. Human life is more important than dividends. Surely the general welfare rises superior to the dividends of the railroads.

Of course I do not complain on account of the railroad officials denouncing me because I signed this just and meritorious measure. But I assure them as the governor of New York, that I am more interested in the conservation of human life, than I am in the conservation of railroad dividends.

Everybody knows that railroad officials are paid very large salaries for looking after the interests of the railroads. The rank and file know that I am paid a small salary in comparison for looking after the interests of the people. When I became governor I said no influence would control me in my official conduct except the influence of my own conscience and my determination to do my duty to all the people as I see the right and God gives me the light.

My duty to the people in this matter was plain and I signed the Full Crew bill, against the protests of the railroad officials, for the greatest good to the greatest number.

These railroad officials are working for the railroads. As the governor of the state of New York I am working for the people. I see things from the people's standpoint and they see things from the standpoint of the railroads. The railroad' officials put the dollar above the man. I put the man above the dollar. A human life to me is worth more than a human dollar, the opinion of the railroad officials to the contrary notwithstanding.

In my judgment if the railroads sufficiently equip their trains with competent crews they will have fewer accidents and less wrecks. This in the end will prove economy to the railroads and prevent them from being subjected to suits for damages and large financial losses necessarily arising therefrom. A year from now I undertake to say that if any attempt is made to repeal this humane Full Crew law the railroads themselves, in the interest of economy, will be the first to object.

WILLIAM SULZER

MESSAGE OF THE GOVERNOR, JULY 23, 1913

STATE OF NEW YORK—EXECUTIVE CHAMBER

Albany, July 23, 1913

To THE LEGISLATURE:

The regular session of this legislature convened this year on January 1, 1913, and it adjourned on May 3, 1913.

Prior to the thirty-day period for the consideration of measures by the Executive, the legislature had passed and sent to the executive, for his consideration, 531 bills. Of these, 442 were approved. A memorandum was filed with 22 of the measures. There were recalled 74 bills; and 15 were vetoed with separate veto messages.

During the thirty-day period the executive had under consideration 701 bills. Of these 351 were approved; and 350 were vetoed, with 19 memoranda of approval and 51 memoranda of disapproval.

All told, 793 bills were enacted into laws, out of a total of 1,232 bills, passed by the legislature and submitted to me for consideration.

The financial bills passed by the legislature, excluding sinking fund and bond interest bills, aggregated a total of $55,108,705.25, made up as follows:

General appropriations.................$30,236,987.29
General supply bill...................... 6,916,922.60
Special appropriations................... 17,954,795.36

I approved $29,825,897.29 of the general appropriation bills; $4,178,505.73 of the general supply bill; and $13,778,862.21 of the special appropriation bills, making a total of $47,783,265.23.

The total of financial items and bills which I vetoed amount to $7,325,440.02.

During the regular session, the legislature having failed to pass a bill for direct primaries, on May 8, 1913, I issued a proclamation convening the legislature in extraordinary session to commence June 16, 1913.

This extraordinary session of the legislature was called for the purpose of considering the people's bill for state-wide direct primaries. It has been in session for a few minutes now and then for a period of over a month, but has signally failed to pass a state-wide direct primary bill, containing provisions which I recommended, and which I believe should be on the statute books of our state.

Since the extraordinary session convened, I have been urged, and for reasons which seemed to me to be quite sufficient, I have recommended for the consideration of the legislature several other measures, concerning each of which I have sent to the legislature a bill with a special message. They relate to the following matters:

On June 18th, recommending the passage of a bill to submit to the voters of the state at the regular election in November, 1913, the question " Shall there be a convention to revise the Constitution and amend the same?"

On June 23rd, recommending temporary legislation relating to maintenance contracts on the highways.

On June 23rd, recommending the passage of a bill for the legal conveyance to the state, by the authorities of the city of New York, of the title to the land and appurtenances of the Long Island State Hospital.

On June 24th, recommending the passage of a measure exempting from sanitary inspection seed oyster beds within the state of New York.

On June 24th, recommending the passage of a bill concerning the extension of the time when the law commonly known as the " Housing Law," being Chapter 774 of the Laws of 1913, shall take effect.

On June 24th, recommending the passage of a bill providing for the direct tax for the payment of interest and principal due on the state debt.

On June 25th, recommending necessary legislation relating to the appropriation by the state of toll bridges crossing the canals.

On June 25th, recommending legislation concerning the operation of the proposed terminal railway in the Borough of Brooklyn.

On June 25th, recommending that Chapter 463 of the Laws of 1913, entitled "An act to amend the Labor Law, in relation to bakeries," should not be effective against cellar bakeries until a certain time after May 9, 1913, when the law went into effect.

On June 25th, recommending necessary legislation to aid the state architect's office in doing its important work.

On July 8th, recommending the enactment of the optional city charter bill.

On July 16th, recommending the enactment of essential legislation to relieve disgraceful prison conditions in the state of New York.

Since the convening of this extraordinary session I have sent the following appointments to the senate for confirmation:

TO BE A TRUSTEE OF CORNELL UNIVERSITY:

John DeWitt Warner, of New York City, a former member of congress, and a well-known lawyer. He is an alumnus of the university and peculiarly qualified for the duties of the office.

FOR COMMISSIONERS OF THE STATE RESERVATION AT NIAGARA:

Elton T. Ransom, of Ransomville, N. Y.

Abram J. Elias, of Buffalo, N. Y.

John L. Romer, of Buffalo, N. Y.

Obadiah W. Cutler, of Niagara Falls, N. Y.

These gentlemen are well-known citizens, who take a deep and an abiding interest in the affairs of this reservation.

FOR PUBLIC SERVICE COMMISSIONERS, SECOND DISTRICT:

William E. Leffingwell, of Watkins, N. Y., to succeed Frank W. Stevens, resigned.

Mr. Leffingwell was formerly a conspicuous member of assembly. He is a successful business man of much experience and well qualified for the position.

Charles J. Chase, of Croton-on-Hudson, N. Y., to succeed Curtis N. Douglas, term expired.

Mr. Chase has been connected with the New York Central and Hudson river railroad for more than twenty years as a locomotive engineer. He is endorsed by railroad organizations, as well as by bankers, merchants, clergymen and distinguished citizens.

For Commissioner of Labor:
James M. Lynch, of Syracuse, N. Y., to succeed John Williams, resigned.

Mr. Lynch is one of the foremost labor leaders in America. He is the president of the International Typographical union, whose membership numbers more than 50,000 enrolled printers. Representatives from the allied printing trades; various labor organizations, and many prominent citizens indorse Mr. Lynch for this important position. It is generally admitted he is well qualified to perform its arduous duties.

For Commissioner of Prisons:
James T. Murphy, of Ogdensburg, N. Y., to succeed Edgar A. Newell, term expired.

Mr. Murphy is a well-known merchant of Ogdensburg, and takes great interest in these institutions.

Rudolph F. Diedling, M. D., of Saugerties-on-Hudson, N. Y., to succeed Simon Quick, term expired.

Dr. Diedling was at one time surgeon of the Elmira reformatory, and is very conversant with the duties of the office for which he has been selected.

For Trustee of the New York State Hospital for the Treatment of Incipient Pulmonary Tuberculosis:
George L. Brown, of Elizabethtown, N. Y., to succeed Martin E. McClary, resigned.

Mr. Brown is a well-known and respected citizen of Elizabethtown; editor of a newspaper, and the present postmaster.

For Trustee of the State College of Forestry at Syracuse University:
Francis Hendricks, of Syracuse, N. Y., to succeed George E. Dunham, heretofore appointed and unable to serve.

Mr. Hendricks is a highly respectable citizen of Syracuse. He was formerly state senator; collector of the port of New York, and state superintendent of insurance.

FOR HELL GATE PILOT:

Albert A. Fordham, of the City Island, N. Y., reappointed. Was appointed in 1912 upon the recommendation of the Board of Port Wardens.

FOR FIRE ISLAND STATE PARK COMMISSIONERS:

Colonel Alfred Wagstaff, of New York city, to succeed Samuel L. Parish, who declined reappointment.

Colonel Wagstaff is too well known to need introduction. He resides on Long Island and is the clerk of the Appellate division, Supreme Court, first department.

James W. Eaton, of Babylon, N. Y., to succeed John H. Vail, term expired.

Mr. Eaton is a large property holder and actively interested in the development of the South Shore of Long Island.

Edward Blum, of the Borough of Brooklyn, reappointed.

Mr. Blum is a prominent business man and has served continuously in this office since its organization in 1908, performing very efficient service.

These recommendations and these nominations speak for themselves; they are made in the interest of the common weal, and I indulge in the hope that the legislature will consider them on their merits, ere the adjournment of this extraordinary session.

Of course I am aware of the inconvenience imposed upon the members of both branches of the legislature through the necessity of their attendance at this extraordinary session, and I appreciate that the consideration of certain charges in the Cohalan case may have prevented the consideration of some of these legislative matters. However, there is no reason now why all these matters should not be speedily considered and promptly disposed of—one way or the other.

The legislature must recognize that its continuance in session adds largely to the burdens of the taxpayers through necessary expense; and while it is proper that the pending matters should receive careful consideration, it is respectfully suggested, in the interest of economy, that they be disposed of at the earliest possible time, and the Legislature then adjourn.

It is useless to deny that at the present season of the year it is extremely difficult to secure the presence of a quorum to pass legislation, but I feel confident that an announcement by the legislative leaders, strictly adhered to, that pending legislation must be promptly considered by the votes of all the members, will accomplish the desired result; and to that purpose, I respectfully urge again that the measures recommended by me receive immediate and favorable consideration.

With a view of assisting the speedy despatch of pending legislative business, and of reducing to a minimum the necessary expense of this extraordinary session of the legislature, I hereby announce, for the information of the members, and all others interested, that I shall recommend to this extraordinary session no further legislation.

For the reasons herein stated, I now earnestly urge the prompt consideration, by this legislature, of pending measures; and by the senate, the early action upon the appointments I have submitted, to the end that the general welfare be promoted; the convenience of the members conserved, and the expenses to the taxpayers of a protracted session reduced to the minimum.

WM. SULZER

THE ARTICLES OF IMPEACHMENT AGAINST
GOVERNOR WILLIAM SULZER

The following are the articles of impeachment against Governor William Sulzer:

Articles exhibited by the assembly of the state of New York in the name of themselves and of all the people of the state of New York against William Sulzer, governor of said state, in maintenance of their impeachment against him for wilful and corrupt misconduct in his said office, and for high crimes and misdemeanors.

ARTICLE I.

That the said William Sulzer, now governor of the state of New York, then being governor-elect of said state for the term beginning January 1, 1913, he having been elected at the general election held in said state on the 5th day of November, 1912, was required by the statutes of the state then in force to file in the office of the secretary of state within twenty days after his said election a statement setting forth all the receipts, expenditures, disbursements and liabilities made, or incurred by him as a candidate for governor at said general election at which he was thus elected, which statement the statute required to include the amount received, the name of the person or committee from whom received, the date of its receipt, the amount of every expenditure or disbursement exceeding five dollars, the name of the person or committee to whom it was made, and the date thereof, and all contributions made by him.

That, being thus required to file such statement, on or about the 13th day of November, 1912, the said William Sulzer, unmindful of his duty under such statutes, made and filed in the office of the secretary of state what purported to be a statement made in conformity to the provisions of the statute above set forth, in which statement he said and set forth as follows, to wit: That all the moneys received, contributed or expended by said Sulzer, directly or indirectly, by himself or through any other person, as the candidate of the democratic party for the office of governor of the state of New York, in connection with the general election held in the state of New

York on the fifth day of November, 1912, were receipts from sixty-eight contributors, aggregating five thousand four hundred and sixty ($5,460) dollars, and ten items of expenditure, aggregating seven thousand seven hundred twenty-four and 9-100 ($7,724.09) dollars, the detailed items of which were fully set forth in said statement so filed as aforesaid.

That said statement thus made and filed by said William Sulzer as aforesaid was false, and was intended by him to be false and an evasion and violation of the statutes of the state, and the same was made and filed by him wilfully, knowingly, and corruptly, it being false in the following particulars, among others, to wit:

It did not contain the contributions that had been received by him, and which should have been set forth in said statement, to wit:

Jacob Schiff, $2,500.
Abram I. Elkus, $500.
William F. McCombs, $500.
Henry Morgenthau, $1,000.
Theodore W. Myers, $1,000.
John Lynn, $500.
Lyman A. Spaulding, $100.
Edward F. O'Dwyer, $100.
John W. Cox, $300.
The Frank V. Strauss Co., $1,000.
John T. Dooling, $1,000.

That in making and filing such false statement as aforesaid, the said William Sulzer did not act as required by law, but did act in express violation of the statutes of the state and wrongfully, wilfully and corruptly; and thereafter, having taken the oath as governor, and proceeded to perform the duties thereof, the said false statement thus made and filed by him caused great reproach of the governor of the state of New York.

Article II.

That the said William Sulzer, governor of the state of New York, then being governor-elect of said state for the term beginning Jan. 1, 1913, he having been elected at the general election held in said state on the 5th day of November, 1912, was required by the statutes of the state then in force to file in the office of the secretary of state within 10 days after his said election, as aforesaid, an itemized statement, showing in detail all the moneys contributed or expended by him, directly or indirectly, by himself or through any other person, in aid of his election, giving the names of persons who received such moneys, the specific nature of each item and the purpose for which it was expended or contributed; and was further required to attach to said statement an affidavit, subscribed and sworn to by him, such candidate, setting forth, in substance, that the statement thus made was in all respects true and that the same was a full and detailed statement of all moneys so contributed or expended by him, directly or indirectly, by himself or through any other person, in aid of his election.

That being thus required to file such statement, and attach thereto such affidavit, on or about the 13th day of November, 1912, the said William Sulzer, unmindful of his duty under such statutes, made and filed in the office of the secretary of state what purported to be a statement made in conformity with the provisions of the statute above set forth in which statement he stated and set forth as follows, to wit:

That all the moneys received, contributed or expended by said Sulzer, directly or indirectly, by himself or through any other person, as the candidate for governor of the state of New York in connection with the general election held in the state of New York on the fifth day of November, 1912, were receipts from sixty-eight contributors, aggregating five thousand four hundred and sixty ($5,460) dollars, and ten items of expenditure aggregating seven thousand, seven hundred, twenty-four and 9-100 ($7,724.09) dollars, the detailed items of which were fully set forth in said statement, so filed as aforesaid.

That attached to such statement thus made and filed by him as aforesaid, was an affidavit, subscribed and sworn to by said William Sulzer stating that said statement was in all respects true and that the same was a full and detailed statement of all moneys received or contributed or expended by him, directly or indirectly, by himself or through any other person in aid of his election.

That said statement thus made and filed by said William

Sulzer, as aforesaid, was false, and was intended by him to be false and an evasion and violation of the statutes of the state and the same was made and filed by him wilfully, knowingly and corruptly being false in the following particulars, to wit:

It did not contain the amounts received by him and which should have been set forth in said statement, to wit:

Jacob Schiff, $2,500.
Abram I. Elkus, $500.
William F. McCombs, $500.
Henry Morgenthau, $1,000.
Theodore W. Myers, $1,000.
John Lynn, $500.
Lyman A. Spaulding, $100.
Edward F. O'Dwyer, $100.
John W. Cox, $300.
The Frank V. Strauss Company, $1,000.
John T. Dooling, $1,000.

That said affidavit thus subscribed and sworn to by said William Sulzer was false and was corruptly made by him.

That in making and filing such false statement as aforesaid, the said William Sulzer did not act as required by law, but did act in express violation of the statutes of the state and wrongfully, knowingly, wilfully and corruptly; and, in making said affidavit, as aforesaid, the said William Sulzer was guilty of wilful and corrupt perjury and of a violation of section 1620 of the penal code of the state; and, thereafter, having taken the oath as governor, and proceeded to perform the duties thereof, the said false statement and affidavit thus made and filed by him, caused great scandal and reproach of the governor of the state of New York.

ARTICLE III.

That the said William Sulzer, then being the governor of the state of New York, unmindful of the duties of his office and in violation of his oath of office, was guilty of mal and corrupt conduct in his office as such governor of the state, and was guilty of bribing witnesses and of a violation of section 2440 of the penal law of said state, in that, while a certain committee of the legislature of the state of New York named by a concurrent resolution of said legislature, to investigate into, ascertain and report at an extraordinary session of the legislature then in session, upon all expenditures made by any candidate voted for at the last preceding election by the electors of the whole state, and upon all statements filed by and on behalf of any such candidates for moneys or things of value received or paid out in aid of his election, and their compliance with the present requirements of law relative thereto, while such committee was conducting such investigation and had full authority in the premises, he, the said William Sulzer, in the months of July and August, 1913, fraudulently induced one Louis A. Sarecky, one Frederick L. Colwell, and one Melville B. Fuller, each, to withhold true testimony from said committee, which testimony it was the duty of said several persons named to give to said committee when called before it, and which, under said inducements of said William Sulzer, they, and each of them, refused to do.

That, in so inducing such witnesses to withhold such true testimony from said committee, the said William Sulzer acted wrongfully and wilfully and corruptly, and was guilty of a violation of the statutes of the state and of a felony, to the great scandal and reproach of the said governor of the state of New York.

ARTICLE IV.

That the said William Sulzer then being the governor of the state of New York, unmindful of the duties of his office, and in violation of his oath of office, was guilty of mal and corrupt conduct in his office as governor of the state, and was guilty of suppressing evidence and of a violation of section 814 of the penal law of said state, in that, while a certain committee of the legislature of the state of New York, named by a concurrent resolution of said legislature to investigate into, ascertain and report at an extraordinary session of the legislature then in session upon any expenditures made by any candidate voted for at the last preceding election by the electors of the whole state and upon all statements filed of such expenditures—while such committee was conducting its investigation and had full authority in the premises, he, then said William Sulzer practiced deceit and fraud and used threats and menaces with intent to prevent said committee and the people of the state from procuring the attendance and testimony of certain witnesses, to wit:

Louis A. Sarecky, Frederick L. Colwell and Melville B. Fuller, and all other persons with intent to prevent said persons named, and all other persons, severally, they or many of them having in their possession certain books, papers and other things which might or would be evidence in the proceedings before said committee, and to prevent such persons named, and all other papers, they, severally, being cognizant of facts material to said investigation being had by said committee from producing or disclosing the same, which said several witnesses named, and many others, failed and refused to do.

That, in thus practicing deceit and fraud and using threats and menaces as and with the intent aforesaid, and upon the persons before named, the said William Sulzer acted wrongfully and wilfully and corruptly, and was guilty of a misdemeanor, to the great scandal and reproach of the governor of the state of New York.

ARTICLE V.

That the said William Sulzer, then being the governor of the state of New York, unmindful of the duties of his office, and in violation of his oath of office, was guilty of mal and corrupt conduct in his office of such governor of the state, and was guilty of preventing and dissuading a witness from attending under a subpoena in violation of section 2441 of the penal law of said state, in that, while a certain committee of the legislature of the state of New York, named by concurrent resolution of said legislature to investigate into, ascertain and report to the extraordinary session of the legislature then in session upon all expenditures made by any candidate voted for at the last preceding election by the electors of the whole state, and upon all statements filed by and on behalf of any such candidate, for moneys or things of value received or paid out in aid of his election, and their compliance with the present requirements of law relative thereto—while such committee was conducting such investigation, and had full authority in the

premises, he, the said William Sulzer, wilfully prevented and dissuaded a certain witness, to wit:

Frederick L. Colwell, who had been duly summoned or subpoenaed to attend as a witness before said committee hereinbefore named for the eighth day of August, 1913, from attending pursuant to said summons or subpoena.

That in so preventing or dissuading said Frederick L. Colwell, who had thus been duly summoned or subpoenaed to appear before said committee on said day named, from attending before said committee pursuant to said summons or subpoena, the said William Sulzer acted wrongfully and wilfully and corruptly and was guilty of a violation of the statutes of the state and of section 2441 of the penal law, and was guilty of a misdemeanor, to the great scandal and reproach of the governor of the state of New York.

That the said William Sulzer, now governor of the state of New York, was duly and regularly nominated by the democratic party of said state as its candidate for governor at a regular convention of said party held in the city of Syracuse, on or about the first day of October, 1912, such nomination having been made on or about the second day of October, 1912, and he was, therefore, until the fifth day of November, 1912, when he was elected to such office of governor, such candidate of said party for said office.

That being, and while such candidate for said office of governor, various persons contributed and delivered money and checks representing money to him, said William Sulzer, to aid his election to said office of governor, and in connection with such election; that said money and checks were thus contributed and delivered to said William Sulzer as bailee, agent or trustee, to be used in paying the expenses of said election and for no other purposes whatever; that the said William Sulzer with the intent to appropriate the said money and checks representing money thus contributed and delivered to him as aforesaid, to his own use, having the same in his possession, custody or control as bailee, agent or trustee as aforesaid, did not apply the same for the uses for which he had thus received the same and appropriated them to his own use and used the same, or a large part thereof, in speculating in stocks, through brokers operating on the New York stock exchange and thereby stole such money and checks and was guilty of larceny.

That among such money and checks thus stolen by said William Sulzer was a check of Jacob H. Schiff for $2,500; a check of Abram I. Elkus for $500; a check of William F. Mc Combs for $500; a check of Henry Morgenthau for $1,000; a check of John Lynn for $500; a check of Theodore W. Myers for $1,000; a check of Lyman A. Spaulding for $100; a check of Edward F. O'Dwyer for $100; a check of John W. Cox for $300; a check of Frank V. Strauss company for $1,000; a check of John T. Dooling for $1,000; and cash aggregating $32,850.

That in so converting and appropriating said money and checks to his own use the said William Sulzer did not act as required by law, but did act wrongfully and wilfully and corruptly, and was guilty of a violation of sections 1290 and 1294 of the penal law, and of grand larceny, and the same was done for the purpose of concealing, and said action and omission of said William Sulzer did conceal the names of persons who had contributed funds in aid of his election and defeated the purposes of the provisions of the statute which require such publication that the people might know whether or not said governor, after he had taken office, was attempting to reward persons who had so contributed in aid of his election, by bestowing official patronage, or favors upon them, and thereafter having taken the oath as governor of the state of New York, and proceeded to perform the duties thereof, the said appropriation to his own use, and his larceny of the same, caused great scandal and reproach of the governor of the state of New York.

ARTICLE VII.

That the said William Sulzer, then being the governor of the state of New York, unmindful of the duties of his office, and in violation of his oath of office, was guilty of mal and corrupt conduct in his office as such governor of the state, and was guilty of the corrupt use of his position, as such governor, and of the authority of said position, and of a violation of section 775 of the penal law of said state, in that while holding a public office, to wit: the office of governor, he promised and threatened to use such authority and influence of said office of governor for the purpose of affecting the vote or political action of certain public officers; that among such public officers to whom the said William Sulzer promised, or threatened to use his authority and influence as governor, for the purpose of affecting their votes, said persons to whom such promises or threats were made, were:

Hon. S. G. Prime, jr., a member of assembly for the county of Essex for the year, 1913, the promise being that if said Prime would vote for certain legislation in which said William Sulzer was interested and, as governor, was pressing to passage, he, said Sulzer, would sign a bill that had already passed the legislature and was pending before him, re-appropriating the sum of about $800,000 for the construction of roads in said county of Essex and counties adjoining thereto, the said governor at the time of said promise well knowing that the said assemblyman, S. G. Prime, jr., was desirous of having said bill for said appropriation for roads signed by the governor.

Hon. Thaddeus C. Sweet, a member of assembly for the county of Oswego for the year 1913, the threat being that if the said Sweet did not vote for certain legislation in which said William Sulzer was interested, and was pressing for passage, the said Sulzer would veto a bill that had already passed the legislature and was pending before him, appropriating moneys for the construction of a bridge in said county of Oswego, the said governor at the time of said threat well knowing that the said assemblyman, Thaddeus C. Sweet, was desirous of having said bill for said appropriation signed.

That in so using the position and authority of the office of governor the said William Sulzer acted wrongfully and wilfully and corruptly and was guilty of a violation of the statutes of the state and of section 775 of the penal law, and of a felony, to the great scandal and reproach of the governor of the state of New York.

ARTICLE VIII.

That the said William Sulzer, then governor of the state of New York, unmindful of the duties of his office, and in violation of his oath of office, was guilty of mal and corrupting conduct in his office as such governor of the state, and was guilty of the corrupt use of his position, as such governor and of the authority of said position and of a violation of section

775 of the penal law of said state, in that, while holding a public office, to wit: The office of governor, he corruptly used his authority, or influence, as such governor, to affect the current prices of securities listed and selling on the New York stock exchange, in some of which securities he was at the time interested and in which he was speculating, carrying, buying or selling, upon a margin or otherwise, by first urging, recommending and pressing for passage legislation affecting the business of the New York stock exchange and the prices of securities dealt in on said exchange, which legislation he caused to be introduced in the legislature, and, then by withdrawing, or attempting to withdraw, from the consideration of the legislature such legislation which was then pending therein. All the time concealing his identity in said transactions by subterfuge. That in so using the position and authority of the office of governor, the said William Sulzer acted wrongfully and wilfully and corruptly and was guilty of a violation of the statutes of the state, and of section 775 of the penal law, and of a felony, to the great scandal and reproach of the governor of the state of New York.

And the said assembly, saving to themselves by protestation, the liberty of exhibiting any other articles of impeachment against the said William Sulzer, governor as aforesaid, and also of replying to the answers which he may make to the impeachment aforesaid, and of offering proof of the said matters of impeachment, do demand that the said William Sulzer, governor as aforesaid, be put to answer all and every of the said matters, and that such proceedings, trial and judgment may be thereunder had and given as are conformable to the constitution and laws of the state of New York; and the said assembly are ready to offer proof of the said matters at such time as the honorable court for the trial of impeachment may order and appoint.

Albany, N. Y., August 12th, 1913.

AARON J. LEVY	JOSEPH V. FITZGERALD
PATRICK J. McMAHON	TRACY P. MADDEN
ABRAHAM GREENBERG	THOMAS K. SMITH
WILLIAM J. GILLEN	HERMAN F. SCHNIREL
THEODORE HACKETT WARD	

Attest: ALFRED E. SMITH, Speaker
          GEORGE R. VAN NAMEE, Clerk

PRESENTMENT OF THE ROCKLAND COUNTY GRAND JURY ON
THE HIGHWAY FRAUDS

The grand jury of the county of Rockland, in session at a term of the New York Supreme Court, held in and for the county of Rockland on the 18th day of August, 1913, do present as follows:

We have had under our consideration a large volume of evidence given before us upon a thorough investigation in relation to the construction and ma'ntanance of certain state roads in the county of Rockland, under the jurisdiction of the highway department of the state of New York; and realizing that the great benefits which are intended to be conferred upon the people through the construction and maintenance of state roads can only be effected by an honest and efficient expenditure of the money voted and appropriated for that purpose, we deem it our duty to call attention to the serious wrongs imposed upon the people of this county by the maladministration heretofore existing in the highway department of the state of New York.

The evidence adduced convinces us that said highway department was in a state of absolute disorganization, and that no means such as would exist in a properly conducted business organization, or which even common prudence would dictate, were invoked, to the end that the money voted and appropriated, for the construction and maintenance of state roads might be expended, so as to obtain the objects intended by the people in consenting to the expenditure of such money through said highway department.

The officials under whom said highway department was conducted at Albany, and upon whose ability, efficiency and loyalty to the state the proper construction and maintenance of said roads in this county, and the proper expenditure of money for that purpose, in the main, legally depended, proceeded largely upon the theory that said highway department was rather a quasi-political organization than a great business supported by the taxpayers and operated under governmental powers.

The highway commission, charged with important duties under the law—duties, which if properly fulfilled, would tend in a large measure to protect the interests of the people—met infrequently considering the volume of business to be transacted and when they did meet, the transaction of their business was done in such a manner as to compel the inference that said commission was striving rather to exhibit a formal compliance with the law than to substantially effectuate the purposes for which sa d commission was created.

The higher the official in said department of highways the less he actually knew as to whether the money paid for the construction and maintenance of state roads was being expended in accordance with the contracts. One of the lowest grade of employees in said highway department was the foreman of laborers, and yet under the pernicious conditions existing, the foreman of laborers was the only employee or official upon whom, according to the evidence before us, the responsibility rested of protecting the people in causing the money voted and appropriated for that purpose to be properly expended for the maintenance of state roads in this county. It is patent that such a condition could not exist unless the high officials of said highway department at Albany were either incompetent or entertained perverted opinions as to the fidelity demanded by the state from its public officers.

Said highway department was more proficient in the dispensation of favors in the form of contracts to contractors having political influence, than it was in requiring integrity in the execution of such contracts. Incompetency prevailed therein where ability was most necessary.

A typical illustration of the inefficient and improper manner in which said highway department was operated is as follows: Contracts were formally entered into between contractors and the state of New York for the performance of work upon state roads and the payment of large sums of money therefor, which were termed supplemental contracts, meaning contracts entered into after the original contract had been made. These supplemental contracts in many instances were made, entered into and signed on or about the day that the payment under the same was made, and long after the time when the work performed, or as is the fact more often pretended to be performed, by the contractors, had passed.

As a result of the above obnoxious conditions in said highway department, cheats and frauds existed to an extent that if a reorganization of the same did not take place, and an honest and effective system for the protection of the expenditure of the people's money inaugurated, the policy of the state of New York to construct and maintain state roads would be thwarted from its commendable purposes and prostituted to subserve venal ends.

EDWARD D. KEESLER—Foreman

THOMAS GAGAN—District attorney

JAMES H. MORRISSEY—Clerk

STATE OF NEW YORK

Rockland County Clerk's office. } *ss.:*

I, Cyrus M. Crum, clerk of said county, hereby certify that I have compared the foregoing copy presentment with the original now on file in said office, and find same to be a true and correct transcript therefrom and of the whole of such original.

In testimony whereof, I have hereunto subscribed my name and affixed the seal of said county this 18th day of August, 1913.

[SEAL] CYRUS M. CRUM—Clerk

COLONEL ROOSEVELT'S FRANK ENDORSEMENT OF GOVERNOR SULZER

THE OUTLOOK

No. 287 Fourth Ave., New York

OFFICE OF THEODORE ROOSEVELT

September 2, 1913

MY DEAR GOVERNOR SULZER.—On my return from Arizona I have received your two letters. I thank you for them. I believe I thoroughly understand the assault that is now being made upon you. I have yet to meet a single person who believes, or even pretends to believe, that a single honest motive has animated the proceedings of your antagonists. From Mr. Murphy himself to the legislators who obeyed his directions, there is no possible question that all of your assailants are the enemies of the public, and that their aim is to acquire the evil domination of the state government, and that the conspiracy against you has not one saving impulse behind it that can in the remotest degree be ascribed to patriotism or civic spirit or anything save the basest impulse of crooked politics. We have never seen a more startling example of the power of the invisible government under the present system. The extraordinary thing is that the "conservative" upholders of this present system should have witnessed the decrees of the invisible government carried out within twenty-four hours, and nevertheless denounce as revolutionary our proposal for changes in the form of government whereby the deliberate judgment of the majority of the voters may be executed within a space of time no shorter than that required for the execution of their deliberate judgment in the choice of a president of the United States.

Let me add one thing, my dear Governor. You owe it to yourself and to all those who have supported you to take the earliest opportunity to answer the charges made against you. That the purposes of those bringing the charges are wholly evil, I am sure that all honest men feel. Moreover, I am sure that honest men feel that the assault made upon you by your foes is due to your having stood up for the principles of good government and decent citizenship even when it was necessary to defy the will of the bosses of the two parties, and especially of your own, and to stand in the way of the success of the corrupt schemes of the party machines' managers. But there is also among honest men a desire for a full and straightforward explanation and answer in reference to the charges made against you, and I very earnestly hope that as soon as possible the explanation and answer will be made.

With all good wishes and regards to Mrs. Sulzer,

Sincerely yours,

(Signed)   THEODORE ROOSEVELT

Hon. William Sulzer

Leading Editorial in the New York American, Tuesday, July 29, 1913
THE PEOPLE'S HOUSE OR FOURTEENTH STREET

The fight between Murphy and the Governor of New York —savage and relentless—presents a crisis as serious and menacing as the Empire State has known within the quarter century.

Suppose that Murphy and Tammany Hall should prevail to destroy the Governor of New York for the simple reason that the Democratic Chief Executive had sincerely and fearlessly advocated the right of the people of New York to vote individually in direct primaries.

What would be the effect of such an unholy triumph?

It would minify and depreciate the power and authority of the Governor of New York now and hereafter.

It would magnify and glorify the power and prestige of Tammany and Tammany's Boss now and hereafter.

It would degrade the State.   It would dignify the Boss and the Machine.

It would make it easier for every subsequent boss to win.

It would make it easier for every subsequent democratic governor to lose.

Since the days of Samuel J. Tilden no democratic governor has ever fought the Tammany machine as the present governor has fought it.   No man has ever fought Tammany in so vital a cause of good government, or burned his bridges so fearlessly behind him in the fight.

If the Tammany boss and the Tammany machine should mass its forces of criticism and abuse and virulent slander, and break the governor's influence and destroy his repute just when it is being used for the public good, then two things are evident.

No other governor is likely to dare the wrath of so deadly and destroying a political organization in the future affairs of the state.

And the baneful influence and power of Tammany and Murphy to-day will be doubled and quadrupled for the future.

It does not matter what the average citizen may think of the governor of New York.   It does not matter what the governor of New York may or may not have been in years past.

It is a fact that just now he is fighting as just and righteous a vital battle for the people as any governor has fought before him. It is a fact that Tammany and Murphy, with all the long evil record of graft and bossism behind them, is making the effort of their lives to destroy the governor of New York, personally and officially, because he is fighting the people's fight against the Tammany machine.

And it does seem evident that every good citizen—or every decent citizen—should in this fight, at least, stand whole-hearted and wholehanded behind the governor and the people against the boss and the machine.

Editorial in the North American, Philadelphia, Wednesday, August 20, 1913

GOVERNOR SULZER'S HEROIC STRUGGLE—THE REAL ISSUE IN NEW YORK

To citizens who had not followed closely recent events in New York the impeachment of Governor Sulzer doubtless seemed an isolated event, the sudden infliction of a spectacular revenge.

But it was, in fact, merely a necessary step toward the culmination of a great conspiracy, the object of which was to murder popular government and seize control of the state's affairs for corrupt Tammany.

This atrocious plot, engineered by boss Murphy in behalf of his criminal organization and his special-privilege backers, has been marked throughout by familiar methods and common-place villainy. But it is unique in one respect—that there is, it is safe to say, not one person in the whole country who believes or pretends that a single honest motive animated the procedure.

Nor could there be found, we think, a reputable citizen who would seriously contend that there was a single participant in the audacious scheme who was moved by patriotism or civic spirit or anything save the basest impulses of crooked politics.

From Murphy himself, notorious as the leader of the world's greatest criminal organization, down to Lieutenant Governor Glynn, the officers of the house and senate and others of his underlings, there is not one who exhibits a redeeming sense of unselfishness or desire to promote the public welfare. And this includes Justice Victor Dowling, now Murphy's candidate for mayor of New York, who attended the boss' secret conference at Delmonico's last May, when the elaborate conspiracy to destroy Governor Sulzer was launched.

That this condition is unique a glance at history will show. There have been political crimes in all ages and all countries, but we recall none which was so desperate or so disreputable that the perpetrators could not enter the plea that at least their aim was the common good.

When Brutus thrust his assassin's knife into Ceasar he struck, he said, because he loved Rome. The blood-crazed mobs of the French revolution, jeering their victims to the reeking guillotine, were inspired with a passion for liberty. Benedict Arnold, we doubt not, believed that what his countrymen called treason was the truest loyalty, which would perpetrate the blessings of monarchy and avert the disasters of republicanism.

The ballot-box stuffer will argue that his irregularities are intended simply to aid the party of peace and prosperity and save the people from their irrational impulses for change. Even Senator Penrose, we are sure, felt no pangs of remorse over taking the oil trust's $25,000, since it was to be used in promoting Republican rule, which notoriously is synonymous with national honor and progress.

But in this Tammany conspiracy every motive is transparently evil. No one has the temerity to assert that there is any honest or patriotic purpose back of it. Even those who cheer on the pursuit of Governor Sulzer admit that his assailants are public enemies and that their aim is to acquire corrupt domination of the state government.

Thus the New York World, which is giving the most effective aid to Murphy's campaign, applauds the impeachment of the Governor as just, lawful and necessary, and at the same time gives this characterization of the gang that committed the assault:

The World agrees with Colonel Watterson, that 'not one of the rogues who voted 'impeachment' cares a jill of beans about the 'crimes' and 'misdemeanors' of William Sulzer.'

"Murphy ordered the impeachment as he would order a beefsteak at Delmonico's, and a servile assembly voted the impeachment with more obsequiousness than a self-respecting French waiter would show to a grand duke.

"The impeachment in itself was the most startling revelation of the degradation of government that New York has ever known. A sordid, corrupt boss at one end of a telephone wire tells the assembly to impeach the governor of the state, and the assembly responds like a trained dog. The assembly obeyed Murphy with the same airy indifference with which the gunmen obeyed Becker when they were told to 'get' Rosenthal.

This is mild language compared to that habitually used concerning Murphy and Tammany by the New York American. That paper had been one of Governor Sulzer's strongest supporters, but in the present controversy it has been strangely indifferent. One explanation for this change may be that Mr. Hearst wanted the Governor to remove Mayor Gaynor; so that he is not in a very good position to denounce another attempt to oust an official elected by the people.

But we shall not argue further that Tammany and its purposes are vicious. Every well-informed citizen must know what no one has the hardihood to deny. The question which the thoughtful American will ask himself is this: How can it be possible for a gang of political freebooters to seize the government of a great state in full view of the people, although their intent is palpably criminal?

The explanation, dear reader, is simple. Tammany is putting through its conspiracy by the strict application of the glorious principles of "constitutional government." Mr. Murphy is demonstrating how admirable are the "orderly processes of the fundamental law," as opposed to such harebrained inventions as the recall, with its dependence upon the " gusty passions of the mob."

Under the Constitution of the State of New York, one more than half of the membership of the assembly can, upon any pretext, impeach the governor. It should be remarked here that the act of impeachment is not conviction, nor even a trial. It is simply a formal accusation, analogous to an indictment. But it operates, according to the interpretation of the Tammany leaders, to remove the governor elected by the people and substitute one more satisfactory to Boss Murphy.

The assembly majority, then, which for years has been controlled absolutely either by the Republican or the Democratic boss, or by the two in concert, can impeach or indict the governor, and thereby—although weeks or months may elapse before the charges are tried—can paralyze the official power of the chief executive and replace him with a serviceable instrument of a corrupt machine.

This is exactly the conservative and highly constitutional course followed by Murphy. First he named a legislative committee to draw up and investigate the charges he supplied. The evidence gathered by Tammany spies and heelers was heard, and impeachment was duly recommended. The assembly majority—some members forced into action only by severe pressure—carried out its part of the orders. And thereupon, still with profound regard to the Constitution, the Murphy forces seized the governorship. The procedure is justly characterized by the legislative reference bureau of the national Progressive party:

A small band of political enemies of the governor were able, by use of their political power, to gather evidence, to present it to their own judgment, and, without any opportunity for either presentation of the other side or the establishment of an impartial tribunal, to condemn their enemy as guilty of the crimes which they themselves had alleged against him, and, according to their claim, to remove him from office.

It is not strange that the "conservative" upholders of "invisible government," which can execute its fiat within twenty-four hours, decry any change in the forms of government whereby the "hasty judgment" of a majority of the voters might be executed within the brief period of two or three months.

But there should be a clear understanding of Tammany's corrupt motives, as well as of its despicable methods. Putting aside entirely the question of Governor Sulzer's guilt or innocence of the charges brought by a servile assembly, the citizen should examine the purposes back of the conspiracy.

It is obvious, first, that Tammany Hall, the most notorious of the agencies of special privilege, would not have nominated this man unless in the belief that it could control him. There-

_ _ _ _ _ _ _ _ _ _ _ _ _ _ _ _ _ _ _, the acts of which
he is accused are venial faults.

But there is not even a pretense that the impeachment was
brought because of the Governor's alleged campaign fund
irregularities. These merely provided the weapons of assassination.

The purpose, of which there is no concealment, was threefold.
First, to wrest from an unsuspectedly honest executive state
departments controlling vast patronage, the award of huge
contracts and the auditing of expenditures; second, to prevent
his forcing the passage of an effective primary law, the enactment of which would be the death warrant of Tammany and
its ally, special privilege; and third, to inflict such punishment
upon the governor as would deter future public officials elected
by the machine from daring to exhibit like proclivities toward
decency and independence.

The real controversy, therefore, is not as to whether Governor
Sulzer's campaign accounts were regular. It is as to whether
corrupt bosses and special privilege shall by "constitutional"
methods strangle popular government in New York State and
perpetuate a system of misrule and public plundering.

E. A. VAN VALKENBURG—Editor

Editorial from the North American, Philadelphia, Monday, August 18, 1913

THE PARADOX OF SULZER—THE TRIUMPH OF DUTY

Boss Murphy's jeering prophecy, that under the very first
assault from Tammany Governor Sulzer would crumple like
a piece of wet paper has been proved false. Even the supreme
exhibition of the criminal machine's malign power—the forcing
of the legislature to commit high treason against the Empire
State—has not broken him down.

We wish it were possible to picture Governor Sulzer as a
knight of stainless virtue defying the hosts of evil, a militant
crusader wielding the sword of righteousness against the powers of darkness.

to congress for nine successive terms, he was stirred to the
depths of his emotional nature. His humane instincts would
for the time being make their wrongs his own.

But he lacked the understanding to perceive that those
wrongs were in large measure due to illicit partnership between special privilege and Tammany, to which organization
he gave allegiance.

In all his makeup there is no spark of militancy. He
would bring about the brotherhood of man by means which
would not remotely approach the kind of fighting required in
the present crisis.

His appearance and mannerisms are far from those of a
resolute champion of desperate causes. Angular, ungainly, not
lacking at times a touch of the grotesque, he seems to take
seriously the suggestions of flattering friends that he has the
personality of a Lincoln or a Clay, and perhaps seeks to enhance the idea by affectations of dress and theatrical emphasis
of voice and gesture.

Yet this man, one most palpably not of heroic mold, who
possesses none of the great qualities needed for this emergency,
the first Democrat of New York state who has been able
to withstand and morally triumph over the combined forces

fore, Murphy felt assured that Sulzer was an infinitely worse man than he would be if every charge in the articles of impeachment were proved to the hilt, for, compared with the treason he was expected to commit or allow, the acts of which he is accused are venial faults.

But there is not even a pretense that the impeachment was brought because of the Governor's alleged campaign fund irregularities. Those merely provided the weapons of assassination.

The purpose, of which there is no concealment, was threefold. First, to wrest from an unexpectedly honest executive state departments controlling vast patronage, the award of huge contracts and the auditing of expenditures; second, to prevent his forcing the passage of an effective primary law, the enactment of which would be the death warrant of Tammany and its ally, special privilege, and, third, to inflict such punishment upon the governor as would deter future public officials elected by the machine from daring to exhibit like proclivities toward decency and independence.

The real controversy, therefore, is not as to whether Governor Sulzer's campaign accounts were regular. It is as to whether corrupt bossism and special privilege shall by "constitutional" methods strangle popular government in New York State and perpetuate a system of misrule and public plundering.

E. A. VAN VALKENBURG—Editor

Editorial from the North American, Philadelphia, Monday, August 18, 1913

THE PARADOX OF SULZER—THE TRIUMPH OF DUTY

Boss Murphy's jeering prophecy, that under the very first assault from Tammany Governor Sulzer would crumple like a piece of wet paper has been proved false. Even the supreme exhibition of the criminal machine's malign power—the forcing of the legislature to commit high treason against the Empire State—has not broken him down.

We wish it were possible to picture Governor Sulzer as a knight of stainless virtue defying the hosts of evil, a militant crusader wielding the sword of righteousness against the powers of darkness.

But to pretend that he appears in such a guise would be folly. In disposition, character and capacity he is almost the antithesis of the figure of knight errantry. Some traces of Don Quixote's spirit constitute his nearest approach to the ideals of chivalry.

He is neither a warrior nor a builder. He is a dreamer. He dreams of such herculean tasks as the liberation of oppressed peoples from tyranny. As a youth he was arrested as a plotter against Spanish misrule in Cuba, and was condemned to be shot. He made his first campaign for congress on the single pledge that he would " free Cuba." It is his chief pride that he introduced the first resolution looking to that end, and his happiest memory is of a banquet given by the government of liberated Cuba in his honor. To this day he corresponds regularly with foreign republicans, even in China.

It may well be believed, then, that as he used to face those throngs of poor folk on New York's East Side, who sent him to congress for nine successive terms, he was stirred to the depths of his emotional nature. His humane instincts would for the time being make their wrongs his own.

But he lacked the understanding to perceive that those wrongs were in large measure due to illicit partnership between special privilege and Tammany, to which organization he gave allegiance.

In all his makeup there is no spark of militancy. He would bring about the brotherhood of man by means which would not remotely approach the kind of fighting required in the present crisis.

His appearance and mannerisms are far from those of a resolute champion of desperate causes. Angular, ungainly, not lacking at times a touch of the grotesque, he seems to take seriously the suggestions of flattering friends that he has the personality of a Lincoln or a Clay, and perhaps seeks to enhance the idea by affectations of dress and theatrical emphasis of voice and gesture.

Yet this man, one most palpably not of heroic mold, who possesses none of the great qualities needed for this emergency, is the first Democrat of New York state who has been able to withstand and morally triumph over the combined forces of corrupt bossism and special privilege.

We tried to explain the other day this splendid paradox. His public and private acts traduced, his errors relentlessly exposed, brought even to the bar of a hostile court of impeachment, he stands immovable. It is because the issue has been clearly revealed to him, once for all. He has seen that for the time being he alone stands between his state and its looters; that to yield or compromise would be the ultimate dishonor. Stolidly, without whimpering and without fury, he plants his feet upon that fact, and there remains.

No doubt there is some truth in the savage sneer of Collier's Weekly that he is "vain, a ranter and poseur." Yet what man in official life, though ever so devoted and sincere, has displayed such courage in the face of merciless odds?

The less venomous of his critics say that he took his stand because it seemed he might win political capital by so doing. But to maintain this theory, they must ignore the facts. For six months he was subject to the secret urgings, cajolements and concealed threats of professed friends, who advised him to yield just enough to secure his own safety; and he refused.

The brutal assaults he endured were never unexpected. He had the chance to prevent by compromise the publication of charges that he had been accused of perjury, the bringing of the breach of promise suit, the pressing of the impeachment. Yet the enemy found the weakling strong, the poseur a man of iron.

But the supreme test was still to come, in a situation more trying than many public men have had to face.

Among the charges against him was that, with other Wall street activities, he operated a gambling account aggregating $50,000. As a fact, this was in no sense a stock account. He owned an equity in certain shares, and for years had used it as security for bank loans. A broker friend offered to take it over and let him draw against it. Not a share of stock was bought or sold. The procedure was legitimate and necessary; many business men follow it, because the stock gamblers have the first call upon money.

The next charge was that his campaign funds were larger than appeared in his sworn return. No one knows all the facts; but it is true that the governor handled no campaign moneys, and that he signed the statement drawn up by trusted friends.

The really serious charge was that some funds were not applied to the campaign at all, but were used in a private account to purchase stocks. When this accusation was first made by the chairman of the Murphy committee, Governor Sulzer denounced it as false, stating specifically that he was never a party to such a transaction and had used no campaign checks privately.

When later, he learned the basis of the charge, he confronted the most searching problem of his career. The acts leading to the only serious charge against him had been those of his wife. Yet, although the result was so perilous for him, he uttered not a word of censure. He never doubted the purity of her motives—that she had believed she was acting in the best possible way honestly to promote his interests.

His enemies believed, of course, that he would make any sacrifice to protect his wife. So the tempters in the guise of friends began to urge him again toward compromise. Surely he was justified, they argued, in adopting any course to save her from publicity.

But they did not know their man. His feet were on the rock of decision. Not to save himself—not to save even the woman who was his dearer self—would he yield to forces when his yielding meant the unrestricted plundering of the state. And during all the weeks of pressure, when he knew that a statement of the facts would in all likelihood avert the final attack, he kept silence.

Not until the legislature was actually assembling to bring the impeachment did he reveal the truth, even to his closest advisers, and then only with the stipulation that it should not be used publicly.

In every turn and twist of the fight the governor and his wife were together, and her word was always to fight. They were in perfect accord, except upon one point she insisted that she should tell her story and clear his name; he resolutely insisted she should not.

But her sense of justice and loyalty was so strong that when the legislature met she sent for a member of the senate, and, against the prohibition of her husband and his advisers, revealed the facts. Her determination buoyed her up to deliver the fateful message; then she collapsed, and now is critically ill.

There have been few more dramatic episodes in our public

life. But it will only be as the people come to be better informed as to the facts that they will realize how heavy has been
the pressure that Governor Sulzer has withstood.

He is fully aware of some of his weaknesses, and discusses
them frankly. He admits that he has not the slightest business
ability or financial foresight. He has always been in debt.
Whenever he had a little money, it went from him rapidly.
In a district where Tammany leaders have grown rich upon
tribute wrung from the unfortunate, he has remained poor, and
what funds he had were always at the service of importunate
constituents.

Mrs. Sulzer took complete charge of his financial affairs, and
tried earnestly to put them on a self-sustaining basis. But
during the campaign the inevitable appeals to which a candidate
is subjected proved stronger than her vigilance. Certain
campaign contributions, therefore—by the advice, it is said, of
friends and even of some of those who sent the money—she
used to make good the drain on her husband's private resources.

No man, we think, would have it in his heart to censure a
woman who had acted from the motives she did, under all the
circumstances. But to the husband, who learned at a late day
how she had been drawn into these acts by attempting to shield
his deficiencies, the proof of her devotion must have made her
doubly dear. And it was she whom, by standing firmly against
the enemies of the state, he was to deliver to suffering and
humiliation.

This man, we have seen, was seemingly quite unfitted to cope
with the overwhelming forces against him. Yet he overcame
something stronger than Tammany; he resisted a pressure more
severe than the fear of losing office and the injury to his public
and private reputation. He put aside the opportunity to
protect his wife, who had imperiled herself in his behalf, because
the price asked was official treason. His enemies might do
their worst. He would not yield.

There are many opinions—most of them, we fear, unflattering
—of William Sulzer's wisdom, capacity and sincerity. But we
think that our public records can be searched for a long time
without finding a demonstration of steadfastness, in the teeth
of certain destruction, more convincing than that which he
has given.   E. A. VAN VALKENBURG—Editor

[From the New York Tribune.]

MURPHY'S POLITICAL UNDERWORLD AND ITS ROSENTHAL

The state is witnessing the most monstrous perversion of its government in its history.

There is a deadlock between the government elected by the people and the invisible government, self-chosen, of the Tammany boss. Even offices that are necessary for the safety of the workers are kept vacant in order that the boss may not lose his hold upon the throat of the state.

The purpose in declining to approve the governor's appointees to the labor commissionership is unconcealed. No bolder or more shameless exh bition of bossism has ever been seen. The senate had nothing against either Mr. Mitchell or Mr. Lynch. On the contrary, there were potent reasons why they should be confirmed. It was Murphy that held them up. His invisible government has come out into the open to fight desperately for its existence.

Hundreds of working people may die any day, as threescore or more died in Binghamton, because of the demoralization in the Department of Labor which the boss keeps up in order to maintain his hold upon jobs and contracts for the Tammany machine.

It was simple justice which led a business man in Ossining to lay the recent mutiny in Sing Sing to Murphyism. The underworld in jail knows what is going on outside. Its revolt was an echo of the fight which Murphy's political underworld is conducting against Sulzer. It was a sympathy strike. The crooks out of jail are in arms against Sulzer. The crooks in jail arose against Sulzer's man, the new warden.

The whole underworld, the political underworld, of which Murphy is the head, and the other underworld, which touches elbows with it in the darkness, is stirred to the depths as a small segment of it was stirred one year ago when the gambler Rosenthal was headed toward the district attorney's office. The underworld of graft and mean politics looks upon the governor as the underworld of gambling looked upon the informer whom it slew—as a traitor, a "squealer," a man to be taught a lesson if the underworld is to survive.

It is possible to smile at Governor Sulzer's story that his life is in danger. The governor is a "movie" melodramatist. But that the underworld of graft and Tammany politics will go so far as character assassination and political blackmail recent events have shown. It will go so far as to imperil the lives of thousands of workers; it will go so far as to bring the state face to face with the danger of jail delivery in its reckless determination to keep its clutches on its dishonest spoils and to "get" the "squealer" whom it hates.

The underworld of graft has tied up the processes of government. Its present challenge to the people of the state is like the challenge to the people of the city when Rosenthal fell on Broadway. How long will the public tolerate this monstrous perversion of its institutions? Whose government is this? The people's or Murphy's and the political underworld's?

HENRY WATTERSON
In the Louisville Courier Journal

"COLLAPSE OF SELF GOVERNMENT VERITABLE VICTORY FOR CRIME "

That the people of New York are incapable of self-government—especially the people of the city which dominates the state of New York–has long been the belief of observant and thoughtful onlookers.

Life is safer among the feudists of the mountains of Kentucky than it is in the Borough of Manhattan. Living is less fuddled in the Bluegrass than the Bronx. Even the scrub politicians who sometimes work into places of emolument and honor here are a trifle cleaner and less ravenous than the wolves who there prowl at all hours of the day and night between the purlieus of the great white way and the legislative red light in the Capitol at Albany.

Judge Herrick talks loftily of "preserving the dignity of the commonwealth." Alack, the day! It has no dignity to preserve. Its dignity was thrown to the dogs years agone. Not one of the rogues who voted "impeachment" cares a hill o' beans about the "crimes" and "misdemeanors" of Sulzer.

The court which tries him will be a mock court, a majority
foresworn. Justice, patriotism, truth have fled to brutish
beasts, leaving graft and grafters to fight over the loot and to
flourish one another in corrupt succession, the people looking on
impotent and dazed.

The opportunities for stealing are so ever-present and easy—
the rewards of theft so enormous—the likelihood of punishment is so slight!

The public debt of the city of New York rivals the national
debt. We read of the Walpole regime in England with a kind of
wonder. It was not a flea bite by comparison with the system
of pillage which holds New York in a grip from which there
seems no escape. Go where one may he encounters its agents
and stumbles over its engineries. Scratch a politician, whatever label he wears, and you find a scamp. Things are every
whit as bad as they were under Tweed. They were amateurs
in those days. A part of their plan was to enjoy life. Wine,
women and song had seats at their tables. Now they are
professionals. Addition, division and silence are ranged about
the board where Fisk said "the woodbine twineth." No
nonsense; just the firm hand, the cold stare, and, where need
be the legend, "dead men tell no tales."

Poor William Sulzer! What siren voice of vanity, what
optimistic simplicity could have lured him to battle on the
off side of a stream having no bridges, his line of retreat leading
through the enemy's country right into the deadly ambus-
cades and yawning rifle pits of Wall Street? One can well
believe he did not wrongfully use a dollar; that the case against
him is a "frame-up;" even that, like the dog in the fable, he
was merely caught in bad company. Did he not know that
Wall street is a house of prostitution? What was he doing
there? Why did he go there? And, knowing the Indians
were on the trail—that proof requiring explanation existed—
had he had a spoonful of common sense it would have warned
him betimes.

A kind of innocent rusticity and childlike egotism plead for
him. But they will plead in vain. Just as they white-
washed Stilwell and Cohalan will they impeach him. Judge
Herrick is a great and noble man; the very synonym of an
old-fashioned jurist and a conscientious Tilden democrat;

but all his learning, his character and his genius would not suffice to save William Sulzer if he were as guiltless as a lamb. whereas the ancient role of guilt presumed by appearance and propinquity puts him at a fatal disadvantage.

It is a veritable victory for crime. The private peccadillo of a weak and erring man who was trying to do right is made the fulcrum from which a gang of grafters are enabled to remove an obstruction to their orgy of pillage. It is here that proof of the incapacity of the people of New York for self-government comes in. They are so at sea—so mis-advised by conflicting counsels—that they tumble about and over themselves like so much wreckage. They are perpetually off the banks and in a fog. They lack the wit to make their way to shore and to find some common ground. Their newspapers tell them nothing. They merely increase the thickness of the weather.

Take for an example the opening chorus of the mayoralty performance in the city of New York. The one visible enemy of good government is Tammany. It can only be overcome by a fusion of all parties. A movement to that end was set on foot. A nominating committee was organized. The names of three good citizens went before it. Each was in honor bound to abide the result, and each did honorably abide the result. Yet there were newspapers claiming to be for fusion and affecting to support this plan of procedure which, after the event, not only drew out, but urged the two aspirants who had contended unsuccessfully to draw out.

To be sure these newspapers then and there proclaimed their own infamy. Yet they continue to appear with regularity and effrontery that goes far to substantiate the doctrine of total depravity and establishes the fact that the people of New York are incapable of self-government. It is a collapse of self-government. Shall it be forever and aye?

BILL SIKES MURPHY—"DON'T I OWN YER?"

From the Albany Knickerbocker Press

HONESTY FIRST MARK OF WILLIAM SULZER

GOVERNOR WOULD HAVE MADE FORTUNE IN CONGRESS
IF STOOPING TO GRAFT

Editorial in Albany Knickerbocker Press, August 12,
by Frank W. Clark, Managing Editor

Governor William Sulzer is a child of nature. He has the enthusiasm of a boy. His heart is great and open. He has trusted mankind because he has faith in and sympathy for humanity. An egotist, like many other public men, he has been susceptible to flattery. His personal vanity has made it easy for unscrupulous persons to win his confidence wholly and implicitly, to play upon his heart strings, to lure him to unwise frankness and open confession of his private affairs. It is such men as these that have led Sulzer into traps. The Judas Iscariots of Tammany have won his confidence and have then betrayed him to their politically vile master. There are no instances of baser treachery in the history of politics in the nation than the treasons of men whom William Sulzer so thoroughly trusted that he would have shed his lifeblood for them. This shameful phase of the tremendous conspiracy which is being laid to grab the government of the greatest state in the union for the benefit and enrichment of the most corrupt political organization of modern history will all be laid before the people of New York before William Sulzer finishes his fight for right and for justice. Governor Sulzer has proofs that from the moment that Charles F. Murphy at the Syracuse state convention consented to his nomination for governor Mr. Murphy's personal spies have dogged his heels. They have searched his life history. They have invented base lies about his past life. They have stolen from his household and from his office in the executive chamber private papers and valuable records. Nor have they stopped there. Personal belongings of Mrs. William Sulzer—a noble woman whose sufferings in these times can be imagined— including jewelry which she prized most highly for its associations, have been ruthlessly taken away or destroyed. Had William Sulzer been a less trusting man he would have discovered before he took the oath of office as governor that the intention of Tammany Hall was to use him as its pawn, or failing to make of him a ready tool, to destroy him. Governor Sulzer, in spite of his human failings, and with full knowledge that he was personally vulnerable in some respects, made up his mind some weeks ago to sacrifice himself for the people of the state of New York. He has said, and he meant it, and he repeats it now, that he does not care what shall become of William Sulzer personally. He has offered himself as a sacrifice upon the altar of good government as an instrument of the people in the war of the honest portion of New York state's electorate against official and unofficial graft and corruption. There is not a dishonest hair in the head of William Sulzer, if we judge him aright. Had William Sulzer been a dishonest man his many years in congress would have seen him a millionaire. Had he been a dishonest man the luxuries which Charles F. Murphy enjoys at Good Ground would not have been denied to William Sulzer. William Sulzer has always been pressed hard financially. He has devoted himself much to ideals and to the sometimes vain pursuits of the gewgaws of ambition and little to practical business affairs. Through carelessness and lack of system of bookkeeping, but not through dishonesty, the financial affairs of William Sulzer have in the past become entangled. But let the people of the state of New York know now that he is an honest man at heart. In the hysteria of the present clamor for his crucifixion let it be understood by the people of the state that if they permit his political destruction at this time, if by breach of law Tammany is permitted to remove him from office, there will be created in American history a real martyr for whom future generations will erect lasting monuments. It is perhaps a good thing for the state of New York that the venomous Tammany is carrying its fight so far and with such high handed unreason, for whatever may be the result of the present battle in the end only good can come. It is too late for a truce. In the first speech which Mr. Justice Charles E. Hughes has delivered in New York state since he left the governor's chair, the speech at Warrensburgh last Friday, Justice Hughes solemnly con-

HONESTY FIRST MARK OF WILLIAM SULZER

GOVERNOR WOULD HAVE MADE FORTUNE IN CONGRESS
IF STOOPING TO GRAFT

Editorial in Albany Knickerbocker Press, August 12,
by Frank W. Clark, Managing Editor

Governor William Sulzer is a child of nature. He has the
enthusiasm of a boy. His heart is great and open. He has
trusted mankind because he has faith in and sympathy for
humanity. An egotist, like many other public men, he has
been susceptible to flattery. His personal vanity has made it
easy for unscrupulous persons to win his confidence wholly and
implicitly, to play upon his heart strings, to lure him to unwise
frankness and open confession of his private affairs. It is
such men as these that have led Sulzer into traps. The Judas
Iscariots of Tammany have won his confidence and have then
betrayed him to their politically vile master. There are no
instances of baser treachery in the history of politics in the
nation than the treasons of men whom William Sulzer so
thoroughly trusted that he would have shed his lifeblood for
them. This shameful phase of the tremendous conspiracy
which is being laid to grab the government of the greatest
state in the union for the benefit and enrichment of the most
corrupt political organization of modern history will all be
laid before the people of New York before William Sulzer
finishes his fight for right and for justice. Governor Sulzer
has proofs that from the moment that Charles F. Murphy
at the Syracuse state convention consented to his nomination
for governor Mr. Murphy's personal spies have dogged his
heels. They have searched his life history. They have invented base lies about his past life. They have stolen from
his household and from his office in the executive chamber
private papers and valuable records. Nor have they stopped
there. Personal belongings of Mrs. William Sulzer—a noble
woman whose sufferings in these times can be imagined—
including jewelry which she prized most highly for its asso-

ciations, have been ruthlessly taken away or destroyed. Had
William Sulzer been a less trusting man he would have discovered before he took the oath of office as governor that the
intention of Tammany Hall was to use him as its pawn, or
failing to make of him a ready tool, to destroy him. Governor
Sulzer, in spite of his human failings, and with full knowledge
that he was personally vulnerable in some respects, made up
his mind some weeks ago to sacrifice himself for the people
of the state of New York. He has said, and he meant it, and
he repeats it now, that he does not care what shall become of
William Sulzer personally. He has offered himself as a sacrifice upon the altar of good government as an instrument of
the people in the war of the honest portion of New York state's
electorate against official and unofficial graft and corruption.
There is not a dishonest hair in the head of William Sulzer,
if we judge him aright. Had William Sulzer been a dishonest
man his many years in congress would have seen him a millionaire. Had he been a dishonest man the luxuries which
Charles F. Murphy enjoys at Good Ground would not have
been denied to William Sulzer. William Sulzer has always
been pressed hard financially. He has devoted himself much
to ideals and to the sometimes vain pursuits of the gewgaws
of ambition and little to practical business affairs. Through
carelessness and lack of system of bookkeeping, but not through
dishonesty, the financial affairs of William Sulzer have in the
past become entangled. But let the people of the state of New
York know now that he is an honest man at heart. In the
hysteria of the present clamor for his crucifixion let it be understood by the people of the state that if they permit his political destruction at this time, if by breach of law Tammany is
permitted to remove him from office, there will be created in
American history a real martyr for whom future generations
will erect lasting monuments. It is perhaps a good thing for
the state of New York that the venomous Tammany is carrying its fight so far and with such high handed unreason, for
whatever may be the result of the present battle in the end
only good can come. It is too late for a truce. In the first
speech which Mr. Justice Charles E. Hughes has delivered in
New York state since he left the governor's chair, the speech
at Warrensburgh last Friday, Justice Hughes solemnly con-

men of
... man of cleaner per-
... with men of char-
... Tammany's
... that through
... committee it
... William Sulzer
... him on the
... New York ... believed,
... Sulzer would be left standing
... a friendless and dishonored man.
... knife
... Had there
... on the part of the
now
... at Albany with a threat
... proceedings, and the ... committee
... in the byways. It sometimes requires an
... to bring out of a man the bigness that is
in hi.   It was a isis of such magnitude that made Abraham
Linco the savi of the nation.   There are indications at
the ; ent crisi at his solemn obligations to the people of
the te will ma . of William Sulzer a capable and efficient
instrument for th delivery of the state for all time from the
clutche of profe nal plunderers of the public treasury and
the r le o olitic bosses who are the partners of shady busi-
e s and c pose e "invisible government" which Theodore
Woosevelt learned know so well and which Woodrow Wilson
we r ng about
inc

BARNES REPAYS DEBT TO CHAF

GIVES ASSEMBLYMAN LEVY ONE

Editorial in Albany Knickerbocker P
by Judge Lynn J. A

Three years ago Governor Charles E.
by William Barnes through the aid of
In the senate of the state of New York,
Murphy Democrats lined up with Re-
licans and sidetracked the bill of direct
Barnes last night repaid his debt to C
furnishing to the Democratic leader
Levy, the only argument which he ha
tention that the assembly might at this
impeach William Sulzer. It was an ed
Barnes which was the foundation of M
which was read in full by Mr. Levy.
said one word as yet in behalf of the peo
York, and it is time for the people of t
the true situation. Last night by track
Levy, the assembly by a majority vote of
the Frawley committee's resolution an
and attested by the secretary of th
This secretary, Matthew T. Horgan.
through certified records of the crimso
of New York to have been convicted
laws of this state. The records show
been pardoned, and yet this same Ho
retary to the Frawley committee, and
of $5,000 a year under a Tammany d
nd economy as deputy commissioner
ance showing the awful condition ca
hen Mr. Murphy resorts to putting
tion of trust how is it possible for

present conditions in politics depress him. He
he fond optimism difficult in these times, and
read the history of the United States to regain
hopefulness for the future of the republic. There
bt the Justice Hughes had in mind the present
im Sizer. But Justice Hughes has read his
il that he knows that in the end right triumphs
ught i the hands of political grafters and cor-
If Wiliam Sulzer had been less stubborn and
n he assumed the governorship of the state, if
about him more trustworthy advisors, men of
h of knowledge and vision, men of cleaner per-
, and if he had about him such men of char-
mmar would not dare attack him. Tammany's
was made because it believed that through
cowardly assaults of the Frawley committee it
a circumstantial case against William Sulzer
ause revulsion of feeling against him on the
peope of New York state. Tammany believed,
elieve that Mr. Sulzer would be left standing
various office, a friendless and dishonored man.
any's plan to plunge its already guilty knife
al heat of a deserted human wreck. Had there
though and less of hysteria on the part of the
ate in the last few days Tammany would not
wve uon the capitol at Albany with a threat
nt proceedings, and the Frawley committee
king in the byways. It sometimes requires an
the crisis to bring out of a man the bigness that is
was a cris of such magnitude that made Abraham
savior of the nation. There are indications at
crisis that his solemn obligations to the people of
ill make of William Sulzer a capable and efficient
for the delivery of the state for all time from the
rofessional plunderers of the public treasury and
tical bosses who are the partners of shady busi-
se the invisible government " which Theodore
arned to know so well and which Woodrow Wilson

BARNES REPAYS DEBT TO

GIVES ASSEMBLYMAN LEVY
FORCE I

Editorial in Albany Knicker
by Judge Lynn

Three years ago Governor Chr
by William Barnes through the
In the senate of the state of New
Murphy Democrats lined up wit
licans and sidetracked the bill of d
Barnes last night repaid his debt
furnishing to the Democratic lea
Levy, the only argument which
tention that the assembly might
impeach William Sulzer. It was
Barnes which was the foundat
which was read in full by Mr. I
said one word as yet in behalf of tl
York, and it is time for the peopl
the true situation. Last night by
Levy, the assembly by a majority
the Frawley committee's resoluti
and attested by the secretary
This secretary, Matthew T. Ho
through certified records of the
of New York to have been com
laws of this state. The records
been pardoned, and yet this man
retary to the Frawley committee
of $5,000 a year under a Tamma
and economy as deputy commis
stance showing the awful conditio
When Mr. Murphy resorts to p
position of trust how is it possi

fessed that present conditions in politics depress him. F
declared that he found optimism difficult in these times, ar
that he had to read the history of the United States to regai
his customary hopefulness for the future of the republic. Thei
can be no doubt that Justice Hughes had in mind the preser
fight of William Sulzer. But Justice Hughes has read h
history so well that he knows that in the end right triumpl
over brutal might in the hands of political grafters and coi
ruptionists. If William Sulzer had been less stubborn an
obstinate when he assumed the governorship of the state, :
he had called about him more trustworthy advisors. men c
greater breadth of knowledge and vision, men of cleaner pei
sonal character. and if he had about him such men of chai
acter today Tammany would not dare attack him. Tammany'
present attack was made because it believed that througl
despicable and cowardly assaults of the Frawley committee i
had built up a circumstantial case against William Sulze:
which would cause a revulsion of feeling against him on th
part of all of the people of New York state. Tammany believed
and may yet believe, that Mr. Sulzer would be left standing
alone in the governor's office. a friendless and dishonored man
It was Tammany's plan to plunge its already guilty knife
into the political heart of a deserted human wreck. Had there
been more of thought and less of hysteria on the part of the
press of the state in the last few days Tammany would not
now dare to move upon the capitol at Albany with a threat
of impeachment proceedings. and the Frawley committee
would be skulking in the byways. It sometimes requires an
overwhelming crisis to bring out of a man the bigness that is
in him. It was a crisis of such magnitude that made Abraham
Lincoln the savior of the nation. There are indications at
the present crisis that his solemn obligations to the people of
the state will make of William Sulzer a capable and efficient
instrument for the delivery of the state for all time from the
clutches of professional plunderers of the public treasury and
the rule of political bosses who are the partners of shady busi‟
ness and compose the " invisible government " which Theodore
Roosevelt learned to know so well and which Woodrow Wilson
 learning about.

depress him. He

in these times, and

States to regain

the republic. There

had in mind the present

Hughes has read his

he end right triumphs

crafters and cor-

less stubborn and

p of the state, if

advisors, men of

man of cleaner per-

such men of char-

k him. Tammany's

that through

Frawley committee it

William Sulzer

against him on the

Tammany believed,

be left standing

and dishonored man.

already guilty knife

wreck. Had there

on the part of the

Tammany would not

Albany with a threat

Frawley committee

times requires an

the bigness that is

that made Abraham

are indications at

to the people of

a capable and efficient

state for all time from the

of the public treasury and

the partners of shady busi-

which Theodore

and which Woodrow Wilson

BARNES REPAYS DEBT TO CHARLES F. MURPHY

GIVES ASSEMBLYMAN LEVY ONE ARGUMENT TO FORCE IMPEACHMENT

Editorial in Albany Knickerbocker Press, August 12,
by Judge Lynn J. Arnold

Three years ago Governor Charles E. Hughes was defeated by William Barnes through the aid of Charles F. Murphy. I the senate of the state of New York, at that time, fourteen Murphy Democrats lined up with fourteen Barnes Republicans and sidetracked the bill of direct nominations. William Barnes last night repaid his debt to Charles F. Murphy in furnishing to the Democratic leader in the assembly, Mr. Levy, the only argument which he had to sustain his contention that the assembly might at this extraordinary session impeach William Sulzer. It was an editorial written by Mr. Barnes which was the foundation of Mr. Levy's speech and which was read in full by Mr. Levy. Mr. Barnes has not said one word as yet in behalf of the people of the state of New York, and it is time for the people of the state to awaken to the true situation. Last night by trickery on the part of Mr. Levy, the assembly by a majority vote of those present adopted the Frawley committee's resolution and report, a resolution and attested by the secretary of the Frawley committee. This secretary, Matthew T. Horgan, was proven yesterday through certified records of the criminal courts of the state of New York to have been convicted as a felon under the laws of this state. The records show that he has never yet been pardoned, and yet this same Horgan is serving as secretary to the Frawley committee, and also drawing a salary of $5,000 a year under a Tammany department of efficiency and economy as deputy commissioner. This is but one instance showing the awful condition existing in this state today. When Mr. Murphy resorts to putting his felon spy in such position of trust how is it possible for any honest Democrat

fessed that present conditions in politics depress him. He
declared that he found optimism difficult in these times, and
that he had to read the history of the United States to regain
his customary hopefulness for the future of the republic. There
can be no doubt that Justice Hughes had in mind the present
fight of William Sulzer. But Justice Hughes has read his
history so well that he knows that in the end right triumphs
over brutal might in the hands of political grafters and corruptionists. If William Sulzer had been less stubborn and
obstinate when he assumed the governorship of the state, if
he had called about him more trustworthy advisors, men of
greater breadth of knowledge and vision, men of cleaner personal character, and if he had about him such men of character today Tammany would not dare attack him. Tammany's
present attack was made because it believed that through
despicable and cowardly assaults of the Frawley committee it
had built up a circumstantial case against William Sulzer
which would cause a revulsion of feeling against him on the
part of all of the people of New York state. Tammany believed,
and may yet believe, that Mr. Sulzer would be left standing
alone in the governor's office, a friendless and dishonored man.
It was Tammany's plan to plunge its already guilty knife
into the political heart of a deserted human wreck. Had there
been more of thought and less of hysteria on the part of the
press of the state in the last few days Tammany would not
now dare to move upon the capitol at Albany with a threat
of impeachment proceedings, and the Frawley committee
would be skulking in the byways. It sometimes requires an
overwhelming crisis to bring out of a man the bigness that is
in him. It was a crisis of such magnitude that made Abraham
Lincoln the savior of the nation. There are indications at
the present crisis that his solemn obligations to the people of
the state will make of William Sulzer a capable and efficient
instrument for the delivery of the state for all time from the
clutches of professional plunderers of the public treasury and
the rule of political bosses who are the partners of shady business and compose the " invisible government " which Theodore
Roosevelt learned to know so well and which Woodrow Wilson
in learning about.

BARNES REPAYS DEBT TO CHARLES F. MURPHY

GIVES ASSEMBLYMAN LEVY ONE ARGUMENT TO FORCE IMPEACHMENT

Editorial in Albany Knickerbocker Press, August 12, by Judge Lynn J. Arnold

Three years ago Governor Charles E. Hughes was defeated by William Barnes through the aid of Charles F. Murphy. In the senate of the state of New York, at that time, fourteen Murphy Democrats lined up with fourteen Barnes Republicans and sidetracked the bill of direct nominations. William Barnes last night repaid his debt to Charles F. Murphy in furnishing to the Democratic leader in the assembly, Mr. Levy, the only argument which he had to sustain his contention that the assembly might at this extraordinary session impeach William Sulzer. It was an editorial written by Mr. Barnes which was the foundation of Mr. Levy's speech and which was read in full by Mr. Levy. Mr. Barnes has not said one word as yet in behalf of the people of the state of New York, and it is time for the people of the state to awaken to the true situation. Last night by trickery on the part of Mr. Levy, the assembly by a majority vote of those present adopted the Frawley committee's resolution and report, a resolution and attested by the secretary of the Frawley committee. This secretary, Matthew T. Horgan, was proven yesterday through certified records of the criminal courts of the state of New York to have been convicted as a felon under the laws of this state. The records show that he has never yet been pardoned, and yet this same Horgan is serving as secretary to the Frawley committee, and also drawing a salary of $5,000 a year under a Tammany department of efficiency and economy as deputy commissioner. This is but one instance showing the awful condition existing in this state today. When Mr. Murphy resorts to putting his felon spy in such position of trust how is it possible for any honest Democrat

fessed that present conditions in politics depress him.   He declared that he found optimism difficult in these times, and that he had to read the history of the United States to regain his customary hopefulness for the future of the republic.   There can be no doubt that Justice Hughes had in mind the present fight of William Sulzer.   But Justice Hughes has read his history so well that he knows that in the end right triumphs over brutal might in the hands of political grafters and corruptionists.   If William Sulzer had been less stubborn and obstinate when he assumed the governorship of the state, if he had called about him more trustworthy advisors, men of greater breadth of knowledge and vision, men of cleaner personal character, and if he had about him such men of character today Tammany would not dare attack him.   Tammany's present attack was made because it believed that through despicable and cowardly assaults of the Frawley committee it had built up a circumstantial case against William Sulzer which would cause a revulsion of feeling against him on the part of all of the people of New York state.   Tammany believed, and may yet believe, that Mr. Sulzer would be left standing alone in the governor's office, a friendless and dishonored man. It was Tammany's plan to plunge its already guilty knife into the political heart of a deserted human wreck.   Had there been more of thought and less of hysteria on the part of the press of the state in the last few days Tammany would not now dare to move upon the capitol at Albany with a threat of impeachment proceedings, and the Frawley committee would be skulking in the byways.   It sometimes requires an overwhelming crisis to bring out of a man the bigness that is in him.   It was a crisis of such magnitude that made Abraham Lincoln the savior of the nation.   There are indications at the present crisis that his solemn obligations to the people of the state will make of William Sulzer a capable and efficient instrument for the delivery of the state for all time from the clutches of professional plunderers of the public treasury and the rule of political bosses who are the partners of shady business and compose the " invisible government " which Theodore Roosevelt learned to know so well and which Woodrow Wilson is learning about.

BARNES REPAYS DEBT TO CHARLES F. MURPHY

GIVES ASSEMBLYMAN LEVY ONE ARGUMENT TO FORCE IMPEACHMENT

Editorial in Albany Knickerbocker Press, August 12, by Judge Lynn J. Arnold

Three years ago Governor Charles E. Hughes was defeated by William Barnes through the aid of Charles F. Murphy. In the senate of the state of New York, at that time, fourteen Murphy Democrats lined up with fourteen Barnes Republicans and sidetracked the bill of direct nominations. William Barnes last night repaid his debt to Charles F. Murphy in furnishing to the Democratic leader in the assembly, Mr. Levy, the only argument which he had to sustain his contention that the assembly might at this extraordinary session impeach William Sulzer. It was an editorial written by Mr. Barnes which was the foundation of Mr. Levy's speech and which was read in full by Mr. Levy. Mr. Barnes has not said one word as yet in behalf of the people of the state of New York, and it is time for the people of the state to awaken to the true situation. Last night by trickery on the part of Mr. Levy, the assembly by a majority vote of those present adopted the Frawley committee's resolution and report, a resolution and attested by the secretary of the Frawley committee. This secretary, Matthew T. Horgan, was proven yesterday through certified records of the criminal courts of the state of New York to have been convicted as a felon under the laws of this state. The records show that he has never yet been pardoned, and yet this same Horgan is serving as secretary to the Frawley committee, and also drawing a salary of $5,000 a year under a Tammany department of efficiency and economy as deputy commissioner. This is but one instance showing the awful condition existing in this state today. When Mr. Murphy resorts to putting his felon spy in such position of trust how is it possible for any honest Democrat

fessed that present conditions in politics depress him. He
declared that he found optimism difficult in these times, and
that he had to read the history of the United States to regain
his customary hopefulness for the future of the republic. There
can be no doubt that Justice Hughes had in mind the present
fight of William Sulzer. But Justice Hughes has read his
history so well that he knows that in the end right triumphs
over brutal might in the hands of political grafters and corruptionists. If William Sulzer had been less stubborn and
obstinate when he assumed the governorship of the state, if
he had called about him more trustworthy advisors, men of
greater breadth of knowledge and vision, men of cleaner personal character, and if he had about him such men of character today Tammany would not dare attack him. Tammany's
present attack was made because it believed that through
despicable and cowardly assaults of the Frawley committee it
had built up a circumstantial case against William Sulzer
which would cause a revulsion of feeling against him on the
part of all of the people of New York state. Tammany believed,
and may yet believe, that Mr. Sulzer would be left standing
alone in the governor's office, a friendless and dishonored man.
It was Tammany's plan to plunge its already guilty knife
into the political heart of a deserted human wreck. Had there
been more of thought and less of hysteria on the part of the
press of the state in the last few days Tammany would not
now dare to move upon the capitol at Albany with a threat
of impeachment proceedings, and the Frawley committee
would be skulking in the byways. It sometimes requires an
overwhelming crisis to bring out of a man the bigness that is
in him. It was a crisis of such magnitude that made Abraham
Lincoln the savior of the nation. There are indications at
the present crisis that his solemn obligations to the people of
the state will make of William Sulzer a capable and efficient
instrument for the delivery of the state for all time from the
clutches of professional plunderers of the public treasury and
the rule of political bosses who are the partners of shady business and compose the " invisible government " which Theodore
Roosevelt learned to know so well and which Woodrow Wilson
is learning about.

BARNES REPAYS DEBT TO CHARLES F. MURPHY

GIVES ASSEMBLYMAN LEVY ONE ARGUMENT TO FORCE IMPEACHMENT

Editorial in Albany Knickerbocker Press, August 12, by Judge Lynn J. Arnold

Three years ago Governor Charles E. Hughes was defeated by William Barnes through the aid of Charles F. Murphy. In the senate of the state of New York, at that time, fourteen Murphy Democrats lined up with fourteen Barnes Republicans and sidetracked the bill of direct nominations. William Barnes last night repaid his debt to Charles F. Murphy in furnishing to the Democratic leader in the assembly, Mr. Levy, the only argument which he had to sustain his contention that the assembly might at this extraordinary session impeach William Sulzer. It was an editorial written by Mr. Barnes which was the foundation of Mr. Levy's speech and which was read in full by Mr. Levy. Mr. Barnes has not said one word as yet in behalf of the people of the state of New York, and it is time for the people of the state to awaken to the true situation. Last night by trickery on the part of Mr. Levy, the assembly by a majority vote of those present adopted the Frawley committee's resolution and report, a resolution and attested by the secretary of the Frawley committee. This secretary, Matthew T. Horgan, was proven yesterday through certified records of the criminal courts of the state of New York to have been convicted as a felon under the laws of this state. The records show that he has never yet been pardoned, and yet this same Horgan is serving as secretary to the Frawley committee, and also drawing a salary of $5,000 a year under a Tammany department of efficiency and economy as deputy commissioner. This is but one instance showing the awful condition existing in this state today. When Mr. Murphy resorts to putting his felon spy in such position of trust how is it possible for any honest Democrat

fessed that present conditions in politics depress him.   He
declared that he found optimism difficult in these times, and
that he had to read the history of the United States to regain
his customary hopefulness for the future of the republic.   There
can be no doubt that Justice Hughes had in mind the present
fight of William Sulzer.   But Justice Hughes has read his
history so well that he knows that in the end right triumphs
over brutal might in the hands of political grafters and corruptionists.   If William Sulzer had been less stubborn and
obstinate when he assumed the governorship of the state, if
he had called about him more trustworthy advisors, men of
greater breadth of knowledge and vision, men of cleaner personal character, and if he had about him such men of character today Tammany would not dare attack him.   Tammany's
present attack was made because it believed that through
despicable and cowardly assaults of the Frawley committee it
had built up a circumstantial case against William Sulzer
which would cause a revulsion of feeling against him on the
part of all of the people of New York state.   Tammany believed,
and may yet believe, that Mr. Sulzer would be left standing
alone in the governor's office, a friendless and dishonored man.
It was Tammany's plan to plunge its already guilty knife
into the political heart of a deserted human wreck.   Had there
been more of thought and less of hysteria on the part of the
press of the state in the last few days Tammany would not
now dare to move upon the capitol at Albany with a threat
of impeachment proceedings, and the Frawley committee
would be skulking in the byways.   It sometimes requires an
overwhelming crisis to bring out of a man the bigness that is
in him.   It was a crisis of such magnitude that made Abraham
Lincoln the savior of the nation.   There are indications at
the present crisis that his solemn obligations to the people of
the state will make of William Sulzer a capable and efficient
instrument for the delivery of the state for all time from the
clutches of professional plunderers of the public treasury and
the rule of political bosses who are the partners of shady business and compose the " invisible government " which Theodore
Roosevelt learned to know so well and which Woodrow Wilson
is learning about.

BARNES REPAYS DEBT TO CHARLES F. MURPHY

GIVES ASSEMBLYMAN LEVY ONE ARGUMENT TO FORCE IMPEACHMENT

Editorial in Albany Knickerbocker Press, August 12, by Judge Lynn J. Arnold

Three years ago Governor Charles E. Hughes was defeated by William Barnes through the aid of Charles F. Murphy. In the senate of the state of New York, at that time, fourteen Murphy Democrats lined up with fourteen Barnes Republicans and sidetracked the bill of direct nominations. William Barnes last night repaid his debt to Charles F. Murphy in furnishing to the Democratic leader in the assembly, Mr. Levy, the only argument which he had to sustain his contention that the assembly might at this extraordinary session impeach William Sulzer. It was an editorial written by Mr. Barnes which was the foundation of Mr. Levy's speech and which was read in full by Mr. Levy. Mr. Barnes has not said one word as yet in behalf of the people of the state of New York, and it is time for the people of the state to awaken to the true situation. Last night by trickery on the part of Mr. Levy, the assembly by a majority vote of those present adopted the Frawley committee's resolution and report, a resolution and attested by the secretary of the Frawley committee. This secretary, Matthew T. Horgan, was proven yesterday through certified records of the criminal courts of the state of New York to have been convicted as a felon under the laws of this state. The records show that he has never yet been pardoned, and yet this same Horgan is serving as secretary to the Frawley committee, and also drawing a salary of $5,000 a year under a Tammany department of efficiency and economy as deputy commissioner. This is but one instance showing the awful condition existing in this state today. When Mr. Murphy resorts to putting his felon spy in such position of trust how is it possible for any honest Democrat

fessed that present conditions in politics depress him. He declared that he found optimism difficult in these times, and that he had to read the history of the United States to regain his customary hopefulness for the future of the republic. There can be no doubt that Justice Hughes had in mind the present fight of William Sulzer. But Justice Hughes has read his history so well that he knows that in the end right triumphs over brutal might in the hands of political grafters and corruptionists. If William Sulzer had been less stubborn and obstinate when he assumed the governorship of the state, if he had called about him more trustworthy advisors, men of greater breadth of knowledge and vision, men of cleaner personal character. and he had about him such men of character today Tammany would not dare attack him. Tammany's present attack was made because it believed that through despicable and cowardly assaults of the Frawley committee it had built up a circumstantial case against **William Sulzer** which would cause a revulsion of feeling against him on the part of all of the people of New York state. Tammany believed, and may yet believe that Mr. Sulzer would be left standing alone in the governor' office, a friendless and dishonored man. It was Tammany's plan to plunge its already guilty knife into the political heart of a deserted human wreck. Had there been more of thought and less of hysteria on the part of the press of the state in the last few days Tammany would not now dare to move upon the capitol at Albany with a threat of impeachment proceedings, and the Frawley committee would be skulking in the byways. It sometimes requires an overwhelming crisis to bring out of a man the bigness that is in him. It was a crisis of such magnitude that made Abraham Lincoln the savior of the nation. There are indications at the present crisis that his solemn obligations to the people of the state will make of William Sulzer a capable and efficient instrument for the delivery of the state for all time from the clutches of professional plunderers of the public treasury and the rule of political bosses who are the partners of shady business and compose the " invisible government " which Theodore Roosevelt learned to know so well and which Woodrow Wilson is learning about.

BARNES REPAYS DEBT

GIVES ASSEMBLYMAN
FORCE

Editorial in Albany Kex
by Judge Ly

Three years ago Governor
by William Barnes through
In the senate of the state of Ni
Murphy Democrats lined up
licans and sidetracked the bill
Barnes last night repaid his
furnishing to the Democratic
Levy, the only argument whi
tention that the assembly mig
impeach William Sulzer.
Barnes which was the
which was read in full by M
said one word as yet in behalf o
York, and it is time for the pi
the true situation. Last nigh:
Levy, the assembly by a majori
the Frawley committee's i
and attested by the secretar
This secretary, Matthew T.
through certified records of tl
of New York to have been
laws of this state. The recor
been pardoned, and yet this
retary to the Frawley comm
of $5,000 a year under a Ta
and economy as deputy co
stance showing the awful
When Mr. Murphy resorts
position of trust how is it po

to remain a member of the so-called Democratic party in the state of New York? Any one who heard the venomous speech made last night by the crazy Cuvillier and the shifty, tricky Levy would unhesitatingly commend Governor Sulzer for absolutely refusing to dignify their attacks or the attacks of the Frawley committee with an answer. The people of the city and county of Albany and of the state of New York have just cause for pride in the position taken by the minority leader, Harold J. Hinman. The assembly of the state of New York needs more men like Harold J. Hinman. If the assembly districts of the state have men of his stamp within their borders they should make certain that they are sent to represent them in the next assembly. It makes no difference whether they are called Democrats, Republicans or Progressives. Such men will never bring shame upon the state. Such men are above petty political trickery. Such men will guard the treasury instead of looting it. The people of the state of New York must sound the note from Montauk Point to Lake Erie which will uphold the hands of Governor William Sulzer and they must strike a note which will terrorize the Frawleys and the Cuvilliers and the Levys and the Wagners and the Al Smiths and drive them forever from the legislative halls.

TICONDEROGA FLAYS MURPHY'S TREASON

MASS MEETING DENOUNCES ATTEMPTED ASSASSINATION OF SULZER'S CHARACTER

JAY W. FORREST SPEAKS

ALBANY LAWYER DECLARES TAMMANY'S MINIONS HAVE PLANNED TO SEIZE AND LOOT STATE

Special to The Knickerbocker Press.

TICONDEROGA, Aug. 24.—Citizens of Ticonderoga registered their emphatic protest against boss rule in the state of New York tonight in a great mass meeting arranged by a committee of 100. Strong speeches were made by leading men and resolutions were passed deploring the conditions that have been brought about in the state through the cohesive power of public plunder and the indifference of the people to the treasonable action of Murphy and his cohorts. The resolutions appeal to the men and women of the Empire State to rise against this insolent usurpation of power.

D. C. Bascom, a life long Republican, was chairman. The meeting from every point of view was a success. It served splendidly to emphasize the fact that in this community there is an overwhelming sentiment against the treasonable act of Tammany Hall and the assault of minions upon constitutional government and the integrity of the governor of the state.

The meeting was opened with prayer by the Rev. C. E. Torrence, who made an appeal for divine guidance in this crisis in our civic life. Mr. Hoffnagle, one of the leading Republican lawyers of Essex county, made a strong appeal for justice to Sulzer and the return of constitutional government, emphasizing the belief of citizens in the governor's honesty of purpose and admiration for the superb courage he has shown in defying the organized forces of graft. The Rev. Dr. de Gruchy sounded a call for the rekindling of the fires of patriotism in the hearts of the people and urged support

of Governor Sulzer in his fight for civic righteousness by every
honest citizen regardless of politics.

Those in the packed auditorium arose and sang "America."
Jay W. Forrest of Albany closed the speaking with a terse
presentation of conditions at Albany and a recital of the
causes which led up to the present situation and a forecast of
the results that would follow the supremacy of the band of
looters. He declared they had planned to seize and rob the
commonwealth. The resolutions were passed with enthusiasm.
The benediction was pronounced by Dr. de Gruchy, which
closed the meeting. The fight in Ticonderoga for the maintenance of constitutional government has only begun, it is
declared on all sides.

RESOLUTIONS ADOPTED

WHEREAS, The deplorable conditions existing in the government of our beloved state today, appeals to the heart of
every patriotic rightminded citizen and cry to high heaven for
relief and correction and,

WHEREAS, These conditions have been brought about to
the shame and disgrace of the citizenship of the Empire state
and the fair name and fame of this great commonwealth, by
a band of men, not inspired by even a false ambition, but
held together solely by the " cohesive force of plunder," the
plunder they already have had and which they hope to secure
by the abuse and misuse of the powers of this state which
they have attempted to seize, and

WHEREAS, Standing with his back against the wall, the
wolfish cry of this pack of bandits, who demand his honor and
his life, if need be, ringing in his ears, stands a man, the constitutional governor of your state, fighting your fight and the
fight of your state for civic righteousness, for common honesty,
for constitutional government; against this horde that repre-
sents today the most effective organization of the " powers
that prey " that exist in the civilized world, and

WHEREAS, Between the honor and solvency of this great
state and a carnival of looting, graft and crime, that will smear
an indelible blot on our shield, stand the great principle of
civic righteousness, for which this man, your duly elected

constitutional governor, is contending almost single-handed and alone, therefor be it

RESOLVED, That the citizens of Ticonderoga, regardless of race, creed or party affiliations, in mass meeting assembled on this evening of the Lord's Day do hereby earnestly and solemnly protest to the manhood and womanhood of the Empire state and the American nation against their seeming indifference in the momentous and unequal struggle for the orderly government by law, under the constitution of this our state, now being led at our capitol by our legal and constitutional governor, William Sulzer, and be it further,

RESOLVED, That we call on the citizenship of this state and nation to uphold the hands of our governor under the law by every legitimate means, in his and their fight against the combined forces of graft and corruption, to the end that civic righteousness and honesty may triumph and the good name of our state may be saved, and be it further,

RESOLVED, That a copy of these resolutions be transmitted to Governor Sulzer, with the assurance of our sympathy, encouragement and continued confidence and support, in his fight against the " Powers that Prey."

CITIZEN'S COMMITTEE
RESIDING IN TICONDEROGA, N. Y.

D. C. Bascom	Wayne B. Simpkins
William W. Jeffers	John C. Munningham
F. B. Wood	T. E. Ward
Roy Lockwood	J. M. C. Thomas
R. J. Bryan	O. C. Badger
M. Mintzer	H. W. Treadway
Dr. Geo. H. Beers	Franklin T. Locke
John G. Hutchinson	Chas. A. Morhous
A. G. Brockney	E. C. Merchant
Sylvester R. Wood	Frank Fish
W. D. McLaughlin	Carlton F. Warner
Judson N. Ross	Daniel Lee
Gordon W. Myott	Frank Wright
John Hyde	Joseph Garrow
Edward S. Bly	G. H. Adkins
C. G. West	William Wicker
L. C. Drake	Palmer Bradford
Robert F. Stott	W. A. E. Cummings
M. Y. Ferris	Jos. A. Wood
Altus B. Adkins	W. G. Wiley
George B. Bryan	Frank H. Grimes
James F. McCaughin	Wilas B. Moore
Edward C. D. Wiley	John A. Briggs
J. H. Clark	Albert Dolbeck

Preston King
Charles G. Wicker
C. E. Bennett
F. B. Wickes
Thomas DeCruchy
W. E. Hildreth
Frederick Flannery
Frederick Ives
S. A. Weaver
James E. Havens
John Hennessy
L. E. Torrance
Myron J. Wilcox
H. D. Hoffnagle

G. D. Harper
Daniel S. Weeks
W. W. Richards
R. V. Smith
I. G. Mason
C. C. Holden
Jackson C. French
R. C. Landon
Alex. Ostiguy
N. P. Dolbeck
- Henry Cowan
Jacob Mintzer
Ben Spearman
C. F. Mercure

RESIDING IN TICONDEROGA, N. Y., R. F. D.

C. E. Burt
Arthur L. Delano
Pell C. Arthur
Thomas J. Cook
Frank Moses
Floyd Densmore
Lester G. Hack

George W. Johnson
Nelson J. Wright
Frank Clark
W. I. Atwood
Bert Shattuck
Palmer Bradford
William Wicker

RESIDING AT CHILSON, N. Y.

Frank Stowell

A FEW LETTERS

FROM THE HUNDREDS RECEIVED BY GOVERNOR SULZER FOLLOWING HIS IMPEACHMENT BY THE ASSEMBLY

Wolcott, N. Y., Aug. 15, 1913.
Governor William Sulzer, Albany, N. Y.

Governor, "hold the fort," for we are coming tens of thousands strong election day. Already we are hearing the dying wails of Tammany in the disgraceful actions of the legislature, their massacre and slaughter of the Constitution to fetter and clog all investigations demanded by the people. We will be heard, for the "mills of the gods may grind slowly, but they grind surely."

E. J. CORNWELL.

Brooklyn, N. Y., Aug. 16, 1913.
To the Honorable William Sulzer, Governor of the State of New York, Albany, N. Y.

As a well meaning citizen and lover of honest government, I take the liberty of congratulating you on the stand you have taken against the lawless proceedings of the foes to the people's cause.

I. J. LEHR.

Cleveland, O., Aug. 16, 1913.
Governor Sulzer, Albany, N. Y.

I am Independent Republican, residing in New York, and wish to extend to you my sympathies in your troubles, with the hope that you will win out against your enemies.

S. SAXE, New York City.

New York, Aug. 15, 1913.
Honorable William Sulzer, Governor, Albany, N. Y.

Don't be discouraged, the public opinion is with you and against the hoodlums who are trying to annihilate everyone that is good and honest.

Everybody hopes to see you cleared at the trial. Be not dismayed, neither be discouraged.

LEAN KARNAIKY,
Publisher Jewish Daily News.

Hagadorns Mills,
Saratoga Co., N. Y., Aug. 15, 1913
Hon. William Sulzer, Governor of New York State.

Stand by your guns to the last ditch. MULFORD NEAHR.

Elmira, N. Y., Aug. 15, 1913.
Hon. William Sulzer, Governor, State of New York, Albany, N. Y.

I take great pleasure in endorsing your administration to date. I feel that you are fighting for a principle. No matter what the outcome of your present trouble, I will still have faith in your honesty of purpose. I was glad to know that our assemblyman, Dr. R. P. Bush, was able to go to Albany and cast his vote for you.

JAMES A. WILMOT.

New Haven, N. Y., Aug. 15, 1913.
Governor William Sulzer, Governor of the state of New York.

I am a republican, but being an honest one, I want to express my regard for you at this time. I regret that you are in your present trouble. It is a shame that men will stoop so low as some have in the Empire state.

WILLIAM BAKER.

New York City, Aug. 15, 1913.
Hon. William Sulzer, Governor State of New York, Albany, N.Y.

We are all with you heart and soul, and sincerely hope that you will eventually win out. We have every confidence in you and your ability to do so, as right and justice always prevails in the long run.

JOHN H. FIFE.

Watertown, N. Y., Aug. 14, 1913.
Hon. William Sulzer, Albany, N. Y.

As one of your constituents, I desire to extend to you my congratulations, for the manner in which you have stood by your principles, for the American manhood which you represent, and for your ability and willingness to fight when fight is necessary to the interests of the people at large. To my mind Tammany is paying tribute to your integrity, and I am not alone in this. Am sure that, generally speaking, the people of the state are back of you in your fight.

Sincerely hoping that when the smoke of battle has cleared away, that your flag will still be flying on the firing line.

CLAUDE M. BURNETT.

Amsterdam, N. Y., R. D. 3,
                Aug. 15, 1913.
Governor Sulzer, Albany, N. Y.

Just a word to let you know there are thousands of men, real men, who did not help you to be elected but who are backing you now to the limit.

F. H. RULISON.

South Bend, Ind., Aug. 13, 1913.
Hon. William Sulzer, Albany, N. Y.

You are deserving of praise, not criticism. You have started out to do a good and great work, let us hope that the result of the trial will be your continuation in office and your continuation to fight.

History will never say it of William Sulzer that he was a coward or that he was dishonest.

FRED. C. GABRIEL.

New York City, Aug. 16, 1913.
Hon. William Sulzer, Governor New York, Albany, N. Y.

I am not a Democrat but a Progressive. The people by an overwhelming vote elected you Governor of this state and I believe in the American doctrine that the voice of the majority is the voice of all. And therefore I am with you to the last ditch. Go it hard and strong and to the limit.

CHARLES EDWIN SUMMERS.

EDWARD A. WALSH, 100 West 91st street, New York city: Permit me to sympathize with you in these dark hours. No man is infallible, but no matter what your faults are, myself and one hundred of my associates believe in you and will fight for you.

ARCHIBALD B. ROSEN-STRAUS, county committeeman, Fallsburg: Hope you win in your fight against the wolves who dare not fight in the open.

M. J. O'CONNELL, Buffalo: Let me offer my sympathy and assure you of my unbounded belief in your honesty and integrity.

DANIEL S. McCORTEL, Wooster, Ohio: The low character and corrupt record of the men who are attacking you is a compliment. Give them rope enough and they will hang themselves. Carry your fight into the assembly districts. Their vote buying will fail when the truth is known.

JAMES A. HARVEY, Yonkers: You are fighting for principle and you are sure to win. I am one of the many who heard your address at Warburton hall on the direct primary bill and I learned there that you meant business.

EDITH A. REIFFERT, New York city: Heretofore I have not been in favor of the recall, but I wish we had it in this state now, then speedy justice would be done you.

P. COHEN, 949 Third avenue, Brooklyn: I have canvassed the opinion of every voter who came to my store and I have found that everybody who is concerned in good government is behind you in this greatest fight that this or any other state has ever had. I didn't vote for you for I thought that Mr. Straus would make a better governor, but hereafter you can count on my support.

REUBEN DORFMAN, 120 Delancey street, New York city: Ninety-nine persons out of one hundred in the city of New York are with you.

GEORGE WAGNER, 194 Second street, New York city: I think your case should be put up to the people that put you in office and want to see you stay there.

BARNET KIRSCHSTEIN, 335 East Houston street, New York city: Do not tremble before the tiger, as the people are with you.

CHARLES BIRD, Rochester: You have acquitted yourself as a man. Continue to act the way you have and hold the fort. Appeal to the brain and the brawn and the judgment of the working people and the verdict in your favor will be a decisive one.

JAMES J. DURNIN, 724 East 11th street, New York city: If Murphy could use you you would be all right with him.

T. C. DORNHEIM, 39 Vandam street, New York city: Do not give an inch to that blackhand bunch.

D. R. WOOD, Mt. Vernon: The majority of the people are for you regardless of their political tendencies. We who know you have no fears for the final verdict.

SILAS MOSTELLER, North Rush: I think you too clean to suit the gang and that is why they planned to throw you over.

ADALBERT PERENYI, 243 East Sixty-first street, New York city: If you need my services among the Hungarian people, I am entirely at your disposal.

GURLUF GUTHORNSEN, 1320 Third avenue, New York city: I thank God we have a governor who will not bow to Tammany Hall.

GEORGE E. GULICK, county committeeman, Lodi: Nine-tenths of the people in this vicinity are with you in this fight.

I. WILLIAM WRIGHT, Buffalo: You have done your duty and it is plain to see that your enemies are not in the open for the public good. Keep on in your battle and history will write you down all right. "Let him that is without fault cast the first stone."

A. D. MARTELL, Sterling, Ill.: I am convinced of your sterling honesty and integrity as are hundreds to whom I have talked and my best wishes go out to you at this time in what I believe to be the greatest struggle a man ever had to preserve his station. It will be a blot on the history of that great state, of which I am proud to be a native, if your enemies triumph.

N. A. HIRSCH, 1200 Madison avenue, New York city: I didn't vote for you but everything is for Sulzer in the places where I go and you ought to feel encouraged.

W. B. FLEMING, Atlantic City, N. J.: You are attacked, not because of any crime you have committed, but because of crimes you refused to commit. Your offense is not the breaking of the law, but breaking with the bosses. Had you obeyed Murphy and sold out the interests of the state to the cowards nothing would ever have been heard of the charges now brought against you. What is the matter with the New York press? Does it all belong to the plutocracy?

L. D. SLADE, Oneonta: You have fought a good fight and won the admiration of the vast army of men and women.

JOHN J. RYAN, Medina: Every legislator who has acted on the order of this contemptible boss impeached himself as an unfit public official and I believe will be dealt with by the public accordingly.

ERNEST H. WOODRUFF, Olean: Congratulations upon your splendid fight for good government, and for manhood.

MILTON ROBE LEE, Scranton, Pa.: How can the people stand idly by and see you crucified? Why don't they rush to your aid? You are the only man who ever sat in the chair of state at Albany and had the nerve to try to get the people a square deal.

W. M. ALDEN, Hyannis, Neb.: I hope to see you come out on top.

CLIFFORD E. CROSS, Washington, D. C.: I ask that you believe me one of the vast number of persons who think you are far above reproach and disloyalty.

C A. TEAGLE, Houston, Texas: We of Texas know what this fight means. We know that the same forces are attacking you that attacked Bryan, Wilson and every man of advanced thought who are willing to stand for the right and for the rule of the people.

T. J. REARDON, Paterson, N. J.: I am only a poor working-man but I want you to know that men like myself are heart and soul with you in this fight against those political gorillas who are trying to ruin and disgrace you.

F. W. LAKEY, New York city: If there is any possible way I can be of service or comfort to you, call on me.

WILLIAM H. SICKLES, New Baltimore: All Democrats who can claim any right to the name in Greene county are with you in your fight for the right.

JAMES S. SEBRING, Corning: I am with you; the people are with you. Fear not, vindication will surely come.

FRANCIS B. KINGSLAND, West Orange, N. J.: Let me show you my appreciation for the stand you have taken for clean government in New York.

WILLIAM LINDSAY, Seattle: This is your opportunity. Be glad of it and make the most of it.

Albany.
Congratulations for the manly stand you have taken in behalf of good government against the gang of freebooters and state treasury looters who have put you in your present predicament.
THOMAS J. KELLY.

WM. LESLIE FRENCH, Tompkinsville, S. I.: Allow me to congratulate you for the unflinching stand you have taken for defense of the rights of the people.

Albany.
My three brothers and three sons are all for you although we did not vote for you.
D. R. HELMES.

New York City.
At a meeting of the advisory board, representing six hundred members of lodge No. 256, O. B. A., it was resolved that Governor Sulzer be commended on the noble fight he is making and that the best wishes of the lodge be extended to him for a complete and speedy victory over his enemies.
JACOB EISENBURG.

Mexia, Texas.
Command me if I can help and I will be with you to the last ditch. Truth never suffered defeat.
M. A. WESTLOW.

Yonkers.
We express our indignation at the outrage committed against you.
PHILIP LUBOOW.

New York City.
This incident will be lost and forgotten when it is shown that you could have had anything if you had only betrayed your state to these highbinders. All the people will be with you when the truth comes out. You will remember how Alexander Hamilton was approached and how it all helped to his glory and success when he stood up for honesty.
W. E. D. STOKES.

New York City.
I am pastor of a church of over seven hundred members. I admire your noble fight against the organized enemies of true democracy. No Sunday morning service has passed in my church in which I have not prayed for you before the congregation.
REV. BARTON M CLARKE·

Ranchester, Pa.
May God bless you and protect
you and give you strength to continue in this fight.
MELVIN T. MILLER.

Sigourney, Iowa.
Once a fellow member of congress
with Governor Sulzer. Let me con-
sole you by saying that there are
those in faraway Iowa who are with
you in this struggle and worry they
cannot be of material benefit to you.
D. W. HAMILTON.

Wyoming, Ohio.
You will be honored and loved
more than ever when this conspiracy has been exposed.
LOUIS HALSEY.

Greenwich, Conn.
I have watched with intense
interest the splendid strength that
you have shown in this great struggle. Surely these are the times that
try men's souls and I pray that
right may prevail.
MRS. WILLIAM C. STOREY.

East Schodack.
Nobody having a share in this
outrage should ever be allowed to
hold office in New York again.
REV. F. W. EDWARD.

Dewitt Memorial Church,
New York city.
In your noble fight against iniquity in high places may you have
the blessing of all the state. "Blessed are they who are persecuted
for righteousness sake."
REV. W. T. ELSING.

Buffalo.
We are all sure of your honesty
and courage.
E. H. BAILING.

Chattanooga, Tenn.
I firmly believe you to be a
square man.
HERBERT W. MORGAN.

Roselle, N. J.
Your boyhood friends in your
old home town are still loyal to you.
LOUIS F. PRICE.

Brooklyn.
My services are at your command. I hear talk in the sixteenth
district of Queens county of meeting to condemn Assemblyman Larrimer for voting for impeachment.
ARTHUR J. STEARN.

Salt Lake City, Utah.
Even if the charges against you
are true, which I do not believe,
there are scarcely ten men in any
state of the Union against whom
worse things could not have been
scented out if the blood-hounds
had been after them as they have
been after you. Be of good cheer,
brave man, all over the world there
are many hearts that thrill at the
spectacle of the splendid fight you
are waging with your indomitable
courage.
MRS. ANNA CLARK SNOW.

New York city.
Five voters in our house are all
pledged to stick to Sulzer through
and through.
R. J. PRICE.

New York city.
The people are waking up. Best
wishes and a prayer for your success in doing away with your
traducers.
C. H. HIBBARD.

Brooklyn.
I assure you of the respect I have
for you and your every act in public life. You are too straight for
convictions by such dirty work.
DR. JOSEPH W. WALSH.

Bainbridge.
My deepest sympathy and ad-
miration.
MRS. ANNA M. DICKINSON.

Philadelphia, Pa.
Your vindication is certain.
EDGAR MELE.

East Orange, N. J.
"All these things do not move me.
Behold all they that were incensed
against thee, shall be ashamed, they
shall be as nothing and they that
strive with thee shall perish."
M. H. COOLEY.

New York city.
My whole soul and energy is in your cause.

EDWARD S. BROWN.

Brooklyn.
Every decent man and woman in this great state are with you, and if this Murphy movement against good government is permitted, it is time for open warfare. I marvel at the patience of the people with this gang of thugs.

MRS. MARY ELIZABETH LEASE.

Buffalo.
By the will of the people you still are Governor. Anyone having any doubt about this should go through the state. I have been at Utica, Rome, Oneida and Syracuse, and believe me you would be the proudest man in this state if you heard what I did. The sentiment is nearly unanimous in your favor. This applies to Republicans, Progressives and Democrats alike.

CHARLES OBERLANDER.

Brooklyn.
You have striven manfully to overthrow this political camorra and deserve the fullest measure of support. Call on me for any help I can give in your war on Murphy and his legislative gunmen.

F. E. AMENT.

Washington.
Hitting below the belt never did pay and never will pay in fighting a man who doesn't scare. I know you will stick and I know you will win.

LOUIS F. POST.

Ithaca.
It takes a strong man to withstand the villainous assaults being made on you, but I have never seen you show a phase of dishonor or a symptom of the white feather.

J. P. MERRILL.

Nyack.
The majority of the Democrats in Rockland county want to see you stamp out corruption and speculation in this state.

FRANK HOFFMAN.

New York city.
Against the workings of the evil forces which came from the depths of the bottomless pits itself, you have proved yourself with bravery the most fearless man who has ever sat in the Governor's chair from General Clinton down, not even excepting that other great champion of the rights of the people, Theodore Roosevelt.

CLARENCE LADD-DAVIS.

New York city.
I am certain that when it comes to the highest authorities you will win out and your treacherous enemies will be exposed. I believe in you and always will, and if there is anything I can do please command me. Keep up your courage and the good will always truimph over the evil in the long run.

OSCAR TOCHIRKEY.

Philadelphia, Pa.
Surely the fates will not be so cruel as to permit your undoing just at the time when you are becoming most useful. You are the fairest and most humane Governor New York has had in many a year. Your courage and independence strikes an exceedingly popular chord in the heart of many.

J. S. STEMONS.

Holley.
I note with keen satisfaction your gritty determination to get to a finish with the bosses of this state.

JAMES F. HOUCHINS.

Seagate.
I know you are brave and fit for the battle.

GEORGE SLATER.

Pheodes, Va.
Like John Paul Jones I know you will never give up the ship while a single spar remains.

GEORGE F. BENSON.

Brooklyn.
We solemnly pledge ourselves to vote against the bosses' ticket this fall in its entirety, even though our best friends may be nominated on it.

HENRY KING.

New York city.
You have done an admirable thing in dragging these scamps out into the open where all may see. They are digging their own political graves.

MORRIS H. MENSCH.

New York city.
The more the hero of a good cause is handicapped the more his deeds are numbered in history. Tenth assembly district will stand on your side and assist you in your battle for more privileges for the people and less for the bosses.

SAMUEL BUCHLER.

New York city.
While I am a Republican in politics I am still with you heart and soul in your purpose to benefit the community at large.

HENRY L. FRANKLIN.

Brooklyn.
As a regular Democrat who comes from a family of regular Democrats in this county for twenty-one years, all of whom have contributed to build up the Democratic organization and none of whom have ever held office, I recognize as the regular elected Governor. I recognize you as the regular elected Governor, I recognize as contemptible the action of the regular so-called leaders and I feel that every Democrat ought to at this time do his duty toward you.

JOHN J. H. ROGERS.

Seattle, Wash.
The people of New York are aroused at the fact that they now have a real champion who cannot be tempted by gold, disturbed by calumny or frightened by threats.

MORRIS D. LEVY.

Skaneateles.
Feeling is running very strong against the assemblyman from this county who voted for impeachment. I attended the State Firemens' convention yesterday at Utica, and it is safe to say that four out of five in attendance were in favor of the Governor.

MARTIN F. DILLON.

New York city.
It is your quality of courage which has won the greatest battles of the world.

WILLIAM BEVERLY HARISON.

Albion.
You were never stronger in Orleans county than you are now. The people on all sides of politics swear by you.

SANFORD P. CHURCH.

Oklahoma.
The Lord loves a cheerful fighter, so get joy in your heart and go forward, it is no disgrace to be impeached by that band of pirates. Don't forget that your enemies are the enemies of the people and good government.

M. L. LOCKWOOD.

Syracuse.
I will not see an effort to befog the public judgment made without lifting up my voice in protest. The thirteen hundred members of the Centenary Methodist Episcopal church are watching every move.

REV. J. H. BRUCHID.

New York City.
The public, irrespective of political party, are ready to crucify those conspirators against the public. They will not allow you to be crucified.

DR. WILLIAM SCIROVICH.

Washington.
I cannot leave on my ship to Europe without expressing to you my belief in your official and personal integrity, all coupled with the earnest hope that you may be able to overcome the vindictive attacks on you.

WILLIAM B. AINEY.

New York City.
My friends believe in you and always have and always will. Do not despair. It is now a fight to the death between you and Murphy. The people will forgive any mistakes on your part if Tammany can be done away with good and all.

JULIUS CHAMBERS.

Fonda.

The people of this town are with you to a man.

DR. A. B. FOSTER.

Washington.

I wish to express my great interest and deep concern in your affairs and Mrs. Sulzer's illness. So far as the charges which have been made against you are concerned, it is hardly necessary to say I do not believe them. The officers whom I meet here believe that when you are heard the charges will fail.

MAJ. GEN. JOHN F. O'RYAN, N. G. N. Y.

Cambridge, Md.

I have not found a man in Maryland who believes for an instant that you are guilty.

J. WATSON THOMPSON.

Lysander.

The real high crimes and misdemeanors upon which you stand indicted in my judgment, are, among others, you are guilty of refusing to appoint criminals and ex-criminals to high salaried offices in this state; you are guilty of making it impossible for Tammany to pollute the state treasury through other departments; you are guilty of the appointment of honest men to office.

CHARLES KING BELL.

Brooklyn.

Although I am a Republican and ran for the assembly under the Republican ticket in the Twenty-third district last election, yet I admire you for having refused to be a pawn of Tammany Hall. I assure you one million of others feel the same way.

JACOB A. FREEDMAN.

Littlestown, Pa.

From the battlefield of Gettysburg we greet you as the champion of right in mortal conflict with might.

D. B. ALLDMAN.

New York city.

You have incurred the hate of the enemies of good government in this state and I believe that in this confused situation at least one thing is clear and that is that you represent the hope of the people of the state to possess and administer their own government. You may count upon me for anything I can do in your aid and support.

BAINBRIDGE COLBRIDGE.

Clay Center, Kansas.

Here's wishing you success. I was a member of the Fifty-fifth congress, and as a congressman I found you right and I believe you are right now.

W. V. VINCENT.

Ticonderoga, Aug. 22.

The citizens' non-partisan committee of Ticonderoga, of which I have the honor to be chairman, are arranging a mass meeting for Sunday evening next at the Wigwam with an overflow meeting across the street to enter the protest of the citizenship of this historic town against the attempted seizure of the state by the Tammany looters and legislative gunmen of their system under the leadership of Murphy and the invisible government that supplies him with brains and power. We send you our assurance of confidence, esteem and respect.

D. C. BASCOM.

Rochester, Aug. 22.

At a meeting of the Prohibition county convention held Tuesday evening, August 19th, the following resolution was unanimously passed and the secretary instructed to send a copy of the same to you.

Resolved, that we recognize the fact that beyond question the Governor of the State of New York, elected by the people of the state— William Sulzer, has been impeached by a hostile assembly, not for high crimes or misdemeanors real or alleged, but for his civic virtues, and that if he had not been true to his preelection pledges to the people of the state, especially to use his influence to secure the enactment of a genuine direct primary law, these impeachment proceedings would not have been thought of, therefore,

Resolved, That we extend to our Governor, William Sulzer, our sympathy, and cordial co-operation in his heroic fight to secure a government of the people, by the people and for the people, to the citizens of the state of New York.

GEORGE H. DRYER, D. D.
WILLIAM SCHALBER.

Brooklyn.
In the name of the twenty-third district, I will say that the impeachment has infuriated its people.

JOSEPH SILVERMANN.

Alma, Mich.
The hearts and sympathies of the great mass of right thinking men throughout our nation are with you in your great fight against the greatest band of political thugs and assassins who ever infested any country.

DE WITT VOUGHT.

Schenectady.
I am not a Democrat and I did not vote for you, but I am for you now.

MARSHALL A. BRADT.

Brooklyn.
All the people that I have come in contact with are with you.

JOHN E. TURLEY.

Rochester.
You have the plain people back of you, want to feel that they are with you and will help you to clean out our state to the last ditch and the last dollar. In every street car and every assemblage of men there is but one feeling here, and that is for you. Partisan feelings have been forgotten and you will be a better man, a better Governor for us and be better yourself when you are through with the tiger.

.   THEO. T. JAGER.

Boxley, Ga.
You are right, and the country is applauding the fight you are so bravely waging. Stick to it until the last friend of Tammany is exterminated.

DAVE M. PARKER.

East Aurora.
I believe you have been deeply wronged.

J. D. WEED.

Pensacola, Fla.
I trust that you will come out victorious.

MAYOR GREENHUT.

Boonville.
You are gaining friends every day. We have a little club here, some forty-two of us, and we want you to know that we are still with you.

GEORGE NELSON.

Savannah.
We hope to defeat your enemies at the primaries and let the real Democrats of Wayne county rule it.

E. M. HARVIE.

Waterloo.
The majority of Democrats of Jefferson county are with you and will be glad to do anything to help you.

C. L. LANSING.

Utica.
Your position would not be heard of if you had been subservient. I believe the people appreciate your courage and tenacity in the struggle.

JOHN L. MAHER.

Rochester.
The people of Rochester are with you in this fight and I personally hope that before you are through, Charles F. Murphy will be in Sing Sing or a similar place where he belongs.

CHARLES RUMPF.

Ballston Spa, Aug. 22.
I am enclosing a copy of a resolution that I introduced yesterday at the annual mid-summer institute of the Charlton Agricultural association. There was an attendance of about 500 people of this vicinity, and I am glad to report that the resolution was heartily adopted without a dissenting vote.

WALTER S. CAVERT.

Baltimore.

Almost without exception the people I meet here are with you in your fight.

THOMAS O. CLARK.

Resolved, That we, the members of the Charlton Agricultural association, at the annual mid-summer meeting assembled, condemn the action of the members of the state legislature who instigated and assisted in the high-handed and hasty impeachment proceedings against Governor Sulzer. We do not believe that a legislature that exonerated Senator Stilwell could be acting with sincere motive in impeaching a governor who is trying to give an honest administration and to expose corruption and graft. Further, we commend those members of the legislature who voted against the impeachment proceedings, and who have acted in good faith in the interests of the people throughout the entire session;

Further resolved, That we heartily favor the adoption of a genuine direct primary bill, and will accept no make-shift substitute therefor;

Still further resolved, That a copy of this resolution be forwarded to Governor Sulzer, and to the senator and assemblyman from this district.

Little Falls, Aug. 22.

I was requested by the trades assembly to write to you and say that they wished to express their confidence and sympathy for you against what they believe to be persecution of your enemies, and pledge our support in your behalf in your effort to give the people of New York state an honest and faithful administration.

CARL CRAMER.

Brooklyn.

Enclosed please find resolutions passed unanimously by a rising vote at the enthusiastic mass meeting held in your behalf Tuesday, August 19.

From the view of the meeting, and the lasting impression made throughout the tenth senatorial district, I can safely state that, at your command, you can have the normal and financial support of this vicinity. There are other meetings of the kind planned by some of your friends in our locality.

It will be a pleasure and an honor to me to be of any personal service to you at any time in any way you may see fit.

VICTOR E. POMERANZ.

At a meeting held at Independence hall, 89 Osborne street, on Tuesday night, August 19, 1913, by the patriotic citizens of the tenth senatorial district, the following resolutions were adopted:

Whereas, The assembly of the state of New York, has at the behest of the "Tammany Boss," and without a proper and fair consideration of the evidence of proof, impeached William Sulzer, the Governor of this state, and brought shame and insult to the honor and dignity of this Empire state, and

Whereas, This unwarranted action was taken solely for the purpose of vindictively punishing the Governor for his independence of character and desire to serve the people in accordance with the light as he saw it, without bending the knee to any "Boss," it is

Resolved, Further, that we sympathize with the Governor in his hour when he is being pilloried because of his loyal devotion to his public trust and his contempt of those men who would prostitute the public offices for their private gain.

Resolved, That we deprecate and condemn the action of the assembly in following with slavish obedience the dictates of one who arrogates to himself the powers and functions entrusted to the representatives of the people.

Resolved, Further, that we pledge our devotion and faith in our Governor and express to him our earnest belief in his patriotic attachment to the welfare of the people, his devotion to public trust and his fearless championing of the people's cause.

Riverhead, Aug. 14.

My dear Governor Sulzer, you have my sincere sympathy.

MELVILLE E. BRUSH.

Buffalo, Aug. 15.

The following resolution was enacted here last night, introduced by J. W. Shields. Resolved that the Sixteenth Ward Democratic Direct Primary league in meeting assembled desires to express its confidence in Governor Sulzer, and its sympathy for him in what it believes to be persecution by his enemies, and we pledge to him our earnest and hearty support.

Resolved that the secretary telegraph this expression of confidence and sympathy to the governor.

EDWARD C. BURGARD.

Chicago, Ill., Aug. 13.

Keep a strong armed guard about your office day and night to prevent others getting possession by trick or force.

ARTHUR C. JACKSON.

Washington, Aug. 14.

I firmly believe you will confound your enemies. Good luck to you in your fight against Tammany.

JOHN CALLAN O'LAUGHLIN.

New York, Aug. 13.

The people love and believe in William Sulzer the man, in Governor William Sulzer a human being like ourselves and therefore liable to human mistakes, the governor who has stood four-square for the platform on which he was elected, who when he came to the parting of the ways chose the straight and narrow path, as did his devoted wife with him, even though it might lead to his crucifixion at the hands of those who would betray the same platform on which they were also elected with him and then stab to its death the new-born progressive democracy which is today the hope of the people of all the world.

WM. OSBORNE McDOWELL.

New York, Aug. 13.

The state road through Islip town will yet be built by and named after Governor Sulzer. Convey my highest admiration to Mrs. Sulzer.

JOHN C. DOXIE.

New York, Aug. 11.

As a taxpayer here, I congratulate you upon stand now taken. May I suggest that your lawyer, by speaking of libel suits against newspapers and other defamators, may change newspapers into valuable assistants in any search for any criminals.

M. A. MOSLE.

Elmira, Aug. 11.

A word from a few of the rank and file; we are with you.

C. FLOSCH,
R. R. WILLIS,
E. ALLEN,
E. D. SCHMIDT,
W. A. WATSON,
W. P. STOUT.

Washington, Aug. 12.

Your twenty-five years ledger account with the people cannot be balanced by one small debit item, the alternate of which would have been their betrayal. Courage governor and above all keep your strangle hold on the tiger.

J. W. FROST.

Corning, Aug. 12.

Stand firm, popular sentiment of this city for you. Keep on firing line.

FREDERICK A. ELLISON.

Cherubusco, N. Y., Aug. 12.

The people are with you.

T. B. HUMPHREY.

New York, Aug. 13.

Men and angels are weeping today over the disgraceful action of Tammany's assembly.

JULE DE RYTHER.

Holley, Aug. 13.

On to victory, am with you to the end. Assemblyman Cole has killed himself here.

J. HOUCHINS.

Washington, Aug. 13.

Fight courageously to ultimate victory. Your true friend in all kinds of weather.

DONALD C. MacLEOD.

Niagara Falls, Aug. 14.
Leave no stones unturned, fight to the last ditch, with right and justice on your side you are bound to win and emerge from the fight bigger and greater than ever.
JOHN F. McDONALD.

Amsterdam, Aug. 13.
The rank and file of the people are expressing themselves in your favor and wish me to express to you to stick tight.
THERON AKIN.

Belfast, Aug. 13.
Your friends prefer to publicly weep over a dead hero than to silently mourn over a living coward. Don't give up the fight. Courage.
Rev. M. J. CORBETT.

New York, Aug. 15.
You are in the right legally and morally, and right must win. The people are with you. You have many friends. You have my sympathy and good wishes.
CHAS. M. KIEFER.

New York, Aug. 13.
Do not abandon your battle for the people's cause. Keep up courage and you will be victorious. The Bronx voters will remain loyal to you and will continue so to the end. We stand ready to assist in this great fight and to wage war against Murphy and trained pups.
JACOB H. GREDINGER.

Babylon, Aug. 13.
Still believing in your honesty and that your impeachment is one of the greatest outrages in the history of our state we assure you that you have our support until it is shown that you are the man that your enemies paint you, our sentiments we believe are the sentiments of the voters of the town of Babylon.
PETER KLEINDENST,
CARL JACKSON,
DAVID SANDMAN,
FRED CARPENTER,
CHAS. R. FLANLY,
LUKE DEVLIN,
JAS. W. EATON.

Chicago, Ill., Aug. 15.
History will show the record that William Sulzer kept faith with the people, and his political assassins will go to oblivion. My heart beats with you and it says courage and hold fast. Command me if there is any service I am able to render. Justice must prevail.
MACKENZIE BYRNE.

Batavia, Aug. 14.
We, the undersigned, citizens of Genesee county hereby pledge our support during the crisis of your fight for the people of the state of New York. The people are with you and we urge you to stand by all you have undertaken.
Dr. John W. Losur, Batavia; G. E. Gubb, Batavia; Thos. J. Gallagher, Batavia; William H. Rial, Batavia; Sidney A. Sherwin, Batavia; Charles R. Gould, Batavia; Allen W. Gillard, Batavia; E. N. Heath, Bergen; William C. Radley, Bethany; The Rev. Jas. C. Crawford, Corfu; E. E. Hotchkiss, Oakfield; John F. Stiles, Penbroke; The Rev. S. J. Clarkson, Batavia; Simeon R. Mattice, Batavia; Albert F. Kleps, Batavia; Ralph P. Young, Batavia; Edward F. Shortt, Batavia; Charles W. Buckheltz, Batavia; Edwin M. Crocker, Bryon; E. W. Dauchy, Bethany; Frank P. Redseal, Batavia; Henry W. Drilling, Darien; Harry J. Howe, Leroy; Gilbert Prolo, Stafford.

Lake Placid, Aug. 13.
More than ever I am your friend and wish I could be of real service.
MRS. DONALD McLEAN.

Fulton, Aug. 13.
I am shocked and grieved at action of assembly.
E. B. NORRIS.

New York, Aug. 14.
You will show lamentable weakness if you give up governor's chair and injure your chance before senate and in public view. Under no circumstances do so. The law, precedent and common sense are opposed to it. If you give up the office it would be equivalent to

surrender and confession. You are
governor until an adverse verdict,
assuming present action legal.
Stand firm and express yourself
in no uncertain terms.

CHAS. H. UNVERZAGT.

Hingham, Mass., Aug. 14.
You have my sympathy.

FRANCIS E. YOUNG.

Hornell, Aug. 14.
The people still believe. Call
all bluffs. You will win.

A. E. COWLES.

Jacksonville, Florida, Aug. 14.
Send message to legislature demanding submission constitutional
amendment providing recall public
officials by popular vote. Protest
against trial by partisan tribunal
carrying out dictates corrupt political machine. People elected you.
People should try you. Play this
card strong. Will put legislature
in hole if people denied this right.

ION L. FARRIS.

Rochester, Aug. 14.
Best wishes from a true friend.

THOMAS J. LADDY.

Lockhaven, Pa., Aug. 14.
All along the line from Lewis-
burgh here popular expression unanimously favors you in your fight
with Tammany detractors and persecutors. My long service in congress with you justifies my implicit
confidence in your high purposes
and desire to serve the people. I
trust the methods of the inquisitors
may not be successful and if you
will permit I will aid in raising a
popular expense fund to help secure
fair play for you in this universally
recognized high-handed blackjack
game designed to encompass your
ruin.

BENJ. K. FECHT.

Glens Falls, Aug. 13.
Keep a steady nerve and fight
hard. You have the sympathy and
will have the support of all Democrats who can claim any right
whatever to the name.

ELMER J. WEST.

New York, Aug. 16.
I believe in you and am your
friend.

SUSAN HILL RUDD.

Riverside, Aug. 15.
The Methodist preachers at Troy
Conference attending annual camp
meeting Riverside unanimously extend sympathy in fight for constitutional government and your heroic
opposition to bi-partisan corruption
in public life. We pray needed
strength may come to you, restoration to health to Mrs, Sulzer.

JOHN LOWE FORT,
District Supt.,
for all the preachers.

Rochester, Aug. 15.
Three thousand voters in mass
meeting assembled pledge you support in your fight against Tammany
for good government.

T. H. ARMSTRONG,
Chairman.

Oklahoma City, Okla., Aug. 15.
You are right. Don't back-
water for a minute.

H. E. MANSFIELD.

Butte, Mont., Aug. 15.
Born in Albany, in 1839, so hold
the fort and stand pat against
Tammany grafters and thieves.
The honest people are with you
sincerely.

ROD D. LEGGATT.

New York, Aug. 16.
The United States Constitution
makes it the duty of the Federal
government to secure to each state
a republican form of government.
That is the government of law,
not of an autocrat. Why not apply
to the Federal court for an injunc-
tion against Glynn on basis of his
letter refusing court jurisdiction.

GODFREY L. CABOT.

New York.
I went on the stump for Strauss,
but you are now in a fight against
the ballot box stuffers and it is a
pleasure to help. Back up your
authority with the bayonet.

L. D. MAYES.

Cazenovia, Aug. 16.
Congratulations on your stand
and sympathy in your distress.
GRANVILLE FORTESCUE.

New York, Aug. 15.
You are only human, the same
as the rest of us, you have made a
bad break or two, but up to date
I am going to give you the benefit
of the doubt like thousands of
others, because you have got the
nerve to put up the final fight
against Tammany. Here's hoping
you win.
M. M. DeCUMP.

Akron, Ohio, Aug. 16.
Since assembly didn't commence
appoint your own pro tem successor
pending trial. Submit this to
Herrick and act at once. This is
from Jack Hazele, telegraph editor
Bacon Journal. After it is all over
send me thanks.
HAZELE.

Chestertown.
Do not give up the fight. Be
governor.
WM. H. FAXON.

New York city.
You may have been unwise, but
I don't believe you are crooked.
Fight right back at them.
PEVERIL MEIGS, JR.

Elmira.
Chemung County Christian
Women's Temperance Union be-
lieves in your honesty and loyalty
to the right.
MRS. J. S. MOTT.

New York city.
Every power to you. May no
traitor be near you.
JOHN A. HAMILTON.

Chatham.
My profound sympathy with
you in the present persecution.
REV. H. P. BAKE.

New York city.
I shall support you with all my
strength believing fully in your
honesty.
CLARKE BELL.

New York city.
How I wish to see you adopt the
methods of Napoleon—arrest the
scoundrels, and if necessary, drum-
head them.
DR. WM. H. McGREEVY.

Richmond Hill.
The people would condone in
you anything from arson to murder
if you can smash the organization
of thugs.
OVAL FELKER.

New York city.
All the Bronx people I meet are
with you.
HENRY K. DAVIS.

Albany.
I am sure that the fall election
will endorse you in a way that will
surprise everybody.
EDWARD M. CAMERON.

Philadelphia.
The source and the venom of the
attack now being made upon you
should rally to your side all right
thinking citizens.
HENRY JOHN S. GIBBONS.

New York city.
I hope you do not intend to drop
the fight now that the real battle
has begun.
SMITH THOMPSON.

Babylon.
Your impeachment is one of the
greatest outrages in the history of
our state.
PETER KLEINDERT.

Circleville, Ohio.
Stand pat and fight the most
corrupt state legislature in the
Union.
HARRY E. WEILL.

Saginaw, Mich.
It is the only clean, good politicians who meet with embarrassment, such as this. Accept our
sympathy.
GEORGE M. WEISNER.

New York city.
Please command me.
MORRIS W. HART.

Canisteo.
You have erred in your judgment, and you may have made mistakes, but that you are guilty of high crimes and misdemeanors, I do not believe.
ALMON W. BURDELL.

Albany.
The people are bigger than Murphy and Barnes combined. Go to it and God bless you.
MORTIMER REDMAN.

New York city.
I am surprised that you did not use the militia to drive that thievish assembly out, as they had no right to sit in judgment of you.
PHILIP HELLER.

Brooklyn.
Do not let the hounds discourage you.
B. S. SANBORN.

Albany.
I am a Republican and voted against you, but I believe you are an honest man.
H. M. BUTTS.

Albany.
In the language of General Bragg, referring to Grover Cleveland, " We love you for the enemies you have made."
J. P. McGARRAHAN.

Jamaica.
I enclose you resolutions adopted by the Hebrews Citizen's association of the Fourth ward, Borough of Queens. They faintly express the disgust of its membership at the attempt of a band of crooks to discredit you for trying to stop the pillage of the state of New York.
JOSEPH KAISER.

Ridgewood, N. J.
What a frightful state of affairs that a man like Murphy should have the power to commit such an act. I do not think that a man with your fine reputation will suffer much from an attack from a man of his type.
ELIZABETH HOWARD ELLIS.

Watkins.
I feel sure that you can count upon the mass of the Republican party to join with your Democratic friends and overthrow your enemies.
C. A. PAYNE.

New York city.
Even if the charges as they appear are true, there can be no justification in the minds of fair and honest men for your impeachment.
ROBERT LEE HARDY.

New York city.
Sit tight, fight back hard; you will win. Public sentiment, the strongest moving force existent, is aroused in your favor.
W. N. AMORY.

New York city.
What counts with the people is the kind of governor you have been for us, and you have more than filled our greatest expectations.
ROBERT TIEMAN.

Jersey City Heights, N. J.
I cried when I read the dreadful news, but it will come out all right.
MRS. J. H. WELLING.

New York city.
Disband the legislature and clean up the state and you will go to history as great as can be.
WILLIAM J. COCHRANE.

New York city.
The editorials in the hired newspapers do not reflect the opinions or the sentiments of the public. You have hazarded your political life for the public interests and do not fear that you will be deserted.
ABRAHAM H. SARASOHN.

New York city.
We German-Americans are with you.
MAX COUNTY LANDOW.

New York city.
You have always held out for the people, and that is why you are marked by those who are false to their trust.
DR. EVERETT FIELD.

New York city.
Why don't you have Murphy and the whole gang arrested and thrown into jail for conspiracy? It makes me ashamed that I am a citizen of a state where such things can be.
F. H. O'NEILL.

Kingston.
The action of the assembly has brought a blush of shame to the face of all good citizens in this state for prosecuting a man whom I believe has always been upright and honest.
SAMUEL STERN, JR.

Glens Falls.
This will make you president.
DR. J. W. DEAX.

Corfu.
My deepest sympathy in your noble warfare against corruption.
REV. J. B. CRAWFORD.

Buffalo.
I have believed in you and your policies and I do now.
E. R. VOORHEES.

Brooklyn.
All right thinking men are with you.
J. VAN VALKENBURGH.

New York city.
You are better off than,if you had compromised with Murphy.
DR. ISADOR N. KAHN.

Naples.
Only the tragedy enacted upon Calvary can equal it.
F. G. PIERCE.

Glens Falls.
You have the sympathy and will have the support of all Democrats who can claim any right whatever to the name.
ELMER J. WEST.

New York city.
If the legislature is using the Cromwell method it will have the ire of the people regardless of all the newspapers against you.
WILLIAM HALPERTY.

Newark.
The fight is against an honest state government and the rights of the people.
JOHN WATSON.

Sodus.
We can not make ourselves believe that you have done wrong.
MILLS BROTHERS.

Kansas City.
We know the charges are not true.
J. L. WOODS MERRILL.

New York city.
I did not.vote for you but I will next time on your present record, and I find lots of people feel the same way.
W. G. YEAMANS.

Poughkeepsie.
They are making you big and more powerful than the party and you shall loom over and above the Frawleys, the Murphys and the Wagners. We will make you our next president.
THOMAS H. LANIGAN.

Thompson Ridge.
The devil never fights a man so small as not to be dangerous to him. I pray for you in public at my Sabbath services.
REV. J. S. E. ERSKINE.

Washington.
I am deeply grieved at your impeachment but the senate and the Court of Appeals have not convicted you and I do not believe they ever will.
JOHN A. JOYCE.

Saint George, Staten Island.
I still believe you are doing more than any other governor to keep your promises to the people.
WILLIAM T. JENKINS.

New York city.
In common with many Democrats I feel very indignant over what I believe is a most wanton attack upon you.
PHILIP VAN ALSTINE.

Troy.

Your battle is the battle of every true and upright citizen of this state.

D. ZEISER.

Rochester.

I did not vote for you last time, but you have won me.

ROSS MATTHEWS.

Brooklyn.

I hope our fellow citizens may see that there is a reasonable side to this matter of personal and incidental expense of an individual holding public office and candidate for another office.

C. AUGUSTUS HAVILAND.

Albany.

I am a Republican and did not vote for you last fall. However, I believe that you are making the greatest fight against graft and grafters that was ever known in political history.

ERASTUS L. POST.

New York city.

The people stand solidly behind you and not only consider the attacks made upon you as unworthy of the notice of decent people, but the machinations of the criminal class you have on the run.

FREDERICK W. PARK.

Albany.

You should consider the impeachment vote this morning by the gang of discredited politicians as an honor, not a disgrace.

REV. O. R. MILLER.

New York city.

I am going to give you the benefit of the doubt like thousands of others, because you have got the nerve to fight Tammany.

M. M. DE CAMP.

Cooperstown.

If I can be of any assistance to you in any way during your coming fight, you may put me on the eligible list without compensation or remuneration.

JAMES J. BYRD, JR.

Riverside.

The Methodist preachers in Troy conferences, attending annual camp meeting here, unanimously extend sympathy in your fight for constitutional government and your heroic opposition to bi-partisan corruption in public life. We pray needed strength may come to you and restoration of health to Mrs. Sulzer.

JOHN LOWE FORT.

Individually

Butte, Mont.

Stand pat against the Tammany grafters and thieves. The honest people are with you.

ROD D. LEGGETT.

New York city.

Thrice armed is he who hath his quarrel just.

JAMES EDWARD GRAYBILL.

Oklahoma City, Okla.

Do not back water for a minute.

H. E. MANSFIELD.

Rochester.

Three thousand voters in mass meeting pledge you support in your fight against Tammany and for good government.

T. H. ARMSTRONG.

Bath, August 25.

Feeling that an injustice has been done in the methods pursued, in the recent action of the legislature of the state of New York, I have interested myself, and caused to be prepared and signed by representative citizens of Bath, a protest which I am herein sending to you. It is our desire that you use this as you may deem for your best interests.

T. M. STEWART.

To the legislature of the state of New York:

We, the undersigned, voters and citizens of the town of Bath, Steuben county, New York, irrespective of party, do hereby take this opportunity to enter a protest against the drastic action taken by the assembly of this state, in its unwarranted, undignified, precipitate action of impeachment of the Governor of this great state. By this we do not attempt to defend any wrongful acts that may have been committed by the Governor, but we believe he should have been given the same treatment that is awarded to the most obscure citizen. Every one charged with offense is presumed to be innocent, under the law, until he is proved guilty.

T. M. Stewart, J. H. Fancett, A. B. Grout, Thomas C. Bassett, John S. Omsby, William Little, J. Robie Griswohl, Stephen S. Read, F. E. Wilkes, F. D. Alden, James Faucett, Jr., W. H. Barr, William S. Shults, F. H. Matthews, F. Myron St. John, Seward Torner, S. Webster, Thomas Scuilun, M. A. Wrightman, Frank E. Rowe, S. E. Morrison, Charles Kausch, Samuel W. Upham, John M. Farr, E. H. Garrison, L. C. Fairchild, F. D. Smith, C. P. Tate, John Snell, W. A. Hommes, Frank C. Hamilton, L. C. Whitford, Ele Bumdage, J. Brownlee, L. M. Ryan, William R. Gundeman, C. M. Hunster, J. W. Wilber, Floyd S. Smith, Harry D. Cohn, D. E. Connie, W. R. Murphy, R. C. Van Patten, W. H. Sharp, H. S. Holcourt, Derward R. Lee, T. O. Burleson, M. D., O. Jay Heinanson, Morris Dunson, A. H. Otis, James A. Hill, William H. Simmons, N. H. Daniels, O. V. Hahn, Walter Longwell, William H. Hicks, E. A. Fuller, H. M. Shannon, E. W. Woodbury, H. N. Daynes, L. S. Warner, J. Lyon Robie, Wallace Ornett, George W. Peck, S. M. Hewlen, B. A. Adams, Robert Leavenworth, H. B. Lee, W. P. Dean, R. B. Oldfield, A. A. Bullard, L. B. Lent, E. F. Smith, E. F. Parker, J. F. Cooper, D. B. Biyou, R. B. Lee, C. R. Smith, A. J. Clark, Van B. Pruyn, B. F. Smith, John H. Bowlby, Charles Allison, James C. Bruder, J. B. Cooley, James L. Whitford, Clinton W. Richardson, John L. Stocum, F. C. Cooper, A. G. Cooper, A. Bowes, John Moore, C. S. Ferris, A. E. McCall, W. R. Sutton, H. R. Daniels, Morton Storphy, George Anna, E. Conley, Henry W. Wildeck, J. B. Scott, Thos. Shannon, Edgar Baggerly, D. Spencer Longwell, E. L. Evans, H. R. Kellogg, C. B. Hadden, A. H. Gardinir, M. C. Shannon, H. T. Shannon, J. Myron Ringer, G. W. Henice, Walter Spraker, R. S. Jones, John Simmons, W. P. Van Seater, Egbert Caster, S. Rothschild, William Memschmitt, W. M. Colley, Louis M. Eshardt, J. C. Carr, George Sutherland, R. Seager, E. D. Sluiny, John T. Cameron, D. W. Thomas, W. H. Morrison, Bernard Arnold, W. Sutherland, Moses Crants, Walter W. Carey, C. B. Townsend, Edward Loveless, H. A. Bill, Frank L. Stocum, James W. Green, W. J. McMahan, Jess M. Pridmore, H. R. Jackson, J. W. Murphy, D. H. Heckman, H. Guy Doris, W. S. Tappany, G. R. Chapman, J. Mark Chamberlain, A. C. Van Loon, O. D. Mickles, Charles Cohn.

FROM GOVERNOR POTHIER OF RHODE ISLAND

My dear Governor Sulzer: I have read your letter of the 23rd instant, as I have also the various newspaper and magazine accounts of the difficulties connected with your administration of your office. I appreciate your position and venture the opinion that you have the sympathy of a majority of the people with you.

Very truly yours,
A. J. POTHIER.

FROM GOVERNOR CRUCE OF OKLAHOMA

My dear Governor: Your letter of the 22nd has just reached me. It seems that affairs of government are undergoing a radical readjustment. The people have grown tired of the old "ring" system of government and are making a winning fight to throw off this domination. The political bosses are making a last desperate stand. Driven to desperation in the unequal contest, they are seizing hold of every possible weapon to use in an effort to perpetuate themselves in power. Men's reputations are sacrificed with ruthless recklessness and nothing is sacred in the eyes of these desperate political tricksters.

The man who stands for honest government and who keeps his face constantly set toward the right is sure to win a signal triumph. The people are not being deceived. The people are intelligent and are becoming active and when thoroughly aroused to their public duties will, in no uncertain way, place their stamp of disapproval upon political bosses and corruptionists. I am

Yours sincerely,
LEE CRUCE.

FROM GOVERNOR BREWER OF
MISSISSIPPI

Dear Governor: I have watched with great interest the fight you are making in New York state, and the opposition. I hope you will succeed in having good government, and that you will come out all right.

Very truly your friend,
EARL BREWER,
Governor.

FROM GOVERNOR HANNA OF
NORTH DAKOTA

My dear Governor: I have your letter of the 22nd inst. and have read it with a great deal of interest.

I have been following the struggle in New York through the press with perhaps more interest than usual, by reason of the fact that I knew you so well while I was with you in congress. I am especially pleased to know there is nothing in the charges which have been made against you.

With kindest regards to Mrs. Sulzer and yourself, I am,

Very sincerely,
L. B. HANNA.

FROM GOVERNOR FERRIS OF
MICHIGAN

My dear Mr. Sulzer: I have your letter of August 22. Mighty glad to hear from me. I glory in your grit. Right will triumph. Sometimes a little time is involved.

For years I have known something about the enemy you are contending with and I am aware that no stone will be left unturned to overwhelm you and crush you. I am hoping and praying that in the trial you will be vindicated. I am having my troubles too, but they are not along the line of fighting political pirates. I have

a copper strike to contend with and any governor who calls out the militia to protect life and property must take his medicine. He at once divides the whole populace.

I have watched your career thus far with interest. I shall continue to watch it and hope for your vindication.

Very sincerely yours,
WOODBRIDGE N. FERRIS,
Governor.

FROM GOVERNOR COX OF OHIO

My dear Governor: I am pleased, indeed to have your letter. There is the fullest measure of sympathy for you here because everyone recognizes the kind of fight you have been in.

Very truly yours,
JAMES M. COX.

LETTER FROM GOVERNOR BLEASE
OF SOUTH CAROLINA

My dear Governor Sulzer: Your letter of August 23 has been received. I am in full sympathy with you, and sincerely hope that you will be able to convince the people of New York and the people of the United States that you are absolutely innocent of any wrongdoing. I myself, last summer, went through just about what you are going through now, except that they did not attempt the impeachment proceedings. I convinced the people of South Carolina that I was being persecuted, and they stood by me, and the main thing for you to do is to let the politicians and ringsters howl and squirm and convince the people that you are right, and they will never forsake you. Trust in God and you will always be a winner.

So far as South Carolina is concerned, you and you alone are looked upon as the governor of New York.

With best wishes,
Very respectfully,
COLE L. BLEASE,
Governor.

JOHNSTOWN DEMOCRAT

Resolutions passed by the Democratic city committee of the city of Johnstown, August 25, 1913.

Dear Sir: At the regular meeting of the Democratic city committee of the city of Johnstown, August 25, 1913, the accompanying resolution was unanimously adopted; and a copy ordered sent to you:

Whereas, The Democratic city committee of the city of Johnstown, N. Y., deeply feels the shame and indignity cast upon the party and upon the state by the attempt that has been made, through a resolution hastily passed by the assembly without consideration for the honor of the party or the welfare of the state, to impeach our honored leader, William Sulzer, governor of New York; therefore, be it

Resolved: That this committee fully believes in the integrity and loyalty of the people's governor, and being assured that the charges made against him are actuated by malice and fear, and have no foundation in fact and are of doubtful legality, hereby extends to William Sulzer, governor of New York, the hearty assurance of its faith in his integrity and its respect for his brave and steadfast support of the principles and pledges of his party and for his devotion to the welfare of the people of the state. Be it further

Resolved: That this committee condemns the rash and ill-advised act of the majority of the assembly, and trusts that a court of higher authority and dignity may fairly weigh the evidence and render a just and impartial judgment upon the issue that has been thrust upon the people of this great commonwealth.

JAMES F. MURRAY.
Secretary Democratic City Committee, Johnstown, N. Y.

YATES PROGRESSIVES

Resolutions passed by the National Progressive County Committee of Yates county, August 26, 1913.

Whereas, The platform of the National Progressive party in this state declares for state-wide primaries, and the vote of all the representatives of said party in the state legislature was in keeping with the platform pledges of the party, and

Whereas, William Sulzer, the duly elected constitutional governor of this state, has fearlessly endeavored to assure the passage of a genuine state-wide direct primary bill, notwithstanding the united opposition of the two party leaders working in collusion to secure its defeat.

Resolved: That we, the members of the National Progressive committee of Yates county, in regular session, hereby commend Governor Sulzer in his efforts to obtain the passage of an honest state-wide direct primary bill, and thus restore to the people the state government which has for so long been controlled by the invisible government at New York, and Albany, and, be it

Resolved: That we likewise condemn the methods used by the political enemies in his own party to discredit him in order to retard the progress of direct primaries, which would allow the political plunderers to continue robbing the tax-payer through the present system of boss control.

STUDENT'S LITERARY CIRCLE

At a mass meeting at the Chrystie Street Settlement house, 186 Chrystie street, under the auspices of the Students' Literary circle, Tuesday, August 26, 1913, the following resolutions were adopted unanimously.

Whereas, William Sulzer, the duly elected governor of New York has lived up to the pledges he has made to the people and in doing so he has committed no crime except in serving the people in an honest, upright and intelligent way. And

Whereas, In discharging his duty as the executive officer of the state of New York, he incurred the enmity of unscrupulous politicians, who, as a result, conspired to remove him from office and gain control of the state government, and,

Whereas, The removal of Governor Sulzer from office would be a great detriment to the state of New York and its citizens, be it therefore

Resolved: That we, citizens assembled here under the auspice

of the Students' Literary circle in
the auditorium at 186 Chrystie
street, city of New York, condemn
the action of the assembly in impeaching Governor Sulzer. And
be it further

Resolved: That we call upon the
members of the senate who are to
try the governor on the alleged
charges, to cast aside all political
prejudices, and be as impartial in
their judgment as the people expect
them. And be it further

Resolved: That one copy of
these resolutions be sent to Governor Sulzer and another to the
press.

L. GOLDMAN,
President.

POUGHKEEPSIE TRADE COUNCIL

Resolutions passed by the Poughkeepsie Trade and Labor Council,
August 27, 1913:

Whereas, Governor William Sulzer of the state of New York has
commended himself to organized
labor by his veto of the vicious
Foley-Walker bill in spite of all
the efforts of casualty insurance
companies in its behalf, and

Whereas, Governor Sulzer has
further expressed himself in favor
of measures urged by the State
Federation of Labor in the interest
of the working class and which is
proven by his signing the full crew
train bill, and nearly fifty other
labor measures passed at the last
session of the legislature, and,

Whereas, Creatures of Charles
F. Murphy in the legislature of the
state of New York, driven by the
whip of a master determined to
continue a system of graft and
spoliation, have shamelessly voted
to impeach a chief executive more
favorable to organized labor than
any hithertofore elected, be it,
therefore,

Resolved, By the Poughkeepsie
Trade and Labor Council, representing twenty-two hundred union
men of this city, that it extends its
support and hearty approval to
Governor Sulzer in his fight against
the domination and dictation of
Boss Murphy and Tammany Hall.

Resolved, That we urge the
organized workingmen of the state

of New York, regardless of political
affiliations, to rally around the
standard of Governor Sulzer in the
present emergency, and to adopt
resolutions of impeachment against
the Tammany state senate, which
refused to confirm John Mitchell
as labor commissioner, and which
has, so far, refused to confirm
James M. Lynch, president of the
International Typographical union;
be it further

Resolved, Inasmuch as the state
senate has no defense and must
plead guilty in refusing to confirm
the appointment of John Mitchell
and James M. Lynch, that we impeach the Tammany senate, and
call upon every central body in the
state to do likewise, and that a
copy of these resolutions be forwarded Governor Sulzer, the State
Federation of Labor, in its convention at Utica, September 9th,
and to the press for publication.

(Signed)   JOHN J. COOK,
President.
PHILIP COOK,
Secretary.

AUBURN BIBLE SCHOOL UNION

At a meeting of the law enforce-
ment committee of the Auburn
Bible School union the evening of
August 27, 1913, in the city of
Auburn, N. Y., the following reso-
lution was introduced by Henry D.
Parsell and adopted unanimously:

Resolved, that we, the members
of the law enforcement committee
of the Auburn Bible School Union
extend to our Governor, William
Sulzer, our loyal support and encouragement in this regrettable
time when his good name and administration are attacked. We very
deeply appreciate his loyalty to our
committee in our efforts to suppress
vice and crime in Auburn during
the past year and furthermore, we
fully believe he will be vindicated
of the charges preferred and will
again be permitted to continue the
good work he so bravely carried on
until suppressed by what we believe
to be an organized alliance of the
enemies of law, order, and public
honor. It is further resolved that
a copy of these resolutions be sent

to Governor Sulzer and a copy be spread on the minutes of the committee.

(Signed) O. C. RULEY,
Secretary Auburn Bible School Union.

YATES COUNTY DEMOCRATS

Resolutions adopted by the Democrats of Yates county. .

Whereas, the people of this state, in accordance with the laws thereof, duly elected and placed in office Governor William Sulzer, who is, as we believe, entitled to act as the executive of this state and should so act without interference excepting through legal channels, and believing that he has honestly, conscientiously, fearlessly and successfully performed his duties as Governor and has acted for the best interest of the people, and that the present attacks upon him are sinister and dishonorable, for the purpose of placing the reins of government in the hands of persons and organizations not elected by the people or in any way authorized to represent them, and to intimidate other officeholders and legislators and to bring the state government under their control and make subservient to selfish and individual interests the chief executive of this state, be it

Resolved, that we believe the attack made upon Governor William Sulzer is as much an insult to every reputable person in the state of New York as to the Governor personally, and should be resented as such, and that we believe that all persons aiding such an attack are guilty of treason in forcing impeachment proceedings against Governor William Sulzer without justice or authority of law, and that any person connected therewith has forfeited any right to our support or to hold office or position as a servant of the people. And be it

Resolved, that we disapprove of the effort used by the enemies of good government to harass, hinder, delay, and thwart the proper, regular and orderly procedure of the state as directed by Governor William Sulzer, which had been used since the present administration entered upon its duties, to the great expense, injury and disapproval of the people.

The Rev. Charles H. Parkhurst, Lake Placid:

The cause which is so close to your heart is also very close to mine and has constantly engaged my thought.

Mrs. Delia A. Howe, Cambridge, N. Y.:

The right will prevail though the road may be rough and stony.

Maurice D. Leehey, Seattle, Wash.:

No government can long prevail under boss rule with its attendant graft and intimidation. But our government will not fail, because men like William Sulzer arise from time to time with courage to defy the martial power of vice and wealth. Men have given their lives to a cause less worthy than that for which you are now engaged. It is not Governor Sulzer who is on trial, but it is the capacity of the American people for self-government.

Samuel Glober Dunseath, Faith Presbyterian church, New York city:

The transgressions with which you are charged, whether they be real or the vicious concoction of a vicious organization, are as nothing compared with the positive sins of that same organization. You are still the people's governor in spite of Murphy and all his allies.

George W. Hills, Albany:

I hope to see Tammany routed on the impeachment proceedings in September and submerged by a tidal wave in November that will sweep the grafting heads of this conspiracy against law and order into Sing Sing, where they all belong.

Miss Emma McCauley, secretary Central Labor union, Newburgh:

The Central Labor union at its meeting on August 28th, passed a motion to give you its approval and endorsement in the fight you are making against political corruption.

Richard Irving, New York city:
I am a Republican, but I will not stand for a lynching bee by either Republicans or Democrats.

The Rev. Donald C. MacLeod, First Presbyterian church, Washington:
I rejoice to see you are holding your own against the unprincipled unscrupulous and resourceful enemy.

The Rev. Madison C. Peters, Brooklyn:
You have more friends than ever.

Alberto Hinman, New York city:
Mr. Five Thousand Dollar Levy is getting weaker every day in his district, and all your enemies are in the same fix or a worse one.

William C. Plum, Washington:
Remember Tilden. When he shook himself loose from Tammany and Tweed, the people rallied to his support. Not even the superb democratic character of such clean men as Horatio Seymour, Sanford Church, Amasa J. Parker, Allan C. Beach, Erastus Brooks, Erastus Corning, Roswell P. Flower and others, who went to the aid of Tammany in its effort to defeat Tilden's nomination for President in 1872, could stem the political tide for Tilden or shake the faith of the people in him. History repeats itself. Tammany and Murphy have no such backing now among such decent people as it had in the days of John Kelly. Tammany Hall under Boss Tweed's rule never approached the rottenness and lawlessness it has under Murphy, and it never betrayed and sold out for cash a Democratic nominee for Presidency as Murphy twice sold William J. Bryan.

Emanuel D. King, Brooklyn:
When you are acquitted of the trumped-up charge, your prestige will be equaled by no one else's in this country.

J. A. Walsh, Philadelphia:
Ninety-five per cent. of the people are on your side.

George M. Donehoo, Owatanna, Minnesota:
Your friends out here trust you.

Hugo Minor, Cannel City, Kentucky:
Nobody out here has ever for an instant doubted your integrity.

Fred. A. Shelley, New Fawne:
I did not vote for you because I thought you were going to be a Tammany tool, but your stand on political questions has convinced me that I misjudged you and I am now heartily with you and I expect to see you triumphantly vindicated.

Stanley C. Tyndall, Yonkers:
The law, the prayers and the sympathetic backing of all people of all parties are with you in this struggle.

Fremont Wilson, New York city:
Your friends are not asleep. They do not propose that you shall have a funeral.

Irving O. Nellis, Utica:
They are beginning to squirm. Keep them under gun.

W. J. Shields, Buffalo:
I have never seen such sentiment for anyone in public life as there is here for you. We will clean out Murphy and Fitzpatrick in this county. It is cheering and wonderful.

William Merrifield, New Brighton:
I have yet to find one man who is not in sympathy with you in the present crisis.

Isidore Rosenbluth, Newark, N.J.
The Independent Order of King Solomon with a membership of three thousand in this city of New Jersey, feel it a duty to express to you through its Grand Lodge, the hope that victory will be with you.

Mrs. J. B. Campbell, Brooklyn:
I go out among the people a good deal and I have yet to hear one unkind word about you. Stick to the chair, don't budge an inch.

L. M. Sweet, Beagle, Oregon:
I am always a friend of old Bill Sulzer, and I have wished many times that I could be there to help you.

———

John A. Sleicher, Editor Leslie's Weekly, New York city:
Stay in, but turn the rascals out.

———

Augustus Townsend Scudder, Brooklyn:
These dark days, when your worries must be great, do not forget that old friends like myself, feel for you and wish to help you wherein they can. You have my best wishes.

———

Henry Wellington Wack, New York city:
I believe a poll of the state would indicate that seventy per cent. or more of its residents are with you.

———

Horace C. King, Bellport, Long Island:
The course of the New York Times against you is infamous. I will gladly do all that you may ask of me.

———

Dudley G. Wotton, Seattle, Washington:
You are paying the penalty of being an honest man surrounded by thieves and blackmailers. Nobody who values courage and constancy in public men believes you are guilty of more than defying the corrupt and crooked despotism of the man that is trying to crush you.

———

Theodore P. Cook, Utica:
The impeachment proceedings have been a farce from the beginning.

———

Daniel Harris, President New York State Federation of Labor:
We are all irrevocably with you in your fight for the people.

———

Harry W. Dryden, Schenectady:
I am sure that enough of the good people of the state will rally to your support to continue you in the office to which you were righfully elected and which you are so eminently qualified to hold.

James E. Schwarzenbach, Hornell:
You have thousands of friends in this section.

———

W. Walton Bryant, Kansas City:
All the good western people send you well wishes. It is a pity that they have not more men who have the courage to do what they know is right.

———

William F. Lareau, Rochester:
You are trying to clean the state of a pest that is worse than any disease which was ever inflicted upon the people of the state of New York. I have canvassed one hundred and seventy-five of my business friends and every one of them is a supporter and well-wisher of yours.

———

W. H. Newton, Earlville:
Nearly everybody in the Chenango valley denounces the outrage against you and admires your backbone.

———

The Rev. George A. McAllister, Chester, N. Y.:
You are bearing a heavy burden now, but it is for the people of the state of New York and you must stand fast. We are praying for you privately and in public.

———

Paul Turner Willis, Lynchburg, Va.:
Be of good heart. You know that although the people are sometimes called fickle on the question of morals and righteousness, they will support the opponents to corruptness and will beyond a doubt stand by you to the end, which end, I believe, may be the absolute disruption of Tammany and all that it stands for.

———

Evelyn S. Garrett, Williamsport, N. Y.:
For years I have resisted the attempt of Mr. Murphy to fasten the grip of Tammany Hall in this county. Mr. Murphy has only half succeeded in dictating Democratic politics here, but if you are allowed to have a few months of power I

am sure Mr. Murphy will be driven out of every county in this state. · Every good citizen should wish you success.

———

Monroe Terwilliger, Goshen:
Keep on investigating until the criminals are where they should be, in prison.

———

Dr. Emma Wing-Thomson, Schenectady:
We are all so thankful to see a man who is loyal and brave at the head of our state.

———

Edward P. Totten, Bowman, North Dakota:
You may rest assured that the thoughtful and progressive Democracy of the country is solidly behind you in your part of the age-long struggle of liberty against privilege. We shall move forward with better thanks because of your brave stand.

———

Former Representative George Fred Williams, of Massachusetts:
I do not need to read the defenses that your friends have put together, because no amount of evidence could shake my faith in your integrity, and I, therefore, am not at all anxious to read your defenses.

I do not think I have known you all these years to be deceived in your high character. If you have made any blunders or others have made them for you, they are a part of everyone's lot; I care not what the tribunals of New York say: George Fred Williams will believe in William Sulzer to the end. Do not lose your courage for I think the people will stand behind you and the best thinking men of the country will give you their co-operation.

———

A. W. Thompson, Preston, Minn.:
I have watched closely the bitter fight that Tammany is making on you and I assure you I deeply sympathize with you, and it is my earnest hope that you will come out victorious in the big struggle. One very gratifying thing about the matter is, that outside of your own state every paper I have seen takes your side in this matter, and there is not much room for doubt but what you are absolutely right and that your daring the Tammany gang they could not run the Governor's office, they are simply determined to crush you. I shall anxiously look forward to your complete vindication.

Sulzer, and I have wish many times that I could be there to help you.

_____

John A. Sleicher, Editor Leslie's Weekly, New York city:
Stay in, but keep the rascals out.

_____

Augustus Townsend Cudder, Brooklyn:
These dark days, when your worries must be great, do not forget that old friends like myself feel for you and wish to help you herein they can. You have my best wishes.

_____

Henry Wellington Wack, New York city:
I believe a poll of the state would indicate that seventy per cent. or more of its residents are with you.

_____

Horace C. King, Bellport, Long Island:
The course of the New York Times against you is infamus. I will gladly do all that you my ask of me.

_____

Dudley G. Wooten, Seattle, Washington:
You are paying the penalty of being an honest man surrounded by thieves and blackmailers. Nobody who values courage and constancy in public men believes you are guilty of more than defying the corrupt and cowardly despotism of the man that is trying to crush you.

_____

Theodore P. Cook, Utica:
The impeachment proceedings have been a farce from the beginning.

_____

Daniel Harris, President New York State Federation of Labor:
We are all irrevocably with you in your fight for the people.

_____

Harry W. Dryden, Schenectady:
I am sure that enough of the good people of the state will rally to your support to continue you in the office to which you were rightfully elected and which you are so eminently qualified to hold.

_____

You have thousands of friends in this section.

_____

W. Walton Bryant, Kansas City:
All the good western people send you well wishes. It is a pity that they have not more men who have the courage to do what they know is right.

_____

William F. Lareau, Rochester:
You are trying to clean the state of a pest that is worse than any disease which was ever inflicted upon the people of the state of New York. I have canvassed one hundred and seventy-five of my business friends and every one of them is a supporter and well-wisher of yours.

_____

W. H. Newton, Earlville:
Nearly everybody in the Chenango valley denounces the outrage against you and admires your backbone.

_____

The Rev. George A. McAllister, Chester, N. Y.:
You are bearing a heavy burden now, but it is for the people of the state of New York and you must stand fast. We are praying for you privately and in public.

_____

Paul Turner Willis, Lynchburg, Va.:
Be of good heart. You know that although the people are sometimes called fickle on the question of morals and righteousness, they will support the opponents to corruptness and will beyond a doubt stand by you to the end, which end, I believe, may be the absolute disruption of Tammany and all that it stands for.

_____

Evelyn S. Garrett, Willia..., N. Y.:
For years I have re... attempt of Mr. Murphy... the grip of Tammany... county. Mr. Murphy... succeeded in dictatin... politics here, but if y... to have a few mon...

IMPEACHMENT OF

CONTRIBUTIONS TO THE ALBANY
KNICKERBOCKER PRESS FUND

"A Friend of Honest Government"...............$100.00		Roy Weedman............	$0.50
Thomas Hunter, Albany...	10.00	A. Echochard.............	.
Elizabeth A. Smart, Tompkinsville, S. I..........	2.00	A. Wilson................	.
		M. A. Dancy.............	2.
Hyman Abramonitz, 75 E. 114th street, New York.	1.50	E. H. Grupe.............	2.
		W. Sutliff................	1.
Hyman Rosefeld, New York	5.00	S. Mathews.............	1.
Ben H. Bearman, New York	5.00	C. Onderkirk............	1.
Samuel Porvancher, New York.................	1.00	H. Sitts..................	1.
		J. McCartney............	1.
J. W. Wiltse..........	10.00	Peter McGinnis...........	1.50
Calvin E. Keach..........	5.00	Gerald H. Goodwin........	1.60
Fred J. Stephens.........	10.00	A. Perkins...............	.50
Theron Akin.............	10.00	T. Quaid.................	.50
Caroline Betz, Albany.....	2.00	A. Lewis.................	.50
Samuel Goldfine, Schenectady....:.........	3.00	L. Smart.................	.50
		L. Millimay..............	.50
William W. Darling, Kingston...................	10.00	Robert McCartney........	.50
		Ed. Doring...............	.50
Arthur W. Weid, Round Lake..................	2.00	Richard Osterhout........	.50
		T. McElroy..............	.50
Naumoff and Loew, Schenectady...............	3.00	H. E. Grupe..............	.50
		T. McCarten.............	.50
"Enemy of Boss Rule and Advocate of Direct Primaries"................	5.	Frank Wilbur.............	.50
		Charles Baer.............	.50
D. Zeiser, Troy..........	10.	Joe Izinka...............	.50
A. E. Roff, Richfield Springs	1.	A. Nickla................	.50
"A Lover of Justice," Albany	10.	J. Closs.................	.50
F. A. W., Binghamton, N.Y.	1.	W. Plumadore............	1.00
"Drive the Grafters Out"..	5.	C. Bellinger..............	1.00
James Burke, Schenectady.	1.	W. L. Nelson.............	1.00
C. Panlier...............	1	Fred Boudreau...........	1.00
William W. Terns.........	1	J. L. Willard, Rochester..:	10.00
Val Nold................	1	Frank Hermans, Troy.....	1.00
A. Taber................	1.	Irving Russell............	5.00
C. Flamburg.............	1	Mrs. A. E. Dyer, Rochester	1.00
William Shultz...........	1	J. F. Trump, Jr., Springfield, O................	1.00
G. Bronk................	1	M. S. Cameron, Albany...	1.00
H. McCartney............	1	Ferdinand Gutman, New York.................	10.00
A. E. Sloeter............	1	O. F. W. Wendt, Albany ..	1.00
H. Ridings..............	1	J. H. Ward, Stephentown..	2.00
N. Hamilton.............	1	"A Friend in Saratoga Co."	10.00
Charles J. McIntyre.......	1	"An Enemy of Boss Rule and Graft".............	1.00
S. Irving................	.00	E. P. Morrison, Ossining ..	5.00
L. Halt.................	.60	E. J. Whitehead, Westfield, N. J..................	10.00
H. Ellerhoff.............	.50	Mrs. Louise Clark, Albany.	1.00
James Bolan.............	.50	Mrs. Edith I. Sill, Albany.	2.00
L. Bovcinck.............	.50	E. Slawsky, Albany........	1.00
I. Stanjues..............	.50		
J. Deskewiez............	.50		

C. Smith, Albany	$1.00	Clinton Clough, Woodstock,	
Wm. Schaff, Schenectady	1.00	N. Y.	$1.00
S. C. A. G. F.	10.00	James F. Leahy, Utica	25.00
George Waldron, Albany	1.00	Ex-member Wichita club,	
F. E. Roff, Richfield Springs	1.00	M. W. G. Garsson, New	
Walter A. Conklin, Catskill	2.00	York	2.00
John Connor, E. Greenwich	2.00	Emil Kovarik, Albany	1.00
Michael Volland, Buffalo	50.00	Charles J. Miller, Newfane,	
Schenectady Citizens	114.12	N. Y.	5.00
Jay A. Robinson, city	1.00	J. F. McClaughry, Hamil-	
R. R. Thompson, city	5.00	ton, Ill.	1.00
C. W. M., city	1.00	A Friend, Troy	1.00
Calvin E. Keach (2nd con-		Old Veteran, Ghent	2.00
tribution)	5.00	Dr. C. McConnell, Hogans-	
H. Fiat, New York	1.00	burg	1.00
Martin Bearman, New York	1.00	Helen A. Winne	1.00
I. Winograd, New York	1.00	A. J. McDonald, Schenec-	
Edward Joseph, New York	1.00	tady	.50
Jacob Lipeles, New York	1.00	D. J. Ross, Amsterdam	1.00
Harry Specter, New York	1.00	S. H., Schenectady	5.00
Harris Goldstein, New York	1.00	Calvin E. Keach (3rd con-	
Robert Jacobson, New York	1.00	tribution)	5.00
R. Wolworth, New York	1.00	A Friend of the Cause	5.62
Geo. W. Bender, Catskill	2.00		

MASS MEETING

NON-PARTISAN CITIZENS COMMITTEE OF ALBANY, N. Y.

Chairman   *Secretary*
HENRY L. KESSLER   JOHN D. CHISM

Treasurer
F. H. BRYANT

ON MATTER OF PROTESTING AGAINST THE METHODS OF THE
IMPEACHMENT OF

GOVERNOR WILLIAM SULZER

Dr. Geo. H. Houghton	Julius F. Harris	Jacob L. Ten Eyck
Solomon Hydeman	George B. Russell	J. C. E. Scott
Walter E. Ward	Eli M. Woodard	O. C. Mackenzie
Thomas Austin	Charles H. Mills	Wm. Lodge
A. Tarsish	Borden H. Mills	A. Brummer
Henry J. Crawford	George A. Harrig	Prof. Frank A. Gallup
H. L. Kessler	E. F. Hunting	Levi Cass
M. Lincoln	M. Schonfeld	Lewis Cass
S. Pierson	Benj. Hensler	Clarence Hotaling
F. W. Cameron, 2d	George T. Clapham	Roland J. Ford
Rev. Charles S. Hager	S. Zuckerman	James J. Fleming
M. T. Adams	A. Levinson	C. E. Lindsay
Dr. C. M. Culver	H. B. McClennan	J. Eicher
John E. Dugan	S. Steinbock	Lewis J. Mackler
Rev. J. Levison	James Ackroyd	Isidor Brooks
John J. Dillon	M. A. Gauntlett	Rev. James N. Knipe
John Hayford	Rev. Roelif H. Brooks	Deny Pollock
George Lawyer	F. H. Bryant	A. Burack
Kassel Simon	Charles J. Davis	J. H. Gillespie
Rev. Arthur M. Ellis	A. Phillips	Edward Gutekunst
James C. Sheehan	Rev. Harold S. Metcalfe	Wm. J. T. Hogan
Jay W. Forrest	Rev. Kingman Colledge	Wm. H. Bond
Smith O'Brien	Wm. J. Coulson	Rev. George Dugan
Dr. Elmer A. Blessing	David J. Fleming	Geo. A. Whish
A. Reiner	Alphonse B. Fisher	Fred J. Riggs
A. U. Wager	Joseph McDonough	Walter J. Eaton
H. Brody	Henry George	U. G. Stockwell
E. A. Doty	E. A. Peck	Robert Stanley Ross
Wm. J. Hough	John J. Murray	Rev. George K. Statham
Robert C. Campbell	A. Yaroslawsky	Byron Holmes
Hyman Alexander	George C. Hisgen	C. A. Covey
Prof. Edward A. Jones	Rev. E. R. James	Philip H. Scott
John D. Chism	Albert Ritchie	A. Redding
Thomas F. Dolan	Clinton Pierce	F. L. McClennan
John Franey	Rev. Wm. H. Hopkins	Charles M. Swan
H. Klein	George Waldron	James T. Townsend
Rev. Charles F. Shaw	George H. McGrew	Amasa J. Parker
	Rev. Charles Graves	

MASS MEETING

ODD FELLOWS HALL—SEPTEMBER 17th, 1913

SPEAKERS

Chairman

REV. WM. HERMAN HOPKINS, D.D.

Hon. George R. Lunn	Hon. Jay W. Forrest
Rev. Madison C. Peters	Hon. Lynn J. Arnold
James S. Sheahan	Hon. Eugene D. Scribner
Rev. Milton B. Pratt	Hon. Jacob L. Ten Eyck
Hon. Samuel B. Thomas	Henry L. Kessler

Long before the hour scheduled for the meeting the hall was filled. Before the Rev. William Herman Hopkins called the meeting to order the rear of the hall was deep with the standing crowd, and police were forced to stand guard at the balcony entrances to prevent more crowding there. Filling the hall and stretching out into Lodge street were more than 400 citizens, unable to gain an entrance, waiting in the rain for the overflow meeting. But few women were in the audience, the crowd for the most part being made up of actual voters who are prepared to endorse their sentiment with ballots at the polls in November.

Mayor George R. Lunn, of Schenectady, the first speaker, said:

" We might inquire what motive actuated the legislature when it moved to impeach Governor Sulzer. Was it purity of politics which was desired? Save the word. What was desired was that Tammany Hall should be able to get its hands on $60,000,000 in good roads contracts, on millions in other contracts—that it should grasp New York state as it has long grasped New York city.

" We have got to get rid of the seventy-six Murphy puppets in the state assembly who are servile enough to take orders. We have got to get rid of all of their ilk. They are the people in their own estimation. But the people of the state think differently, only they have not yet had the courage to come out and stand against such sort of government."

TAMMANY'S TREASON

NON-PARTISAN CITIZENS COMMITTEE OF ALBANY, N. Y.

Chairman
HENRY L. KESSLER

Secretary
JOHN D. CHISM

Treasurer
F. H. BRYANT

ON MATTER OF PROTESTING AGAINST THE METHODS OF THE
IMPEACHMENT OF

GOVERNOR WILLIAM SULZER

Dr. Geo. H. Houghton	Julius F. Harris	Jacob L. Ten Eyck
Solomon Hydeman	George B. Russell	J. C. E. Scott
Walter E. Ward	Eli M. Woodard	O. C. Mackenzie
Thomas Austin	Charles H. Mills	Wm. Lodge
A. Tarsish	Borden H. Mills	A. Brummer
Henry J. Crawford	George A. Harrig	Prof. Frank A. Gallup
H. L. Kessler	E. F. Hunting	Levi Cass
M. Lincoln	M. Schonfeld	Lewis Cass
S. Pierson	Benj. Hensler	Clarence Hotaling
F. W. Cameron, 2d	George T. Clapham	Roland J. Ford
Rev. Charles S. Hager	S. Zuckerman	James J. Fleming
M. T. Adams	A. Levinson	C. E. Lindsay
Dr. C. M. Culver	H. B. McClennan	J. Eicher
John E. Dugan	S. Steinbock	Lewis J. Mackler
Rev. J. Levison	James Ackroyd	Isidor Brooks
John J. Dillon	M. A. Gauntlett	Rev. James N. Knipe
John Hayford	Rev. Roelif H. Brooks	Deny Pollock
George Lawyer	F. H. Bryant	A. Burack
Kassel Simon	Charles J. Davis	J. H. Gillespie
Rev. Arthur M. Ellis	A. Phillips	Edward Gutekunst
James C. Sheehan	Rev. Harold S. Metcalfe	Wm. J. T. Hogan
Jay W. Forrest	Rev. Kingman Colledge	Wm. H. Bond
Smith O'Brien	Wm. J. Coulson	Rev. George Dugan
Dr. Elmer A. Blessing	David J. Fleming	Geo. A. Whish
A. Reiner	Alphonse B. Fisher	Fred J. Riggs
A. U. Wager	Joseph McDonough	Walter J. Eaton
H. Brody	Henry George	U. G. Stockwell
E. A. Doty	E. A. Peck	Robert Stanley Ross
Wm. J. Hough	John J. Murray	Rev. George K. Statham
Robert C. Campbell	A. Yaroslawsky	Byron Holmes
Hyman Alexander	George C. Hisgen	C. A. Covey
Prof. Edward A. Jones	Rev. E. R. James	Philip H. Scott
John D. Chism	Albert Ritchie	A. Redding
Thomas F. Dolan	Clinton Pierce	F. L. McClennan
John Franey	Rev. Wm. H. Hopkins	Charles M. Swan
H. Klein	George Waldron	James T. Townsend
Rev. Charles F. Shaw	George H. McGrew	Amasa J. Parker
	Rev. Charles Graves	

MASS MEETING

ODD FELLOWS HALL—SEPTEMBER 17th, 1913

———

SPEAKERS

Chairman

REV. WM. HERMAN HOPKINS, D.D.

Hon. George R. Lunn	Hon. Jay W. Forrest
Rev. Madison C. Peters	Hon. Lynn J. Arnold
James S. Sheahan	Hon. Eugene D. Scribner
Rev. Milton B. Pratt	Hon. Jacob L. Ten Eyck
Hon. Samuel B. Thomas	Henry L. Kessler

Long before the hour scheduled for the meeting the hall was filled. Before the Rev. William Herman Hopkins called the meeting to order the rear of the hall was deep with the standing crowd, and police were forced to stand guard at the balcony entrances to prevent more crowding there. Filling the hall and stretching out into Lodge street were more than 400 citizens, unable to gain an entrance, waiting in the rain for the overflow meeting. But few women were in the audience, the crowd for the most part being made up of actual voters who are prepared to endorse their sentiment with ballots at the polls in November.

Mayor George R. Lunn, of Schenectady, the first speaker, said:

"We might inquire what motive actuated the legislature when it moved to impeach Governor Sulzer. Was it purity of politics which was desired? Save the word. What was desired was that Tammany Hall should be able to get its hands on $60,000,000 in good roads contracts, on millions in other contracts—that it should grasp New York state as it has long grasped New York city.

"We have got to get rid of the seventy-six Murphy puppets in the state assembly who are servile enough to take orders. We have got to get rid of all of their ilk. They are the people in their own estimation. But the people of the state think differently, only they have not yet had the courage to come out and stand against such sort of government."

Jay W. Forrest of Albany declared that William Sulzer
would be acquitted of the charges against him, and the audience
backed up the sentiment with hearty applause. Mr. Forrest
confined himself, for the most part, to a recital of past deeds
of Martin H. Glynn. He sprung a little surprise in reading
extracts from a letter written from New York to Eugene D.
Woods, formerly of Albany.

"They had a meeting Wednesday at Delmonico's," wrote
Mr. Woods. "Glynn and McCabe were present, as was
McCall, McCooey, Wagner and Murphy."

"Sulzer could have retired from office with his share of the
public plunder," said Mr. Forrest, "if he had stood with
Murphy, Glynn and McCabe et al. But he refused and this
fight is your fight."

Rev. Milton B. Pratt of Amsterdam said in part:

"If this thing were not such a deep, dark tragedy, it would
be a screaming farce. I am a minister and I talk a good deal
about heavenly crowns. Well, I venture to suggest a crown
for Charles F. Murphy—a crown of asbestos with a mica top.
Wagner and Levy and a few others should order the same kind.
They will need them."

Jacob L. Ten Eyck of Albany, the next speaker, said:

"The state assembly is a grand jury in this instance. What
did the state assembly act upon—the report of a joint committee headed by a member of the state senate, now sitting as a
member of the court of impeachment, and having as its members other senators who are now also judges.

"What a farce to suppose that this court can deliver an impartial verdict with members upon it who have already declared their convictions? These men sought evidence—heard
testimony—and now they are to sit as 'impartial' judges in
what is termed the highest court in the land.

"I recall a bit of old history. Before Justice Barnard, a
member of the supreme court, and Justice Peckham, also a
member of that court, had had some personal trouble. When
Justice Barnard was impeached Justice Peckham was a member of the Court of Appeals, and as such was to sit on trial of
his former colleague. What did Justice Peckham do? He told
the Court of Appeals that he did not want to sit—he said that
his verdict might be influenced by past events. Can you

imagine Frawley or Wagner or any of the others doing that tomorrow, when the Court of impeachment convenes? But the court should purify itself by debarring these men from sitting. That must be plain to everyone. If Frawley and Wagner attempt to sit, I want to tell you that the American people won't stand for it.

"There are some things about this court of impeachment that I, as an American citizen, want investigated. I am told that Charles F. Murphy was on the telephone for hours, talking to members of the assembly. If Murphy attempted to influence the votes of any of these assemblymen he should be called to account for it. The assembly lost its identity as a legislative body the moment it began to consider these articles of impeachment and it became a judicial body. It was a grand jury, nothing more nor less. If Murphy did this—if votes were influenced, then this case should be thrown out of court, as would be the case in any court of law under similar circumstances."

Following the last speaker, the Rev. J. Addison Jones, pastor of the Madison Avenue Reformed church, of Albany, offered the resolutions which were adopted by the meeting.
In placing the motion, Dr. Hopkins asked the audience to vote assent by both standing and saying " aye." Like one person the audience rose, and shouted a thunderous " aye," adopting the following:

Resolved, that we affirm our confidence in Governor Sulzer and extend to him our support in his efforts to maintain the dignity of the state government and to rid the public service from boss rule and unworthy servants.

Resolved, that we deplore the aggressions of Tammany Hall and its efforts to seize the government as inimical to the best interests of the citizenship of this state and as subversive of the fundamental principles of popular rule. We urge all citizens, irrespective of party affiliations, to join in opposition to the band of political pirates and marauders, who are now assuming to dictate the offices and the policy of the state.

Resolved, treason to the state must stop. The leaders of Tammany Hall should profit from the example of Tweed. The people of the state of New York are still fit for self-government.

We further pledge ourselves to support as candidates for members of assembly at the coming election only such candidates as shall favor the interests of the people in affording to every voter the widest expression in the choice of candidates for public office.

Resolved, that a copy of these resolutions be forwarded to Governor Sulzer.

INDEX

	Page
Allds, Jotham P., political effect of trial	21
Arnold, Lynn J., his editorial on Barnes and Murphy	415
Ashurst, Henry S., U. S. Senator of Arizona writes Sulzer	370
Bayne, Howard R., introduced hydro-electric bill in 1912	86
Beardsley, S. A., opposes hydro-electric bill	89
Belmont, August, attacked by Bryan at convention	25
Blake, George W., Murphy opposes his appointment as secretary	38
Murphy demands his investigation of prisons cease	63
Report on Auburn prison	303
Brady, Anthony N., interest in hydro-electric bill	86
Bryan, William J., his attack on Murphy at Baltimore	25
Brackett, Edgar T., speech against Sulzer in court	240
Brewer, Governor of Mississippi, writes to Sulzer	367
Carlisle, John N., Sulzer wanted him recognized by organization	39
· Appointed chairman of inquiry committee	47
Appointed highway commissioner	103
Clark, Champ, his defeat for nomination at Baltimore	26
Clark, Frank W., editorial in " Knickerbocker Press "	412
Cobalan, Daniel F., his trial by legislature	110
Conger, Senator Ben, witness in Allds trial	21
Conners, William J., quarrels with Charles F. Murphy	23
Connolly, John A., witness against Cohalan	110
Croker, Richard A., relations with Sulzer	20
Callanan & Prescott, Capitol contractors	287
Colquit, O. B., Governor of Texas, writes Sulzer	368
Cox, Governor of Ohio, writes Sulzer	365
Cruce, Lee, Governor of Oklahoma, writes Sulzer	366
Crater, David S., Secretary of State of New Jersey, writes Sulzer	366
Delaney, John H., appointed on inquiry committee	48
Appointed commissioner efficiency and economy	103
Loans M. T. Horgan to Frawley committee	116
His conversation with Sulzer taken by detectaphone	164
Delmonico conference of bosses to " get Sulzer "	73
Democratic state convention, 1912, at Syracuse	32
Direct primary meeting in executive chamber	72
Dix, John A., nomination for governor	22
Administration controlled by Murphy	23
Favors Sheehan for United States senator	24
One of Murphy's wax figures at Baltimore	25
Direct primaries, names of men who attended Sulzer conference	319
Vote on Sulzer in legislature	327
Donohue, Frank J., Secretary of State of Massachusetts, writes to Sulzer on direct primaries	367
Douglas, Curtis, public service commissioner	49
Dunn, Bart, Tammany state committeeman, indicted for highway frauds	295

Page

Editorials from leading newspapers of country on Sulzer case........397–416
Eisner, Mark, introduces Sulzer bill in assembly..................... 101
Fielder, James F., Governor of New Jersey, to Sulzer................ 369
Fitzpatrick, W. H., Murphy makes him his Erie county agent......... 24
    Member of Delmonico conference............................ 73
Forrest, Jay W., independent candidate for congress................. 28
    Direct primary speech, Schenectady......................... 346
Frawley, James J., Chairman of Frawley committee................. 75
    Committee delves into Sulzer accounts....................... 116
    Impeachment report to assembly........................... 121
    Meeting in Saratoga Springs............................... 135
    Objected to as member of court............................ 154
    Asks for and receives pen used to sign certificate of Sulzer's re-
    moval.. 180
Full crew bill for railroads... 374
Gaffney, James E., Murphy urges his appointment for highway com-
    missioner... 59
    " Gaffney or war ".. 61
Glynn, Martin H., his ambition to be governor..................... 22
    Predicts he will be nominated at Syracuse.................. 27
    Refers to possibility of removal of governor................. 27
    Knows Tammany plans early in 1912....................... 28
    Praises Dix at Syracuse convention......................... 34
    Urges Sulzer to come out strong for direct primaries........... 47
    Asks Sulzer to appoint McCabe public service commissioner.... 50
    Predicts in February, 1912, he will be governor.............. 52
    Advises Forrest to stop being independent................... 52
    Refuses to help Sulzer's direct primary fight................ 72
    His editorial for direct primaries in 1909................... 80
    Said most of the bosses are vampires....................... 81
    His interest in hydro-electric bill.......................... 89
    " Government by investigation must now cease "............. 143
Hearst, William R., breaks with Sulzer on McCall appointment....... 49
Hennessy, John A., appointed executive auditor.................... 48
    Receives letter from Eugene D. Wood....................90, 92, 93
    Report on Capitol contracts............................... 279
    Spies put on his trail..................................... 95
    Report on highways....................................... 295
Herrick, D- Cady, chief counsel for Sulzer, speech in court........... 225
Hall, Luther E., Governor of Louisiana, writes to Sulzer............. 368
Hitchcock, Gilbert M., U. S. senator, Nebraska, to Sulzer........... 365
Hollis, Henry F., U. S. senator, New Hampshire, to Sulzer........... 365
Hinman, Harvey D., speech for Sulzer in court..................... 209
Impeachment articles... 383
Mack, Norman E., arranges meeting between Sulzer and Murphy..... 66
    Accepts and then declines to serve on primary committee....... 101
McKnight, John W., introduced Sulzer bill in senate................ 101

Page

Editorials from leading newspapers of country on Sulzer case........397–416
Eisner, Mark, introduces Sulzer bill in assembly.................... 101
Fielder, James F., Governor of New Jersey, to Sulzer................ 369
Fitzpatrick, W. H., Murphy makes him his Erie county agent......... 24
    Member of Delmonico conference............................ 73
Forrest, Jay W., independent candidate for congress................ 28
    Direct primary speech, Schenectady........................ 346
Frawley, James J., Chairman of Frawley committee................. 75
    Committee delves into Sulzer accounts..................... 116
    Impeachment report to assembly........................... 121
    Meeting in Saratoga Springs.............................. 135
    Objected to as member of court........................... 154
    Asks for and receives pen used to sign certificate of Sulzer's removal.. 180
Full crew bill for railroads.. 374
Gaffney, James E., Murphy urges his appointment for highway commissioner.. 59
    " Gaffney or war "...................................... 61
Glynn, Martin H., his ambition to be governor..................... 22
    Predicts he will be nominated at Syracuse................. 27
    Refers to possibility of removal of governor.............. 27
    Knows Tammany plans early in 1912........................ 28
    Praises Dix at Syracuse convention....................... 34
    Urges Sulzer to come out strong for direct primaries..... 47
    Asks Sulzer to appoint McCabe public service commissioner.... 50
    Predicts in February, 1912, he will be governor.......... 52
    Advises Forrest to stop being independent................ 52
    Refuses to help Sulzer's direct primary fight............ 72
    His editorial for direct primaries in 1909............... 80
    Said most of the bosses are vampires..................... 81
    His interest in hydro-electric bill...................... 89
    " Government by investigation must now cease "........... 143
Hearst, William R., breaks with Sulzer on McCall appointment...... 49
Hennessy, John A., appointed executive auditor.................... 48
    Receives letter from Eugene D. Wood................90, 92, 93
    Report on Capitol contracts.............................. 279
    Spies put on his trail................................... 95
    Report on highways....................................... 295
Herrick, D- Cady, chief counsel for Sulzer, speech in court........ 225
Hall, Luther E., Governor of Louisiana, writes to Sulzer.......... 368
Hitchcock, Gilbert M., U. S. senator, Nebraska, to Sulzer......... 365
Hollis, Henry F., U. S. senator, New Hampshire, to Sulzer......... 365
Hinman, Harvey D., speech for Sulzer in court..................... 209
Impeachment articles.. 383
Mack, Norman E., arranges meeting between Sulzer and Murphy..... 66
    Accepts and then declines to serve on primary committee...... 101
McKnight, John W., introduced Sulzer bill in senate............... 101